Pacific Northwest Line Drawing

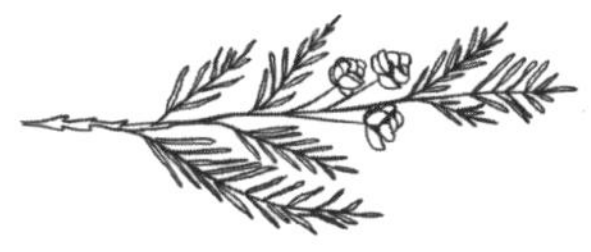

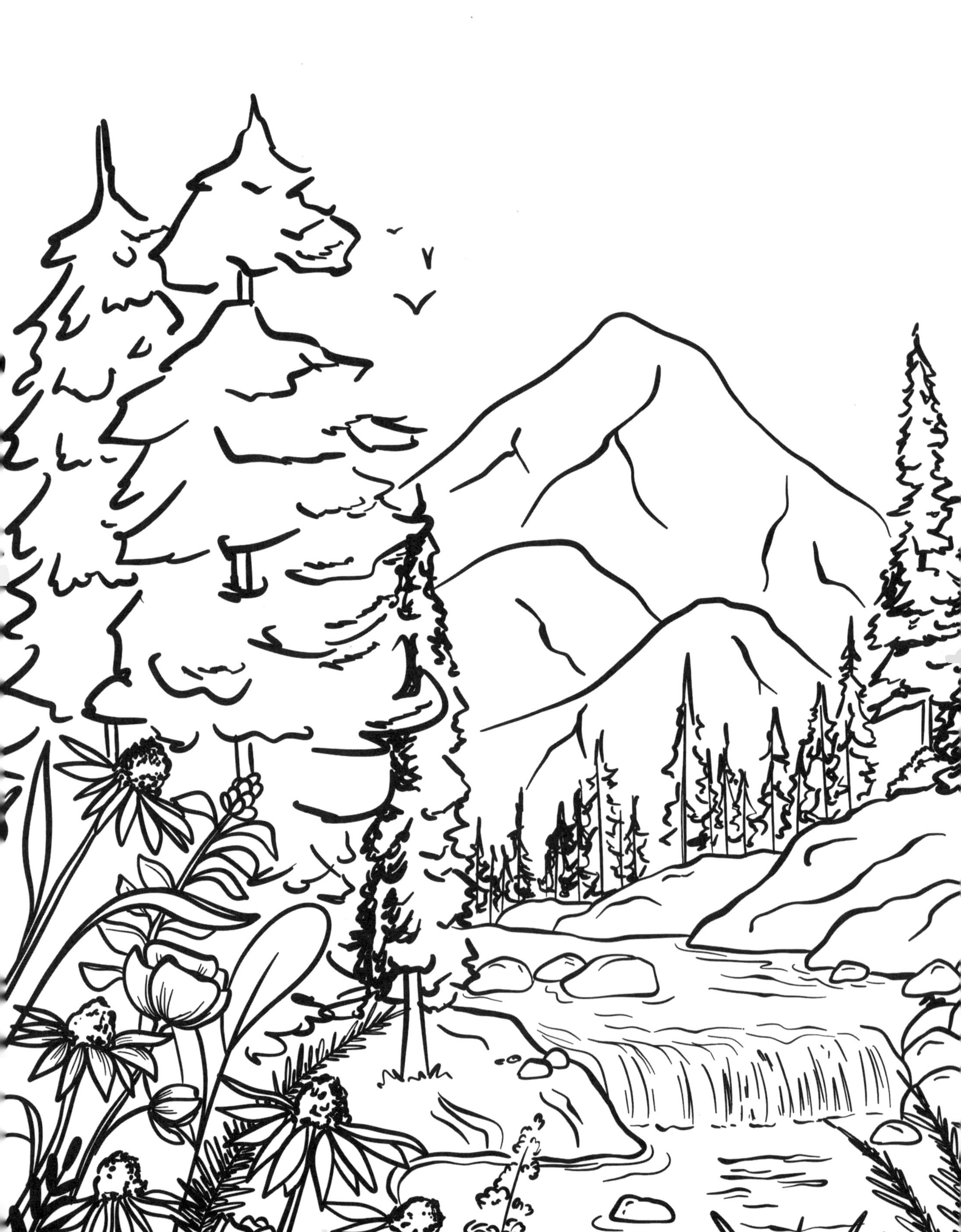

Pacific Northwest LINE DRAWING

HOW TO DRAW
Flowers, Trees, Mushrooms, Birds, Animals, Landmarks, and More

PEGGY DEAN

SASQUATCH BOOKS | SEATTLE

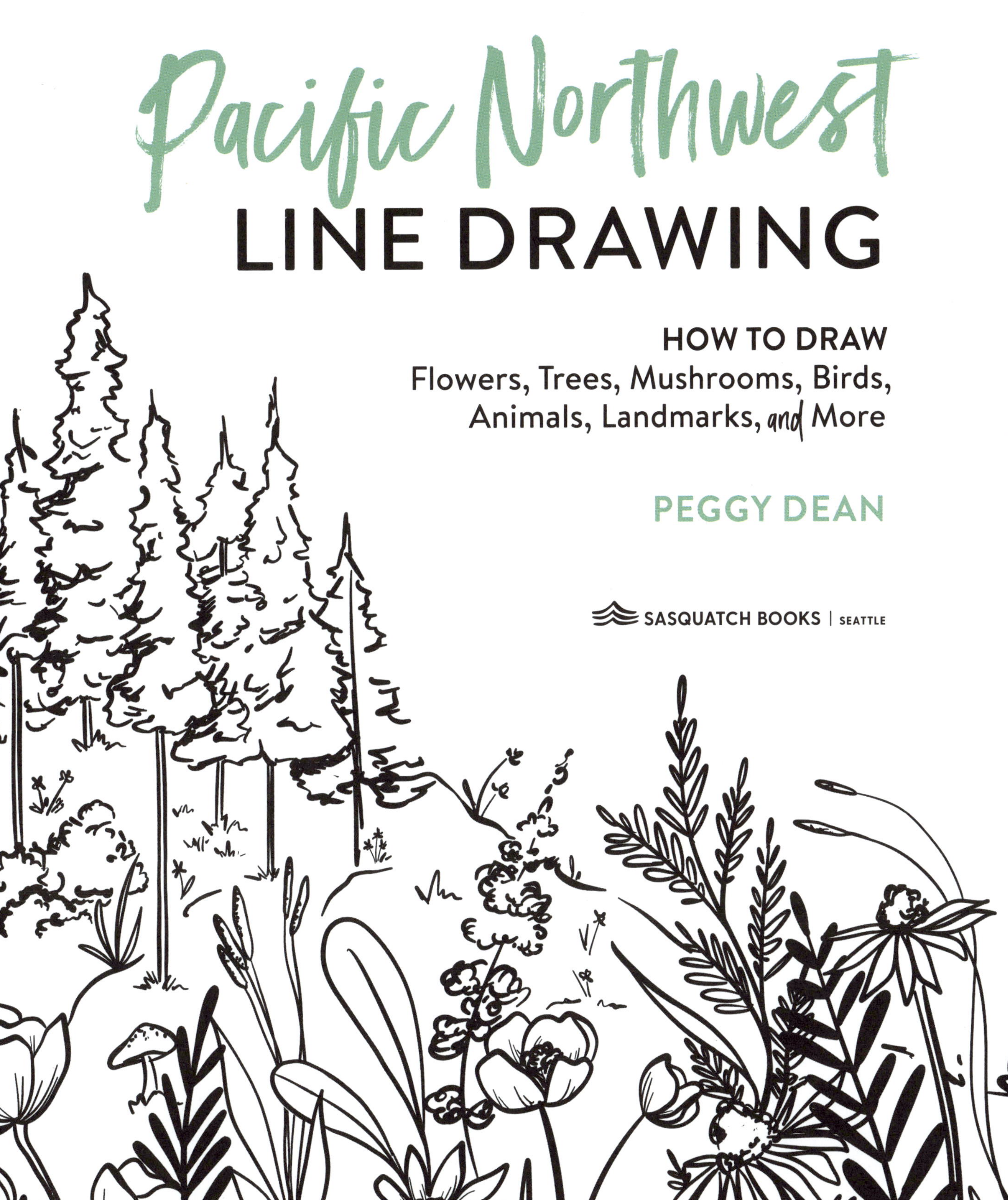

Contents

Illustration Catalog

FLORA

FAUNA

LANDMARKS

Introduction

Welcome to the Pacific Northwest, a land of boundless beauty. The drawings on the following pages are a love letter to the region that has captured my heart and soul. I had the privilege of growing up exploring the Pacific Northwest's diverse ecosystems, from the towering evergreen forests to the rugged coastline, from the majestic mountains to the tranquil rivers. I love how every season brings its own palette of colors, textures, and sensations—the scent of old-growth forests, where moss-draped branches of ancient trees touch the sky; the taste of wild berries plucked from the underbrush, bursting with the essence of summer; and the feeling of cool, misty rain on your skin, a gentle reminder of all the ways this region can inspire us.

This book is organized into three main sections: Flora, Fauna, and Landmarks of the Pacific Northwest. Each section contains step-by-step drawing instructions for various subjects, accompanied by fun facts that might surprise you! Whether you're a beginner or an experienced artist, feel free to start anywhere that inspires you. Remember, the goal is to enjoy the process and capture the essence of the Pacific Northwest through your own unique perspective.

Peggy Dean

About Line Drawing

The magic of line drawing often lies in simplicity—capturing the essence of a subject with just a few strokes. When I first started practicing line drawing, I quickly realized that it wasn't about making perfect replicas of what I saw. It's about capturing the way I wanted to interpret my surroundings. My lines were wobbly and imperfect, and as I progressed and my skills improved, I found myself returning to those wobbly lines because that's what I liked most about drawing. It was freeing—not worrying about precision, and just enjoying the process.

In this book, you'll be guided simply, line by line, and I encourage you to make it your own. We'll explore different objects in nature, animals, and places that you can draw with only a few lines.

Over my years of practice, I've discovered that mastering a few key techniques can significantly enhance your drawing experience and results.

Let me share some insights to help you on your line drawing journey.

Holding Your Pen

How you hold your pen can dramatically affect the control and fluidity of your lines. For detailed work, try holding your pen close to the nib. For looser, more expressive lines, grip it further back. Experiment to find what feels most comfortable and natural to you.

Controlling Line Weight

Varying line weight adds depth and interest to your drawings. While using pens with different tip sizes is one method, you can also achieve this by adjusting the pressure you apply. Light pressure creates thin, delicate lines, while heavier pressure produces bold, striking ones. Practice transitioning smoothly between these pressures to master dynamic line work.

Creating Texture

Textures bring your line drawings to life. Experiment with techniques like hatching (parallel lines), cross-hatching (intersecting lines), stippling (dots), and scumbling (scribbled lines) to add dimension and detail. Each texture technique can convey different surfaces and materials, so experiment to see what works best for your subjects.

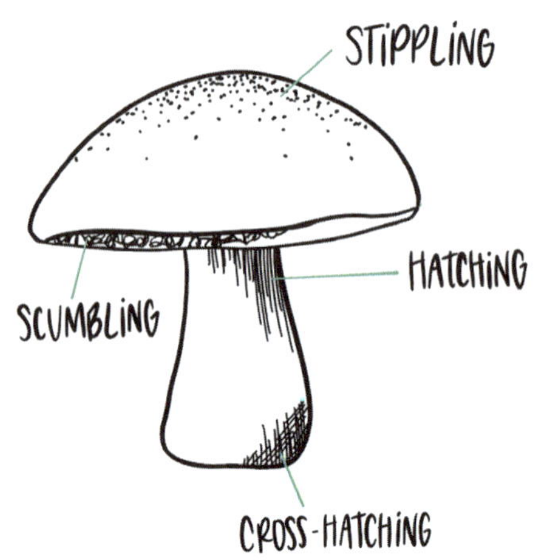

Applications
Line drawings have a unique way of adding charm and personality to everything they touch. You can incorporate them into handmade cards, journals and planners, standalone art pieces, craft projects, digital media and graphic design, marketing and branding, tattoo art, and even educational materials! The versatility of line drawing allows it to enhance virtually any creative endeavor.

Finding Your Flow
One of the most rewarding aspects of line drawing is entering the flow state while creating. This mental state of deep focus and immersion can be achieved by starting with simple subjects, allowing yourself to draw without judgment. Let your hand move freely and embrace mistakes as part of the process. Remember, the beauty of line drawing lies in its imperfections. Each line, whether deliberate or accidental, adds character and energy to your work.

Embracing Imperfections
My favorite way to draw is to jump in with a pen, embrace imperfections that come up, and capture the energy of the moment. Line drawing allows us to exist in a place of creative play, without the need for a ton of art supplies. I present line drawing literally—line by line—to help you view seemingly complicated objects in a simpler form.

Through the step-by-step drawings in this book, you'll see how each line builds upon the previous one, culminating in a charming final piece.

Building Confidence
As you practice, your confidence in line drawing will naturally grow. Keep a dedicated sketchbook for your line drawings, filling it with quick sketches and detailed studies alike. Over time, you'll see your progress and identify the techniques and subjects you enjoy the most.

Every line you draw is a step toward improving your skills and developing your unique style. By focusing on simplicity, practicing key techniques, and embracing imperfections, you can create beautiful and meaningful drawings.

I encourage you to use this book as both a guide and inspiration as you embark on your line drawing journey. Remember, the most important thing is to enjoy the process and let your creativity flow.

So, grab your sketchbook and let's get started. You don't need to be a pro to enjoy this—just dive in and have fun. The Pacific Northwest is full of inspiration, and I can't wait for you to see it through your own line drawings.

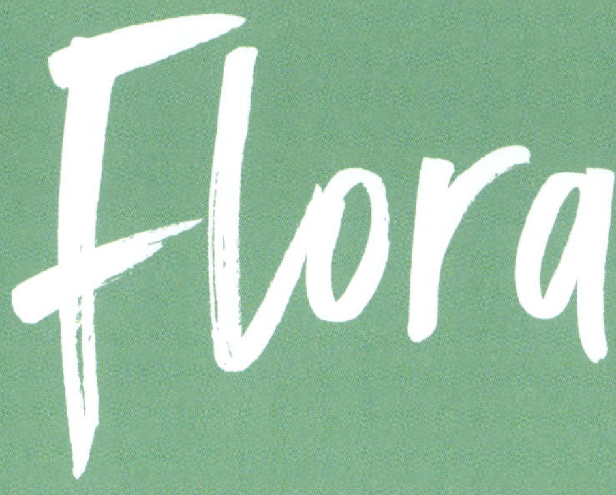

In the Pacific Northwest, plants do more than just color the landscape green; they're the backbone of the ecosystem. Native plant species are essential, providing food and shelter to a wide range of wildlife, from the tiniest insects to the largest mammals.

Towering evergreens form the iconic canopy of Northwest forests. These giants create a unique microclimate, offering shade and cooler temperatures that help other species flourish. Then there are the understory plants and wildflowers, adding layers of diversity beneath the canopy. These plant species offer critical nesting sites and foraging grounds for birds, insects, and mammals.

Amid this verdant world, wildflowers emerge in springtime like colorful confetti, while mosses and lichens paint the rocks and trees in hues of green and silver.

As you draw these plants, observe how their shapes and structures reflect their roles in the ecosystem. Notice how the sturdy trunks of evergreens, the delicate petals of wildflowers, and the intricate patterns of moss each require different line techniques to capture their essence.

Trillium

Trillium ovatum

STEP 1

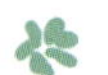

STEP 2

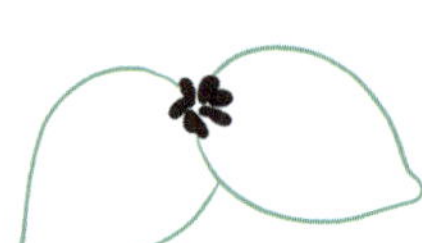

STEP 3

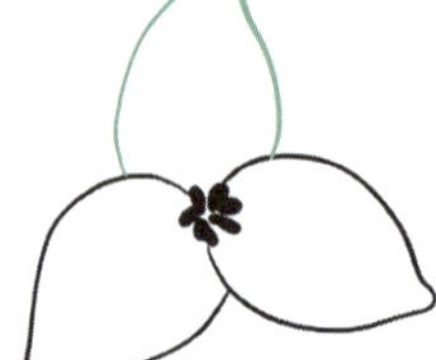

STEP 4

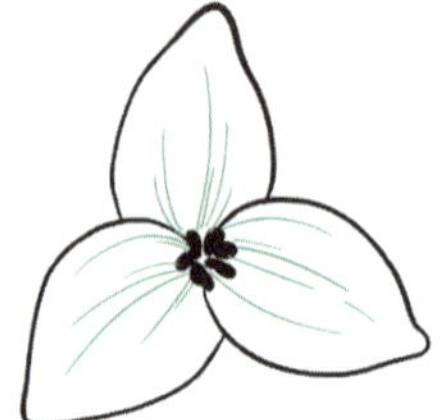

STEP 5

STEP 6

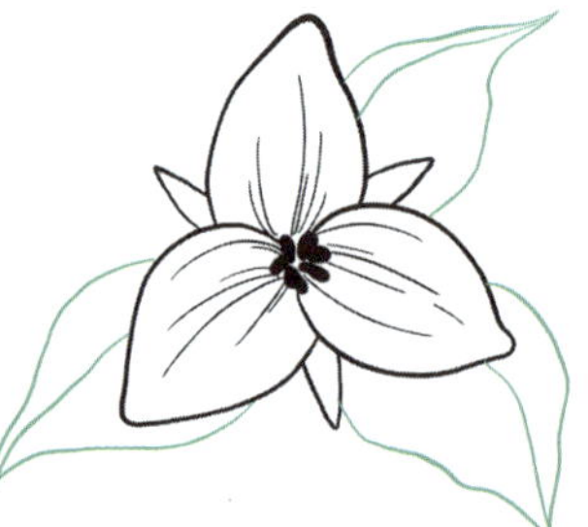

STEP 7

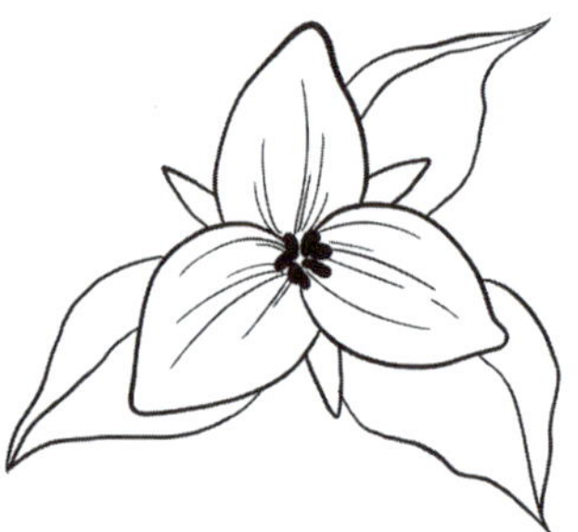

FUN FACT!

Trilliums are considered the heralds of spring, as they bloom early, before the trees' first green leaves appear.

Lupine

Lupinus oreganus

STEP 1

STEP 2

STEP 3

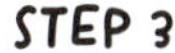

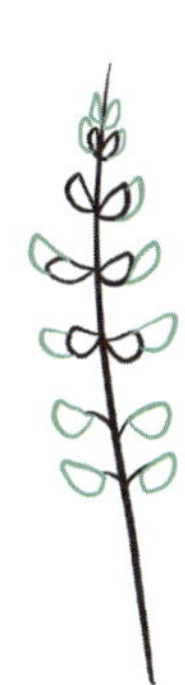

STEP 4

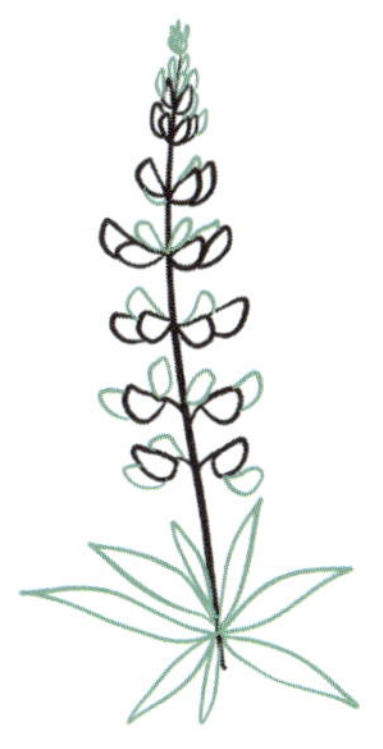

STEP 5

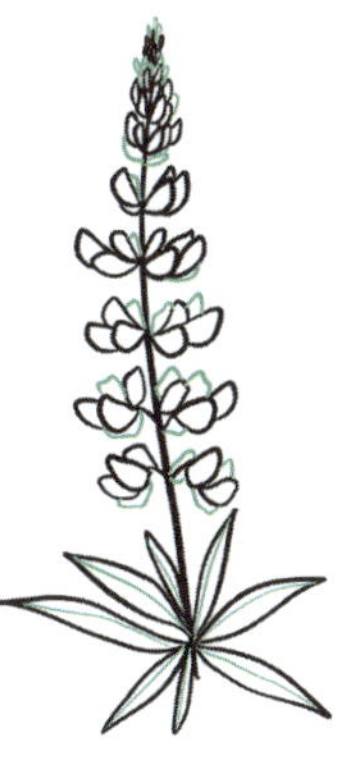

STEP 6

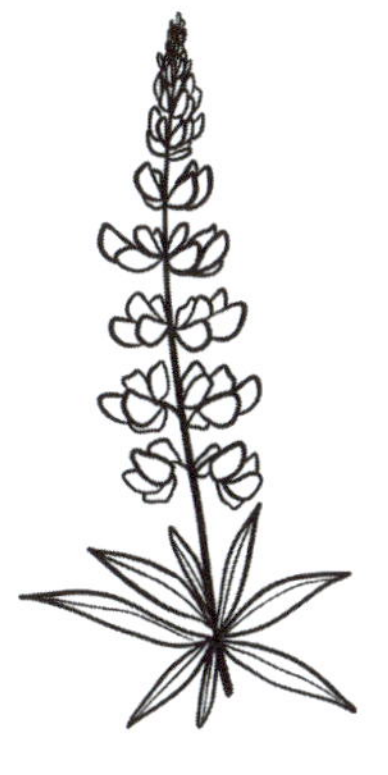

FUN FACT!

Taking its name from the Latin for "wolf," the lupine flower has the ability to enrich soil by fixing nitrogen, which, together with bacteria, allows it to convert nitrogen from air into plant nutrients.

Pacific Rhododendron

Rhododendron macrophyllum

STEP 1

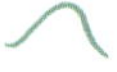

STEP 2

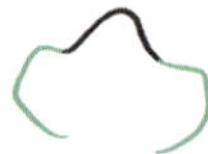

STEP 3

STEP 4

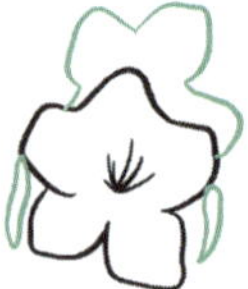

STEP 5

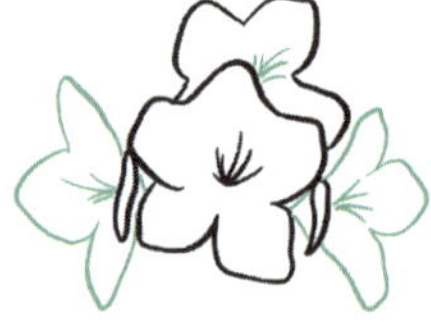

STEP 6

STEP 7

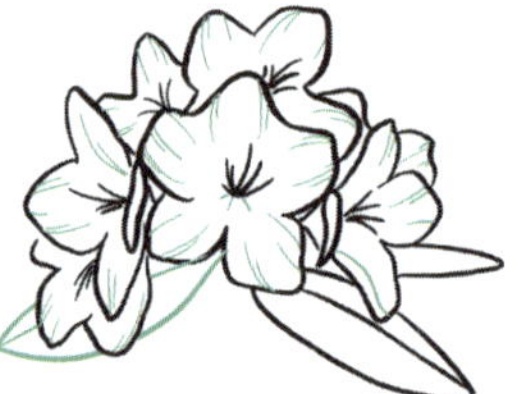

STEP 8

FUN FACT!

More than eight hundred species of rhododendrons are found around the world (except in Africa and South America).

Oregon Grape

Mahonia aquifolium

STEP 1

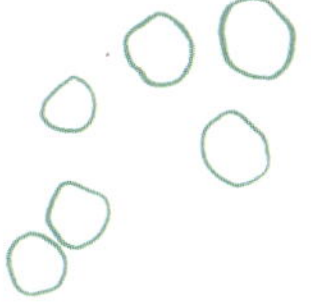

STEP 2

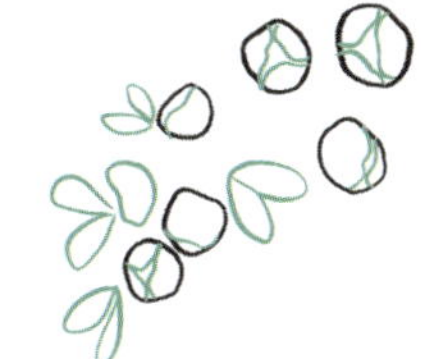

STEP 3

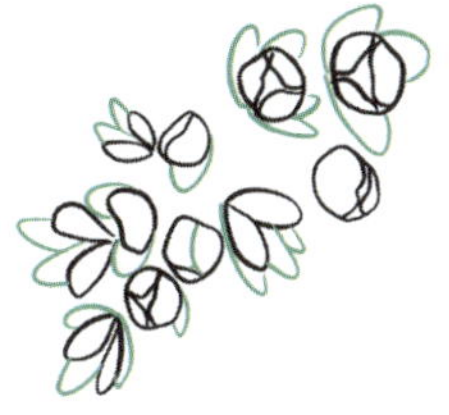

STEP 4

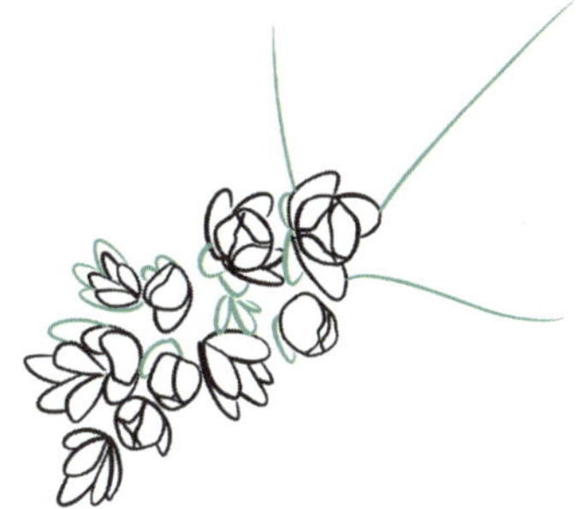

STEP 5

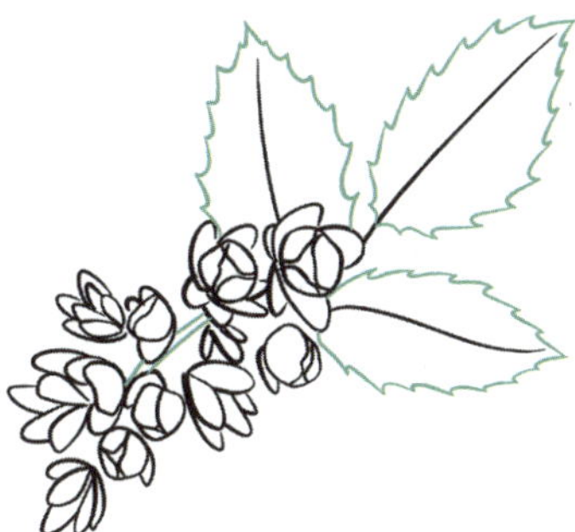

STEP 6

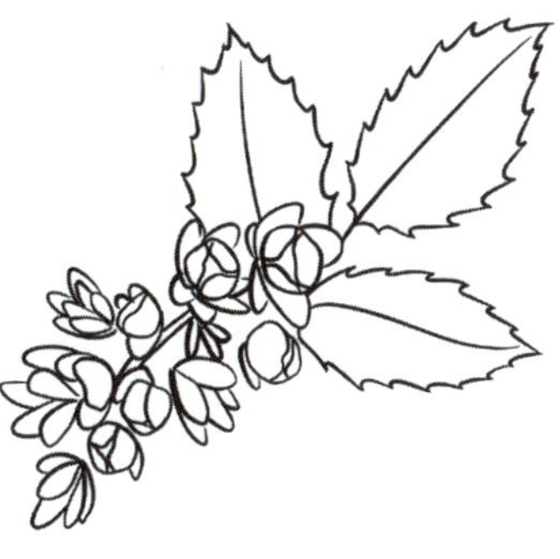

FUN FACT!

The flower of this plant is the Oregon state flower, and the roots have been used as a natural remedy to treat a variety of ailments, including tuberculosis.

Syringa

Philadelphus lewisii

STEP 1

STEP 2

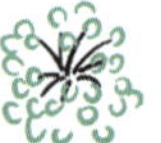

STEP 3

STEP 4

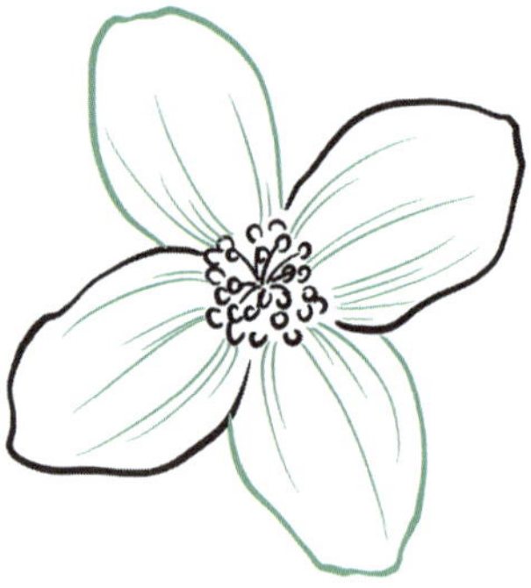

STEP 5

FUN FACT!

The scientific name of this white-flowered shrub commemorates the Egyptian king Ptolemy Philadelphus, who is said to have been a garden lover.

Red Columbine

Aquilegia formosa

STEP 1

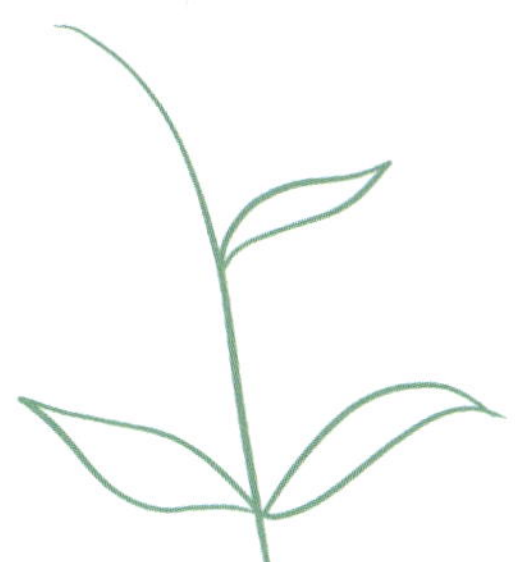

STEP 2

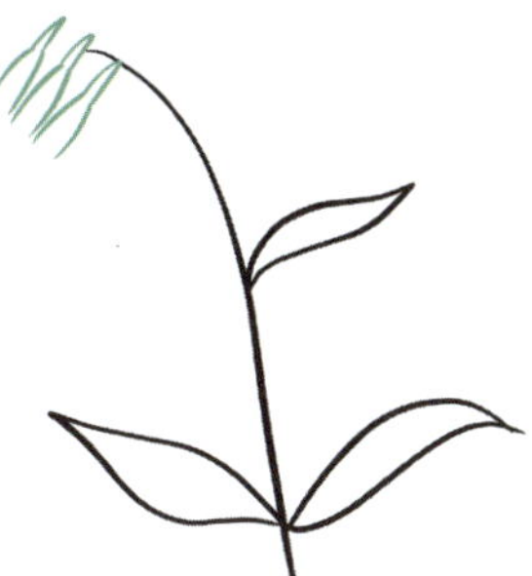

STEP 3

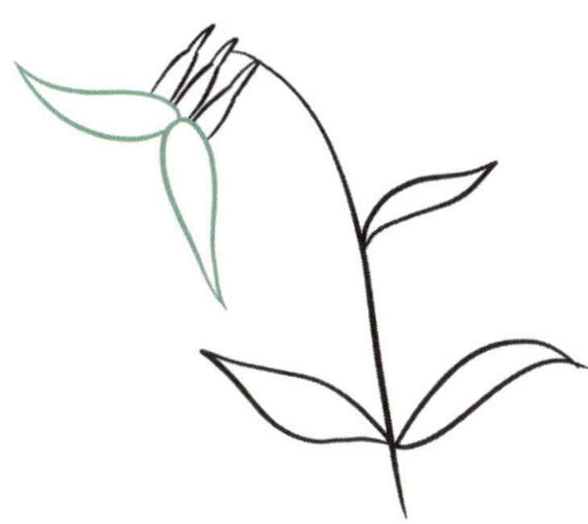

STEP 4

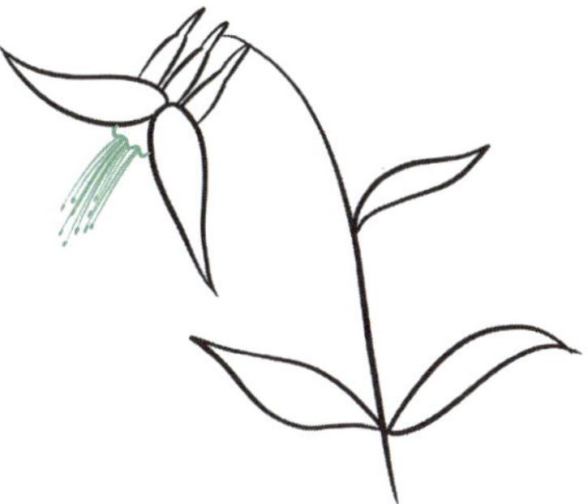

STEP 5

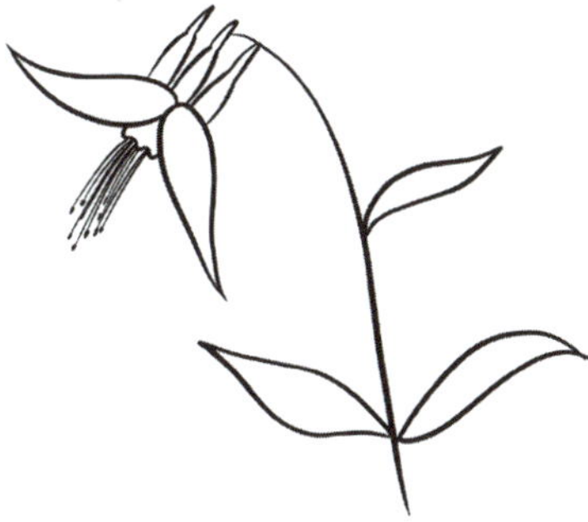

FUN FACT!

The clawlike spurs at its base resemble eagle talons and give this flower its scientific name (*Aquila* is the golden eagle's genus). Its inverted shape resembles clusters of doves and gives it its common name (*Columba* means "dove" in Latin).

Snow Buttercup

Ranunculus nivalis

STEP 1

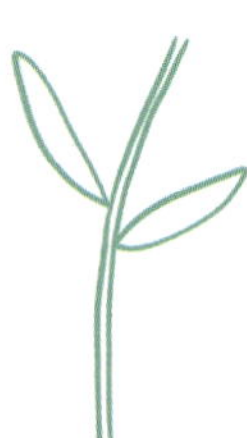

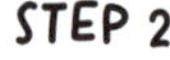

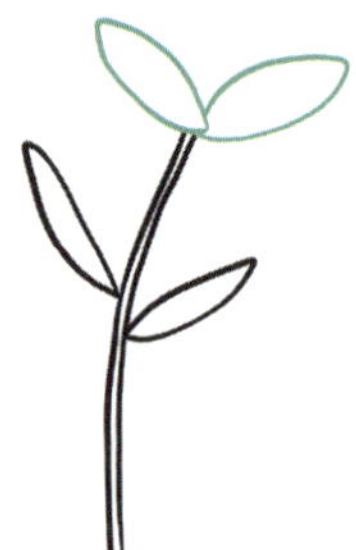

STEP 3

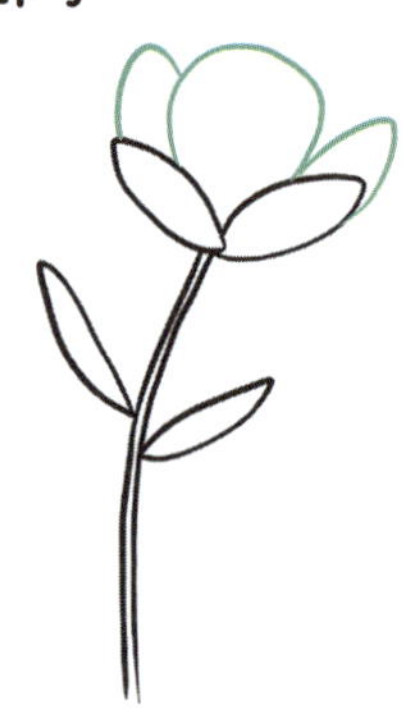

STEP 4

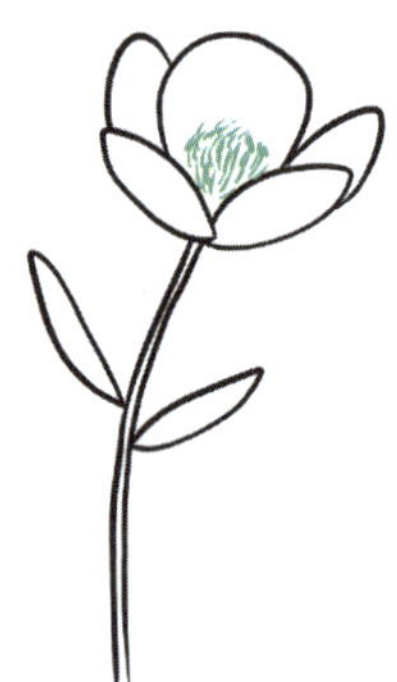

STEP 5

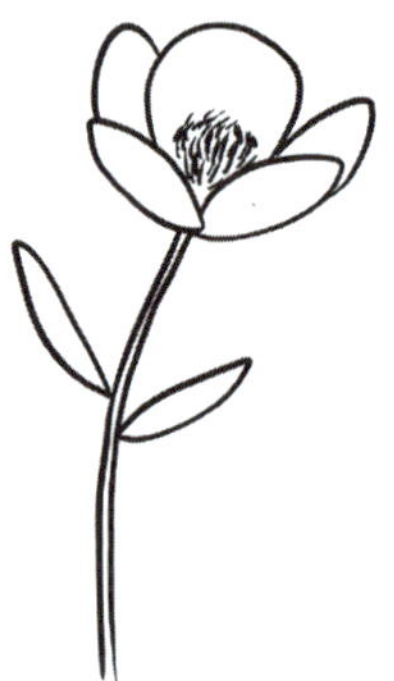

FUN FACT!

Despite its charming, bright yellow appearance, the snow buttercup is poisonous to humans.

Coast Silk Tassel

Garrya elliptica

STEP 1

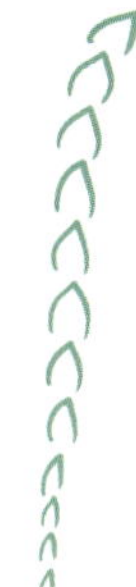

STEP 2

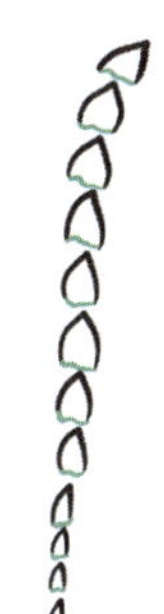

STEP 3

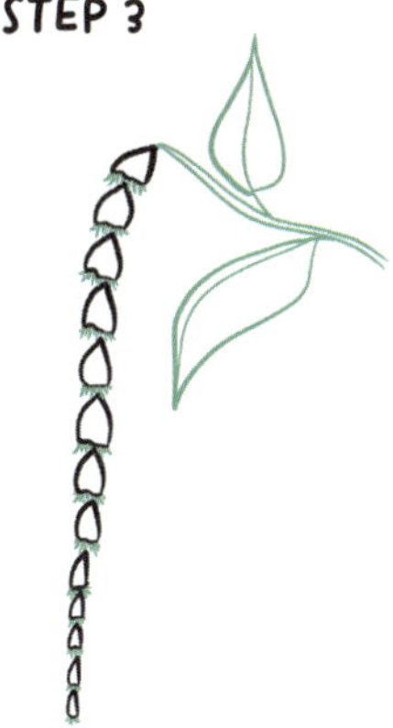

STEP 4

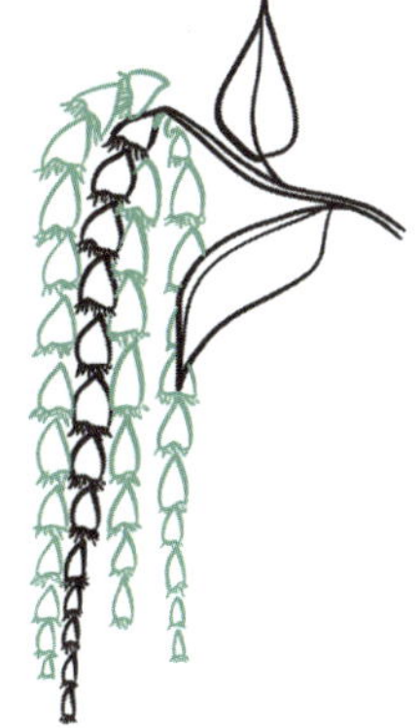

STEP 5

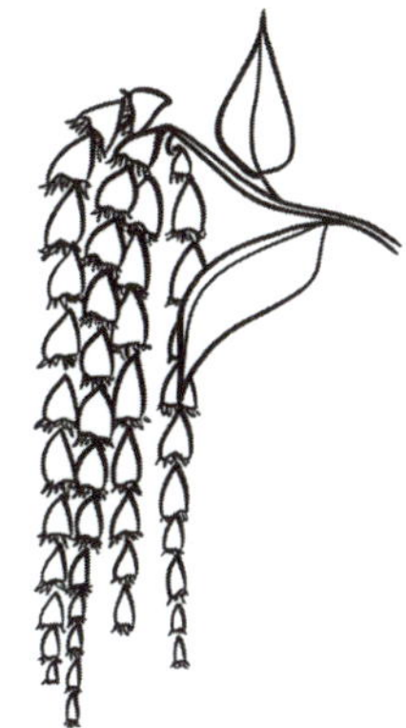

FUN FACT!

This species is dioecious, meaning individual plants are either male or female, with stamens or pistils, respectively.

Western Yarrow

Achillea millefolium var. occidentalis

STEP 1

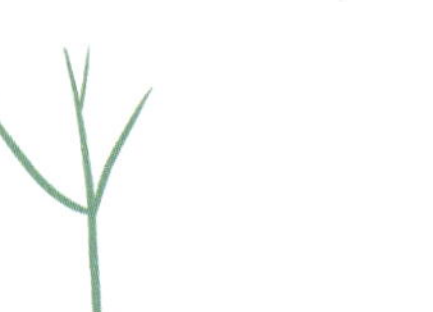

STEP 2

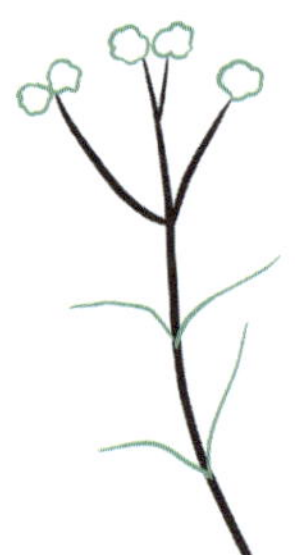

STEP 3

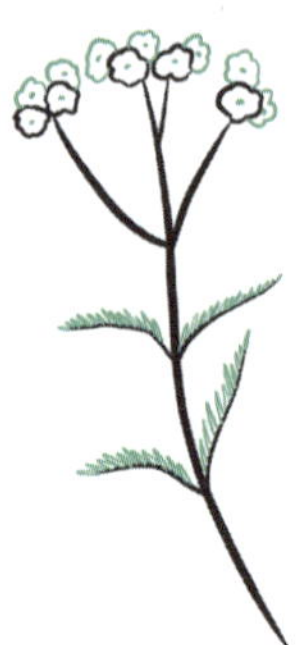

STEP 4

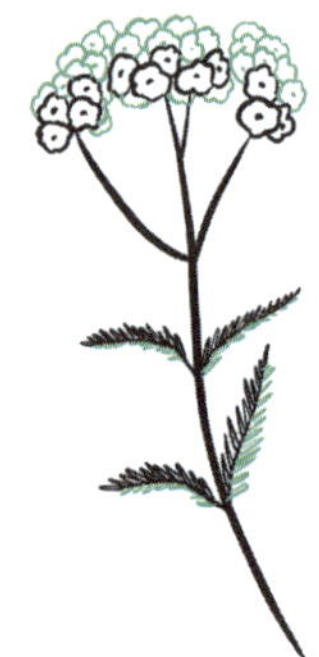

STEP 5

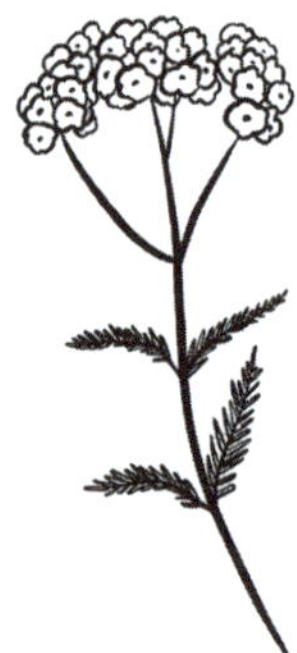

FUN FACT!

This plant is great at attracting beneficial insects and repelling pests.

Yellow Marsh Marigold

Caltha palustris

STEP 1

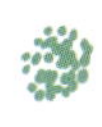

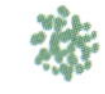

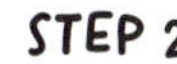

STEP 3

STEP 4

STEP 5

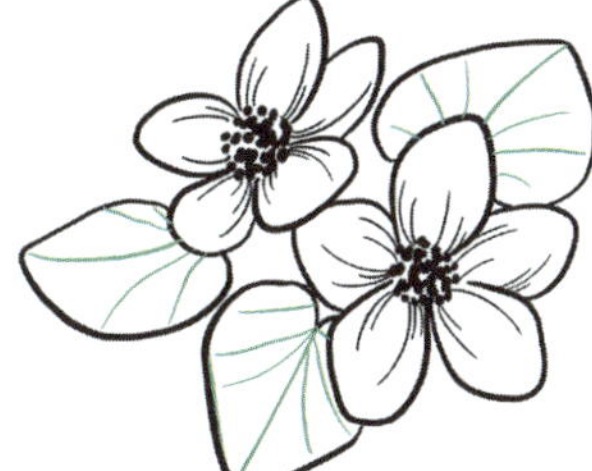

STEP 6

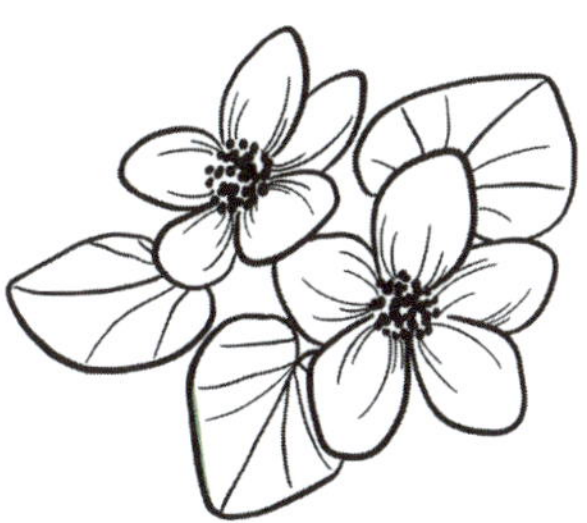

FUN FACT!

With its bright yellow flowers, the marsh marigold is often associated with bravery and courage. It was even believed to have protective powers that ward off evil spirits.

Bleeding Heart

Dicentra formosa

STEP 1

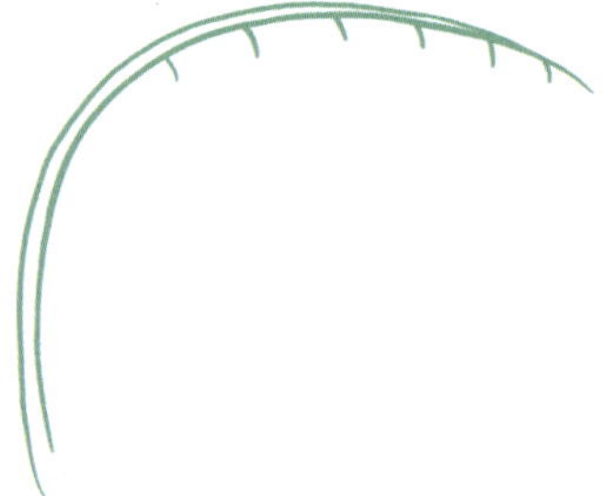

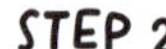

STEP 2

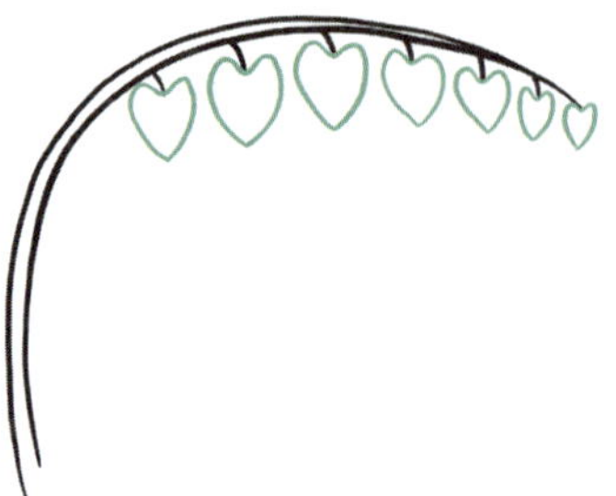

STEP 3

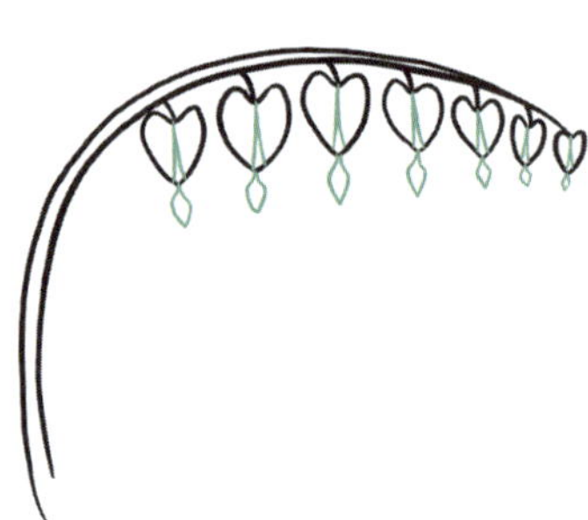

STEP 4

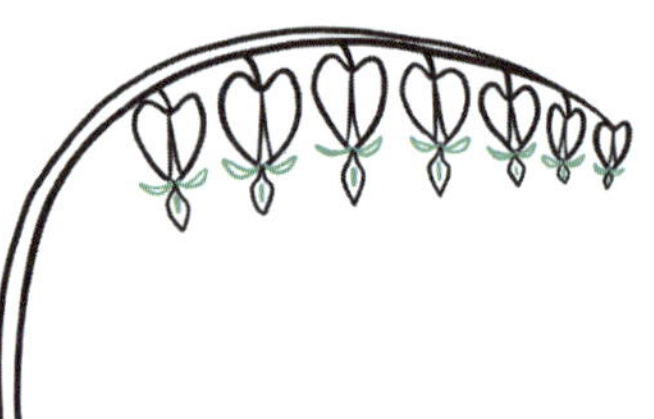

STEP 5

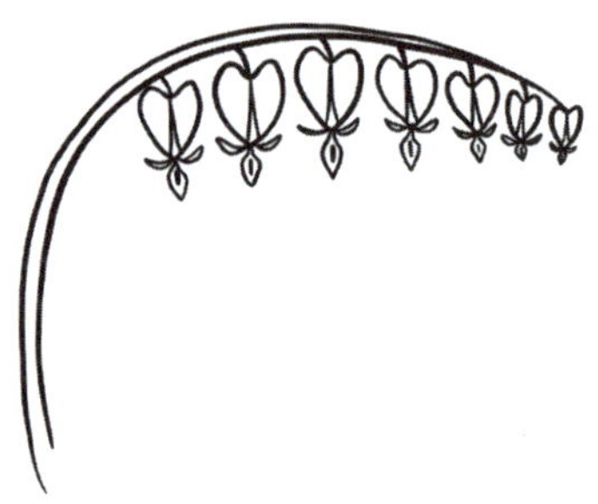

FUN FACT!

Various Native American tribes chewed the roots of this plant to alleviate toothaches.

Broad-Leaved Starflower

Trientalis latifolia

STEP 1

STEP 2

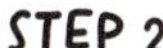

STEP 3

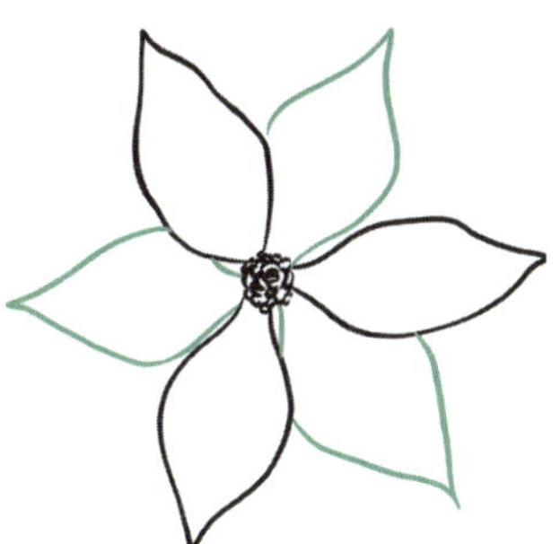

STEP 4

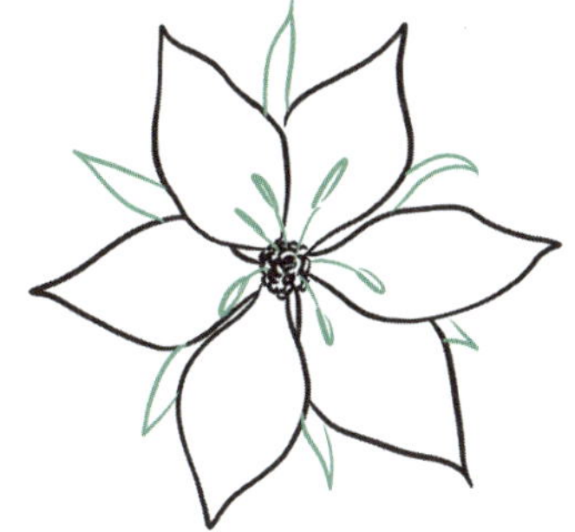

STEP 5

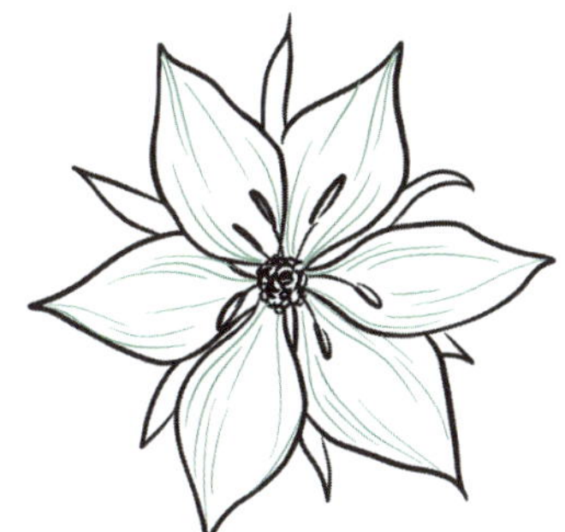

STEP 6

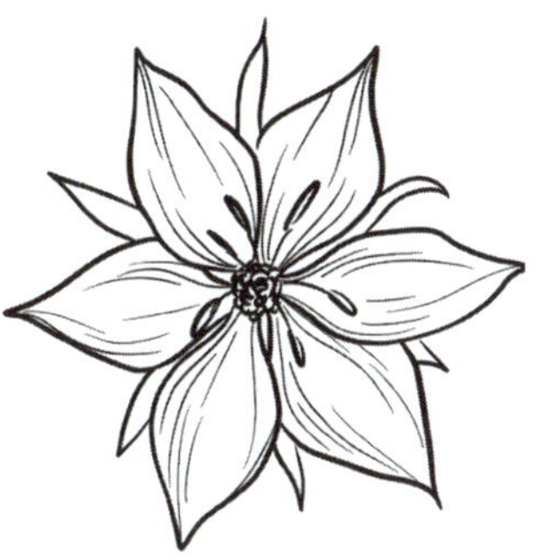

FUN FACT!

While each plant can be expected to live only around three years, it grows in persistent dense patches that will continue expanding as a self-sustaining colony.

Yellow Monkeyflower

Mimulus guttatus

STEP 1

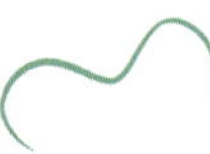

STEP 2

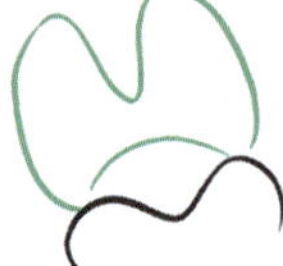

STEP 3

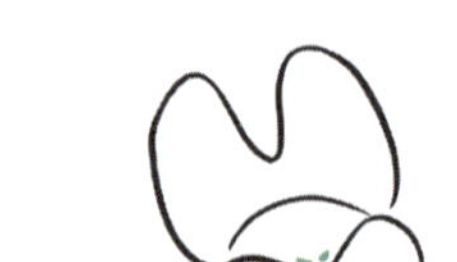

STEP 4

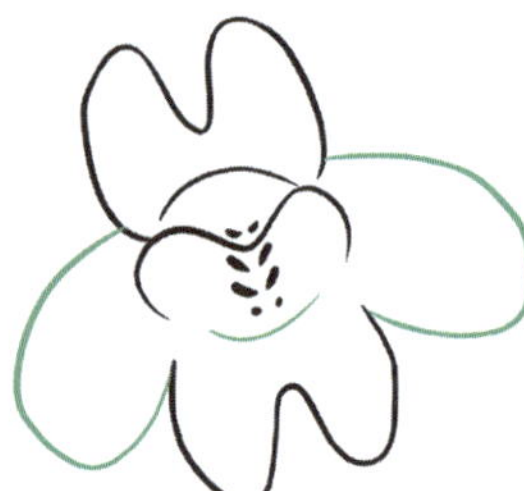

STEP 5

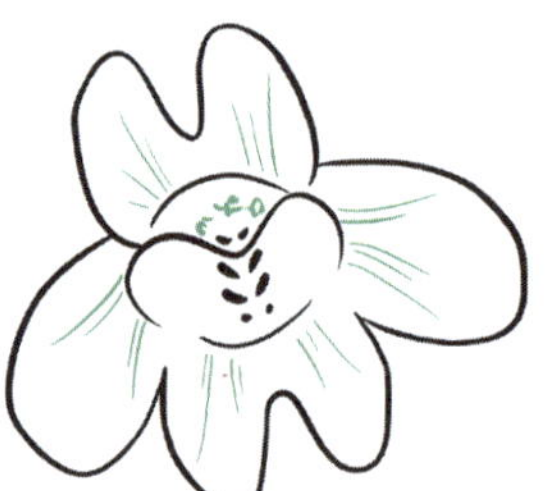

STEP 6

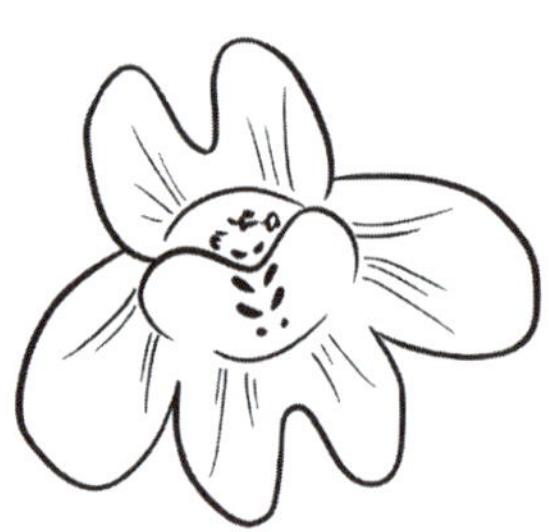

FUN FACT!

This damp-loving flower got its name because some of its species resemble a monkey's face.

Satin Flower

Olsynium douglasii

STEP 1

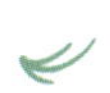

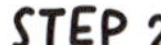

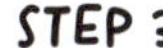

STEP 4

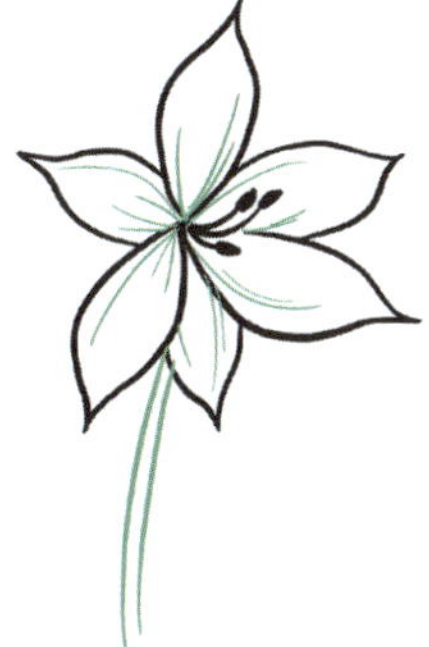

STEP 5

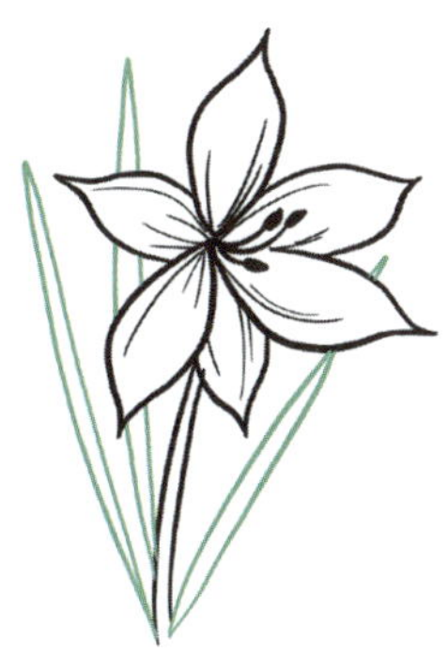

STEP 6

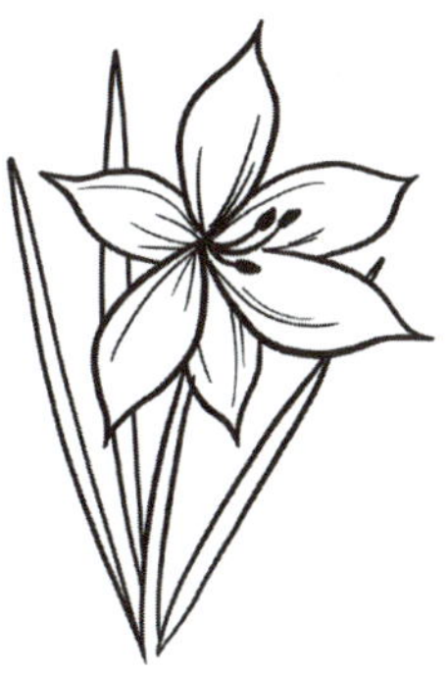

FUN FACT!

Also known as grass widow or purple-eyed grass, this flower often grows in rugged areas, giving the surroundings a beautiful splash of purple.

Henderson's Shooting Star

Dodecatheon hendersonii

STEP 1

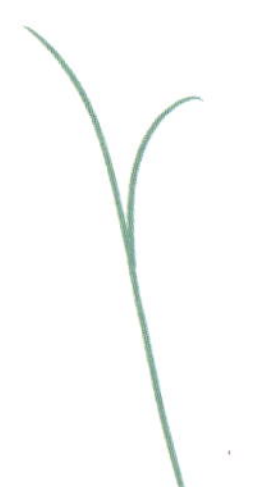

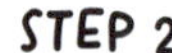

STEP 3

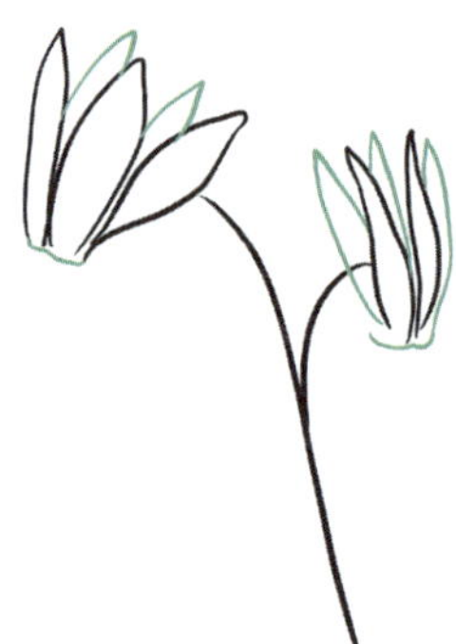

STEP 4

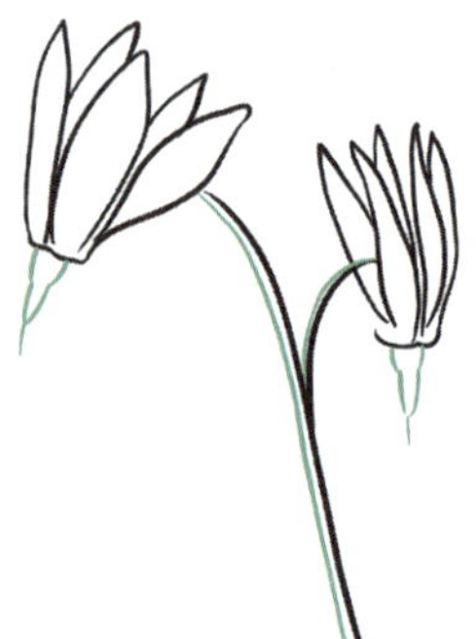

STEP 5

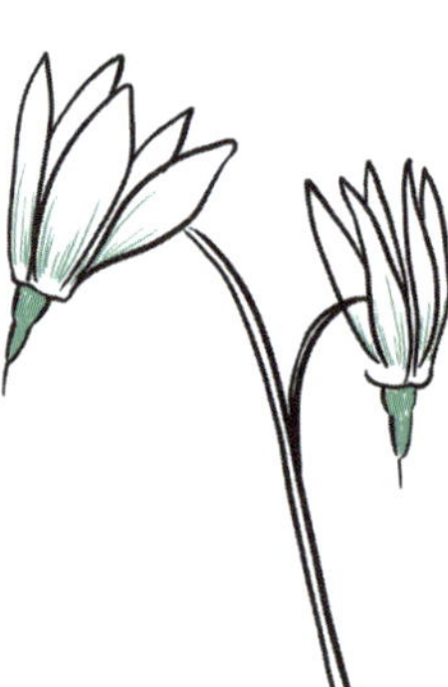

STEP 6

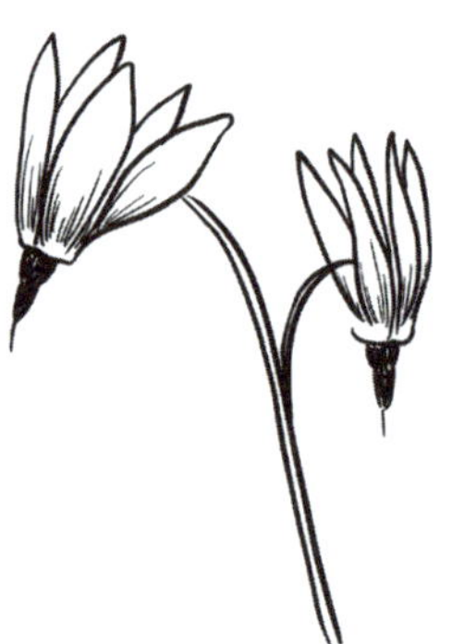

FUN FACT!

The petals and stamens of this flower create an illusion of pink shooting stars. To add even more magic, its scientific name means "flower of twelve gods" in Greek.

Checker Mallow

Sidalcea malviflora

STEP 1

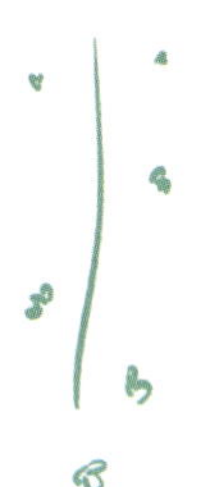

STEP 2

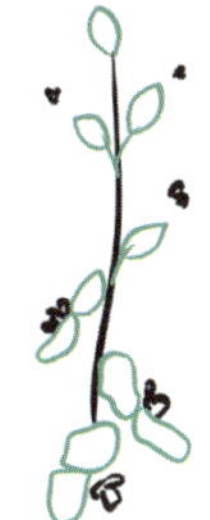

STEP 3

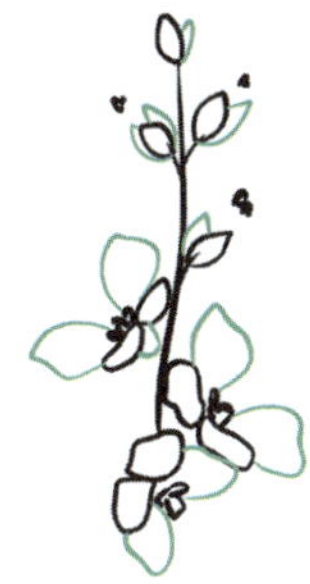

STEP 4

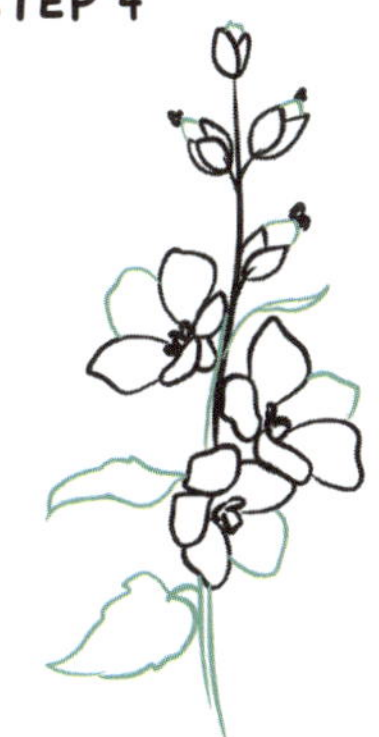

STEP 5

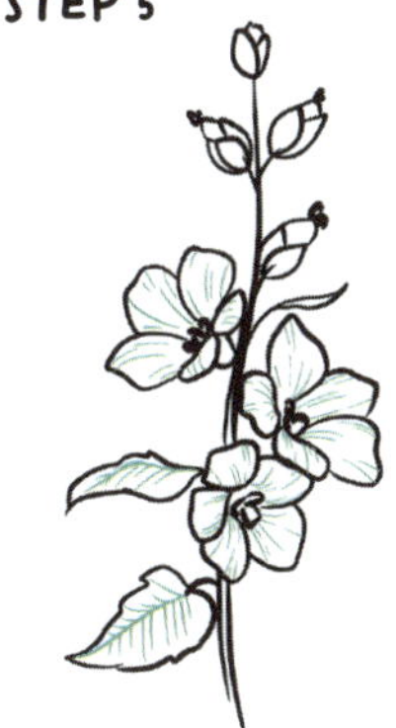

STEP 6

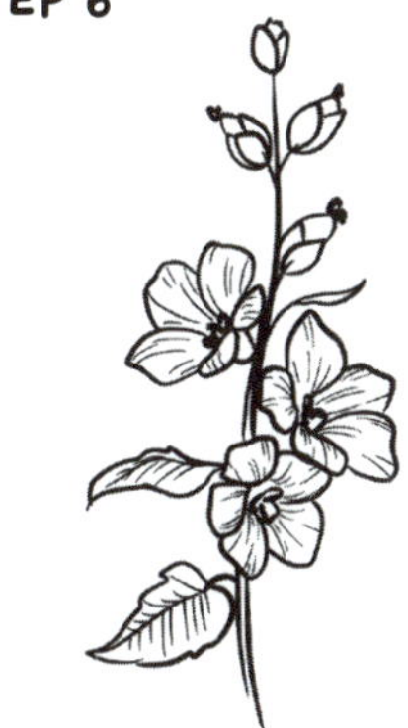

FUN FACT!

As a gynodioecious species, this plant can have either perfect (male and female) or pistillate (female) flowers.

White Mountain Heather

Cassiope mertensiana

STEP 1

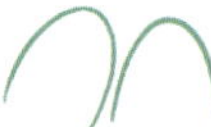

STEP 2

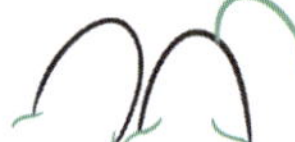

STEP 3

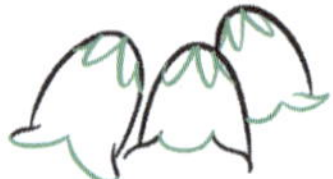

STEP 4

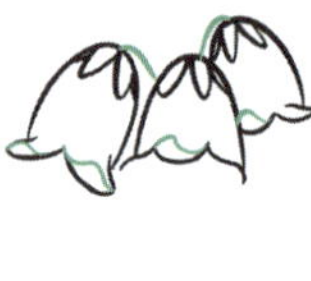

STEP 5

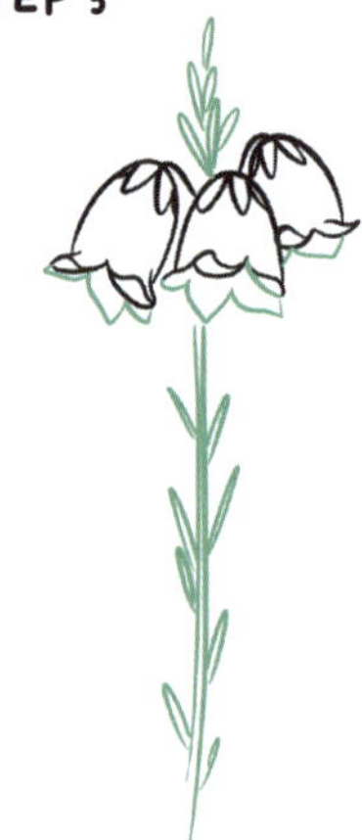

STEP 6

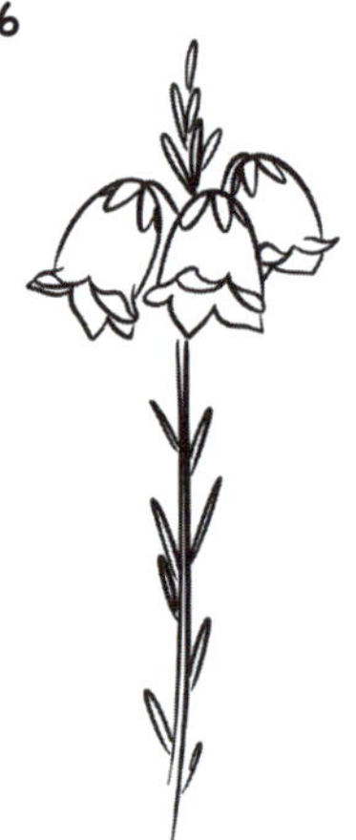

FUN FACT!

A slow grower (a small shrub can be up to twenty years old!), white mountain heather can be used to produce a golden-brown dye.

Oregon Oxalis

Oxalis oregana

STEP 1

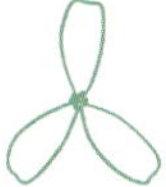

STEP 2

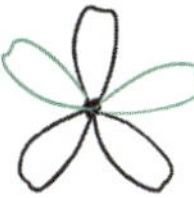

STEP 3

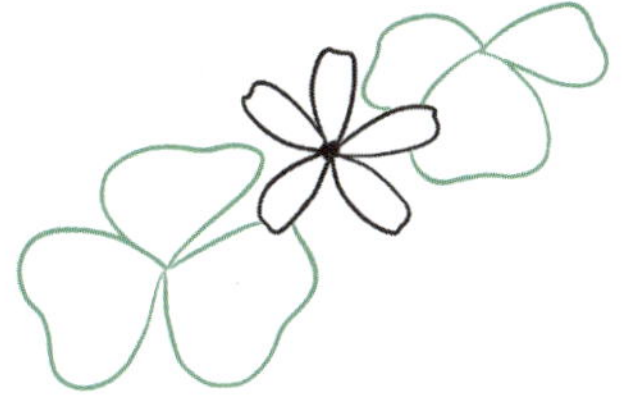

STEP 4

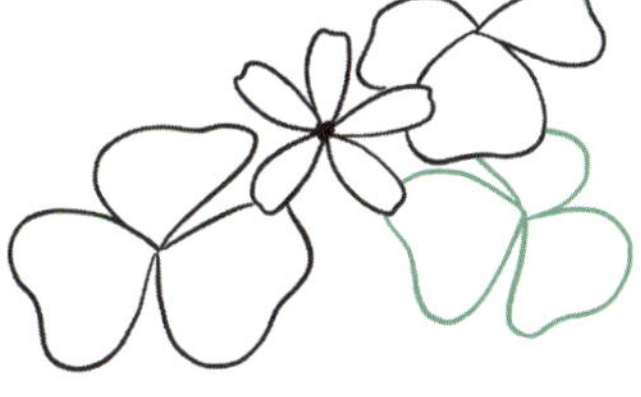

STEP 5

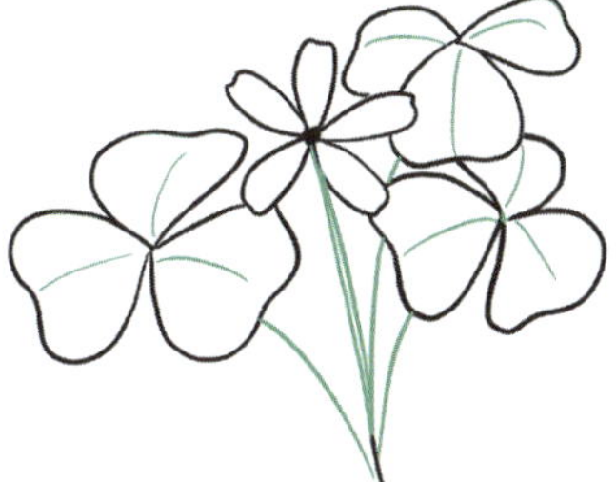

STEP 6

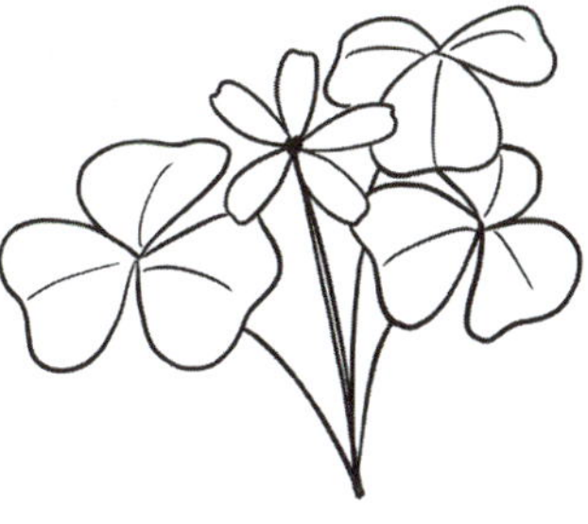

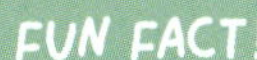

This plant's delicate leaves fold down into a tiny pyramid to protect themselves from direct sunlight.

Oregon Iris

Iris tenax

STEP 1

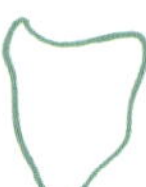

STEP 2

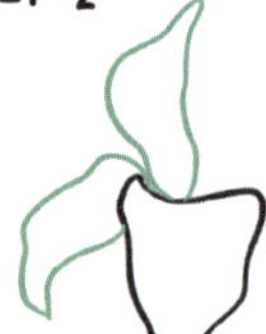

STEP 3

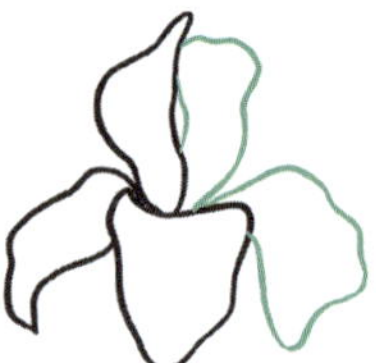

STEP 4

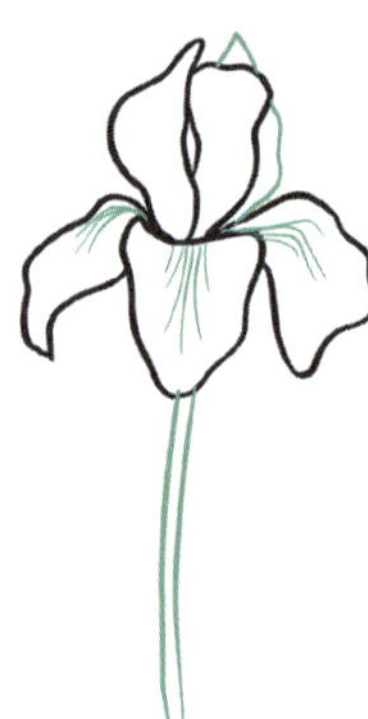

STEP 5

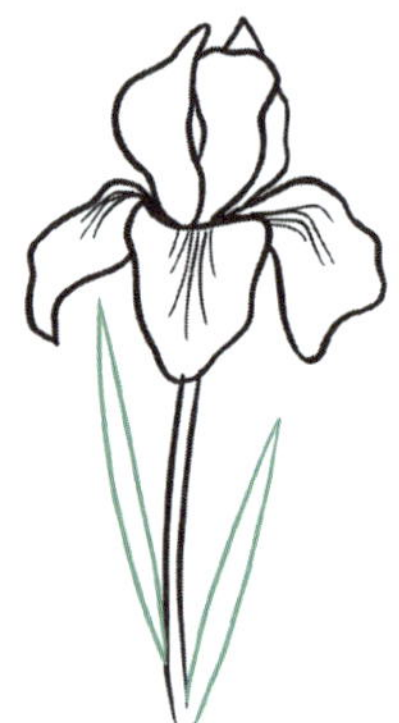

STEP 6

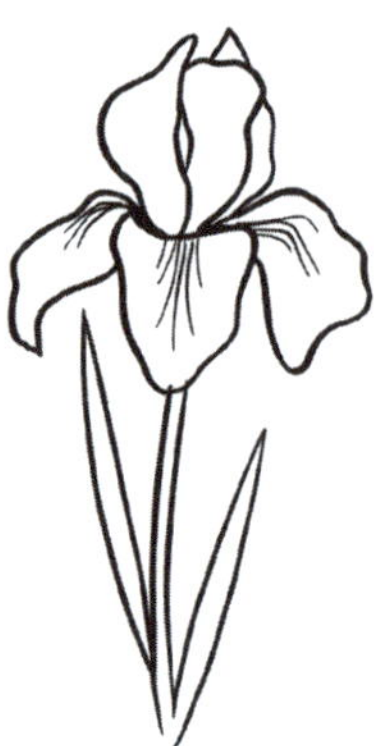

FUN FACT!

The strong fibers of this plant's leaves have been used to make ropes, nets, and string.

Mariposa Lily

Calochortus luteus

STEP 1

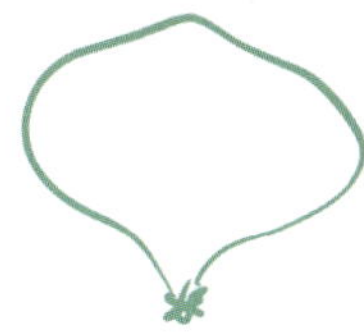

STEP 2

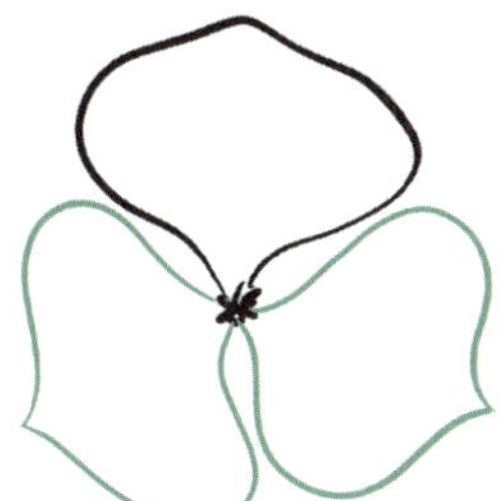

STEP 3

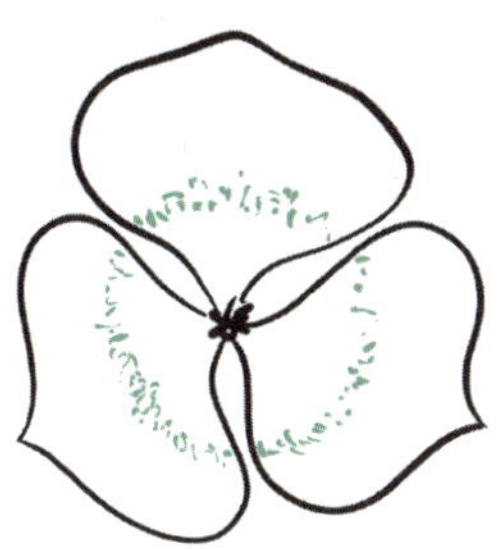

STEP 4

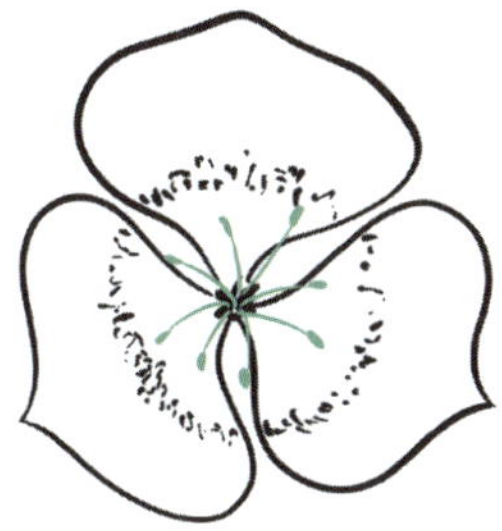

STEP 5

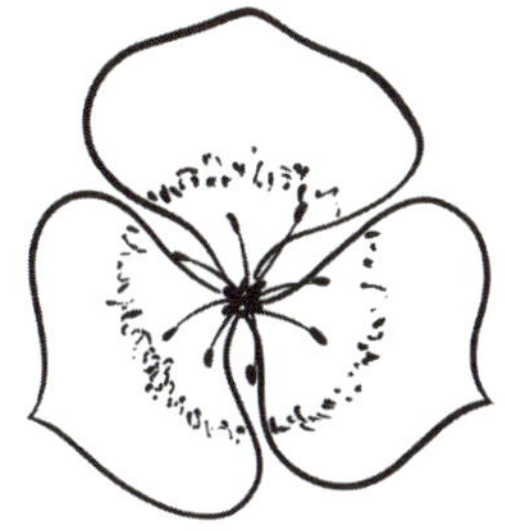

FUN FACT!

Because this flower grows from a bulb, it can survive most wildfires even when the exposed part of the flower is burned.

Arrowleaf Balsamroot

Balsamorhiza hookeri

STEP 1

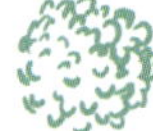

STEP 2

STEP 3

STEP 4

STEP 5

STEP 6

FUN FACT!

This plant is also known as the Oregon sunflower.

Fireweed

Chamerion angustifolium

STEP 1

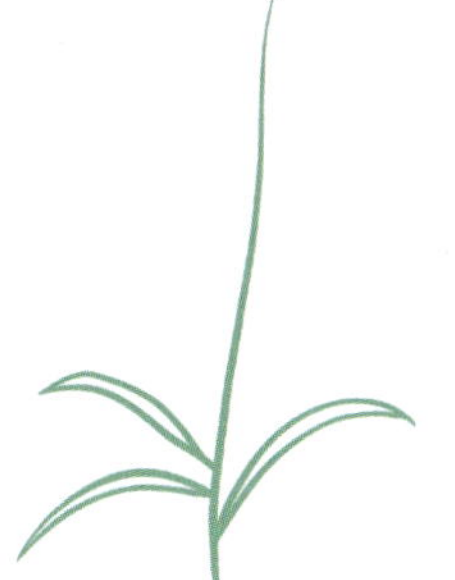

STEP 2

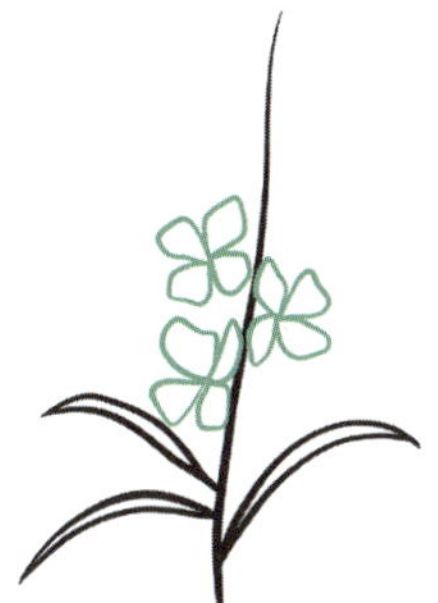

STEP 3

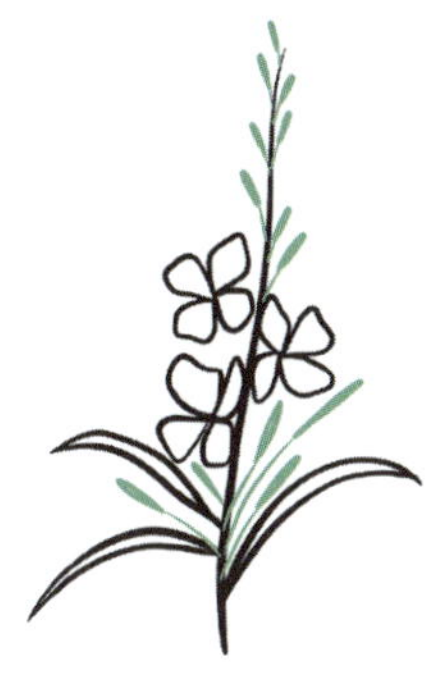

STEP 4

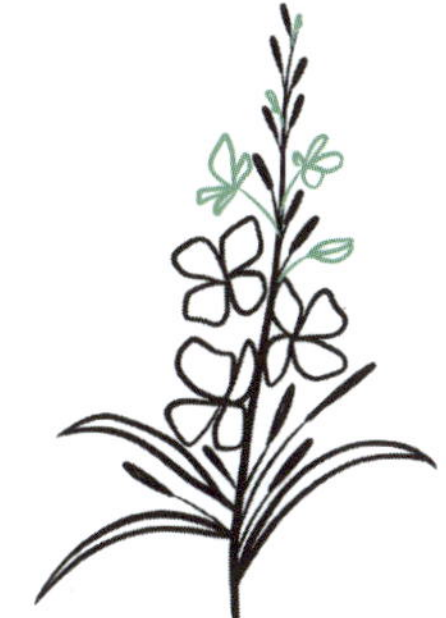

STEP 5

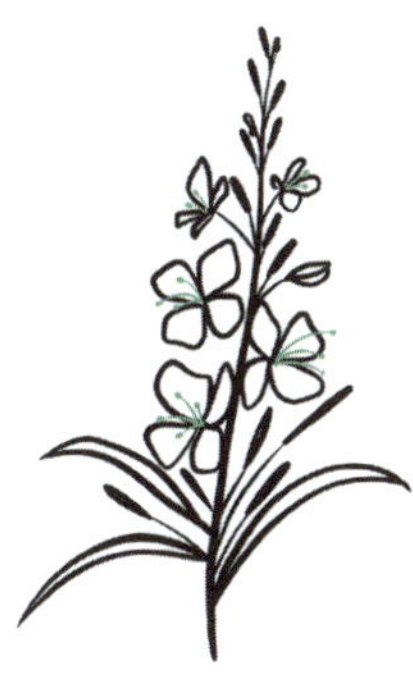

STEP 6

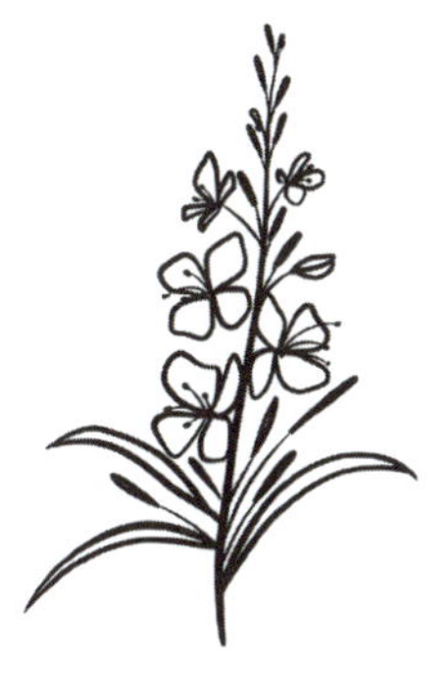

FUN FACT!

This charming purple-flowered plant is named for its ability to quickly colonize areas cleared by a fire.

Western Anemone

Anemone occidentalis

STEP 1

STEP 2

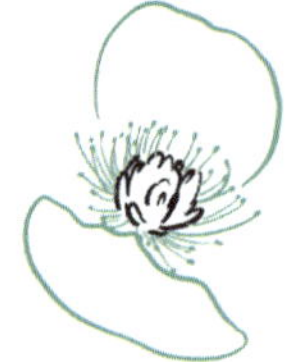

STEP 3

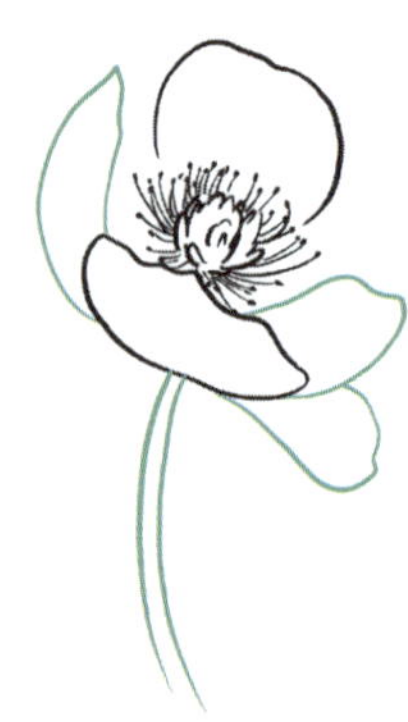

STEP 4

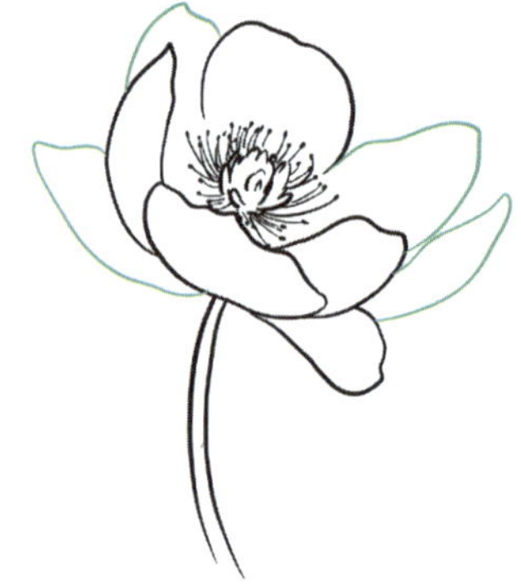

STEP 5

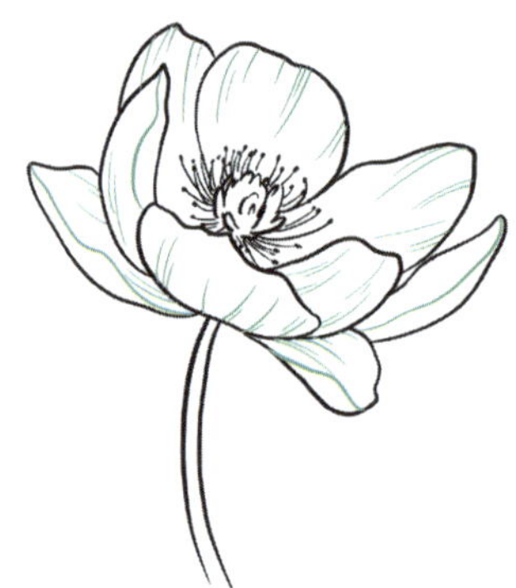

STEP 6

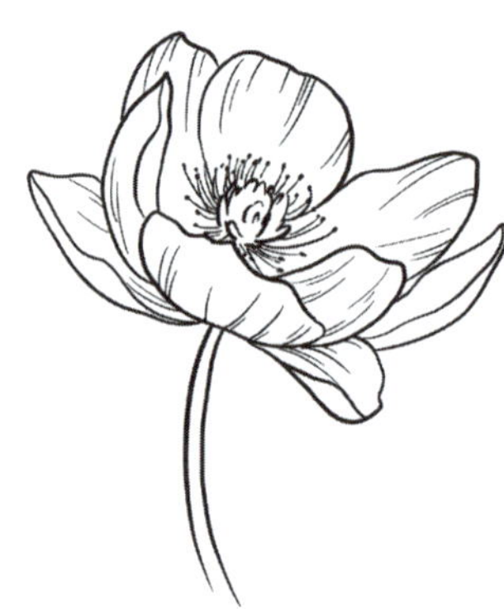

FUN FACT!

After blooming, its white flowers turn into distinctive fluffy seed heads, earning it the nickname "old man of the mountain."

Indian Paintbrush

Castilleja spp.

STEP 1

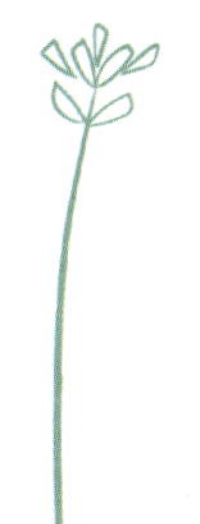

STEP 2

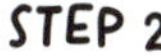

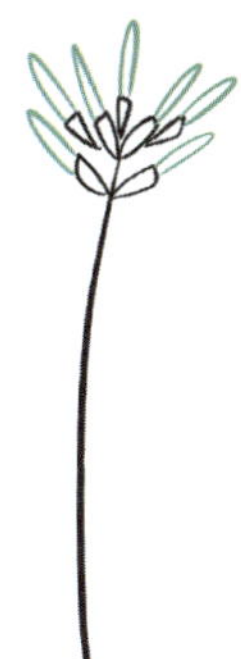

STEP 3

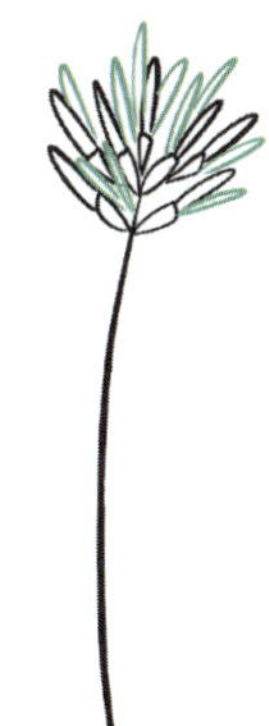

STEP 4

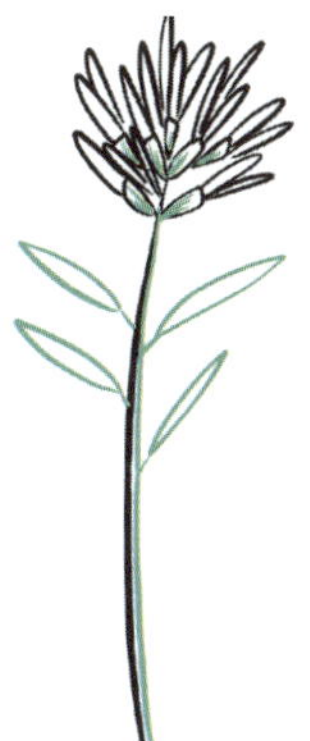

STEP 5

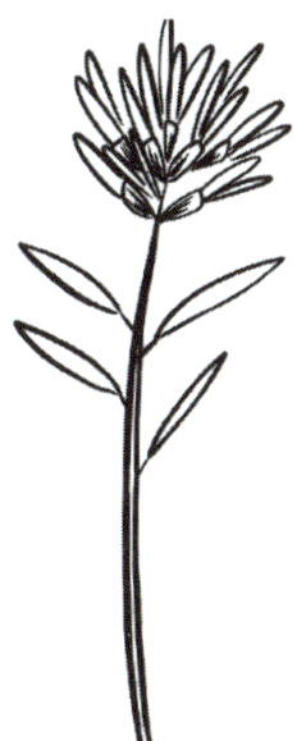

FUN FACT!

This plant's striking red-orange flowers look like they have been dipped in paint.

Nootka Rose

Rosa nutkana

STEP 1

STEP 2

STEP 3

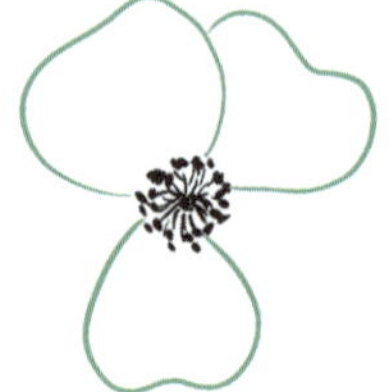

STEP 4

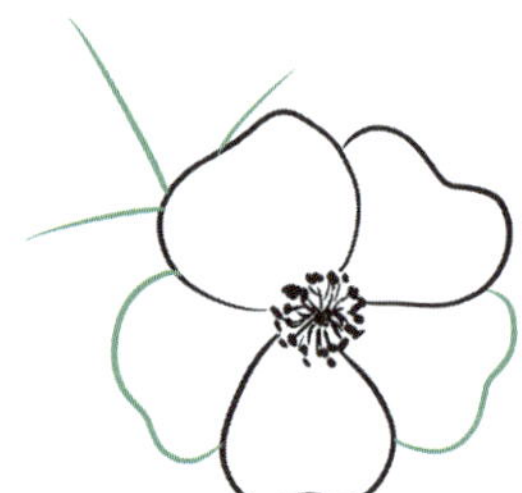

STEP 5

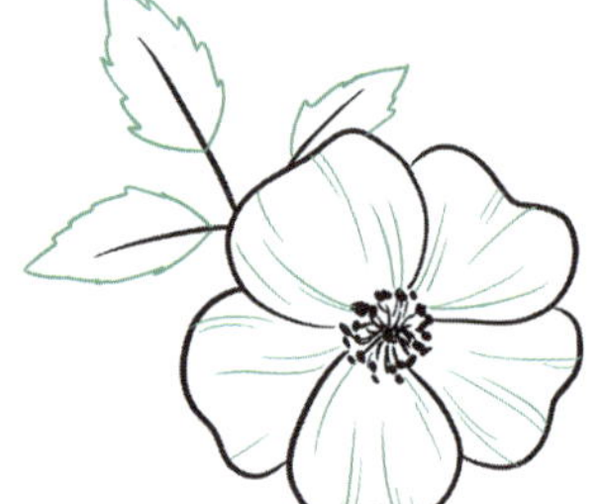

STEP 6

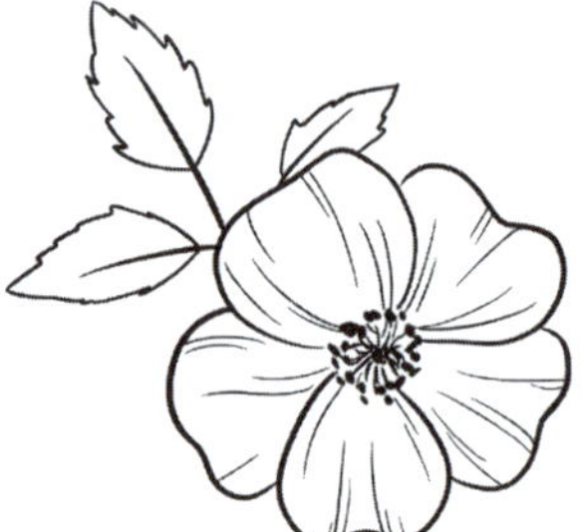

FUN FACT!

This pink-flowered plant is used to control erosion on hillsides, road cuts, and stream banks because of its rapid growth and ability to produce extensive rhizomes.

Fairy Slipper

Calypso bulbosa

STEP 1

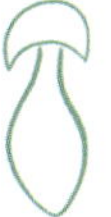

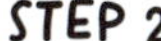

STEP 2

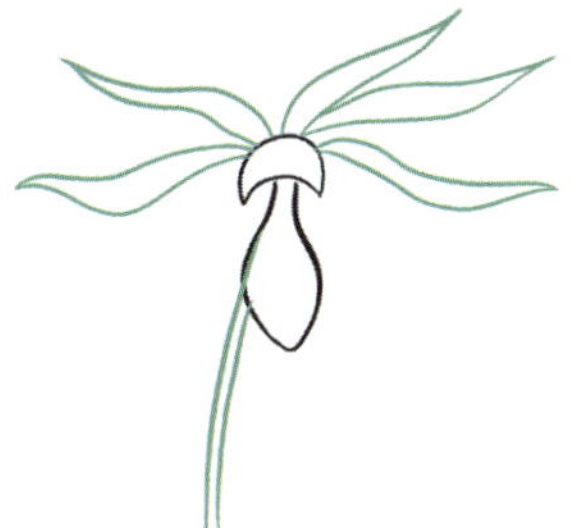

STEP 3

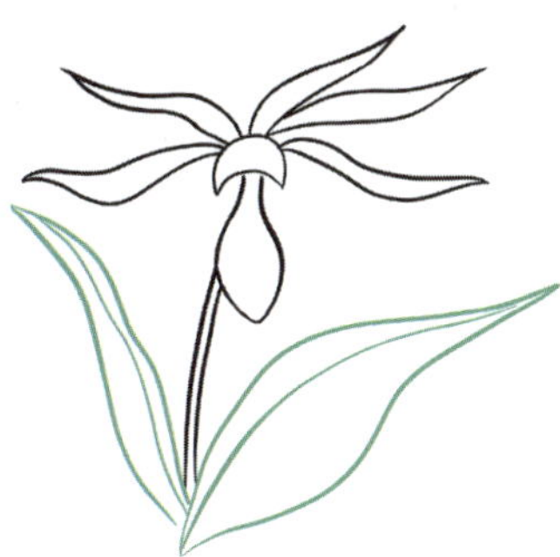

STEP 4

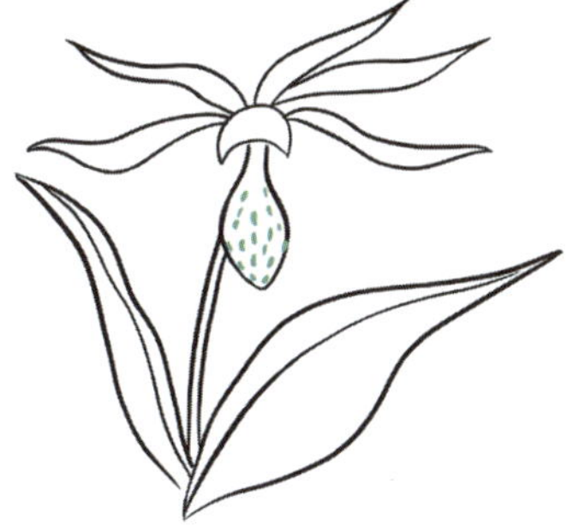

STEP 5

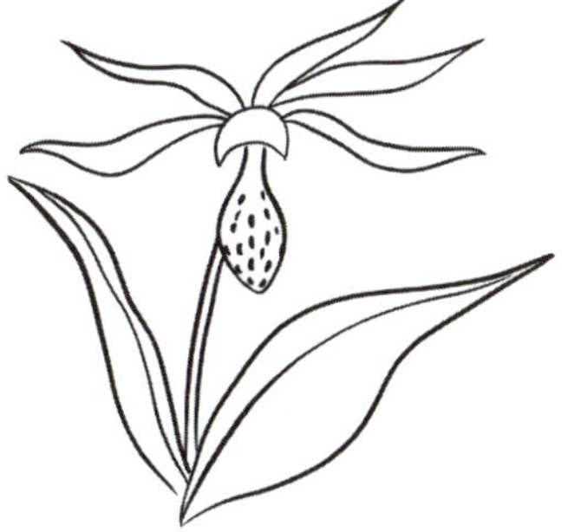

FUN FACT!

Seeing this pinkish-purple orchid is said to indicate that morels are nearby.

Twinflower

Linnaea borealis

STEP 1

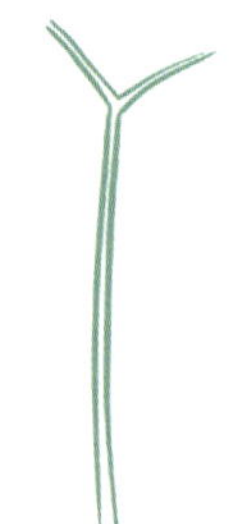

STEP 2

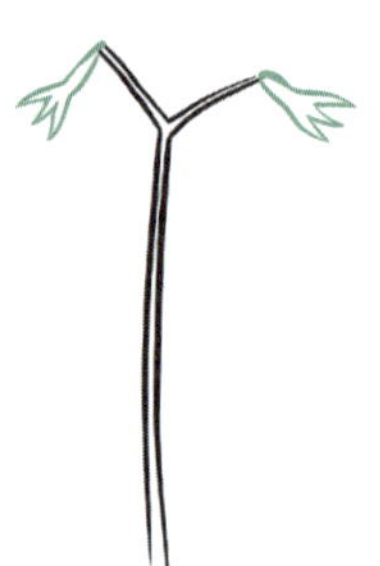

STEP 3

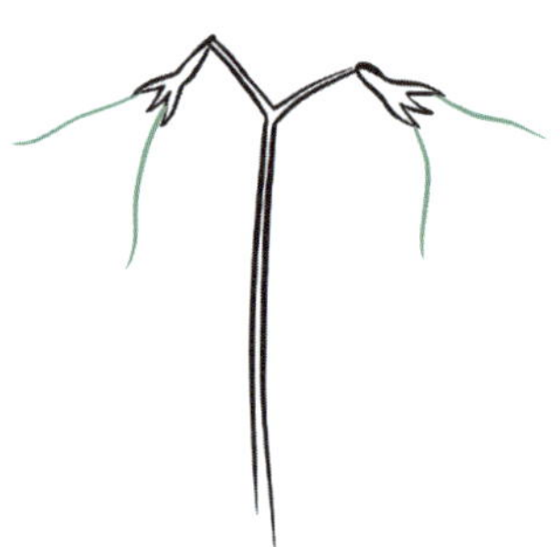

STEP 4

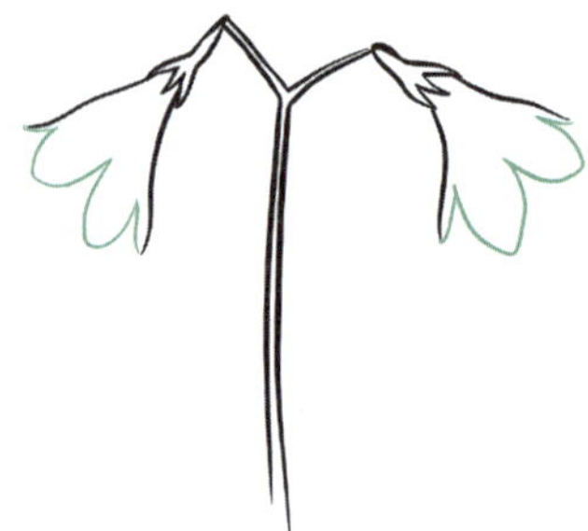

STEP 5

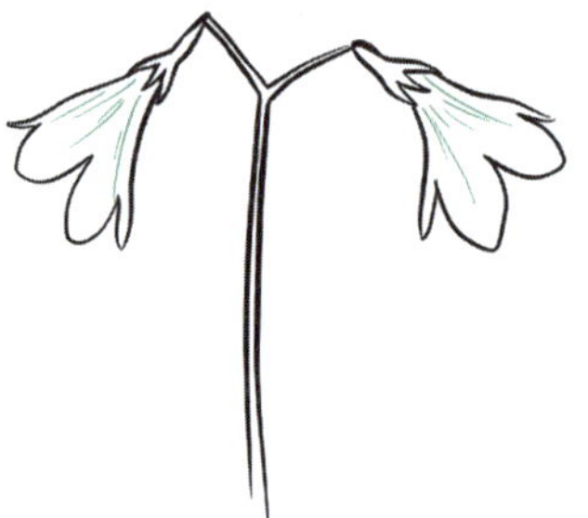

STEP 6

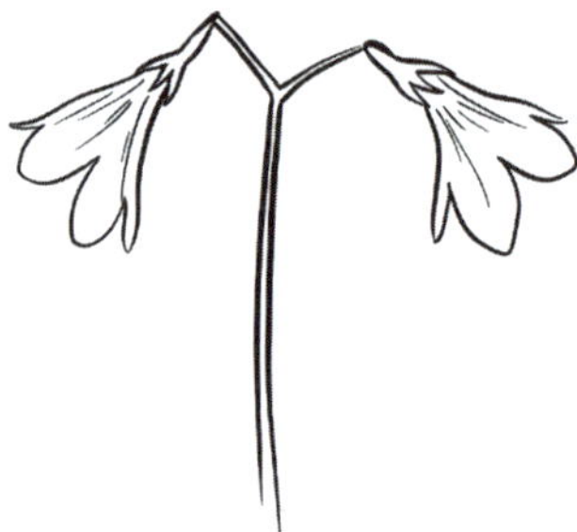

FUN FACT!

Technically, this white- or pink-flowered pineland native member of the honeysuckle family is a small shrub.

Skunk Cabbage

Lysichiton americanus

STEP 1

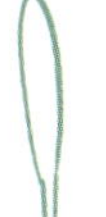

STEP 2

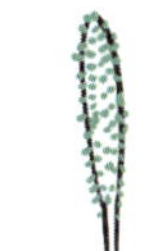

STEP 3

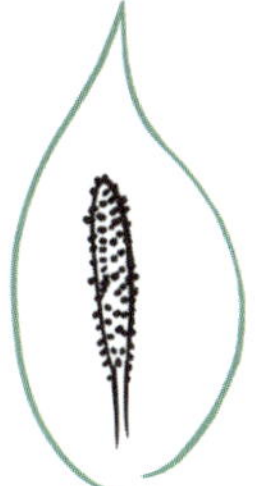

STEP 4

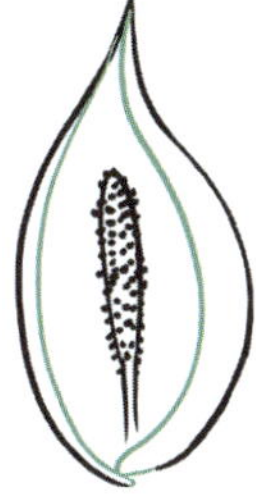

STEP 5

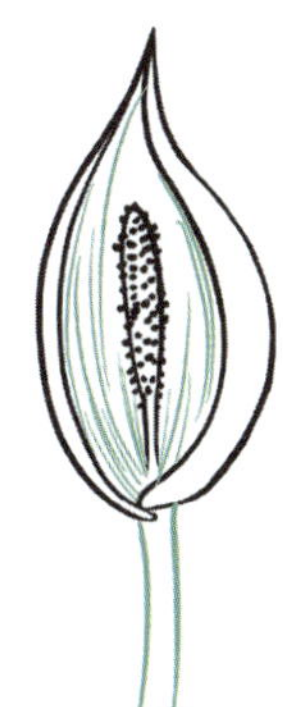

STEP 6

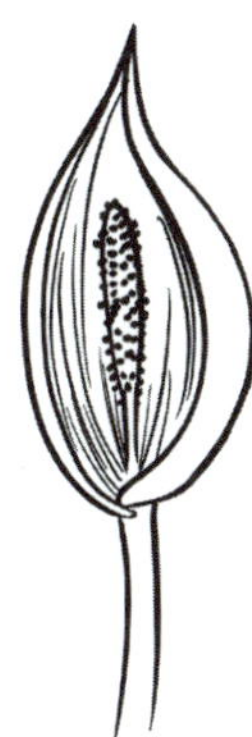

FUN FACT!

As the name suggests, this plant is named for its distinctive skunky odor (you'll instantly know when you've encountered it).

Woolly Sunflower

Eriophyllum lanatum

STEP 1

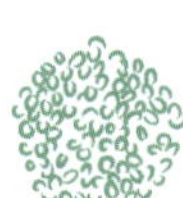

STEP 2

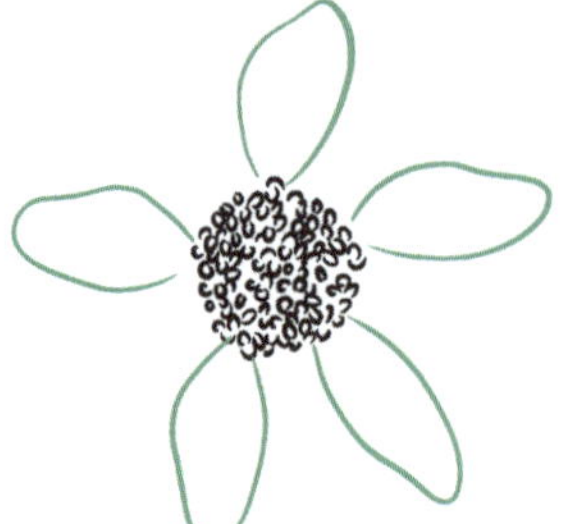

STEP 3

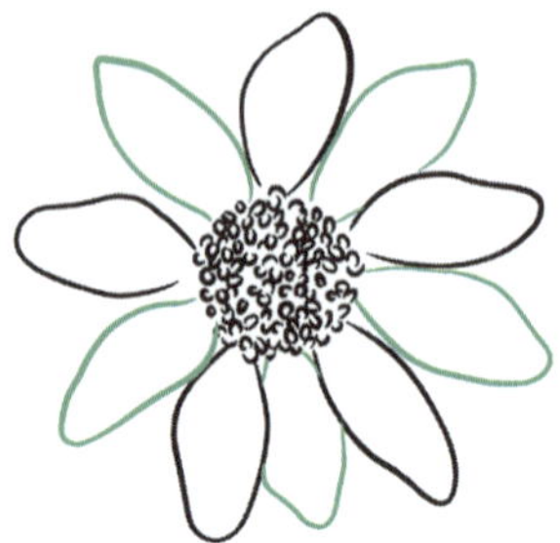

STEP 4

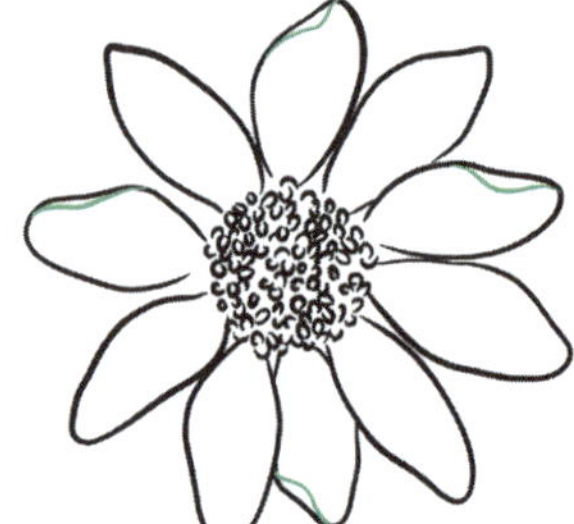

STEP 5

STEP 6

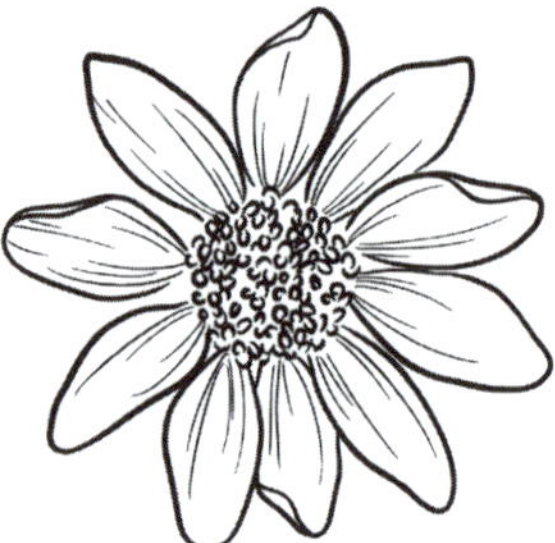

FUN FACT!

Also known as Oregon sunshine, this tiny yellow flower tolerates a variety of climates.

Common Camas

Camassia quamash

STEP 1

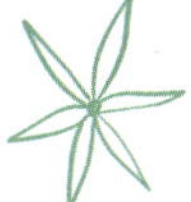

STEP 2

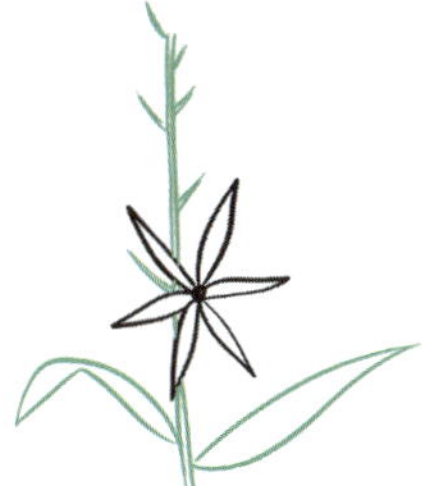

STEP 3

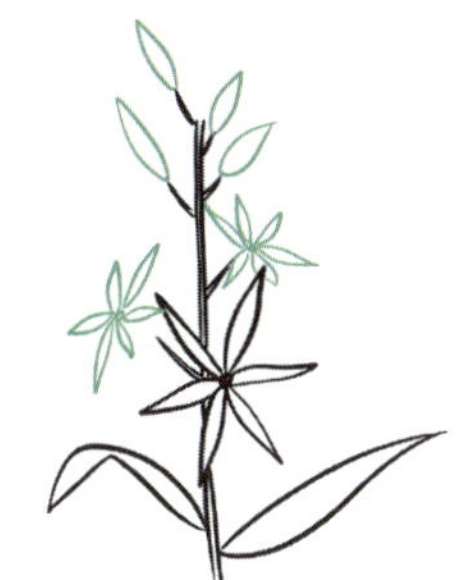

STEP 4

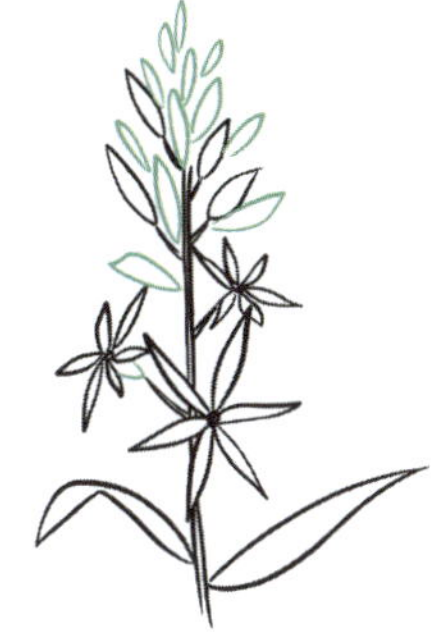

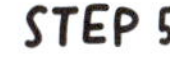

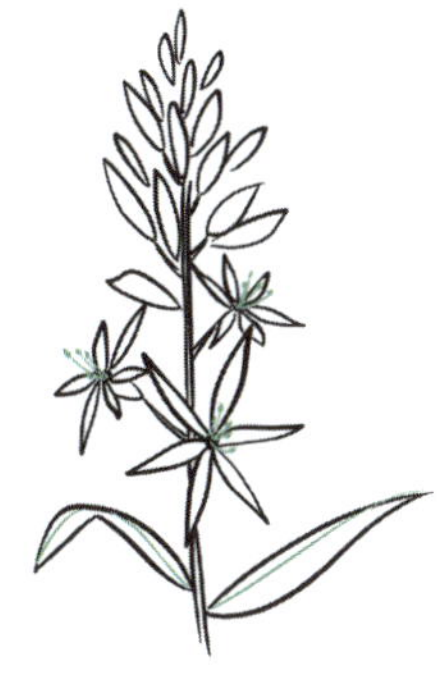

STEP 6

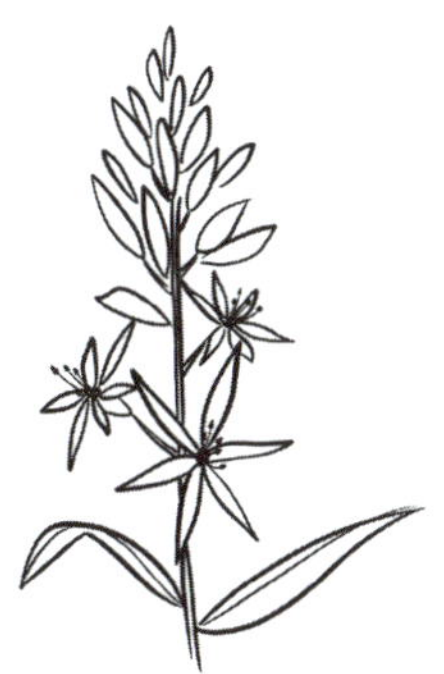

FUN FACT!

The bulbs of this plant have long been an important food source for Native people of the Pacific Northwest.

Sword Fern

Polystichum munitum

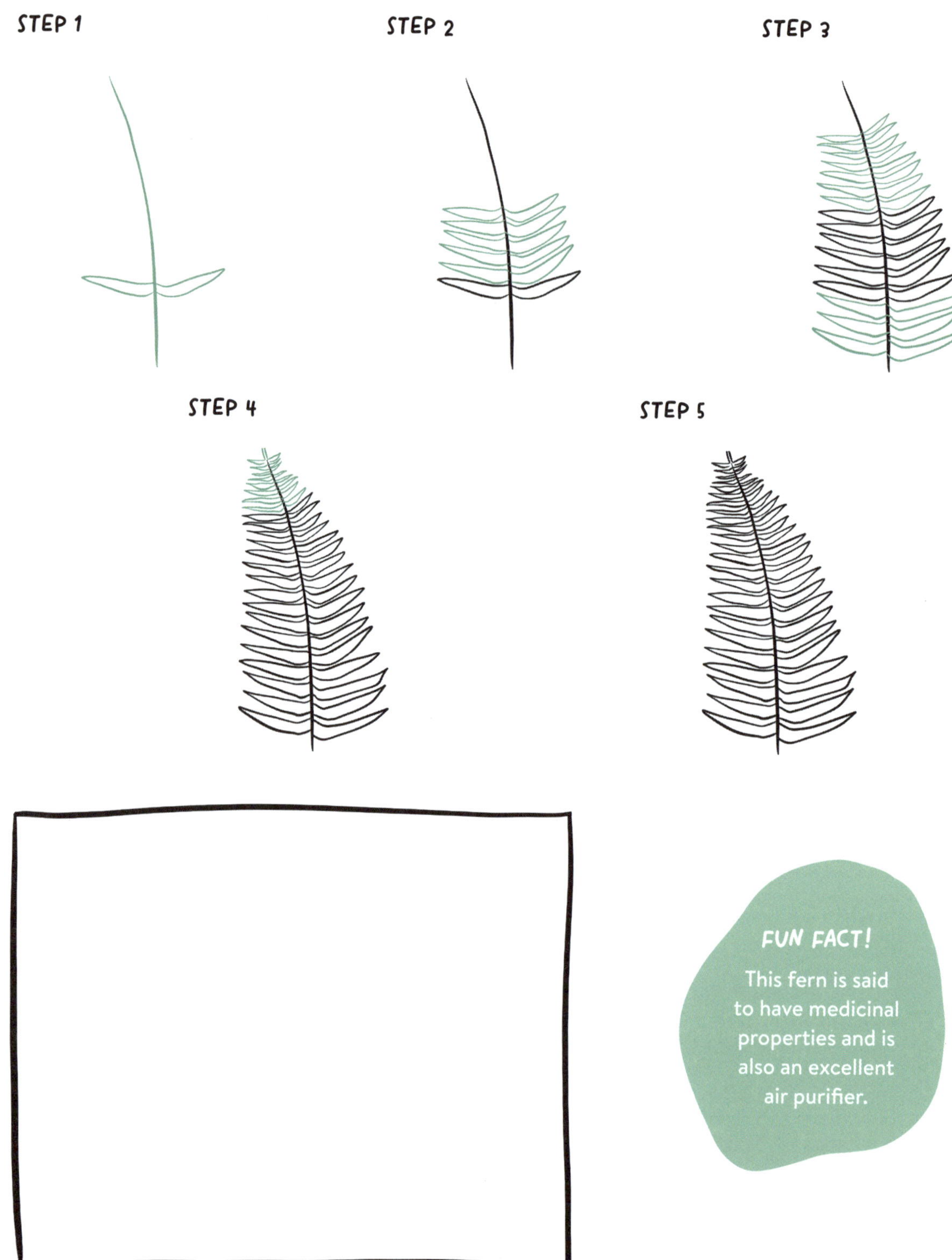

FUN FACT!

This fern is said to have medicinal properties and is also an excellent air purifier.

Common Fiddleneck

Amsinckia intermedia

STEP 1

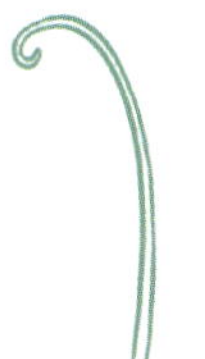

STEP 2

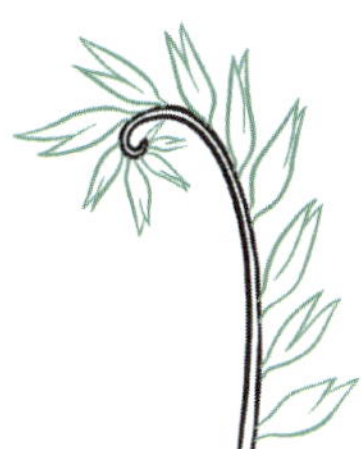

STEP 3

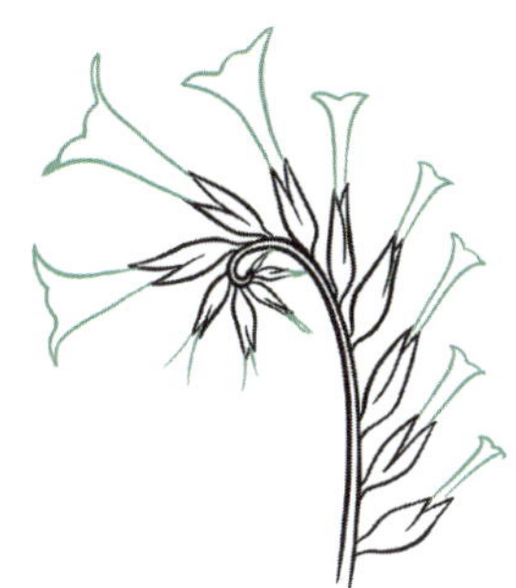

STEP 4

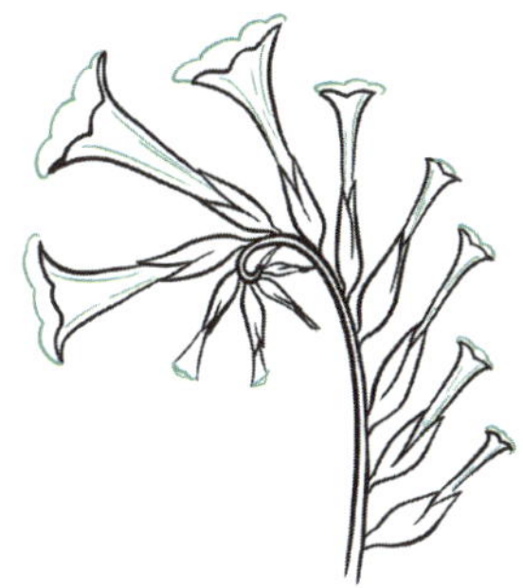

STEP 5

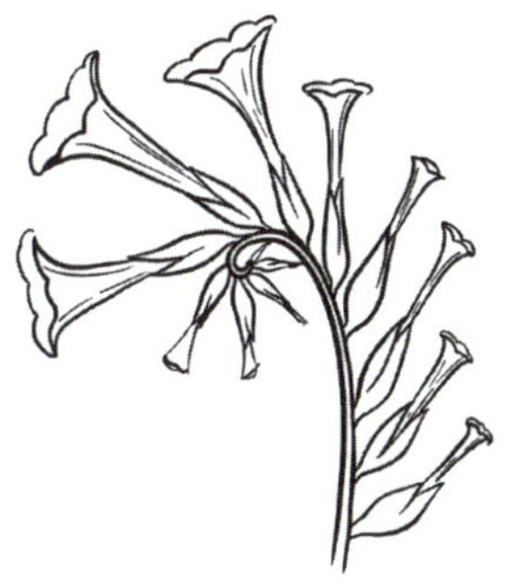

FUN FACT!

This plant got its name from the way its stems curl at the top, resembling the neck of a fiddle.

Maidenhair Fern

Adiantum aleuticum

STEP 1

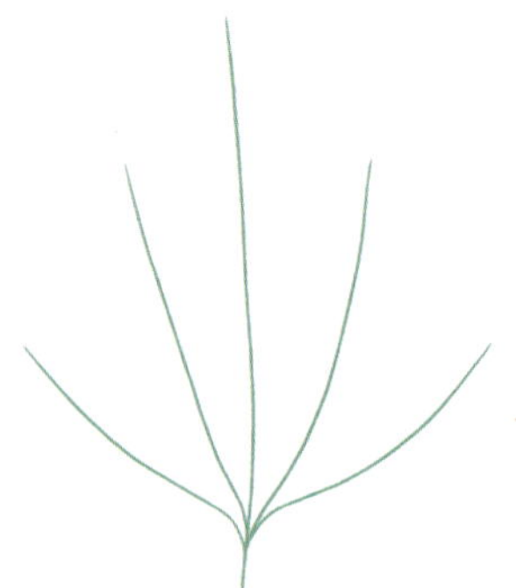

STEP 2

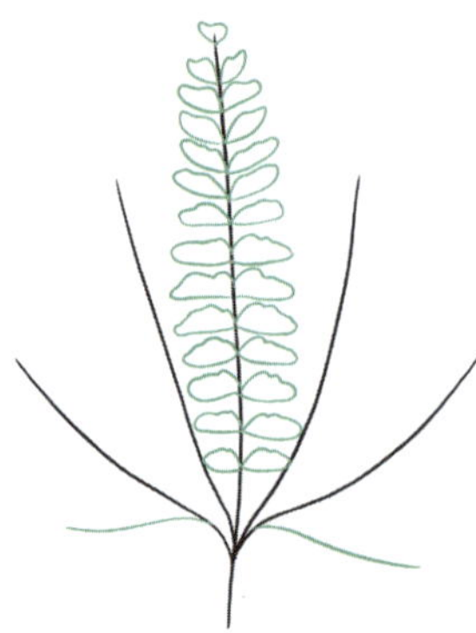

STEP 3

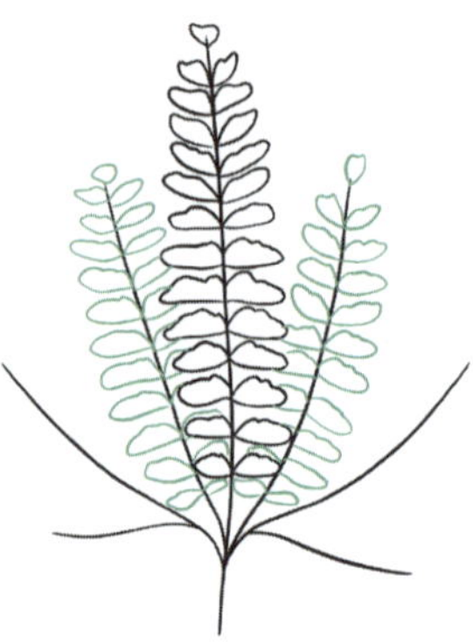

STEP 4

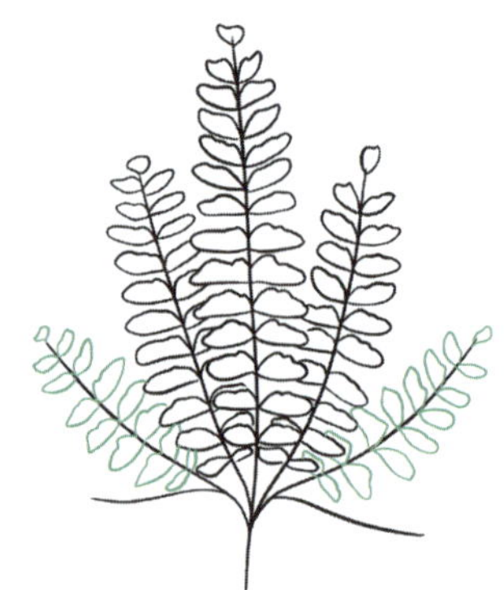

STEP 5

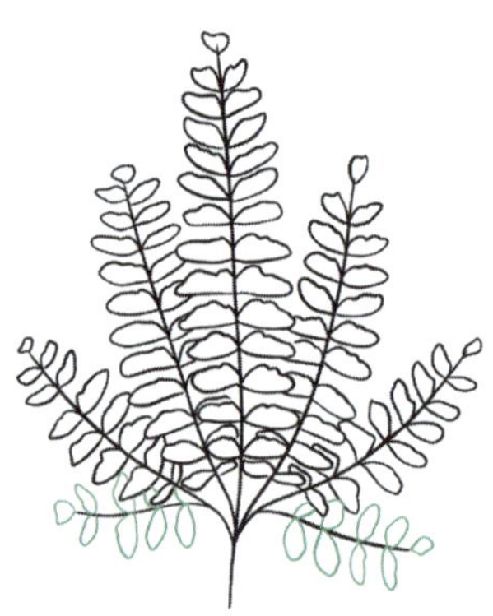

STEP 6

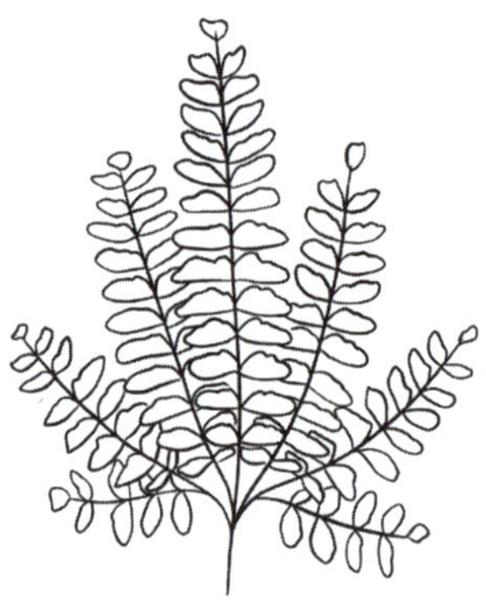

FUN FACT!

Maidenhair fern is my favorite plant! Its soft, delicate fronds are supported by shiny black stems.

Licorice Fern

Polypodium glycyrrhiza

STEP 1

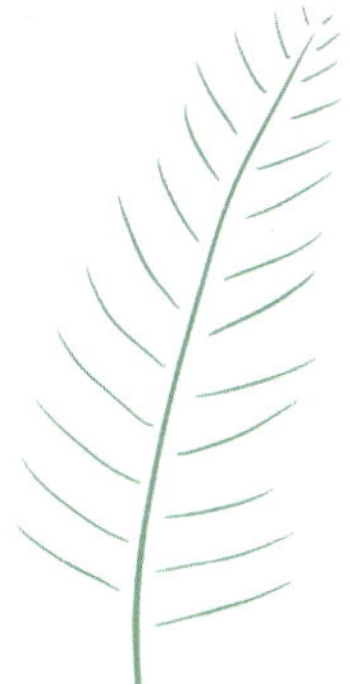

STEP 2

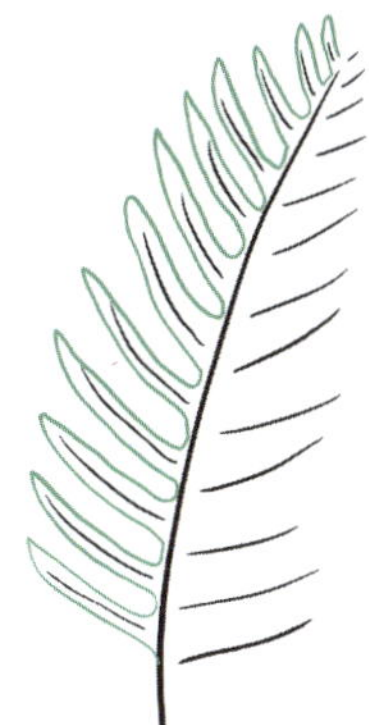

STEP 3

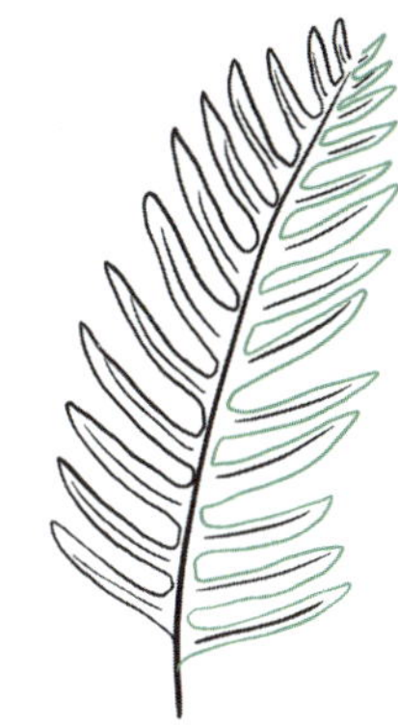

STEP 4

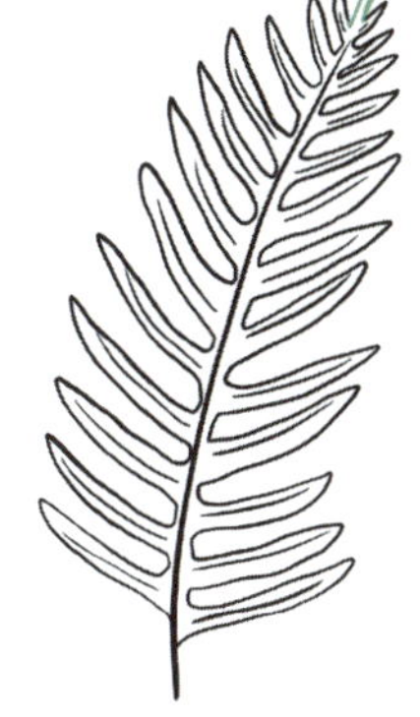

STEP 5

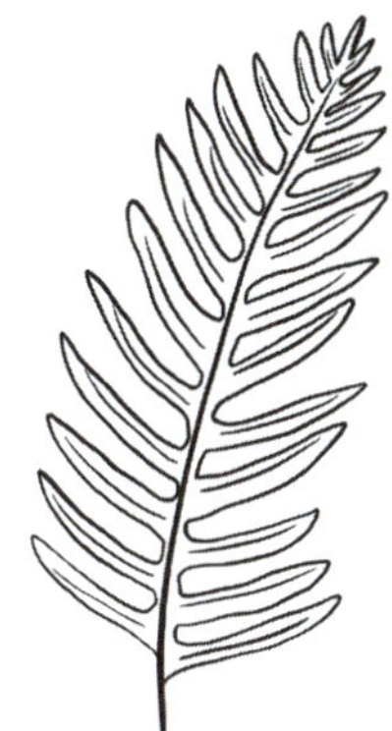

FUN FACT!

Named after the taste of its rhizomes, this fern is commonly used as a natural remedy.

Bracken Fern

Pteridium aquilinum

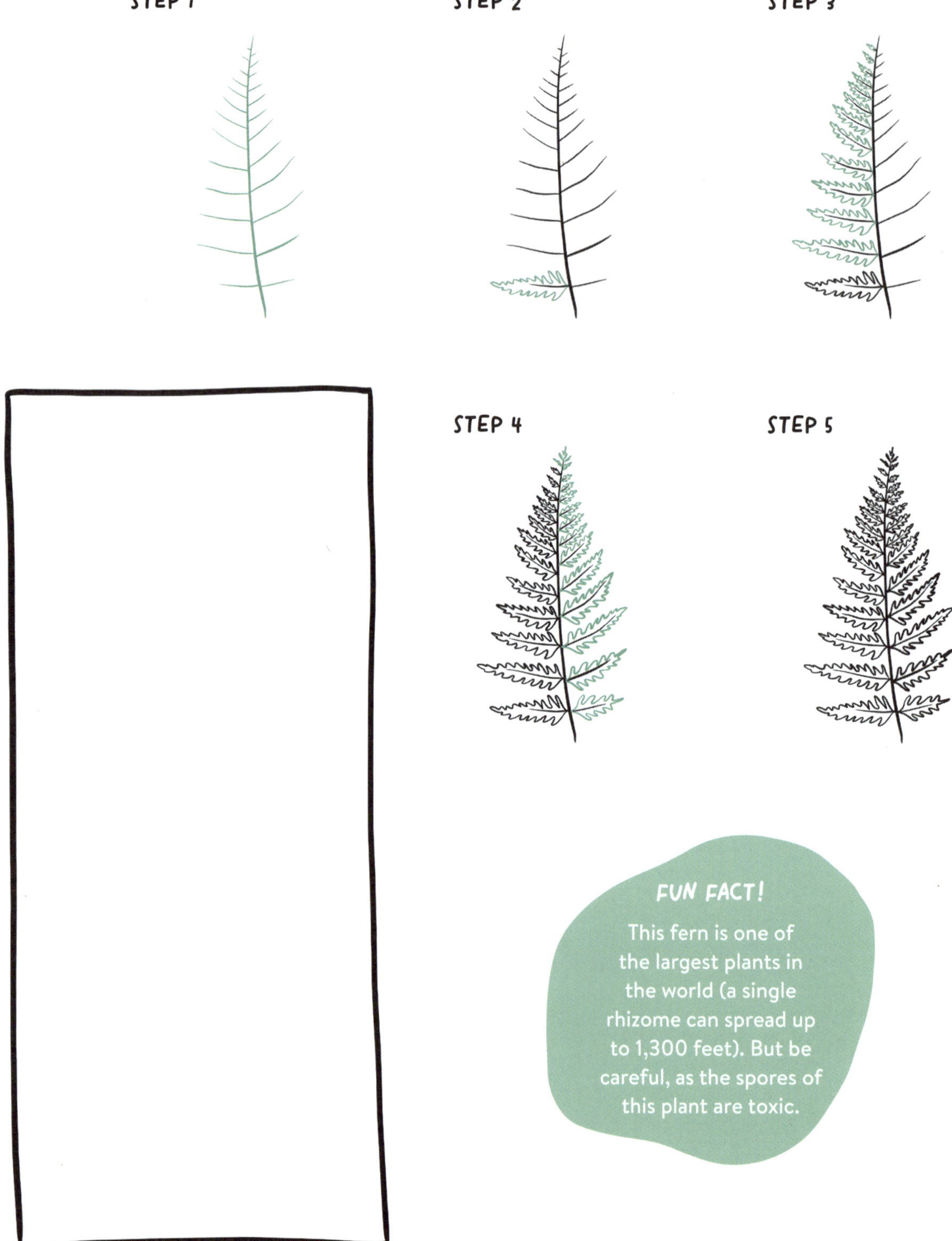

FUN FACT!

This fern is one of the largest plants in the world (a single rhizome can spread up to 1,300 feet). But be careful, as the spores of this plant are toxic.

Stinging Nettle

Urtica dioica

STEP 1

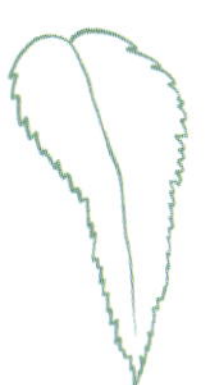

STEP 2

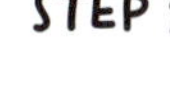

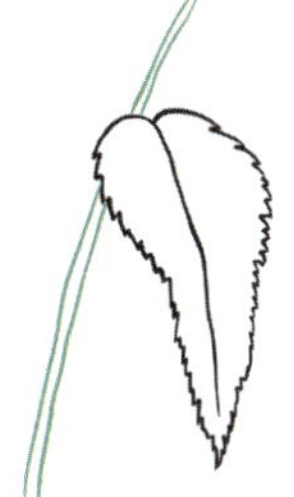

STEP 3

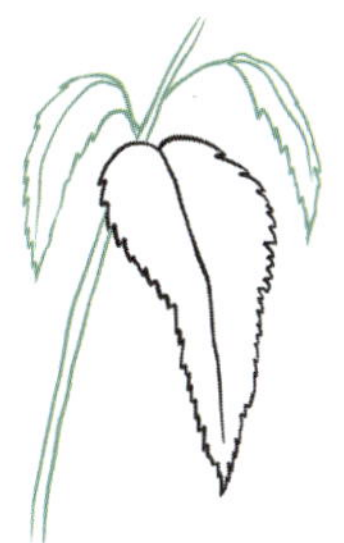

STEP 4

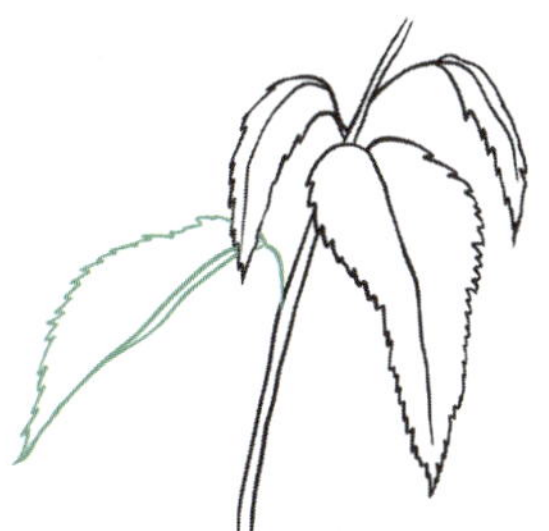

STEP 5

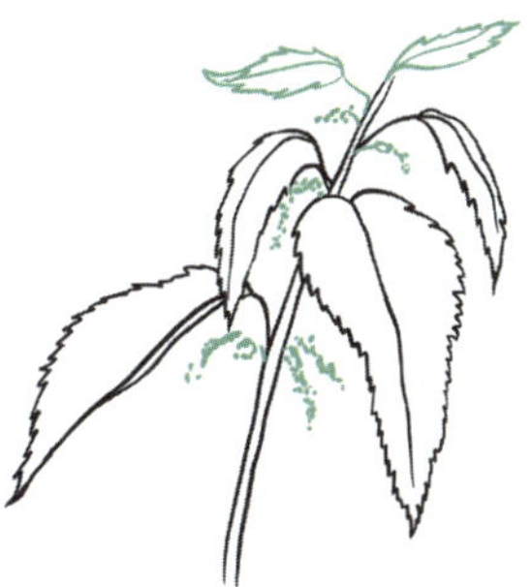

STEP 6

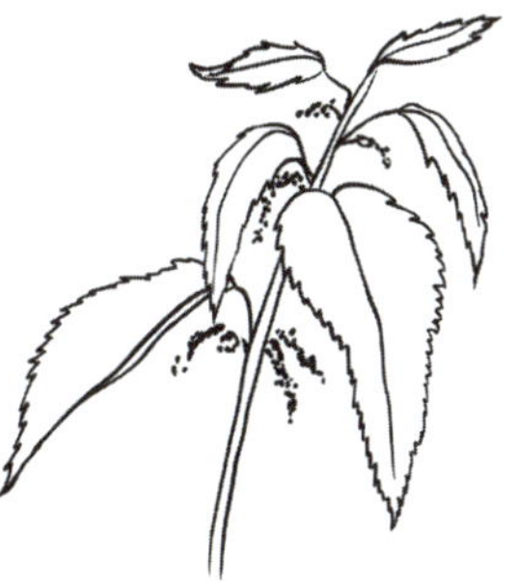

FUN FACT!

Often called a weed, stinging nettle has been used in traditional medicine for hundreds of years. During World War II, children were encouraged to collect it to make dye for camouflage.

Beargrass

Xerophyllum tenax

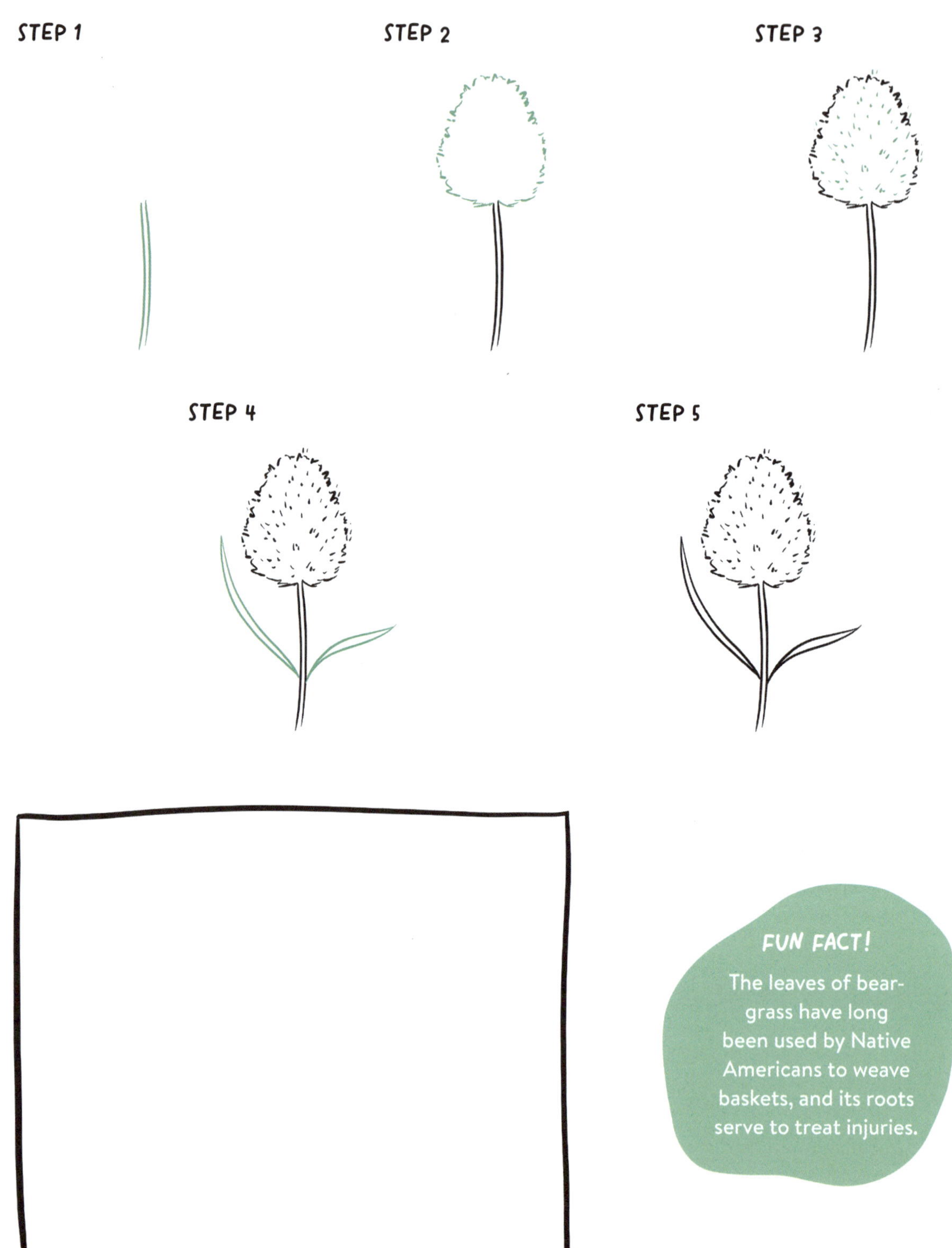

FUN FACT!

The leaves of beargrass have long been used by Native Americans to weave baskets, and its roots serve to treat injuries.

Sea Thrift

Armeria maritima

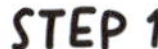

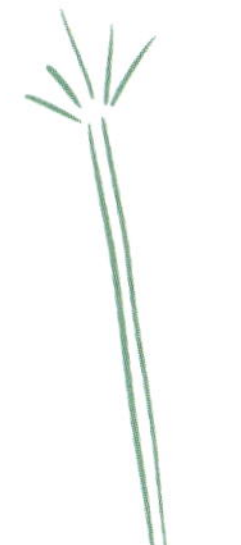

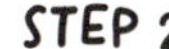

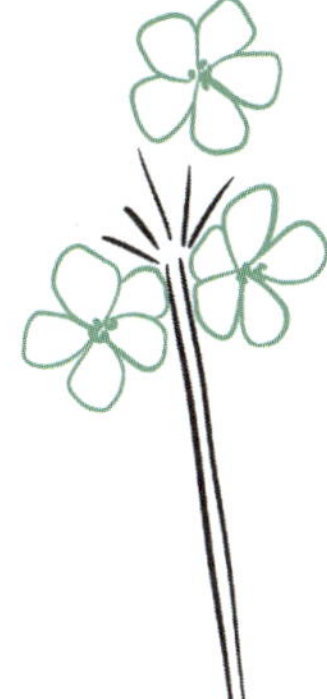

STEP 3

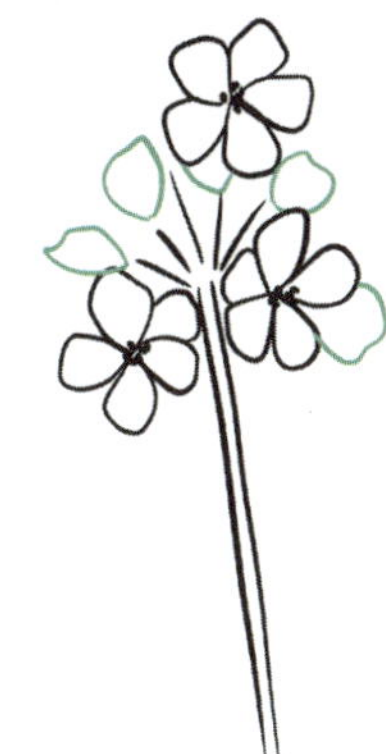

STEP 4

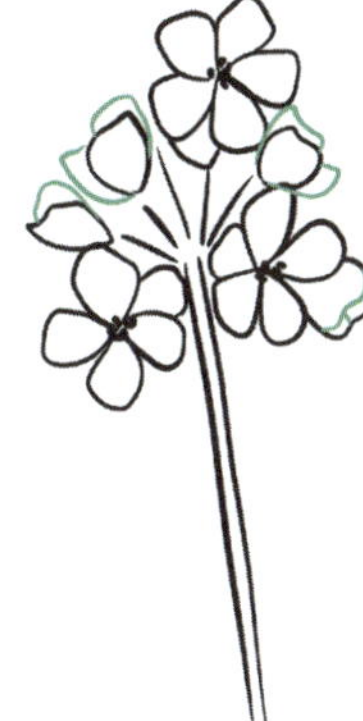

STEP 5

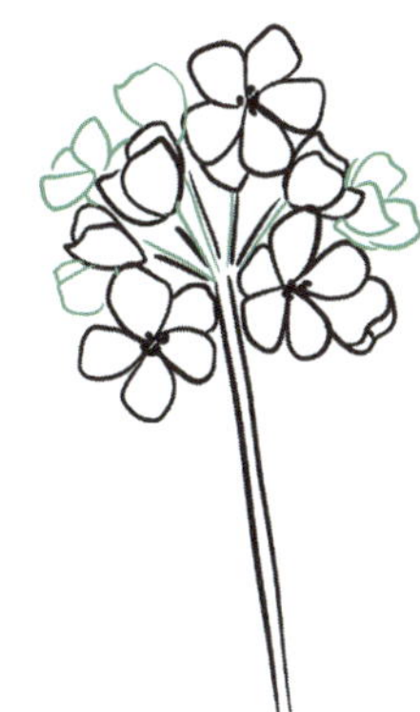

STEP 6

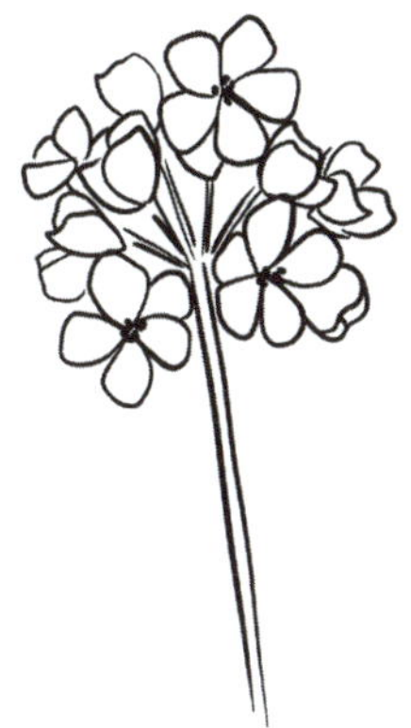

FUN FACT!

Its scientific name, *Armeria*, means "armor," referring to the toughness of the plant.

Fawn Lily

Erythronium oregonum

STEP 1

STEP 2

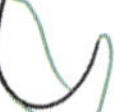

STEP 3

STEP 4

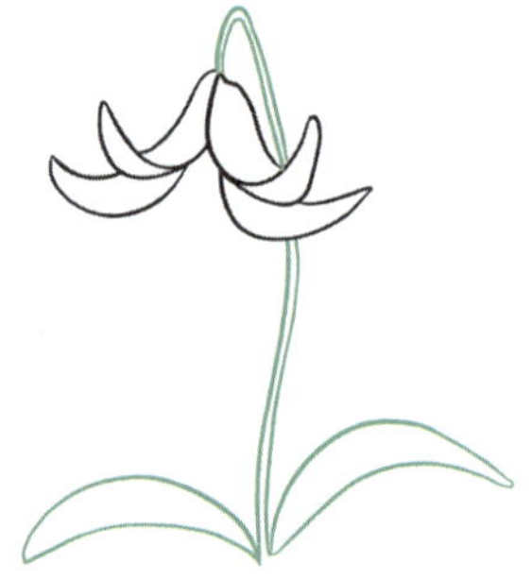

STEP 5

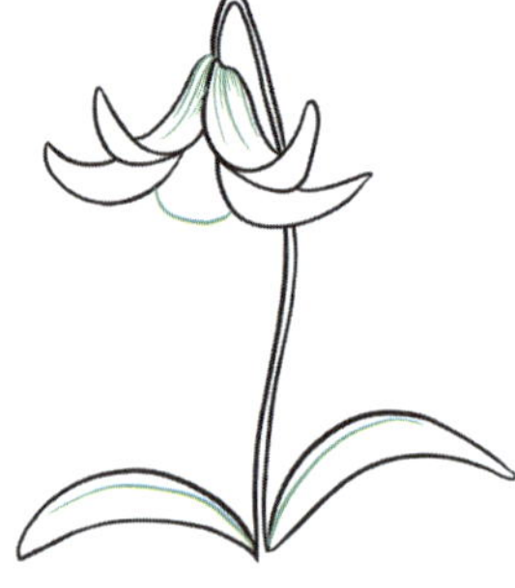

STEP 6

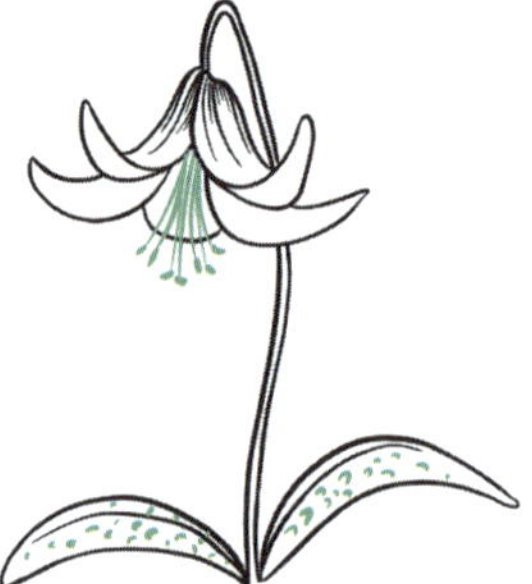

STEP 7

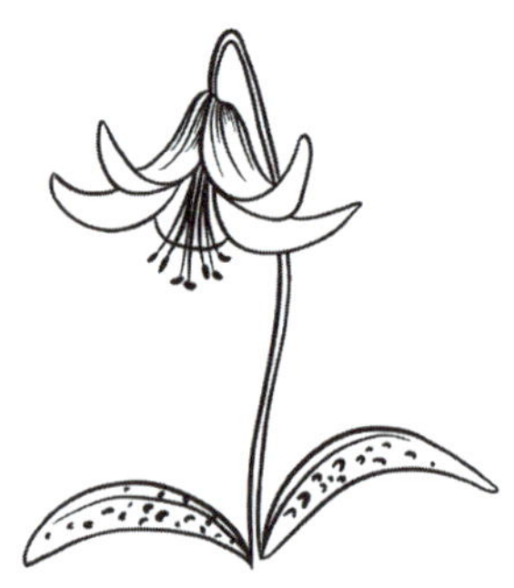

FUN FACT!

This flower looks like it's straight out of a fairy tale, but it has a little botanical secret: its recurved petals are actually tepals (when petals and sepals, modified leaves that form the outer whorl of the flower, cannot be differentiated).

Bearberry

Arctostaphylos uva-ursi

STEP 1

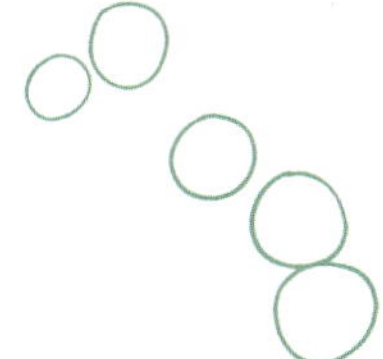

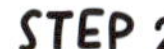

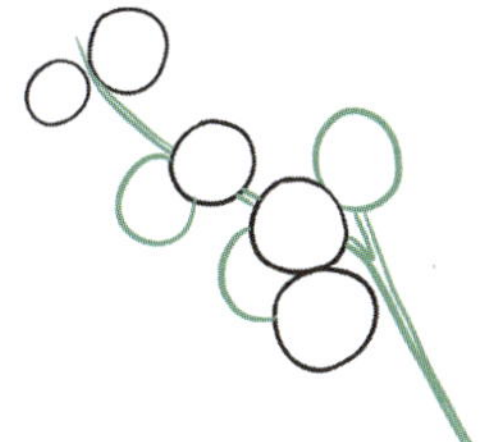

STEP 3

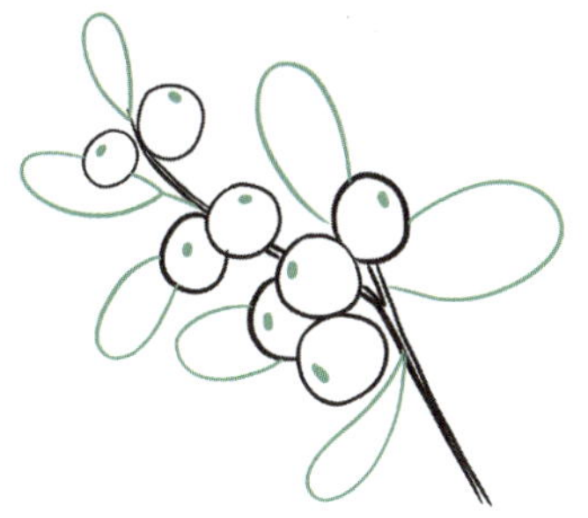

STEP 4

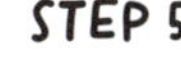

FUN FACT!

This plant can stay alive even in freezing temperatures, making it a bear's favorite and giving it its name.

Western Azalea

Rhododendron occidentale

STEP 1

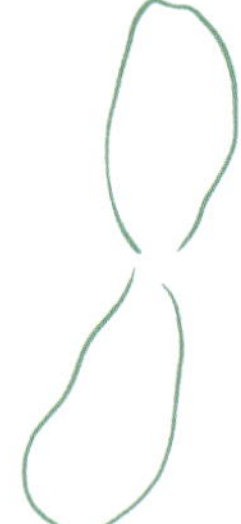

STEP 2

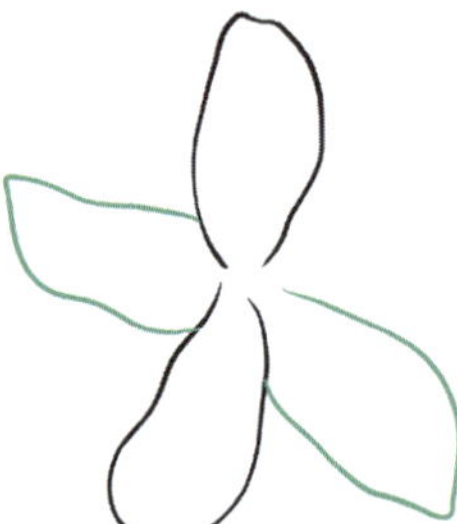

STEP 3

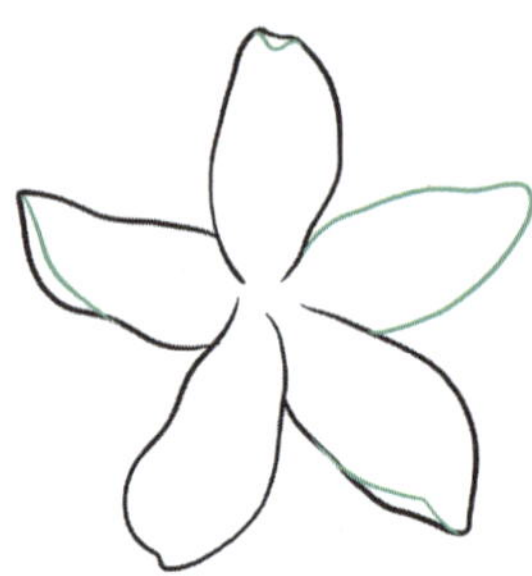

STEP 4

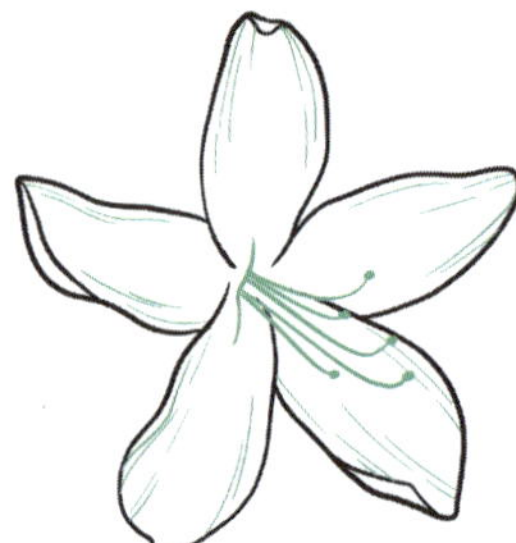

STEP 5

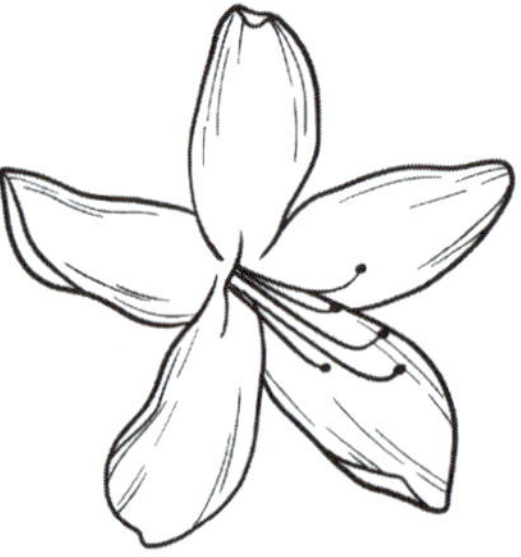

FUN FACT!

This species is the only azalea native to the Pacific Coast.

Pacific Dogwood

Cornus nuttallii

STEP 1

STEP 2

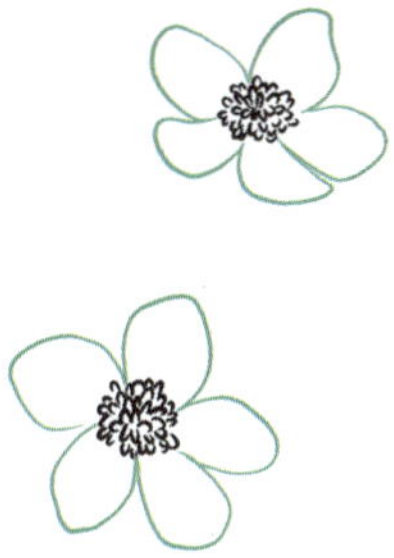

STEP 3

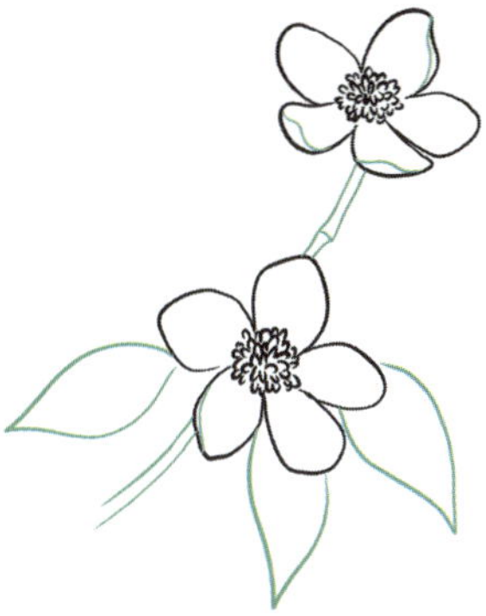

STEP 4

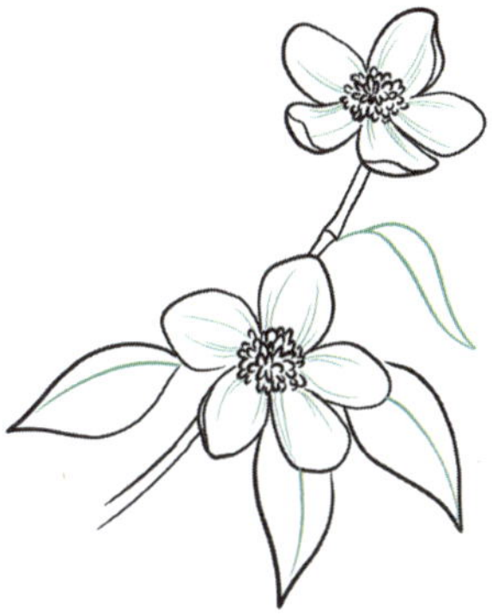

STEP 5

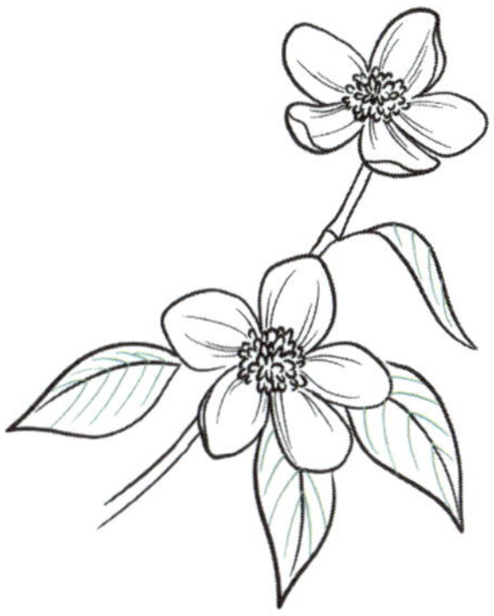

STEP 6

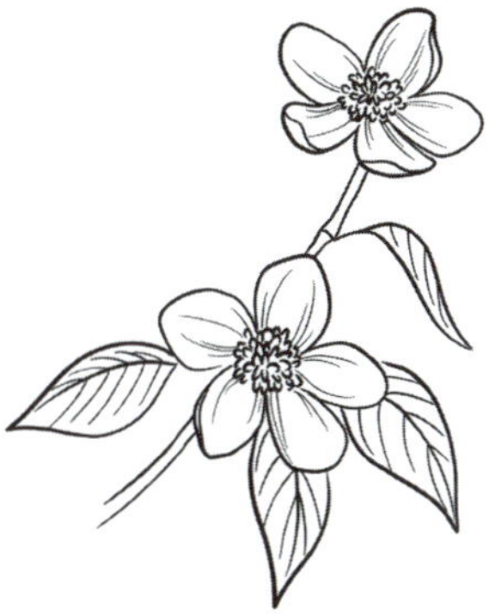

FUN FACT!

Adopted as British Columbia's floral emblem, this flower can live up to 150 years and is often used to make natural brown dye.

Oakmoss

Evernia prunastri

STEP 1

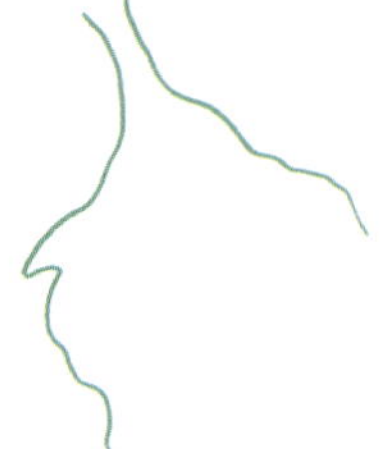

STEP 2

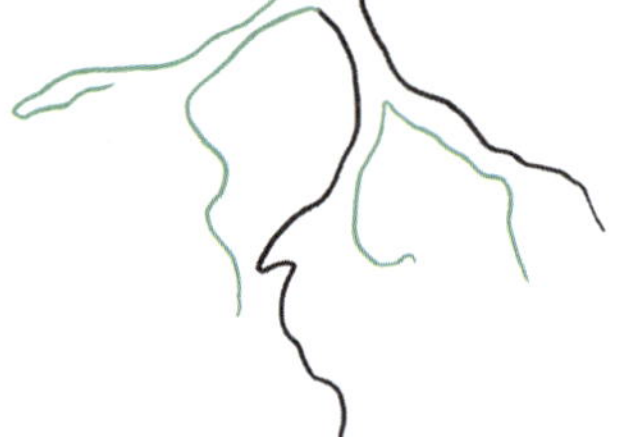

STEP 3

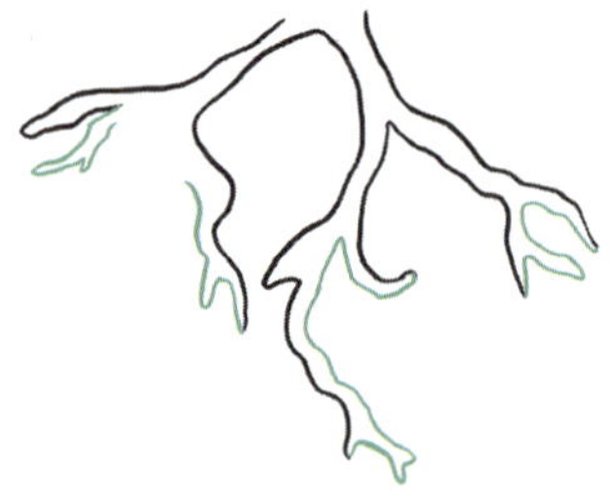

STEP 4

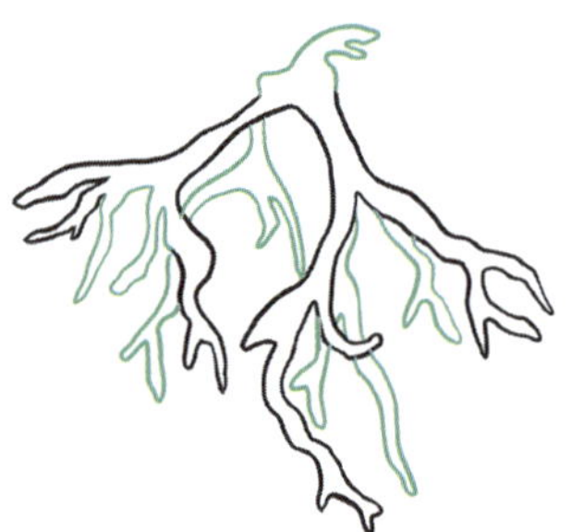

STEP 5

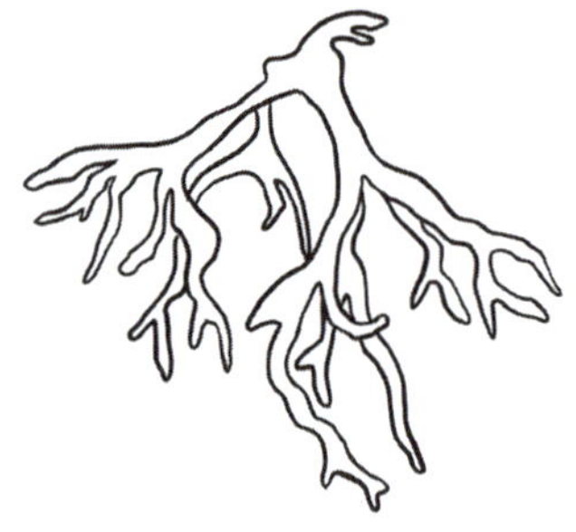

FUN FACT!

The common name of this plant is a misnomer: it's a lichen, not a moss, and it grows on many trees besides oak.

Bryum Moss

Bryum argenteum

STEP 1

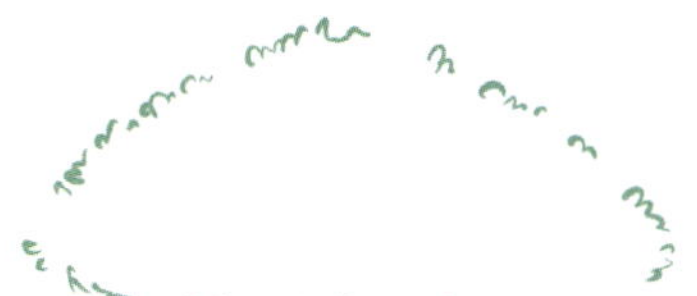

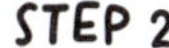

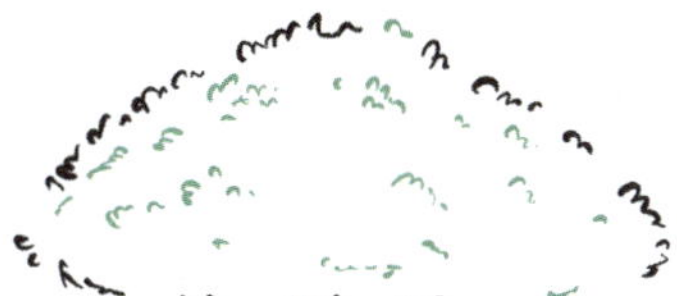

STEP 3

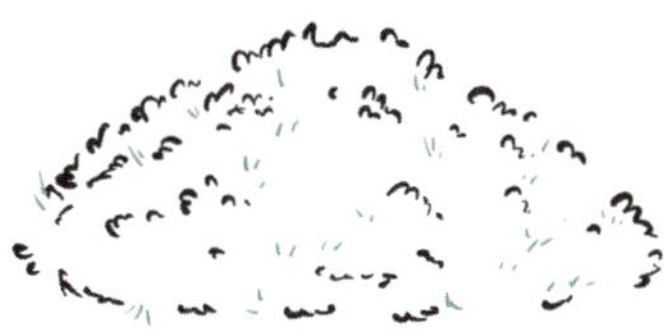

STEP 4

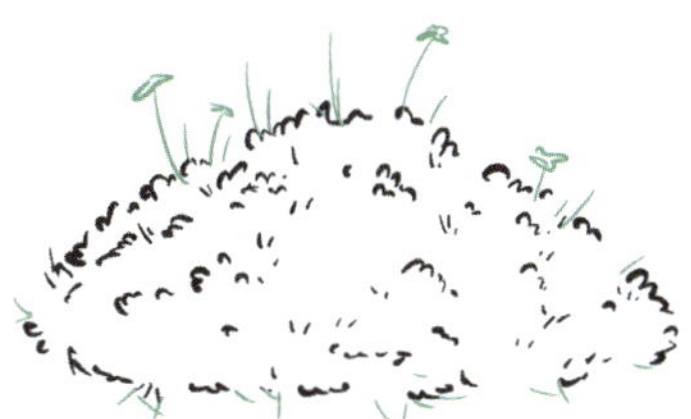

STEP 5

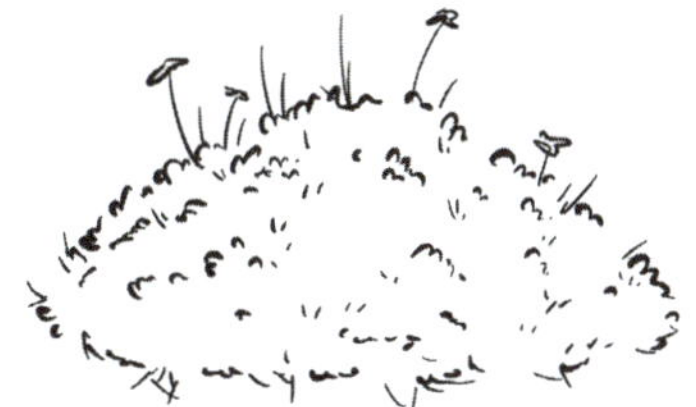

FUN FACT!

Mosses do not have roots. Instead, they have tiny threadlike structures called rhizoids that help them attach to surfaces and absorb water and nutrients.

Chanterelle

Cantharellus cibarius

STEP 1

STEP 2

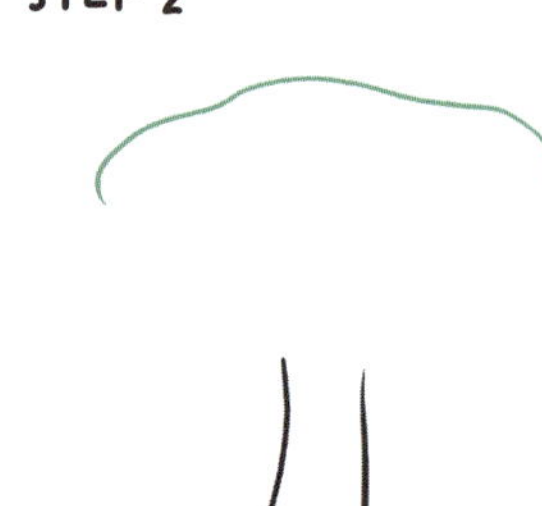

STEP 3

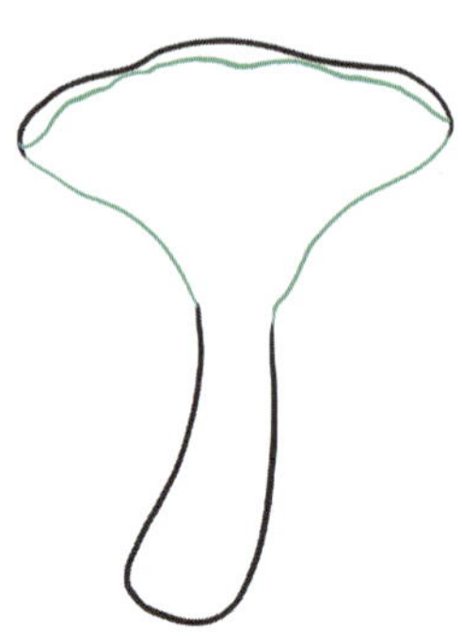

STEP 4

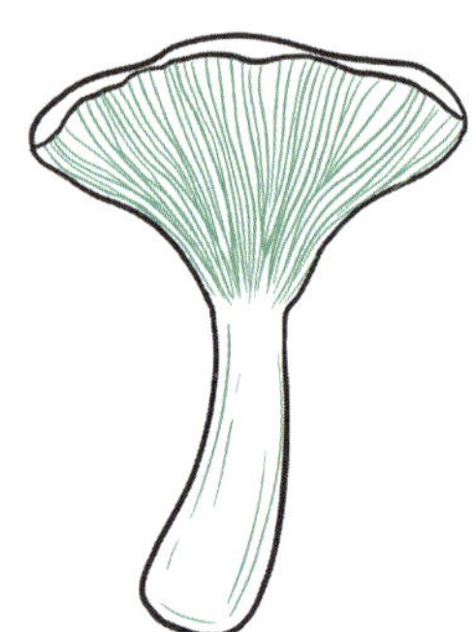

STEP 5

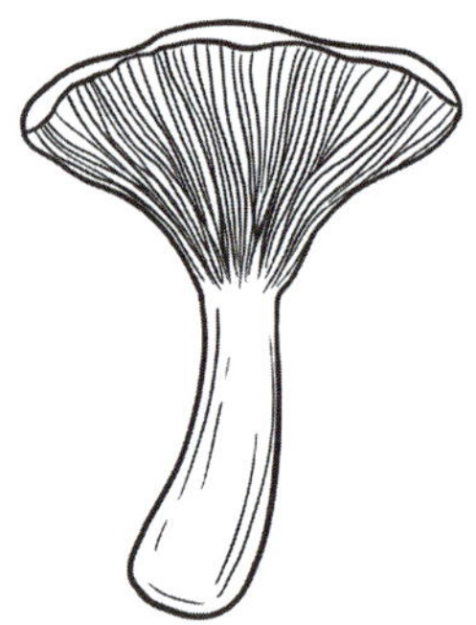

FUN FACT!

Considered a gourmet fungus, this mushroom also has antiviral and antibacterial properties.

Morel

Morchella esculenta

STEP 1

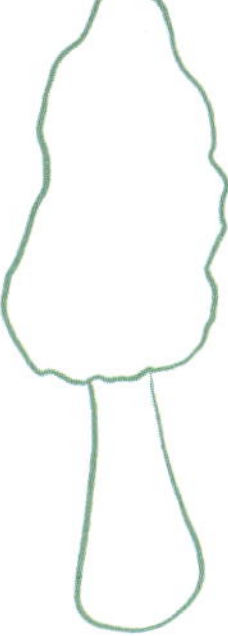

STEP 2

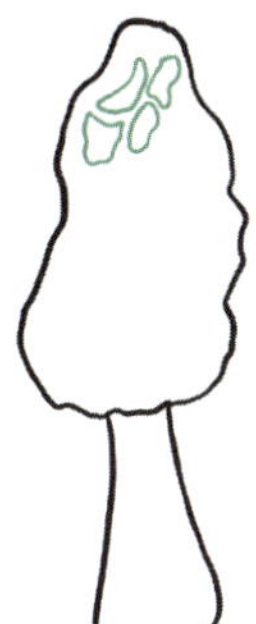

STEP 3

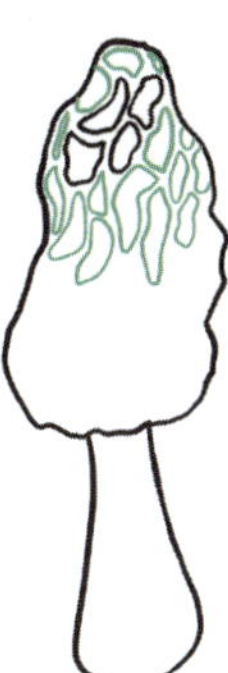

STEP 4

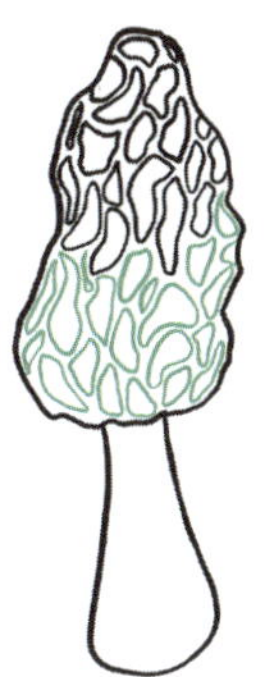

STEP 5

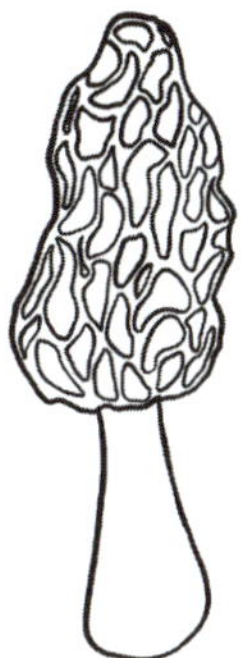

FUN FACT!

It's said that the darker the morel, the more intense the flavor.

Fly Agaric

Amanita muscaria

STEP 1

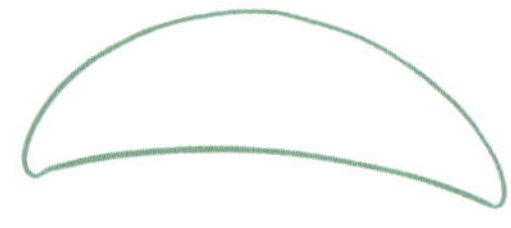

STEP 2

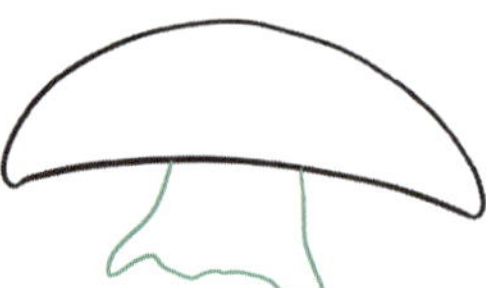

STEP 3

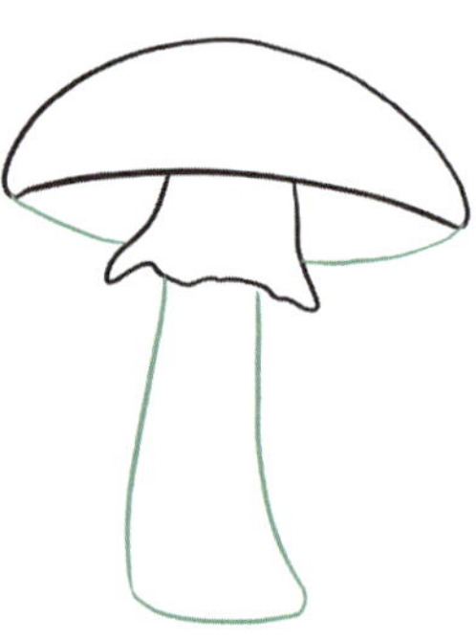

STEP 4

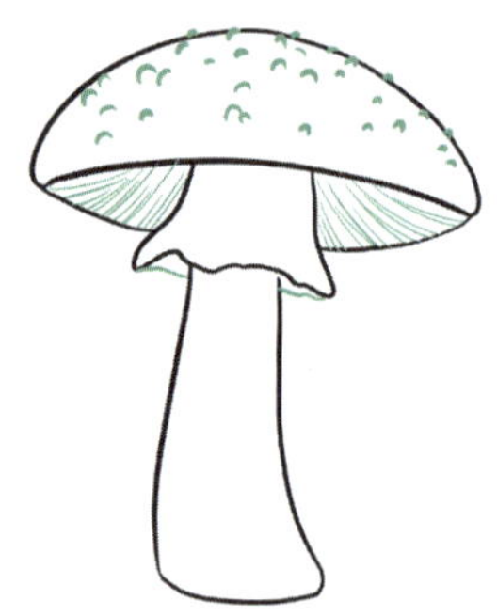

STEP 5

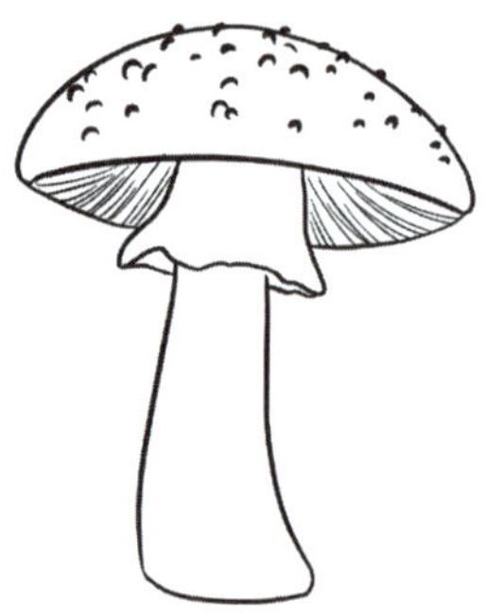

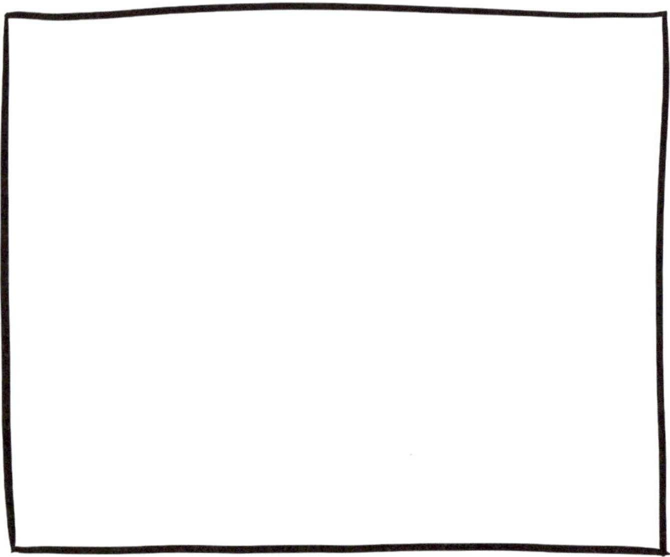

FUN FACT!

This toxic mushroom is often depicted in fairy tales and folklore.

Turkey Tail

Trametes versicolor

STEP 1

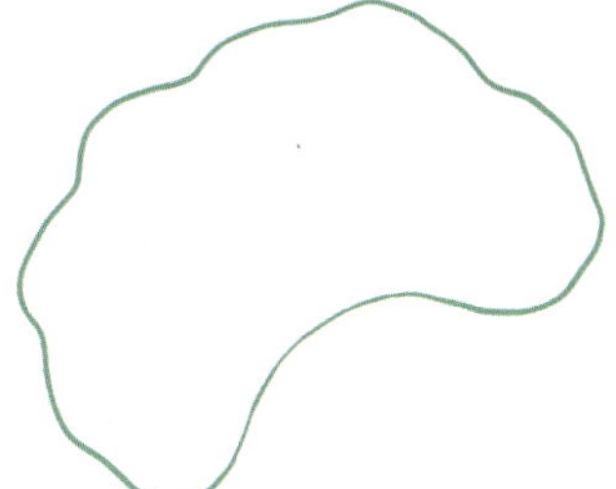

STEP 2

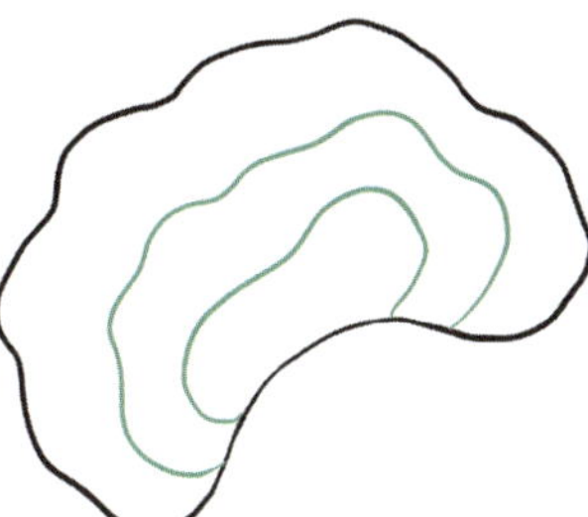

STEP 3

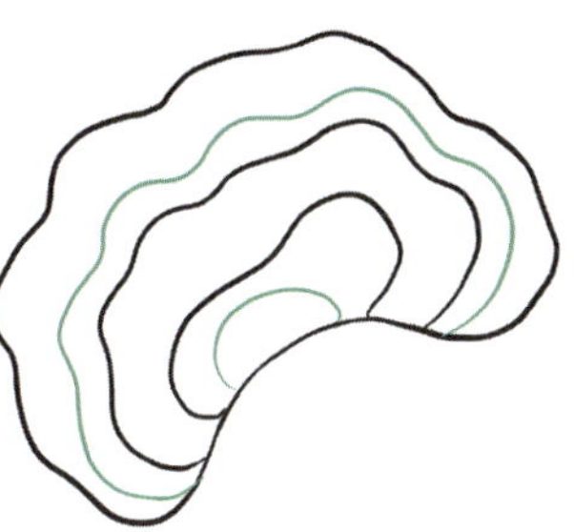

STEP 4

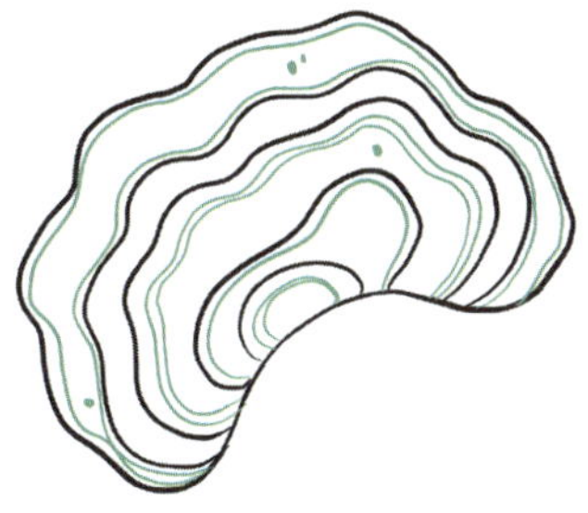

STEP 5

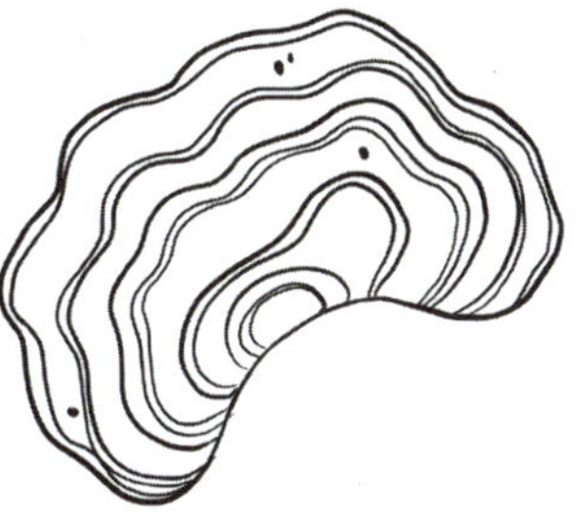

FUN FACT!

This mushroom's scientific name, *verisolor*, means "several colors," as it can appear gray, brown, green, ochre, and even blue.

Black Trumpet

Craterellus cornucopioides

STEP 1

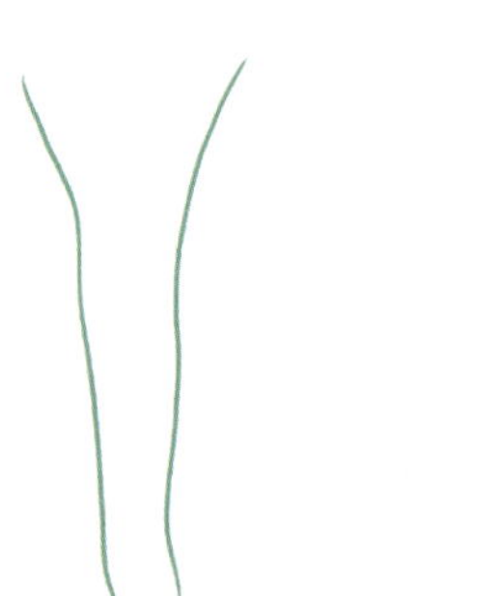

STEP 2

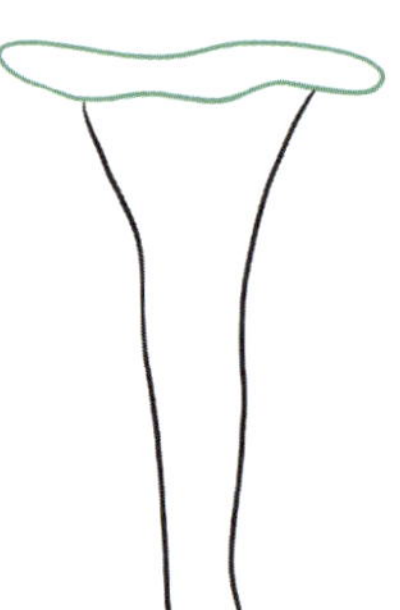

STEP 3

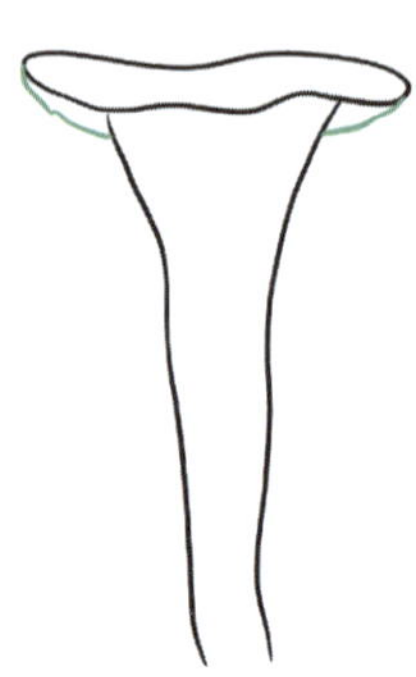

STEP 4

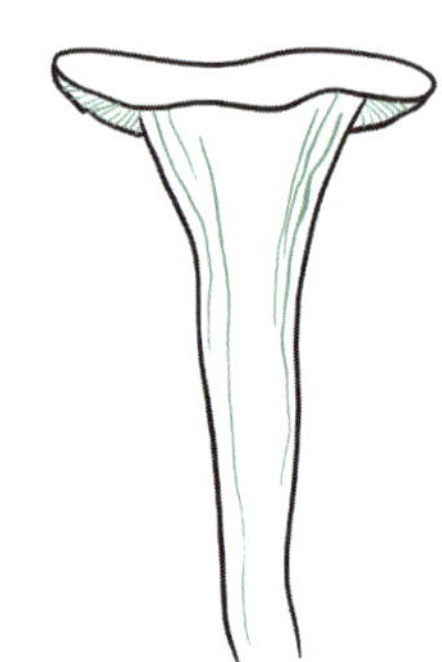

STEP 5

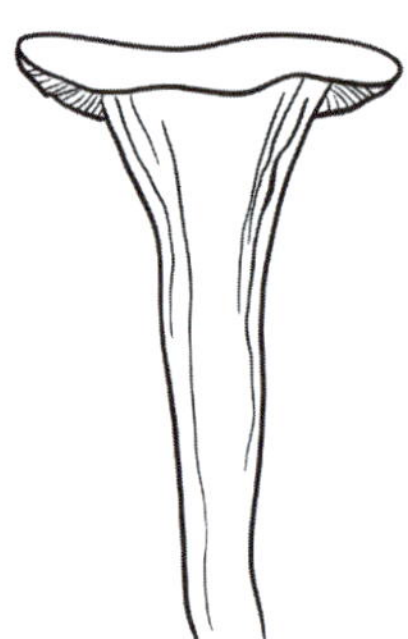

FUN FACT!

A common fungus found in humid forests, it is also known as "trumpet of death" because of its ominous appearance.

Inky Cap

Coprinopsis atramentaria

STEP 1

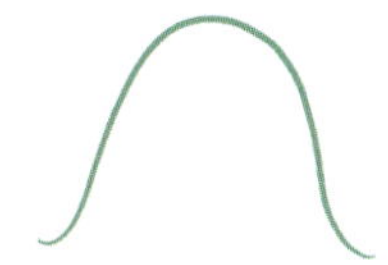

STEP 2

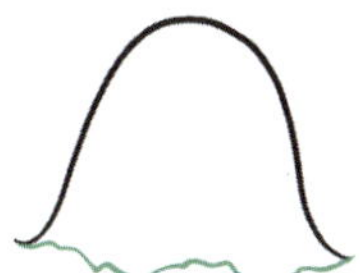

STEP 3

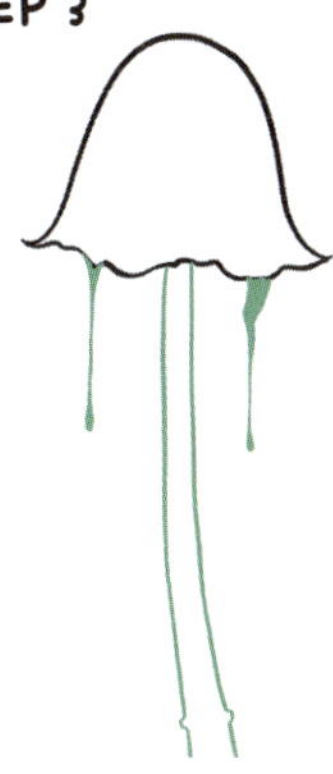

STEP 4

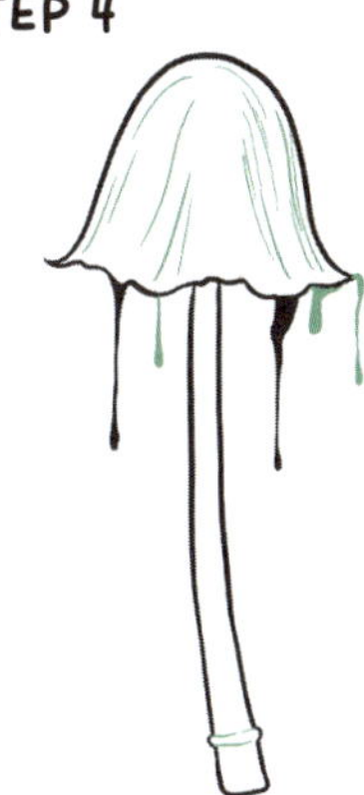

STEP 5

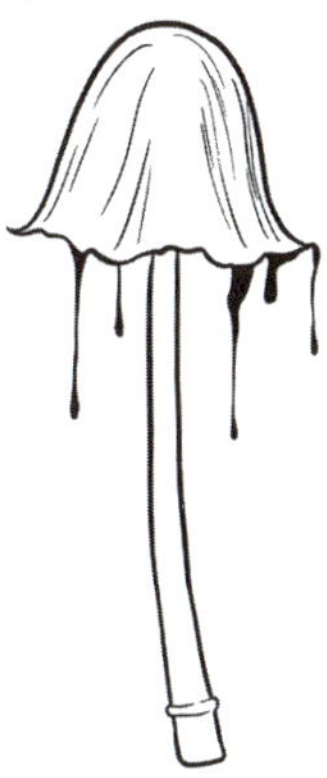

FUN FACT!

Known for its unique self-digesting mechanism, the cap of this mushroom dissolves into an inky substance after spore dispersal.

Bear's Head

Hericium americanum

STEP 1

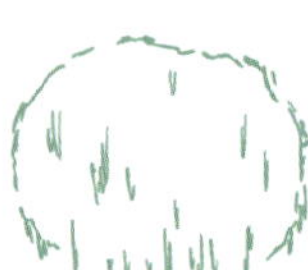

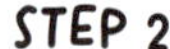

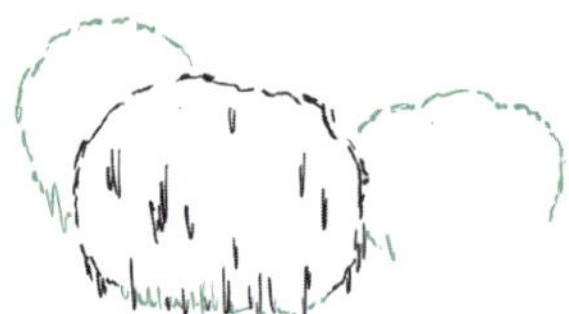

STEP 3

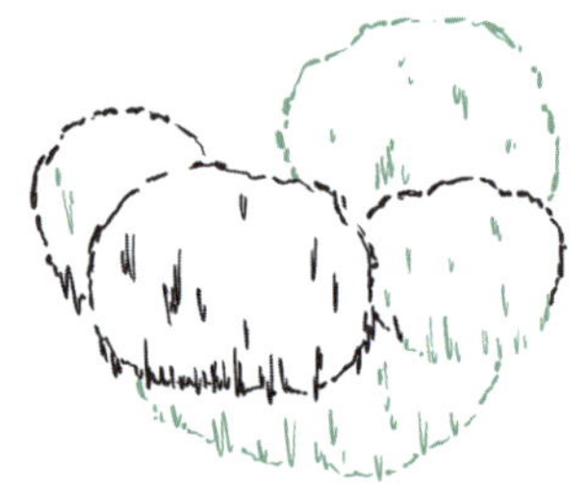

STEP 4

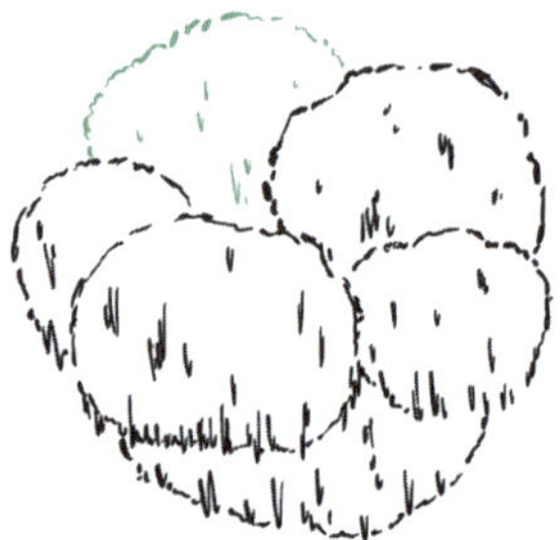

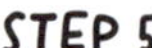

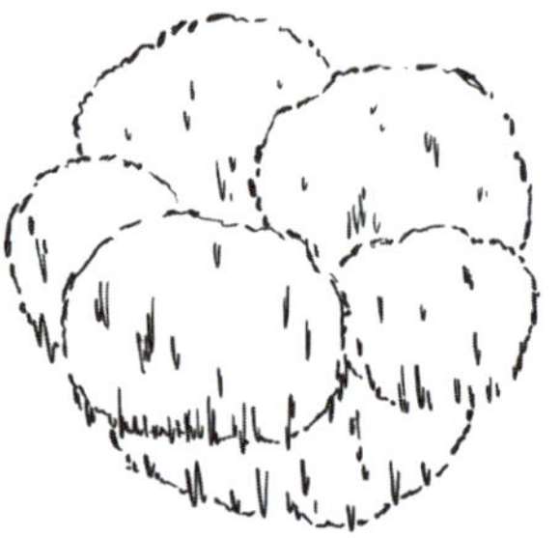

FUN FACT!

Named for its resemblance to the elongated claws and teeth of bears, this mushroom contributes to the decomposition process of wood.

King Bolete

Boletus edulis

STEP 1

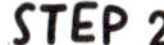

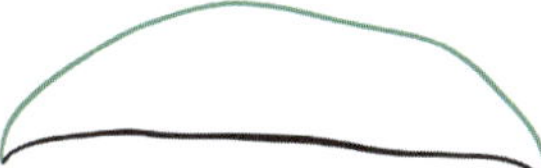

STEP 3

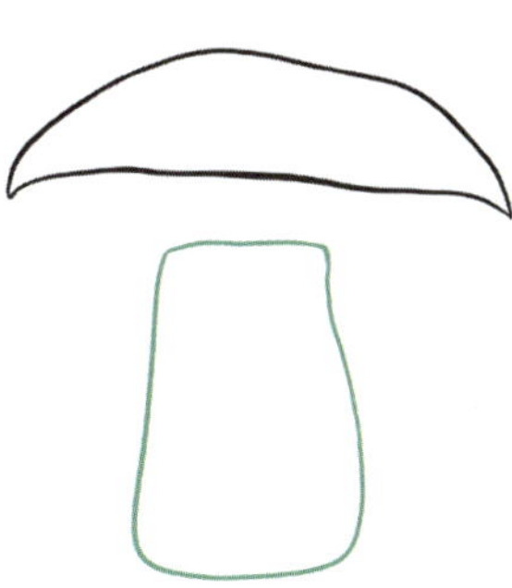

STEP 4

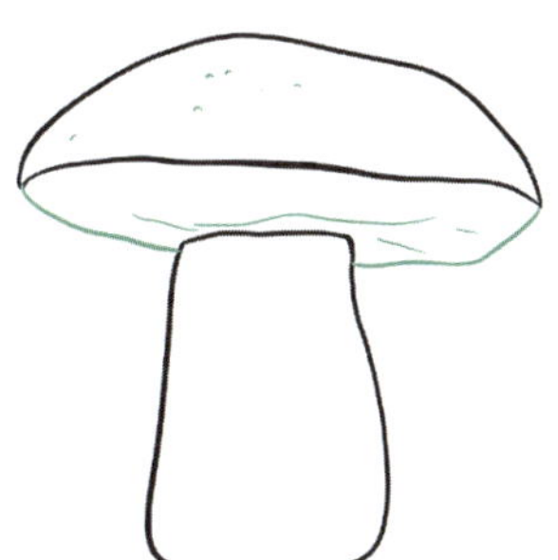

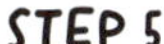

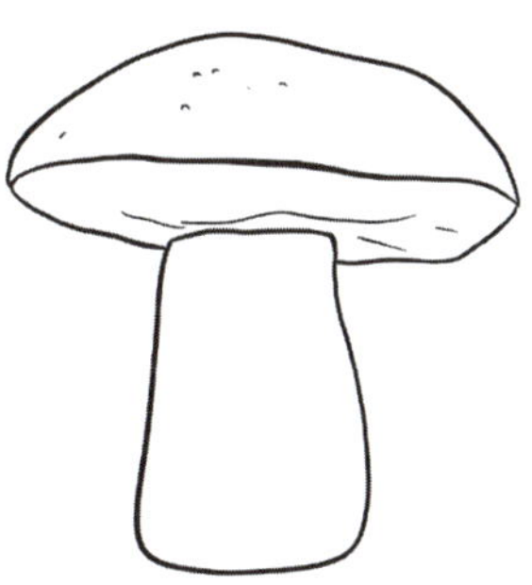

FUN FACT!

One of the most prized edible fungi, the underside of this mushroom's cap features a spongelike surface instead of gills.

Douglas Fir

Pseudotsuga menziesii

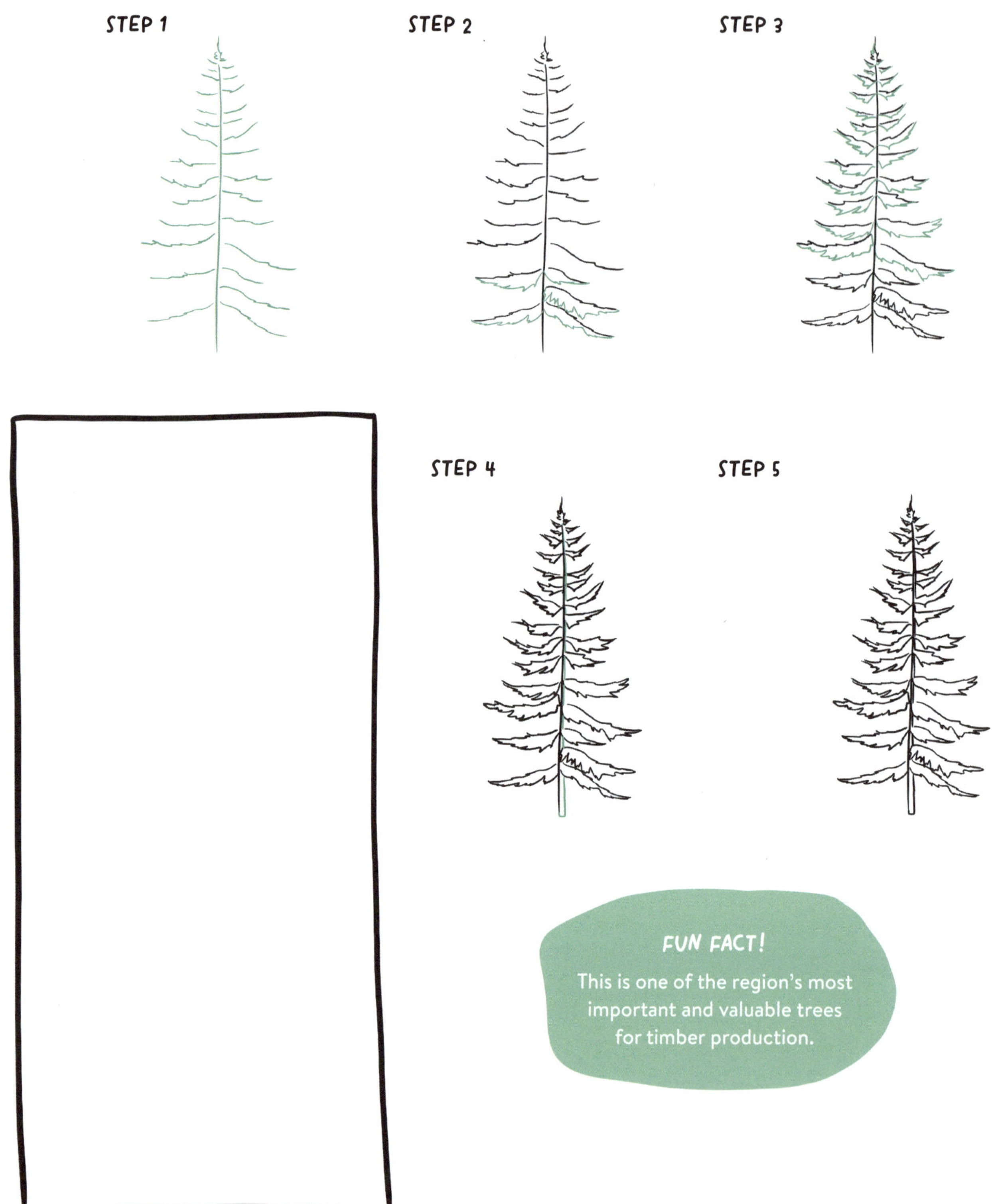

FUN FACT!

This is one of the region's most important and valuable trees for timber production.

Douglas Fir Cone

STEP 1

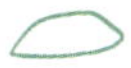

STEP 2

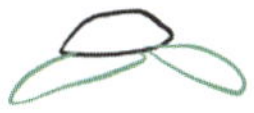

STEP 3

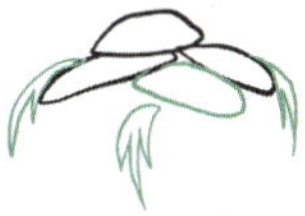

STEP 4

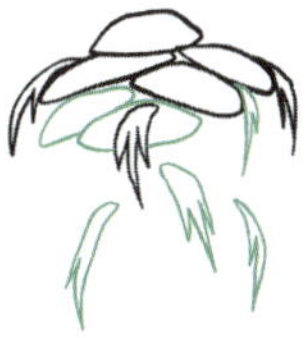

STEP 5

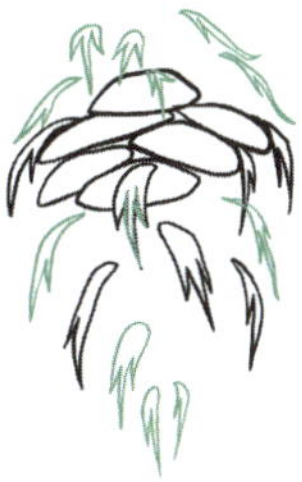

STEP 6

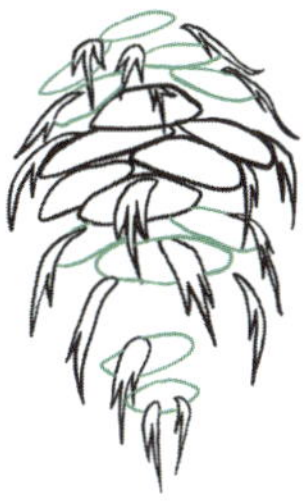

STEP 7

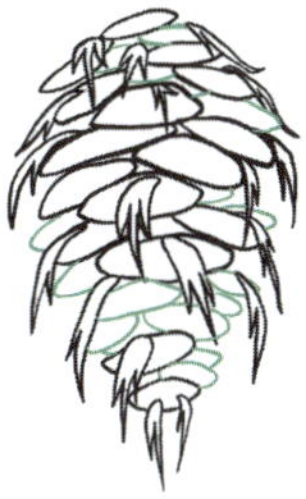

STEP 8

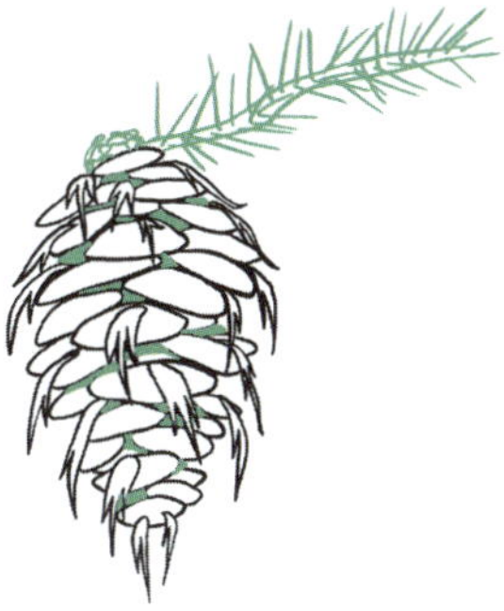

STEP 9

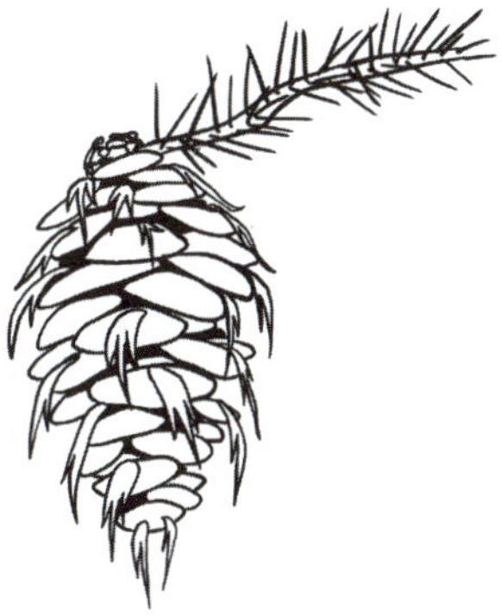

Western Redcedar

Thuja plicata

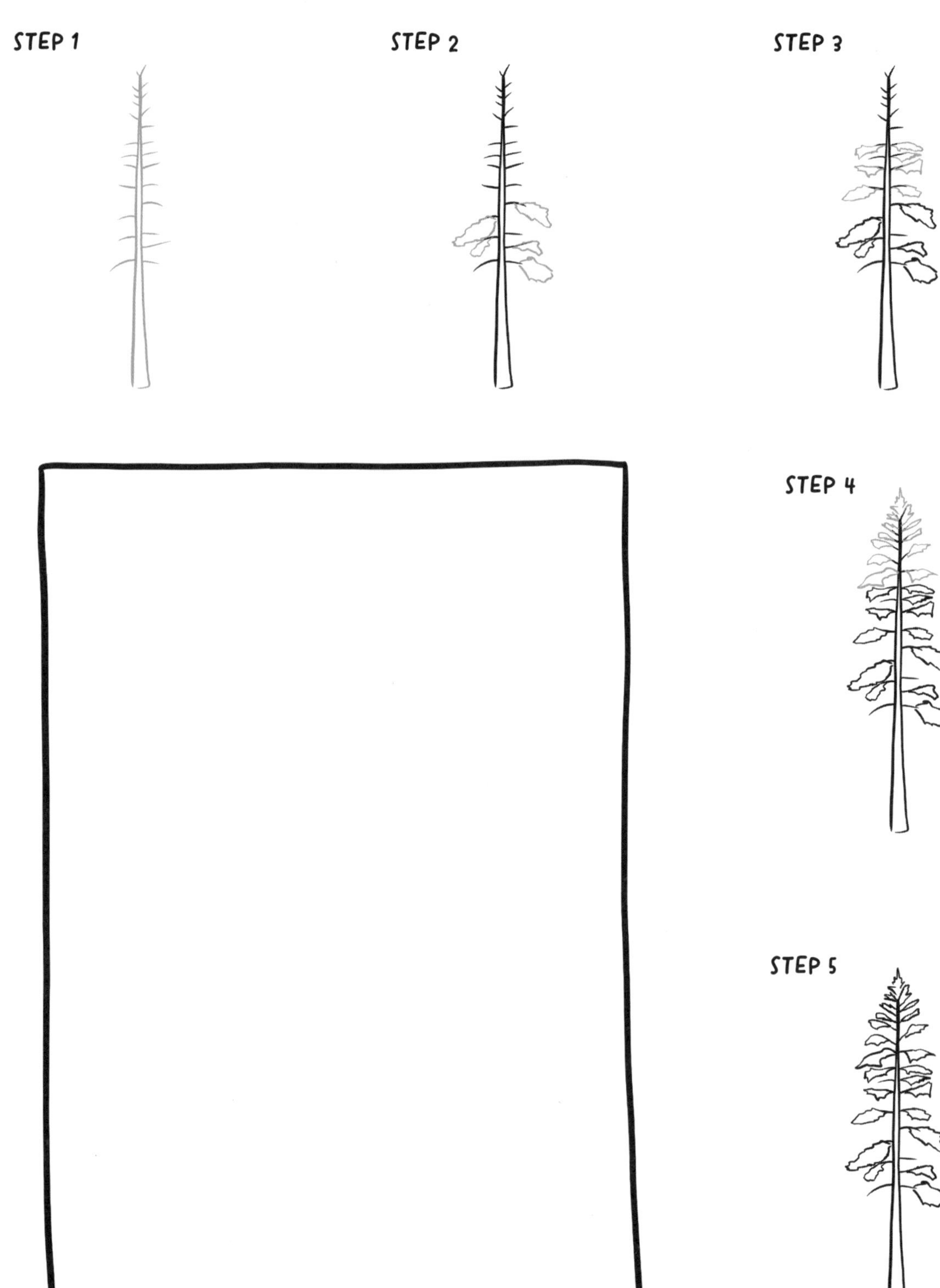

Western Redcedar Branch

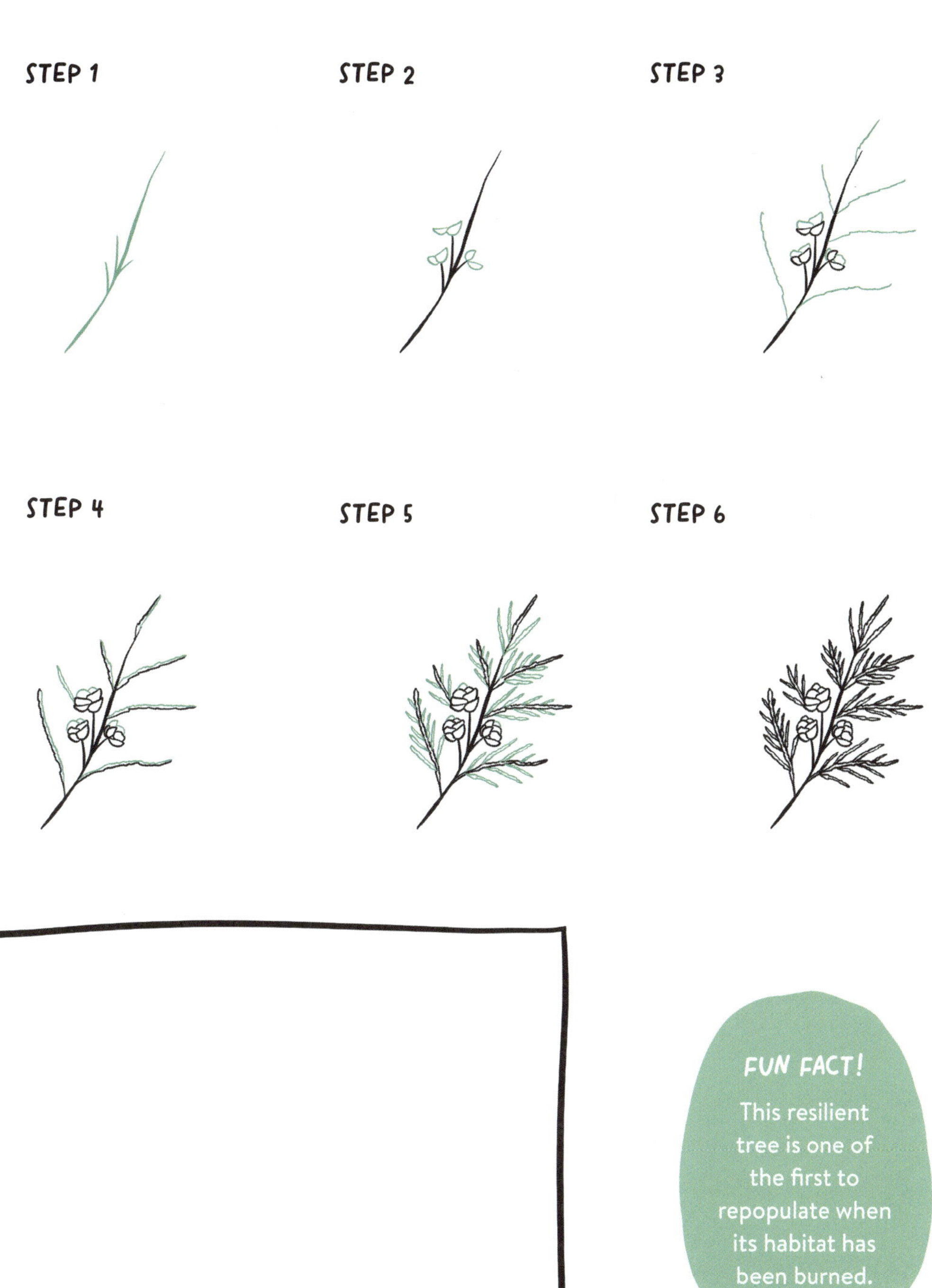

FUN FACT!

This resilient tree is one of the first to repopulate when its habitat has been burned.

Western Hemlock

Tsuga heterophylla

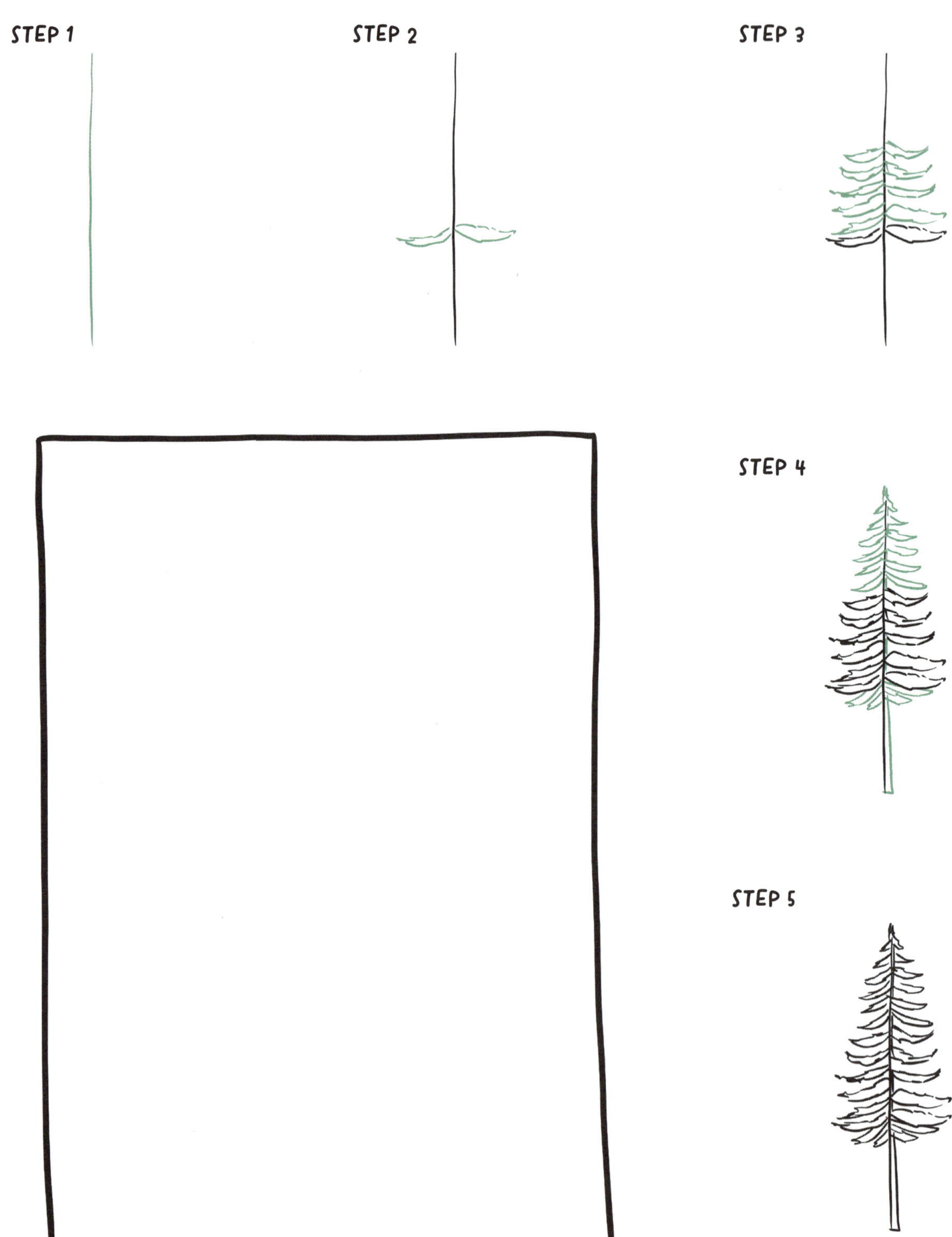

Western Hemlock Branch

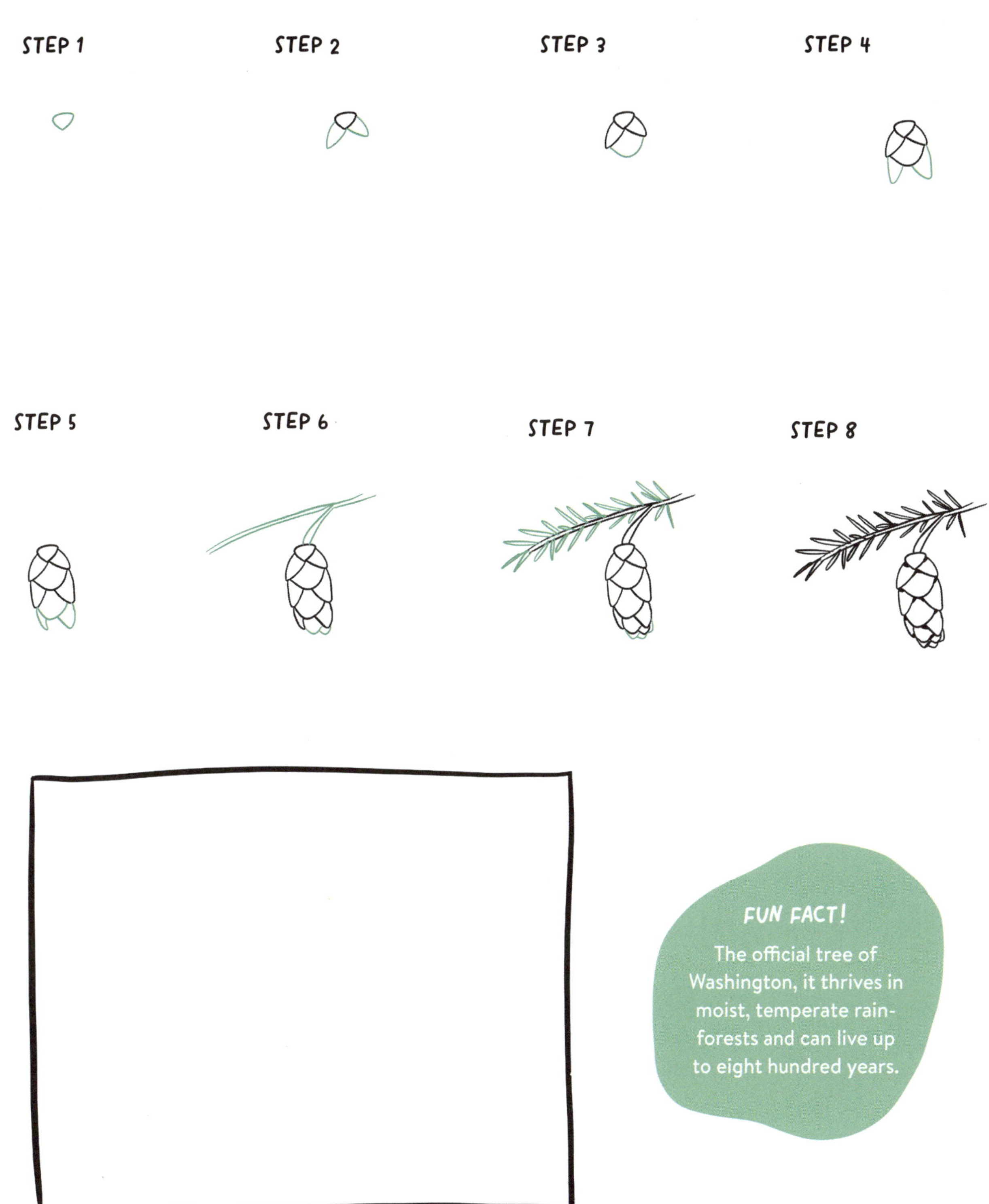

FUN FACT!

The official tree of Washington, it thrives in moist, temperate rainforests and can live up to eight hundred years.

Bigleaf Maple

Acer macrophyllum

STEP 1

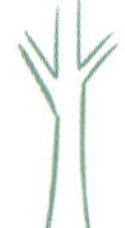

STEP 2

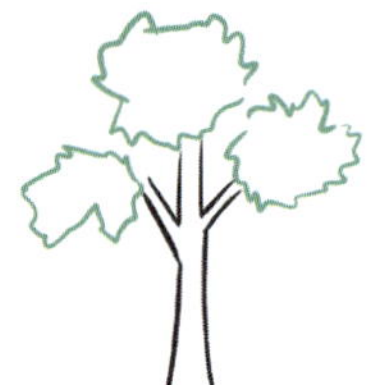

STEP 3

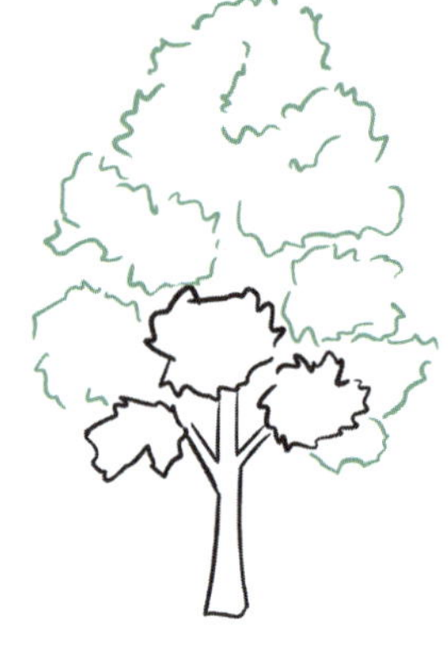

STEP 4

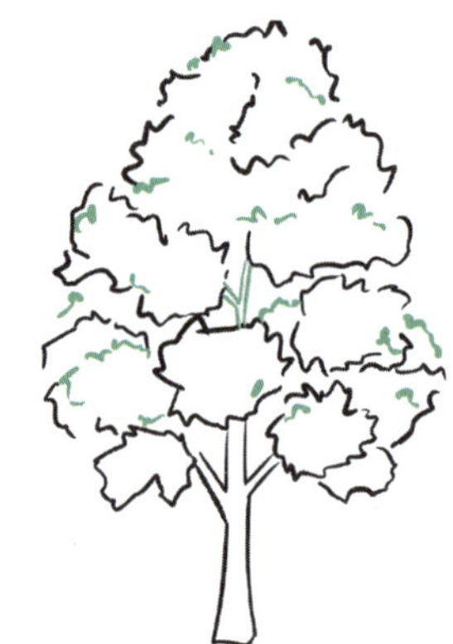

STEP 5

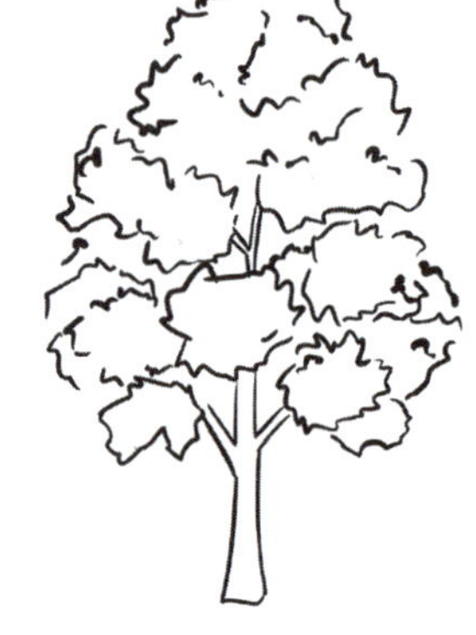

Bigleaf Maple Leaf

STEP 1

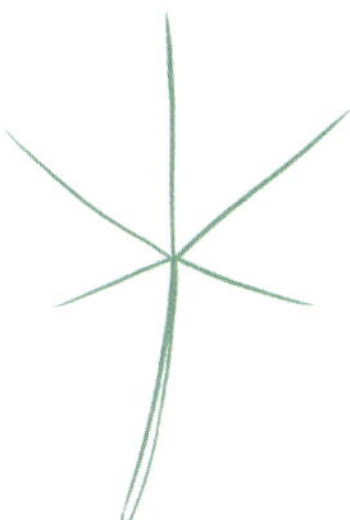

STEP 2

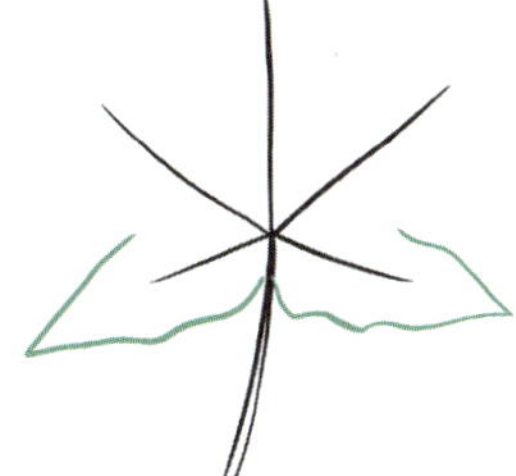

STEP 3

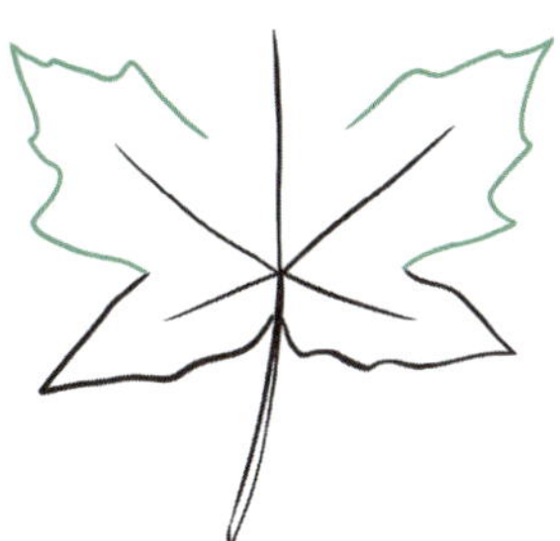

STEP 4

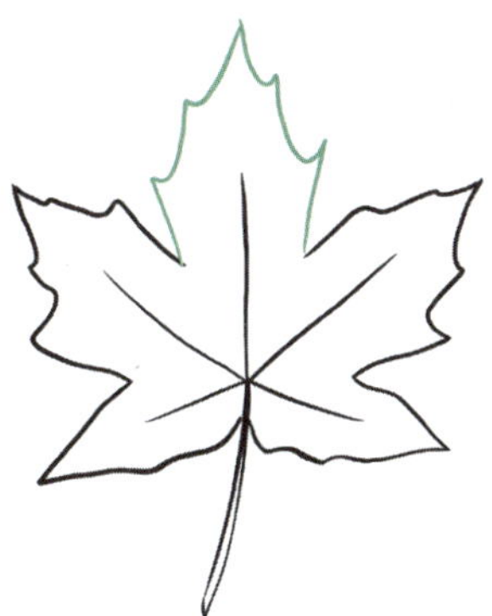

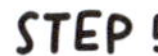

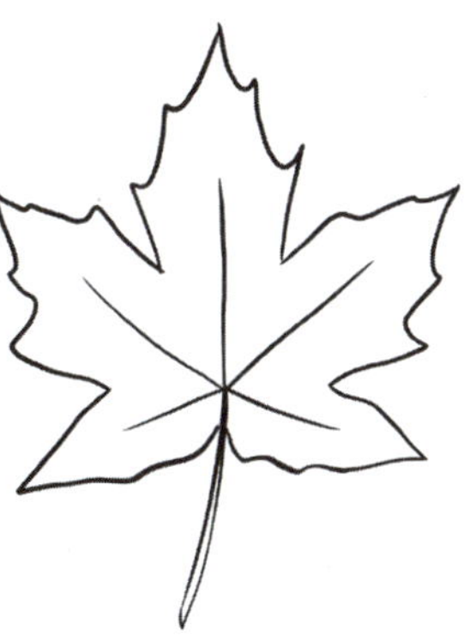

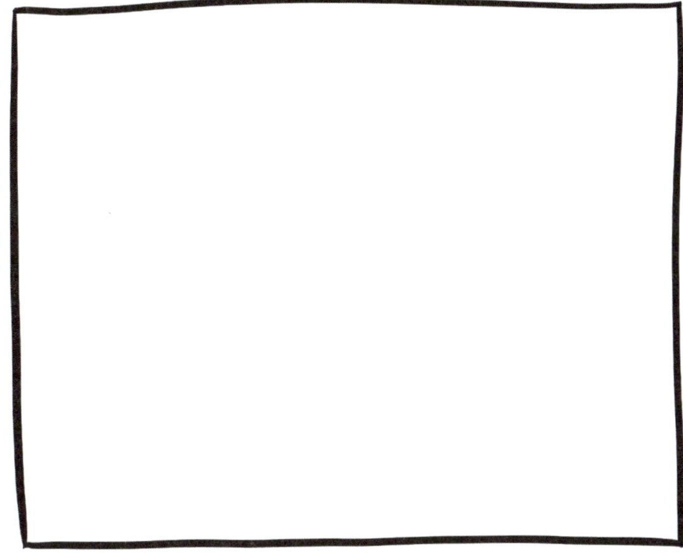

FUN FACT!

This tree's sap can be made into maple syrup, but the tree can take up to thirty years to start producing.

Vine Maple

Acer circinatum

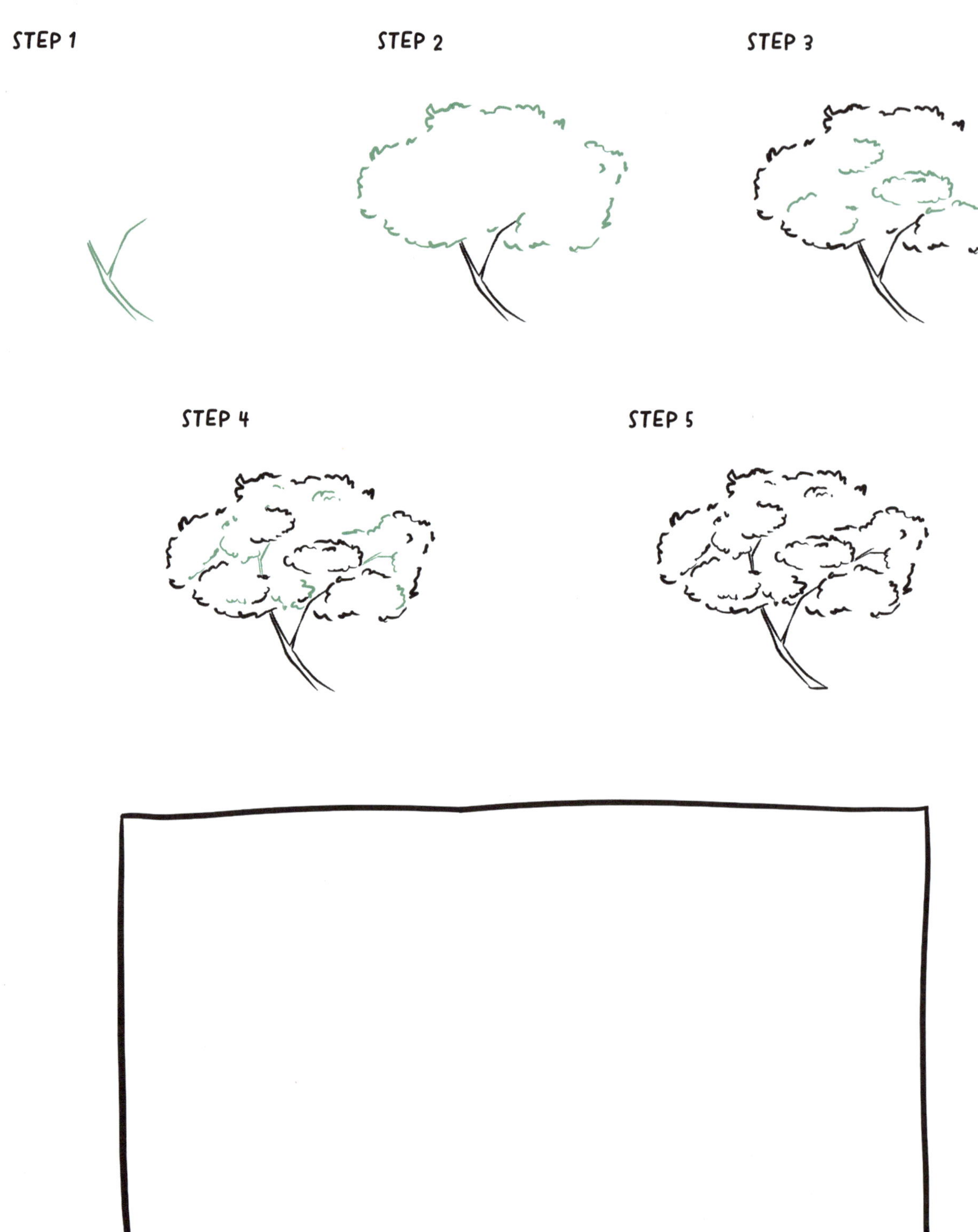

Vine Maple Leaf

STEP 1

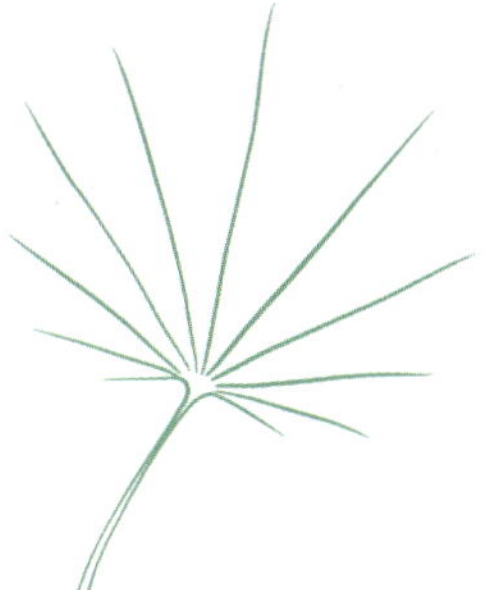

STEP 2

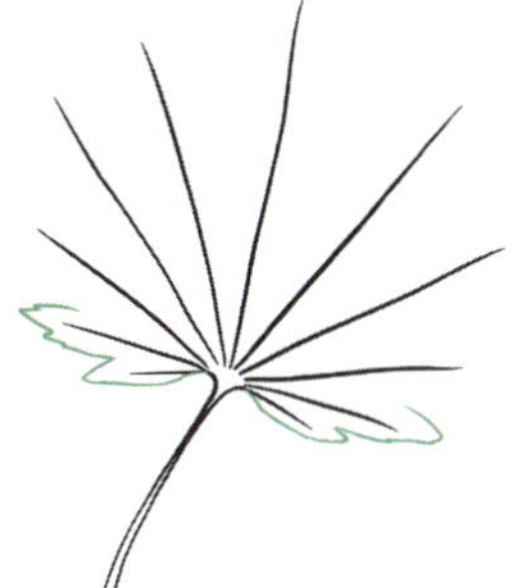

STEP 3

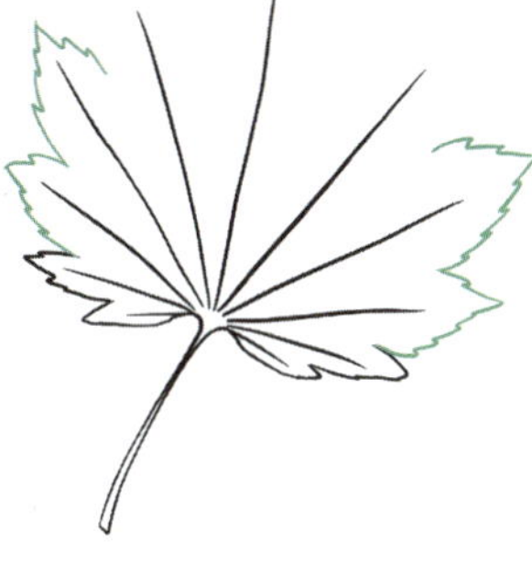

STEP 4

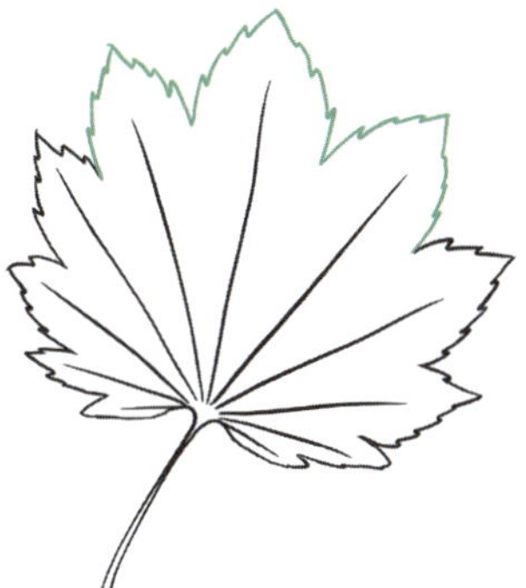

STEP 5

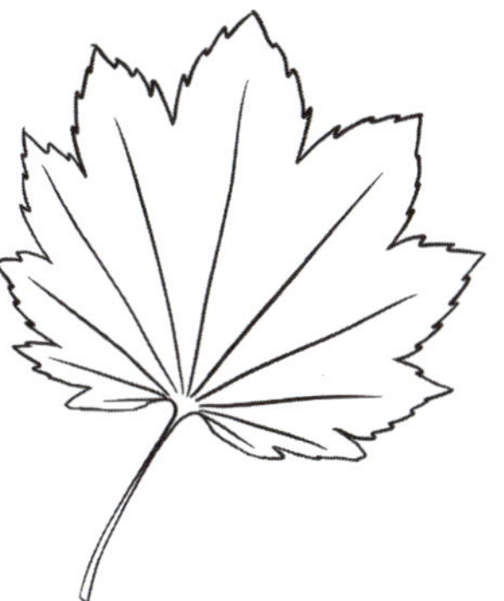

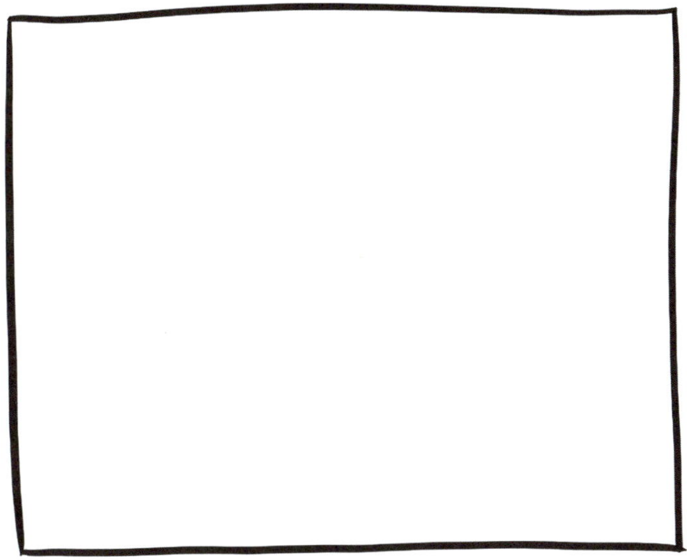

FUN FACT!

This tree has been used by Native people of the Northwest to make bows, frames for fishing nets, snowshoes, and cradle frames.

Pacific Madrone

Arbutus menziesii

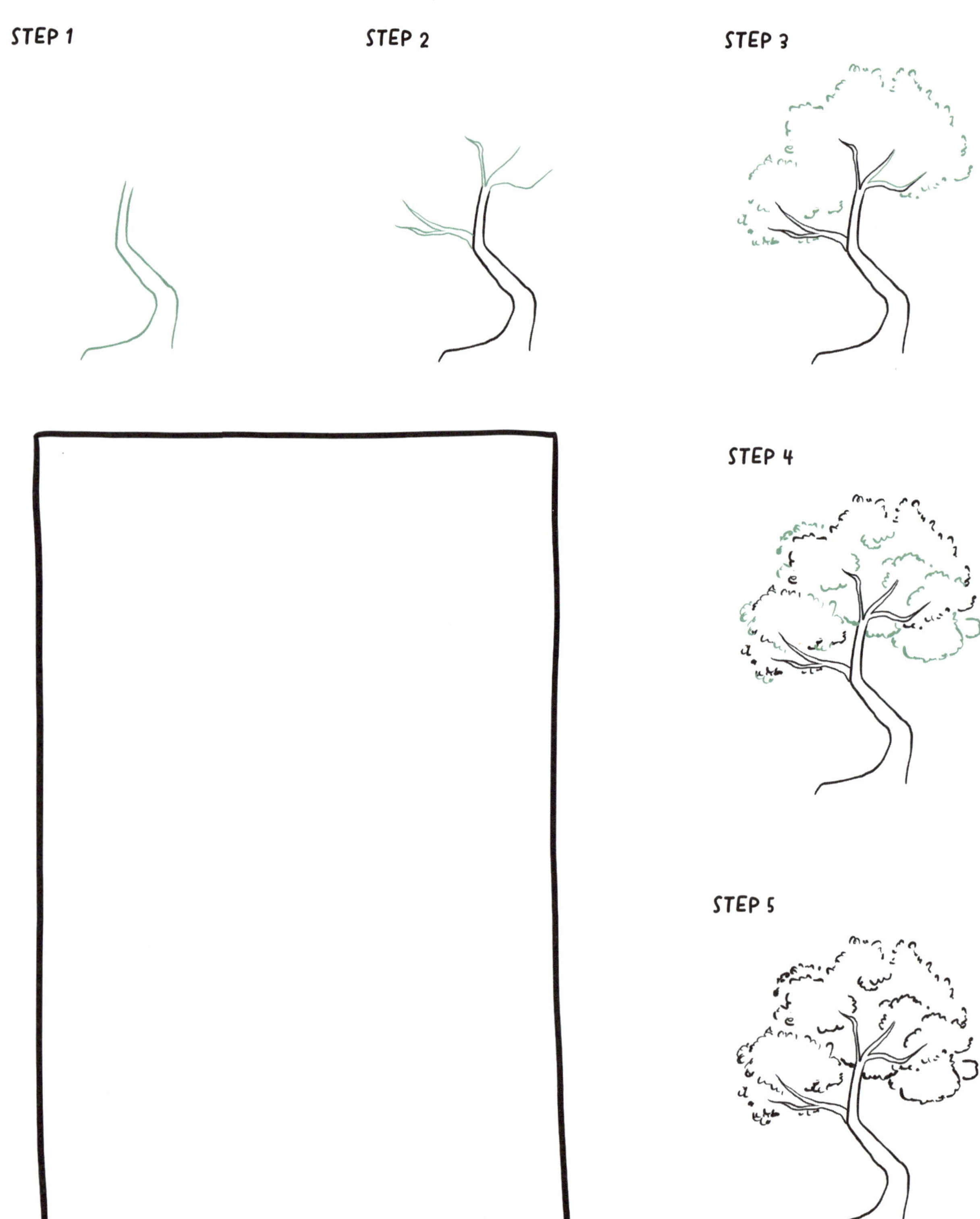

Pacific Madrone Flower

STEP 1

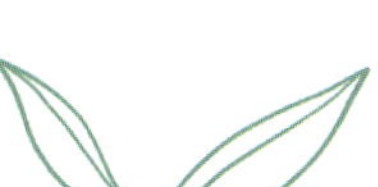

STEP 2

STEP 3

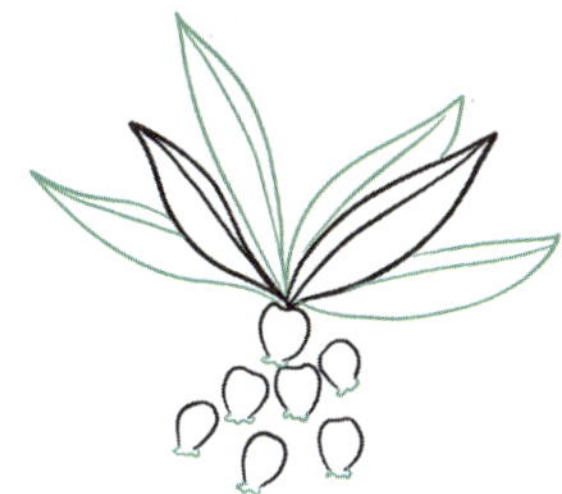

STEP 4

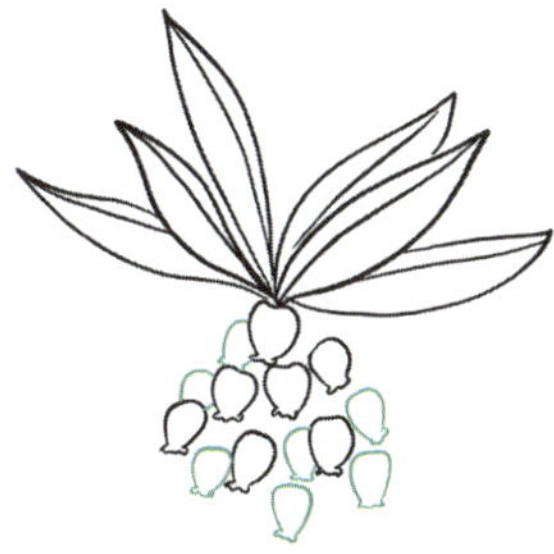

STEP 5

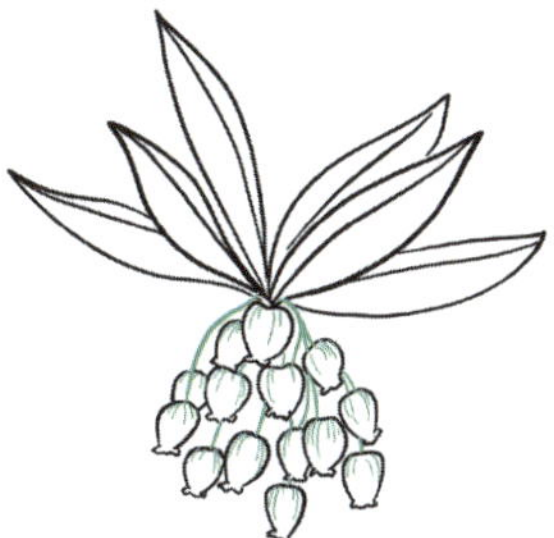

STEP 6

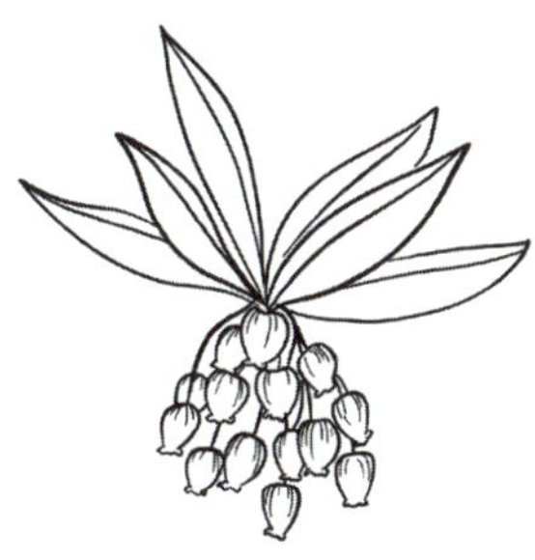

FUN FACT!

A symbol of strength and resilience, this tree produces sweet-smelling flowers around May that attract hummingbirds and honeybees.

Ponderosa Pine

Pinus ponderosa

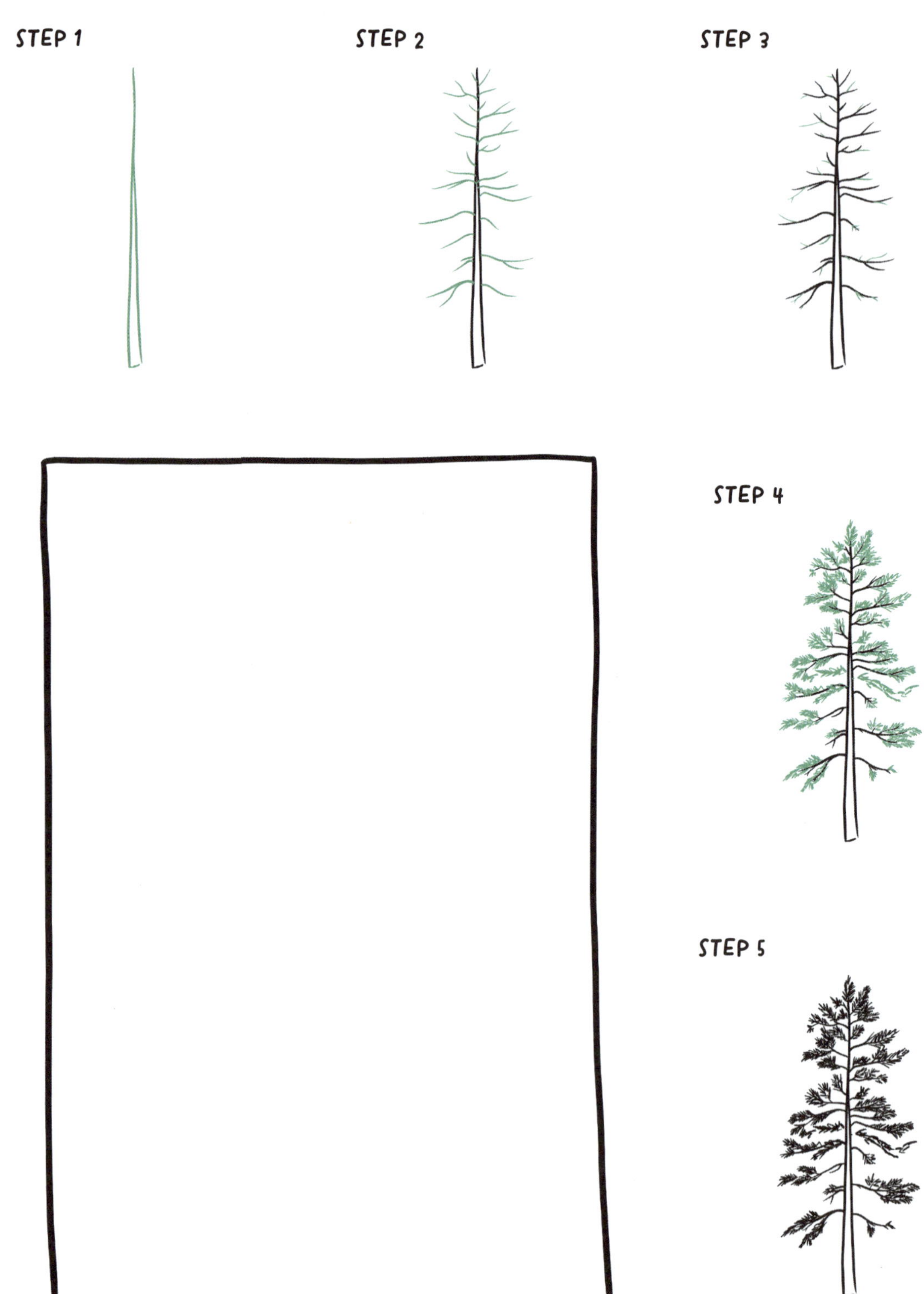

Ponderosa Pine Cone

STEP 1

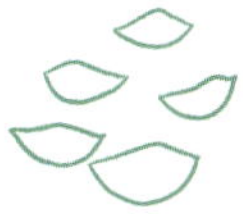

STEP 2

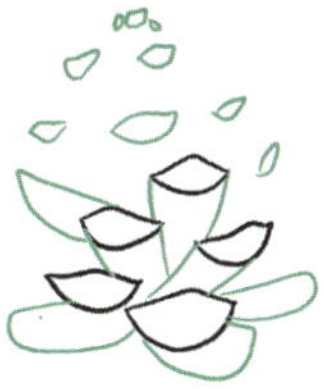

STEP 3

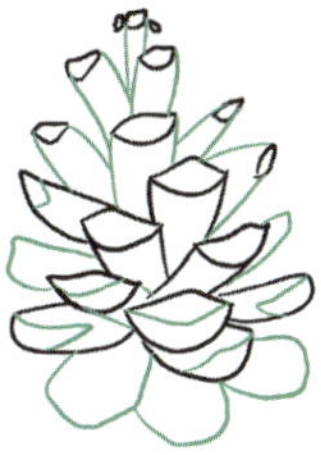

STEP 4

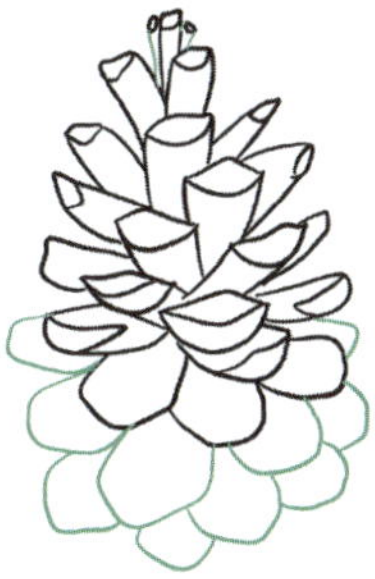

STEP 5

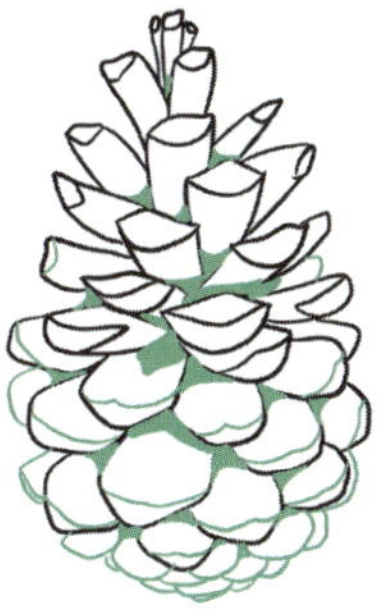

STEP 6

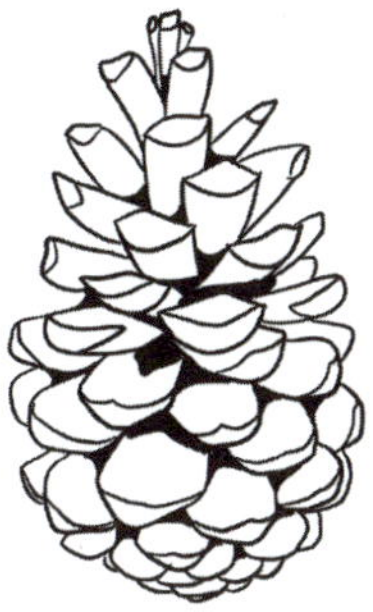

FUN FACT!

Its bark smells like vanilla or butterscotch when warmed by the sun.

Coast Redwood

Sequoia sempervirens

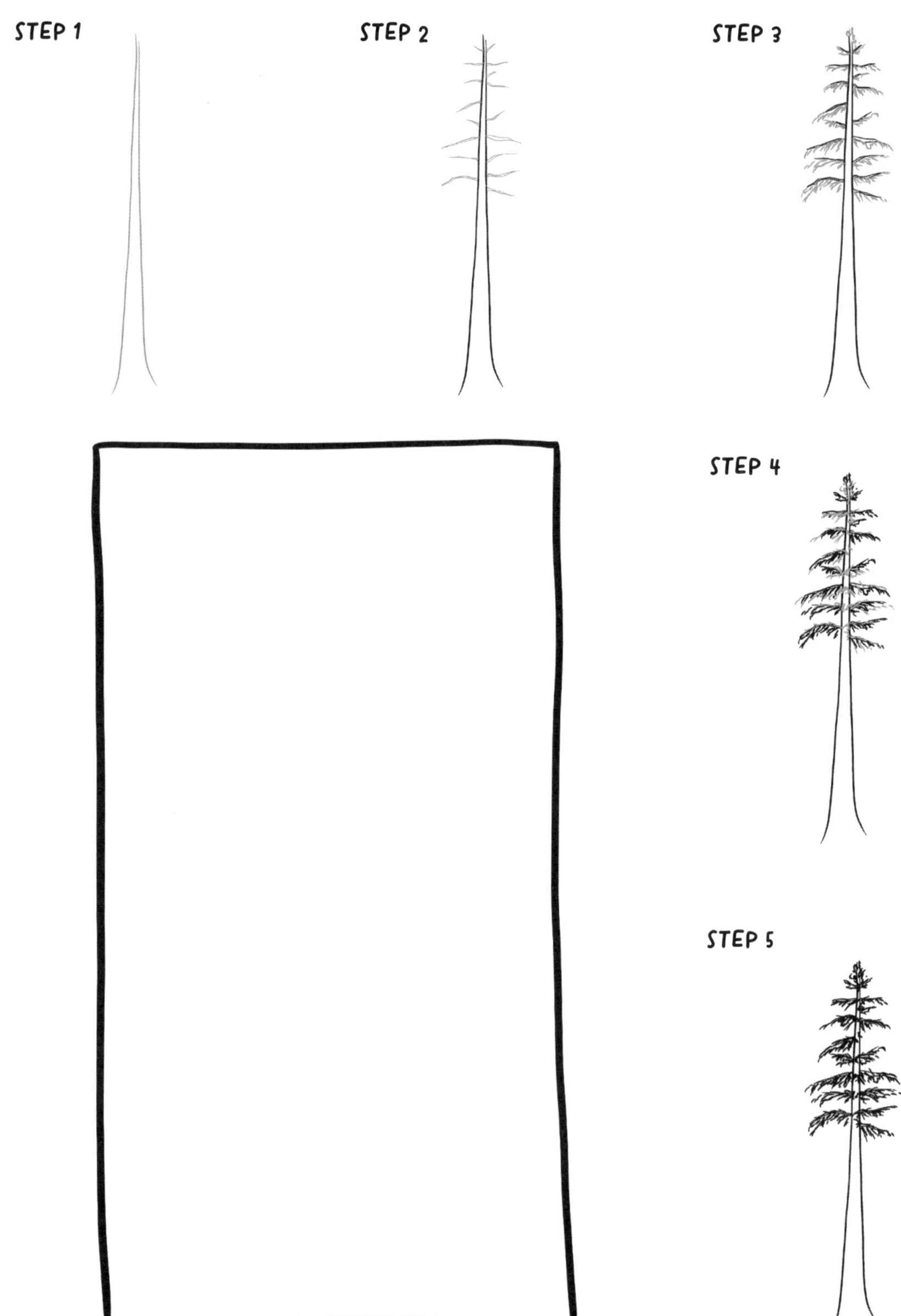

Coast Redwood Branch

STEP 1

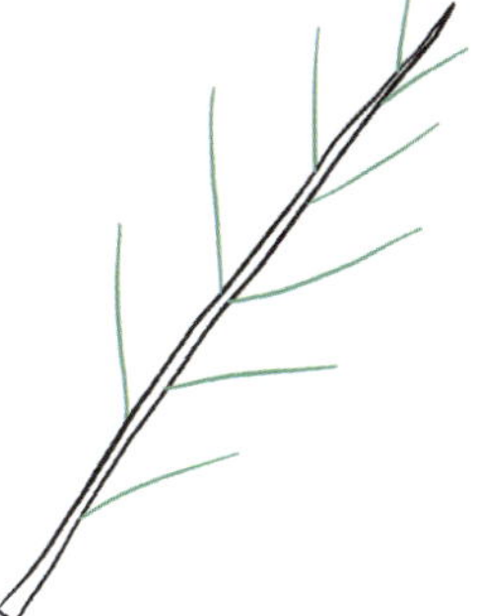

STEP 2

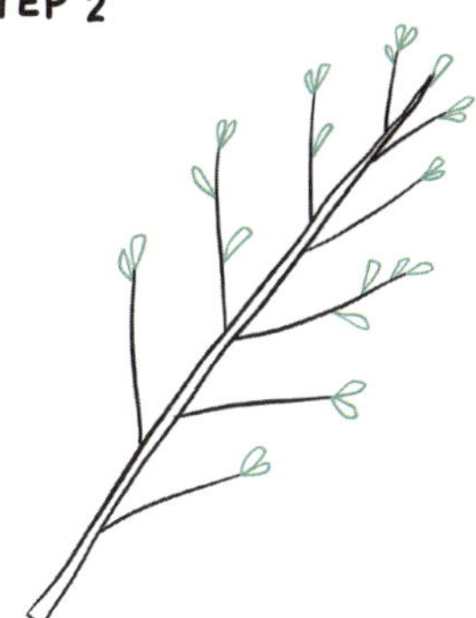

STEP 3

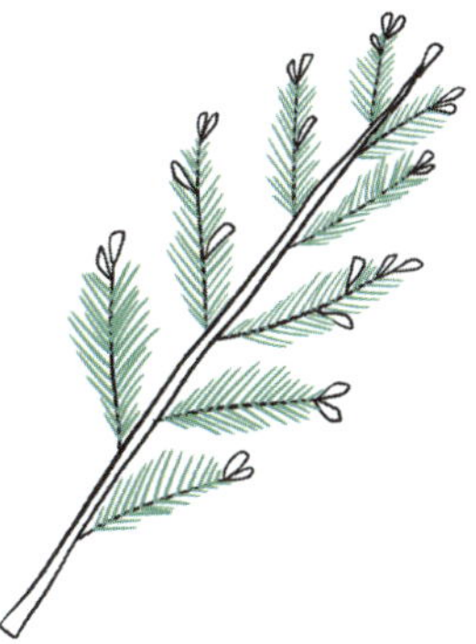

STEP 4

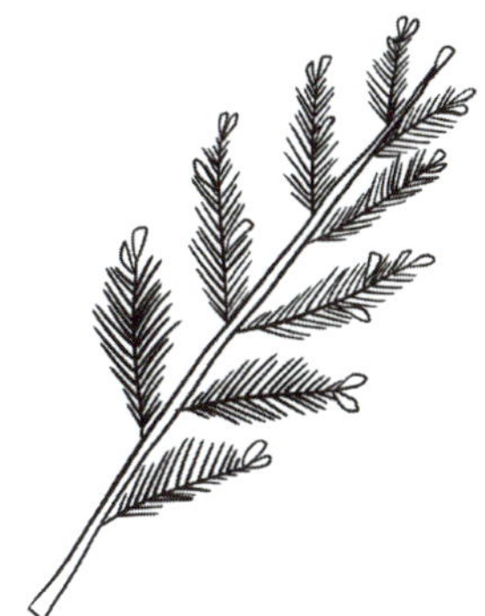

FUN FACT!

This tree can live for thousands of years and is the tallest tree on Earth.

Western Larch

Larix occidentalis

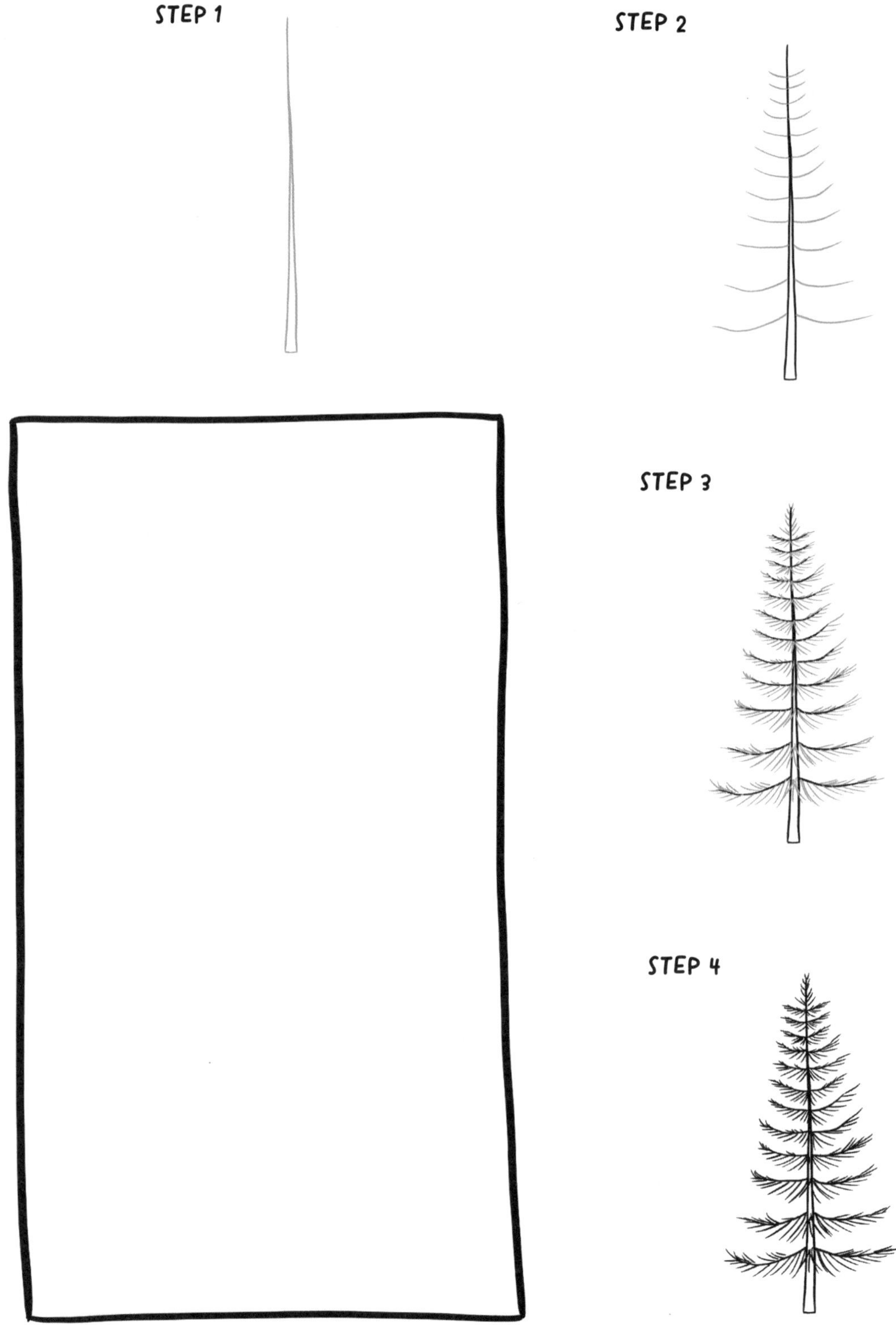

Western Larch Branch

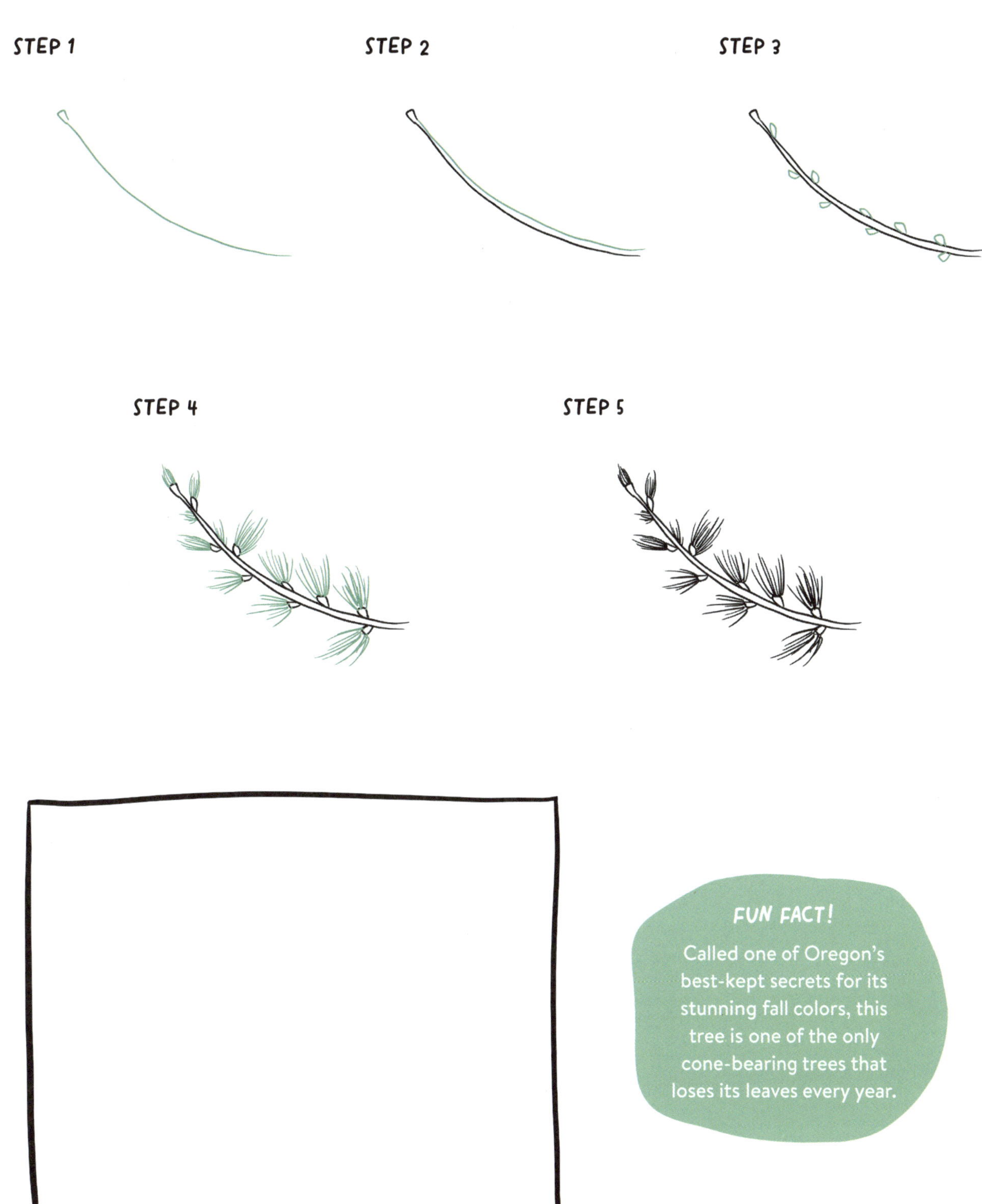

FUN FACT!

Called one of Oregon's best-kept secrets for its stunning fall colors, this tree is one of the only cone-bearing trees that loses its leaves every year.

Red Alder

Alnus rubra

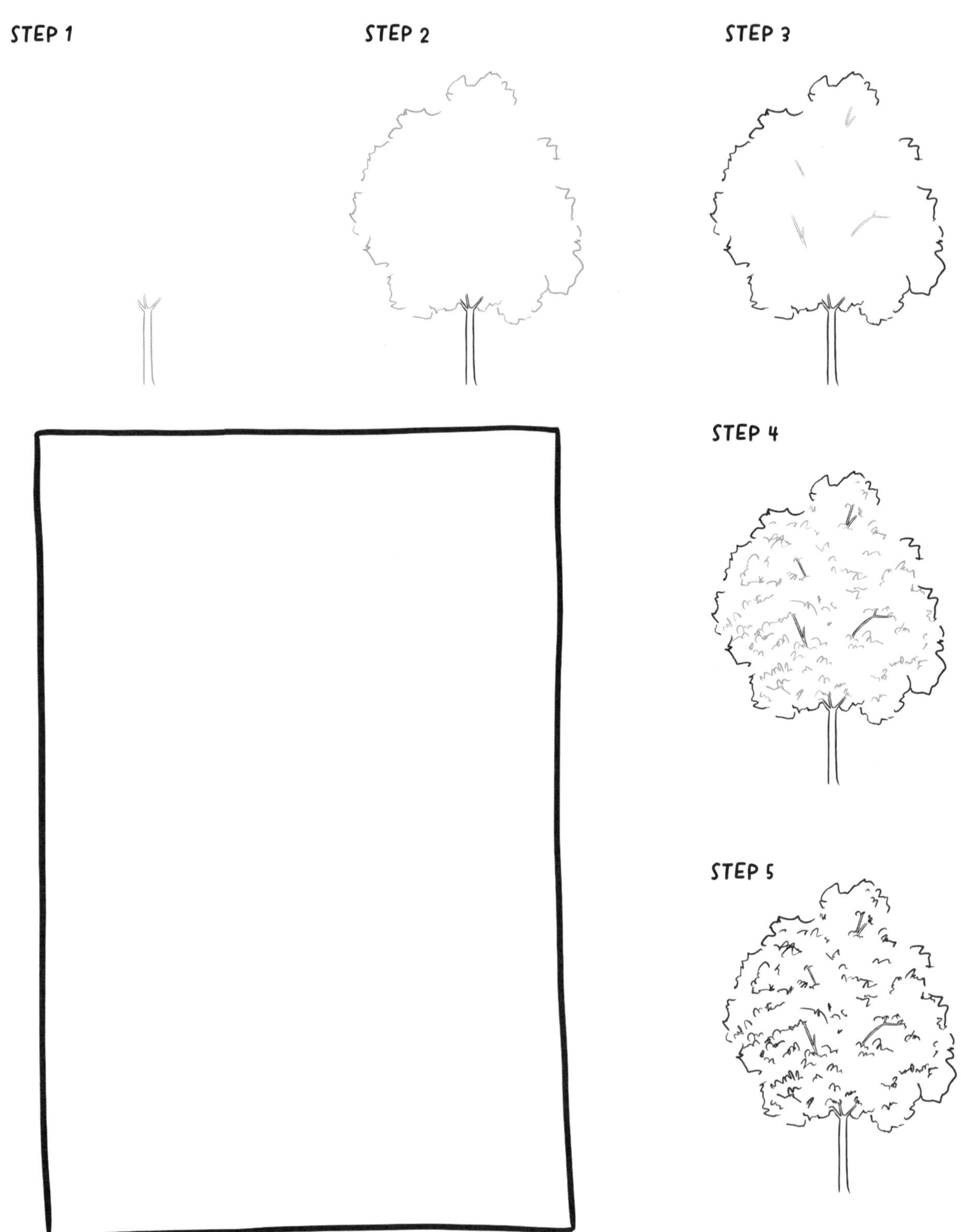

Red Alder Catkins

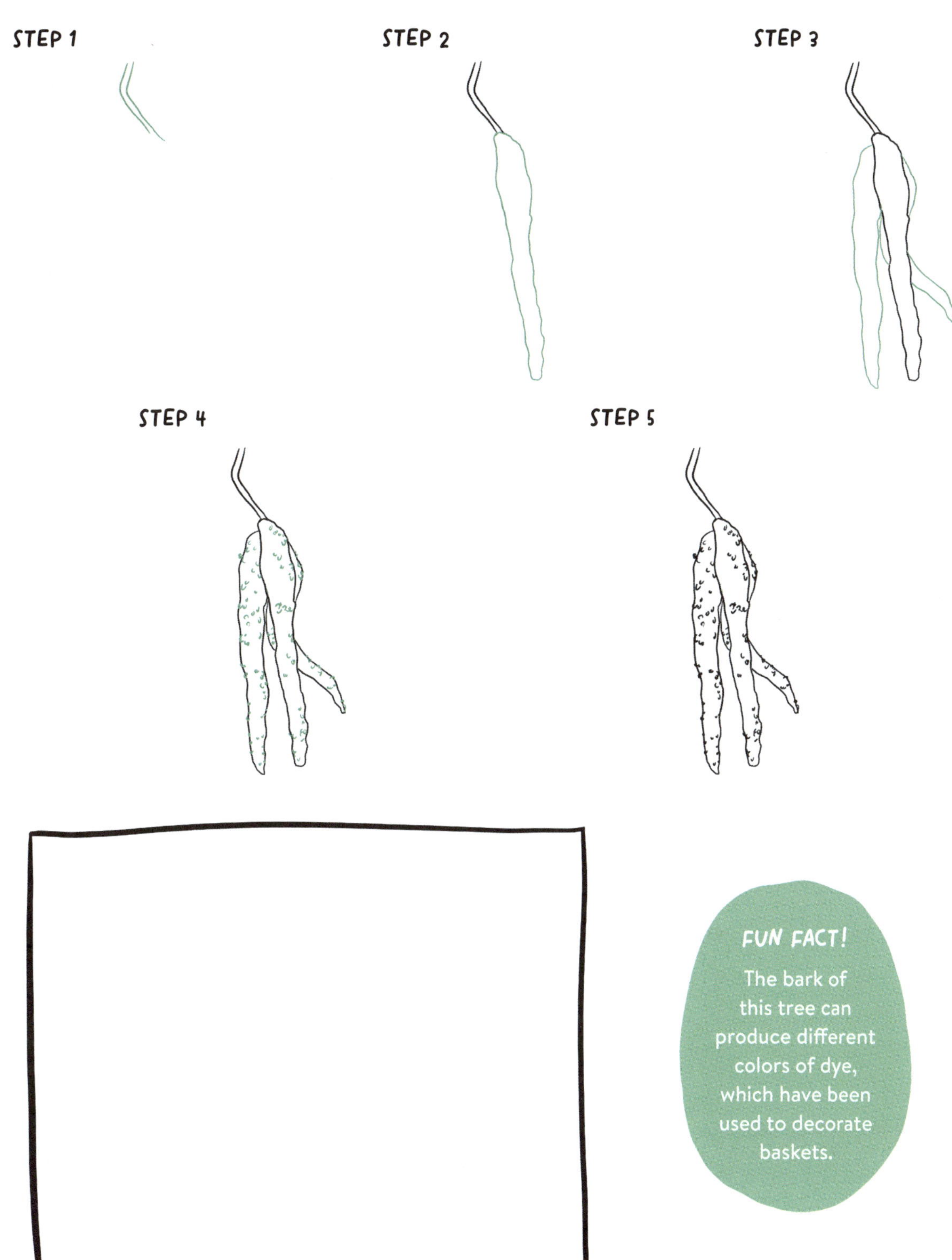

FUN FACT!

The bark of this tree can produce different colors of dye, which have been used to decorate baskets.

Black Cottonwood

Populus balsamifera ssp. trichocarpa

STEP 1

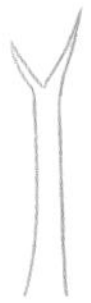

STEP 2

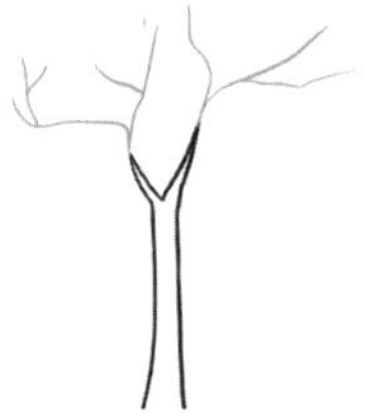

STEP 3

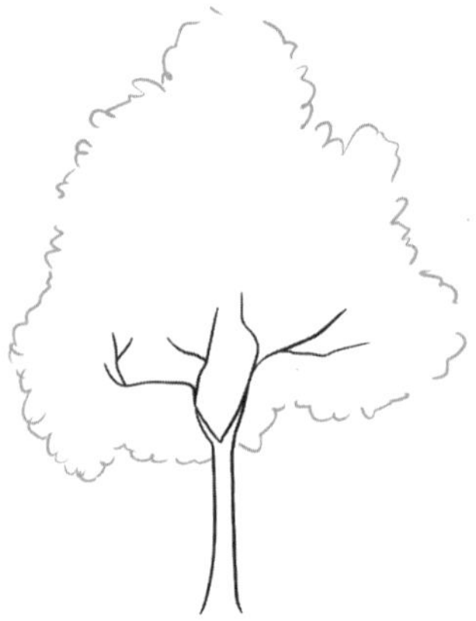

STEP 4

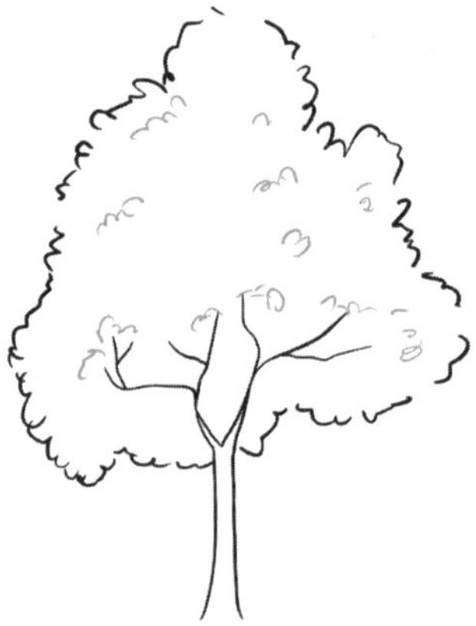

STEP 5

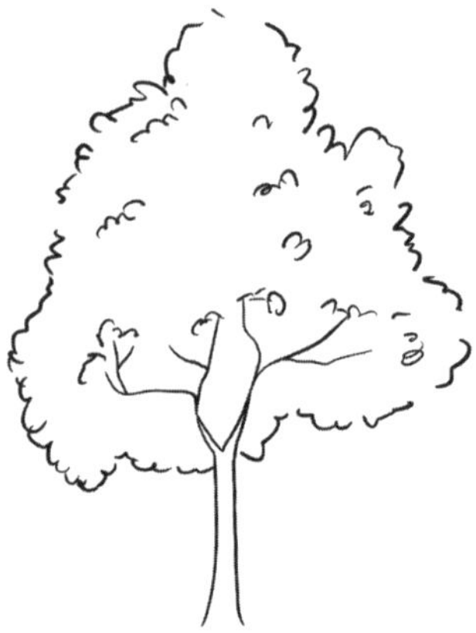

Black Cottonwood Branch

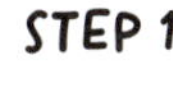

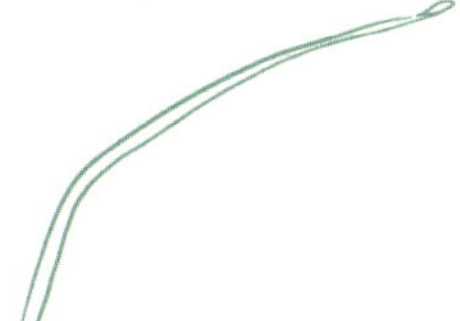

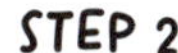

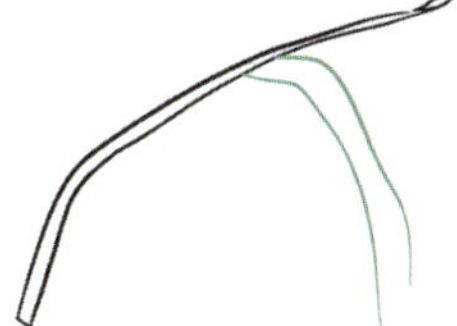

STEP 3

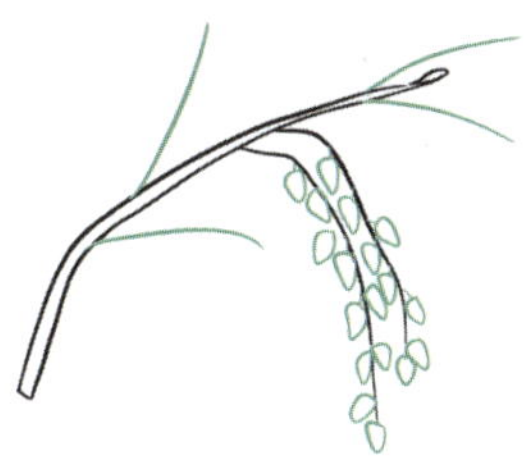

STEP 4

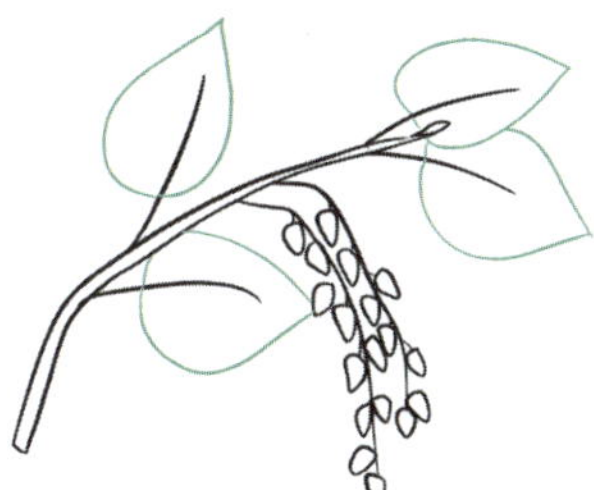

STEP 5

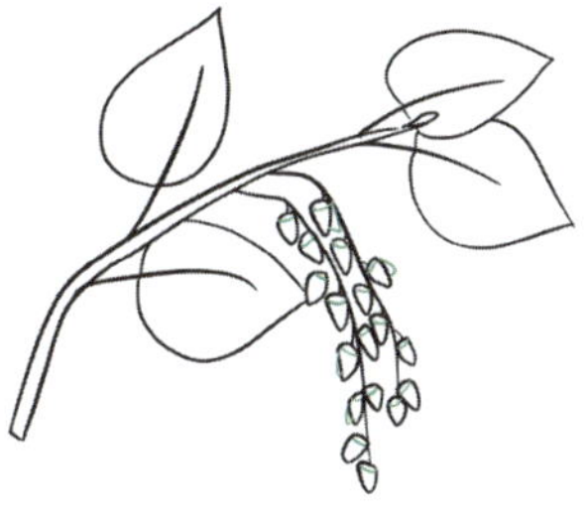

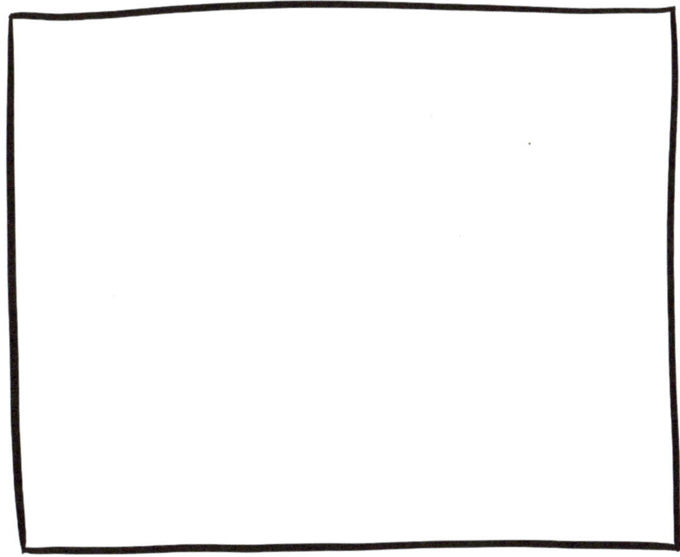

FUN FACT!

The buds of this tree are covered in resin to protect them from insects.

Western Redbud

Cercis occidentalis

STEP 1

STEP 2

STEP 3

STEP 4

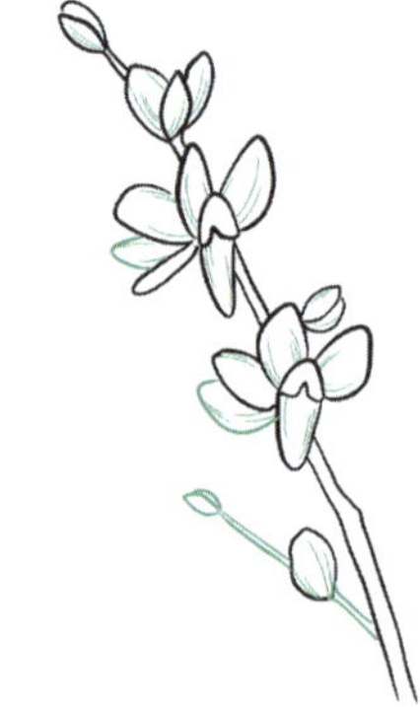

STEP 5

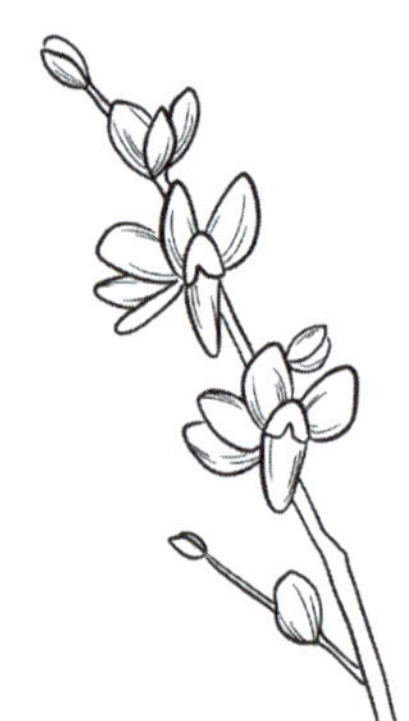

FUN FACT!

This tree is truly versatile. Different parts of it have been used for their medicinal purposes, as well as in food and crafts.

Salmonberry

Rubus spectabilis

STEP 1

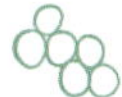

STEP 2

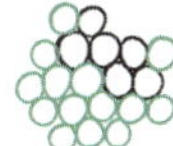

STEP 3

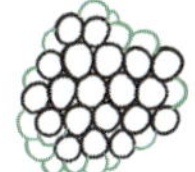

STEP 4

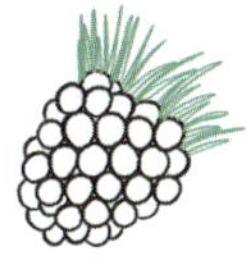

STEP 5

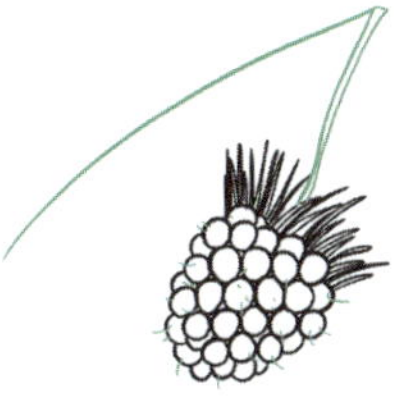

STEP 6

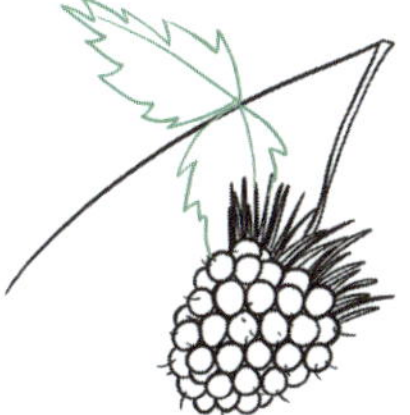

STEP 7

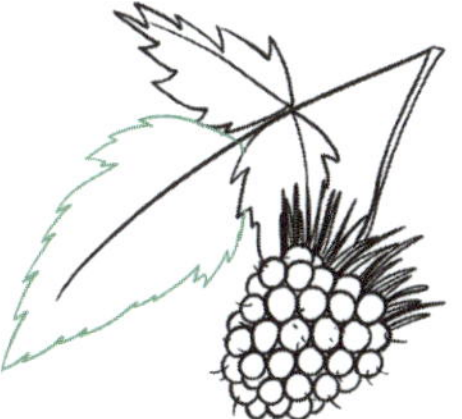

STEP 8

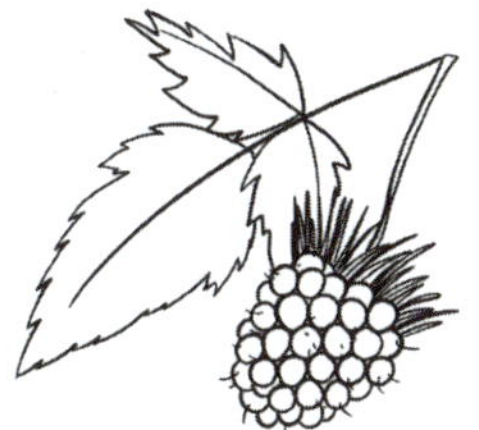

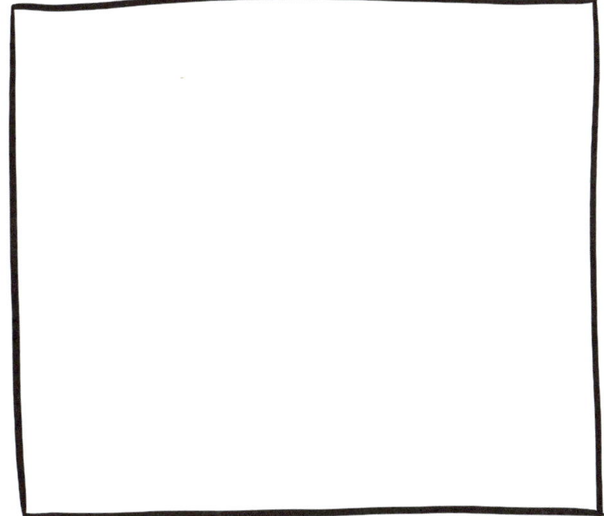

FUN FACT!

Used to flavor beer and wine, this berry is found in moist forests and along stream banks.

Thimbleberry

Rubus parviflorus

STEP 1

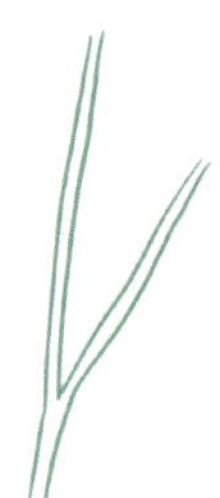

STEP 2

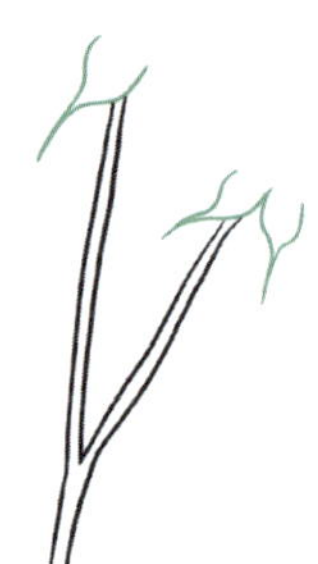

STEP 3

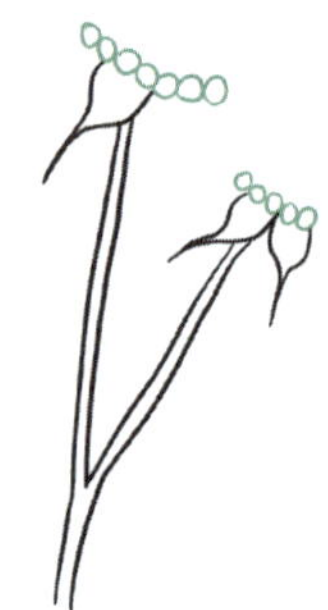

STEP 4

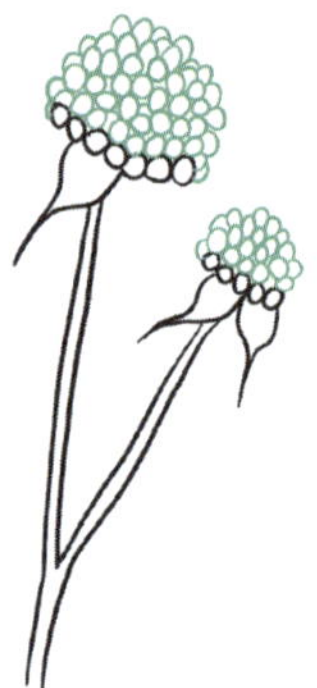

STEP 5

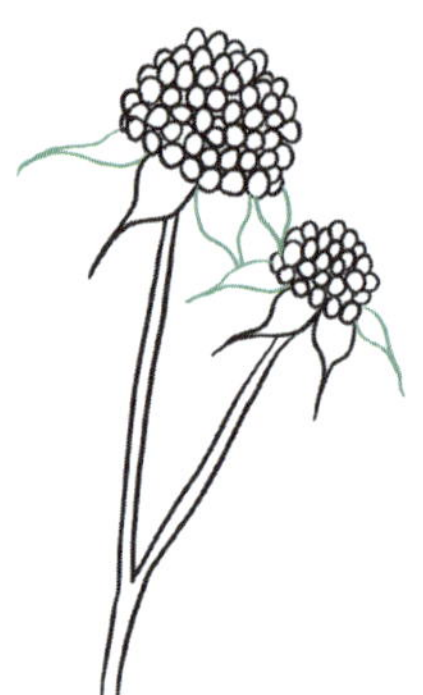

STEP 6

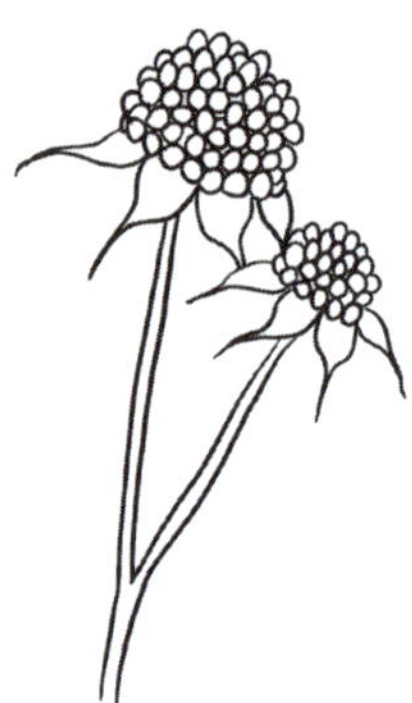

FUN FACT!

This indecisive plant needs both shade and sun and is named for its resemblance to a thimble.

Salal

Gaultheria shallon

STEP 1

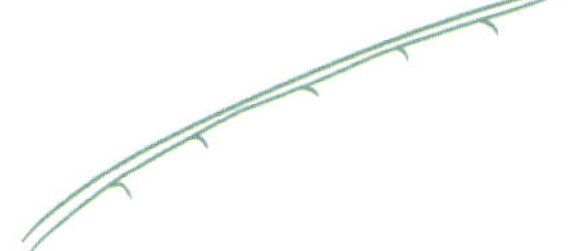

STEP 2

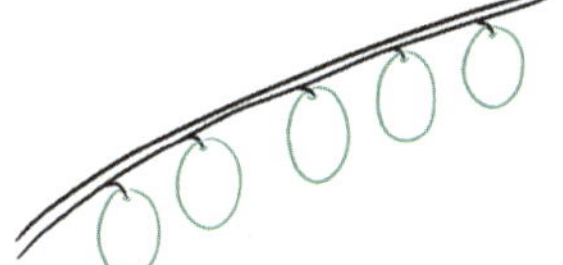

STEP 3

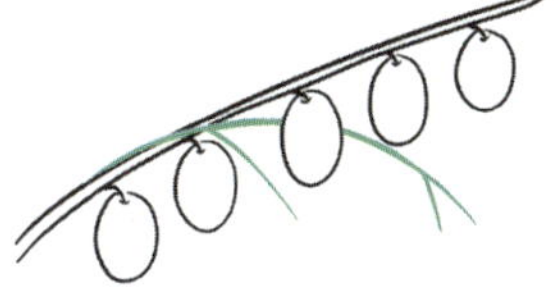

STEP 4

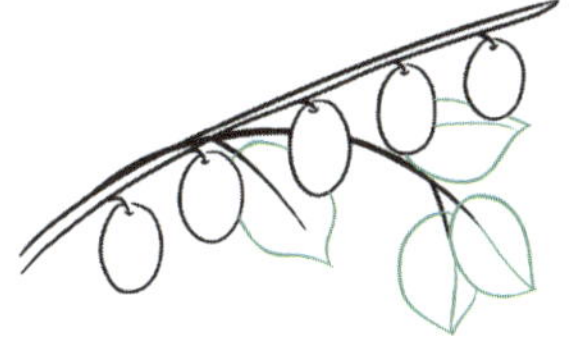

STEP 5

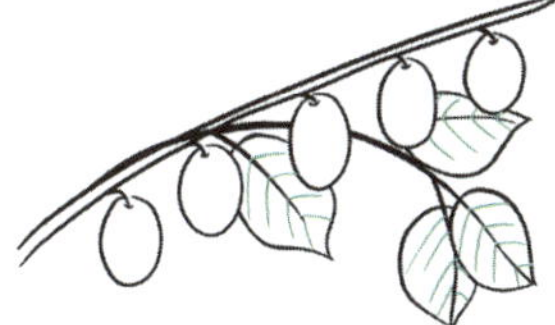

STEP 6

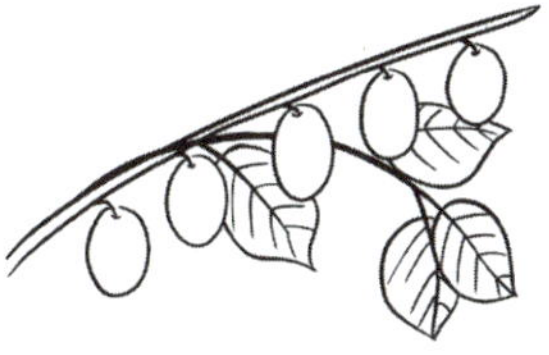

FUN FACT!

Salal's leaves and berries feed a variety of animals, including deer, elk, bears, and chipmunks.

Marionberry

Rubus ursinus

STEP 1

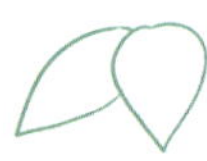

STEP 2

STEP 3

STEP 4

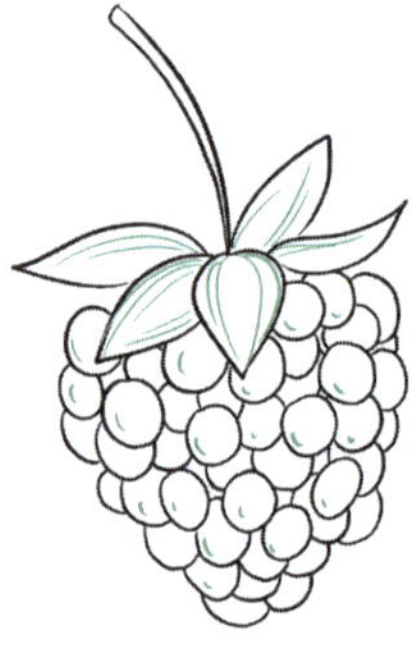

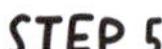

STEP 5

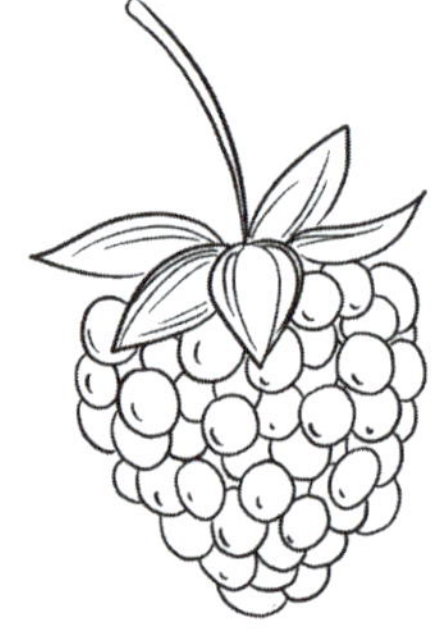

FUN FACT!

Marionberry is a cultivar of blackberry grown almost exclusively in Oregon, and it owes its existence to the native trailing blackberry.

Huckleberry

Vaccinium spp.

STEP 1

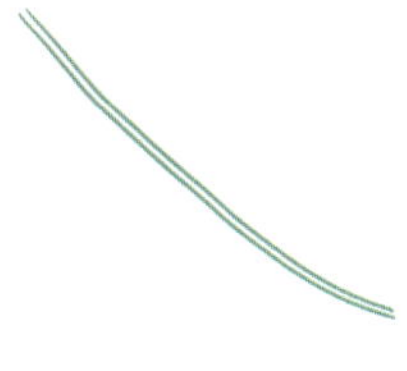

STEP 2

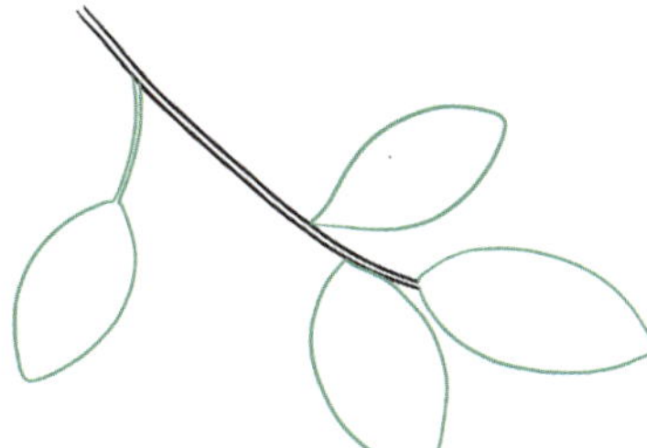

STEP 3

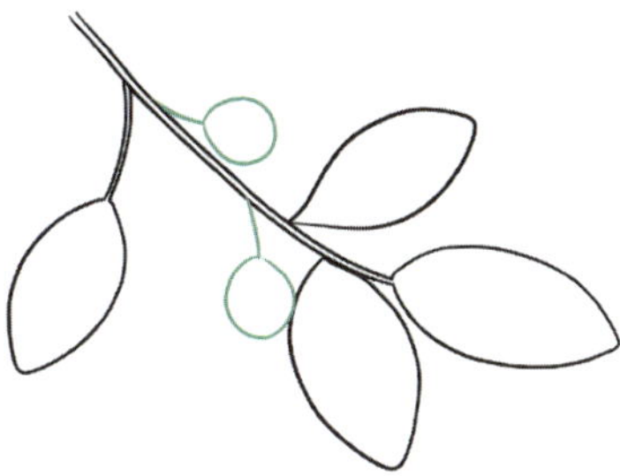

STEP 4

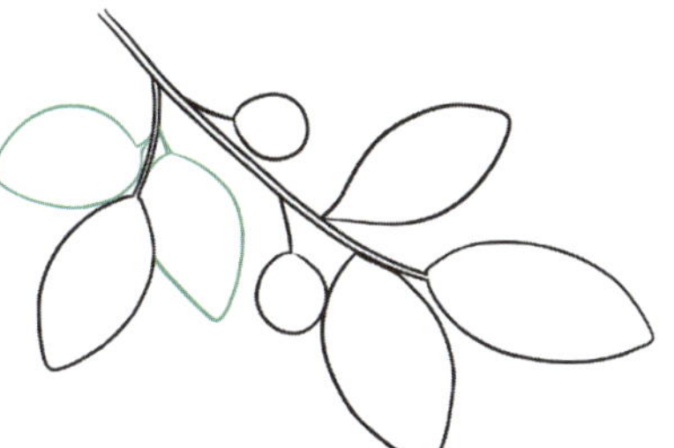

STEP 5

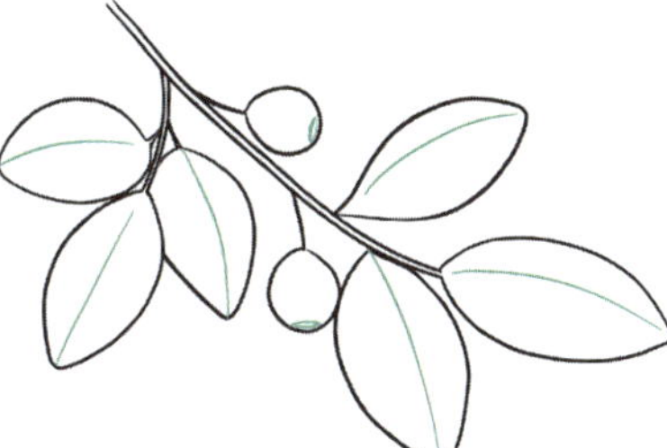

STEP 6

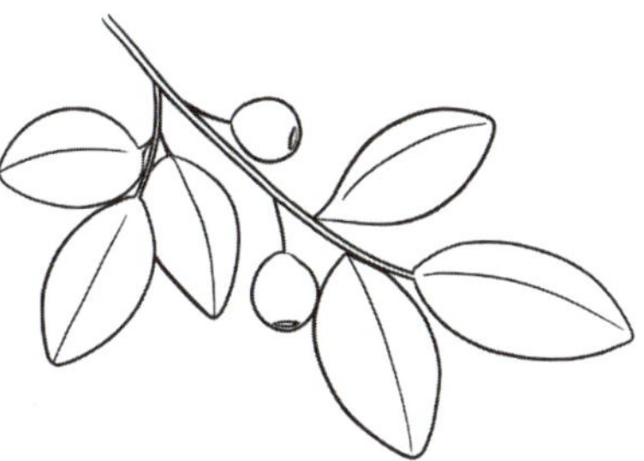

FUN FACT!

There are more than twelve species of huckleberries in the Pacific Northwest. Though they are popular, they cannot be grown commercially.

Rainier Cherry

Prunus avium 'Rainier'

STEP 1

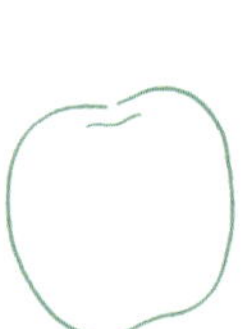

STEP 2

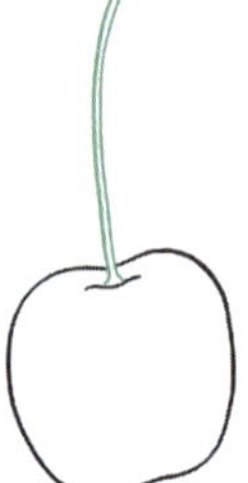

STEP 3

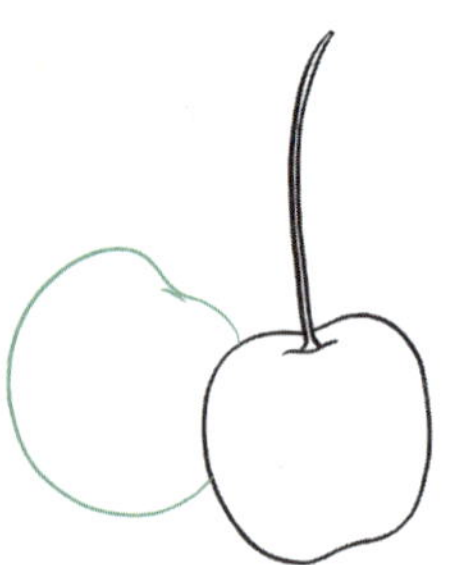

STEP 4

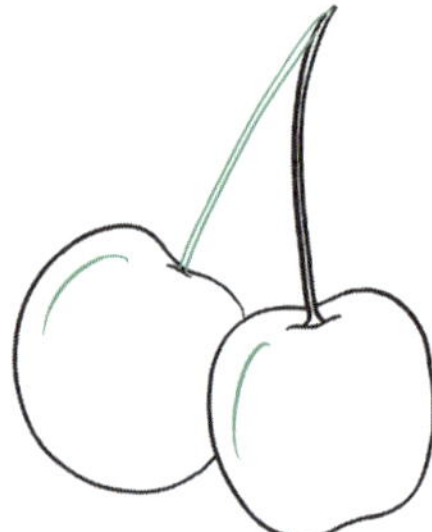

STEP 5

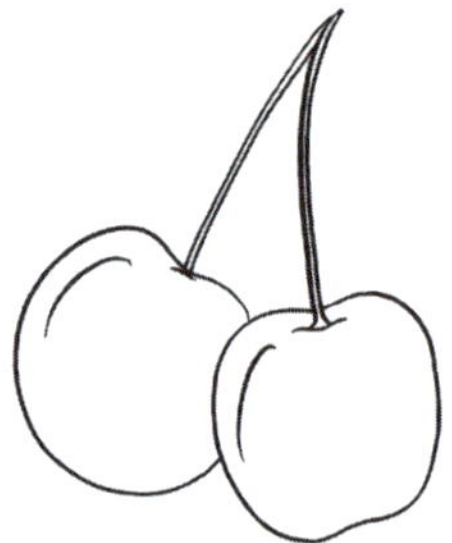

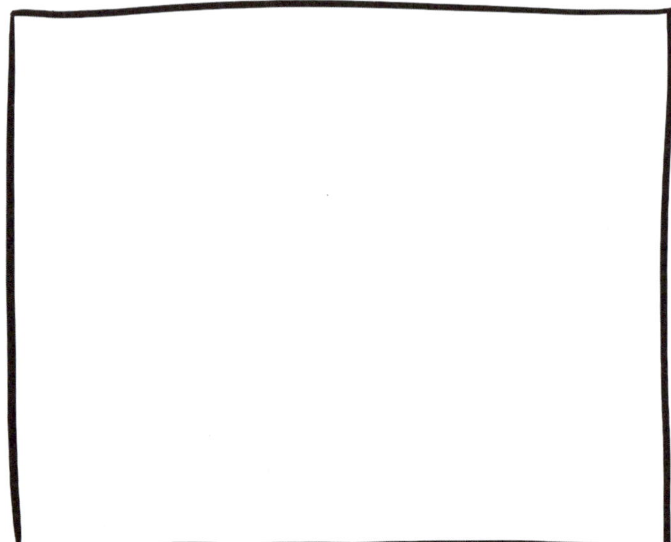

FUN FACT!

A cross between the 'Bing' and 'Van' cultivars, this cherry is named after Mount Rainier.

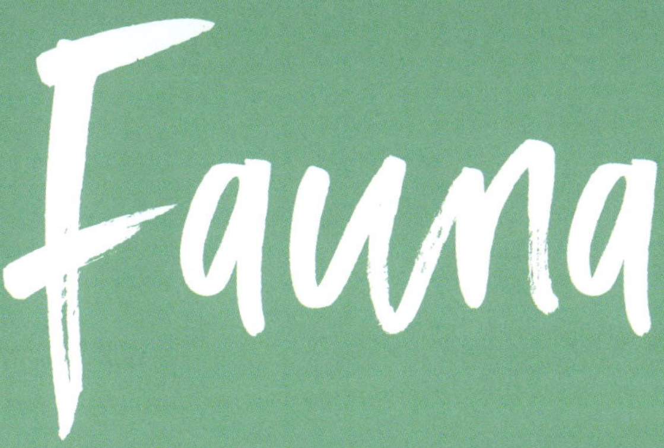

Fauna

In the Pacific Northwest, the animal kingdom is as varied and complex as the region's geography. Dense forests, expansive coastlines, and rushing rivers are not just scenic backdrops but vital habitats supporting a diverse array of wildlife. Each species, from the smallest insect to the largest predator, plays a crucial role in the ecosystem's health.

Fauna in the region shape the landscape through their activities, regulate populations of other species to maintain balance, and facilitate the pollination of plants and dispersal of seeds.

While sketching these diverse creatures, pay attention to how their forms and features are adapted to their environments. From the sleek lines of aquatic animals to the robust shapes of land mammals, each drawing will help you appreciate the incredible diversity of Pacific Northwest wildlife.

American Beaver

Castor canadensis

STEP 1

STEP 2

STEP 3

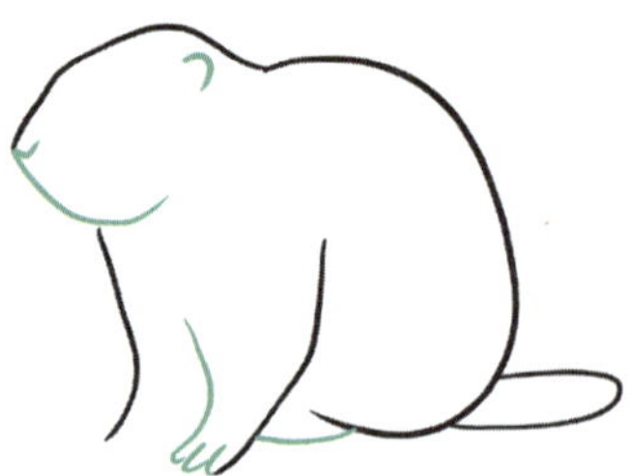

STEP 4

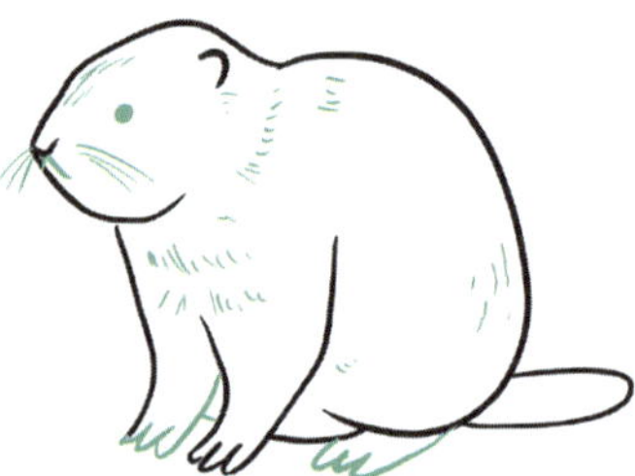

STEP 5

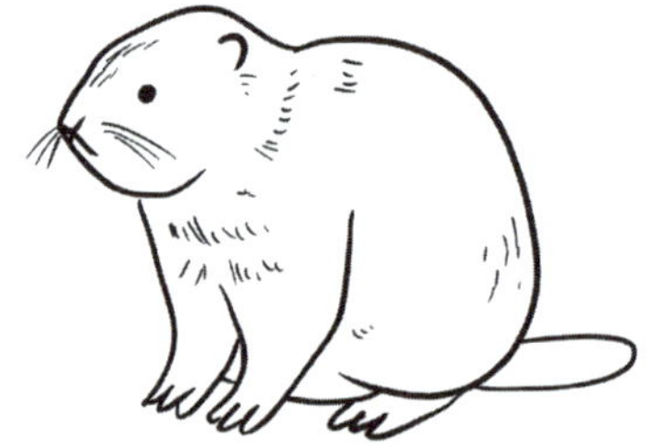

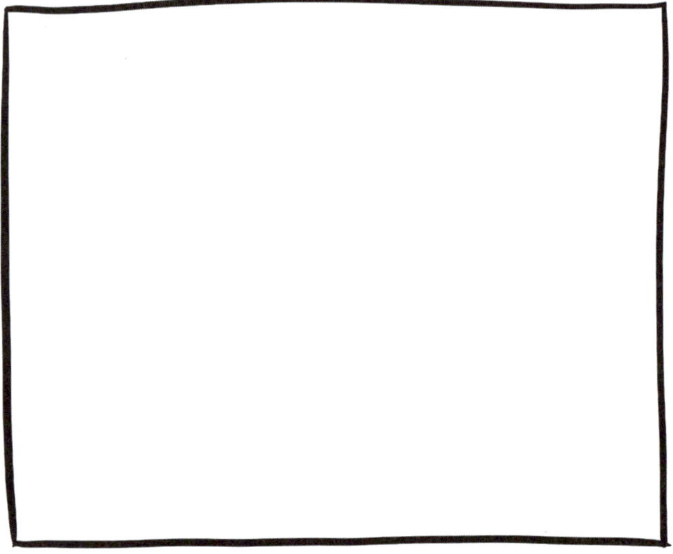

FUN FACT!

The official Oregon state animal, the beaver's dam-building activities help filter and purify water.

Olympic Marmot

Marmota olympus

STEP 1

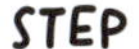

STEP 2

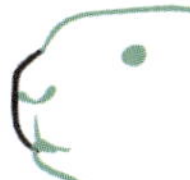

STEP 3

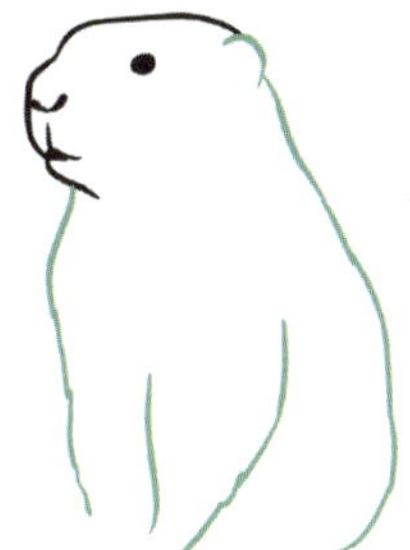

STEP 4

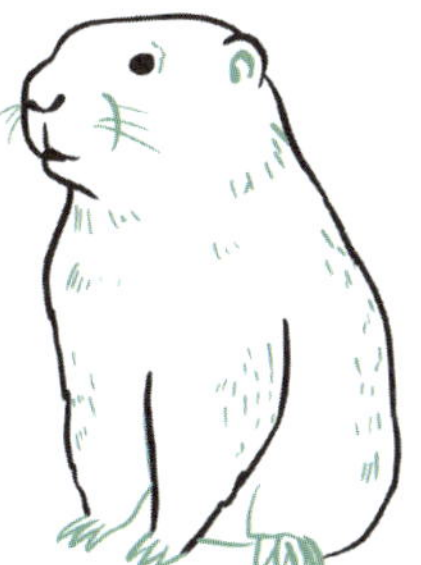

STEP 5

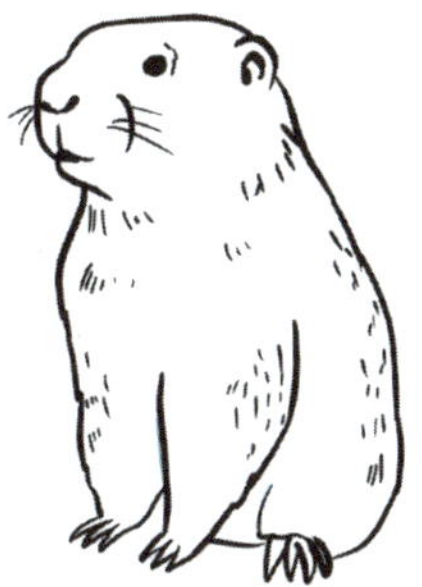

FUN FACT!

Although they hibernate seven to eight months a year, when they're awake, marmots aerate the soil by digging, which helps plant growth.

Appaloosa

Equus ferus caballus

STEP 1

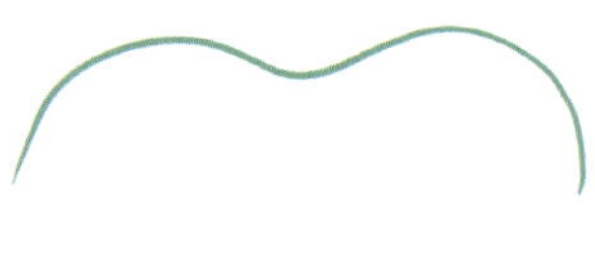

STEP 2

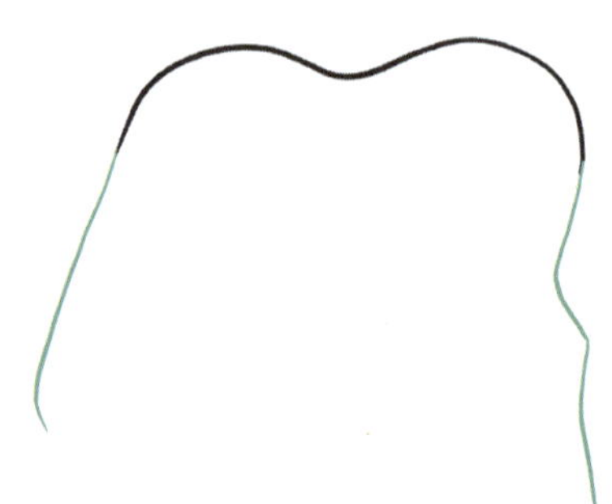

STEP 3

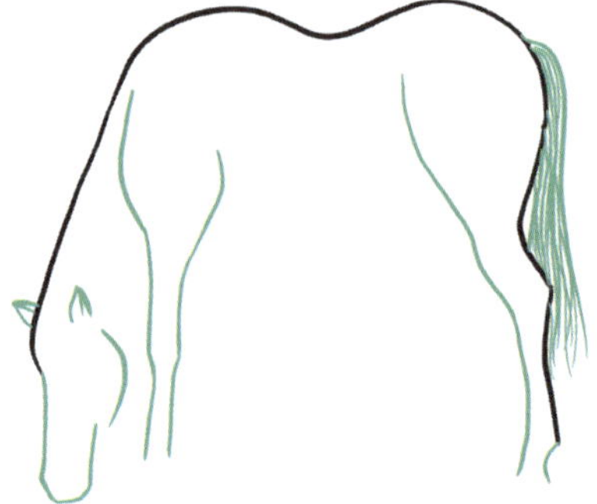

STEP 4

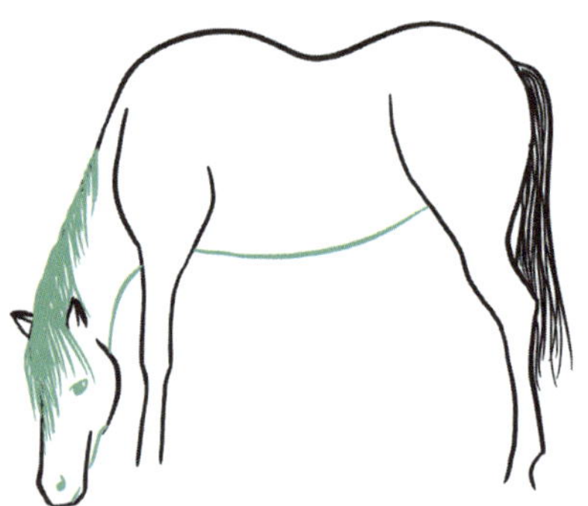

STEP 5

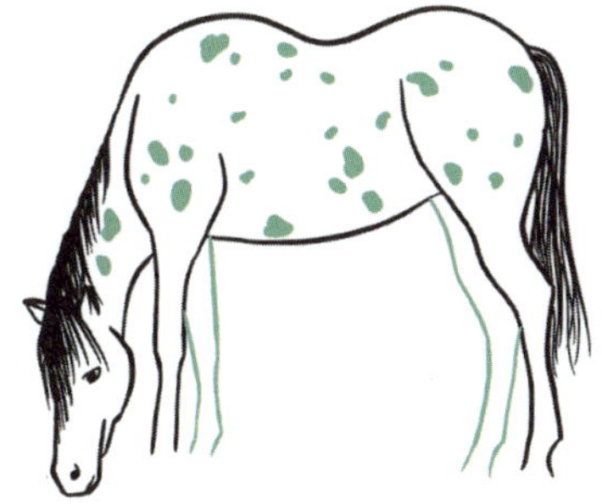

STEP 6

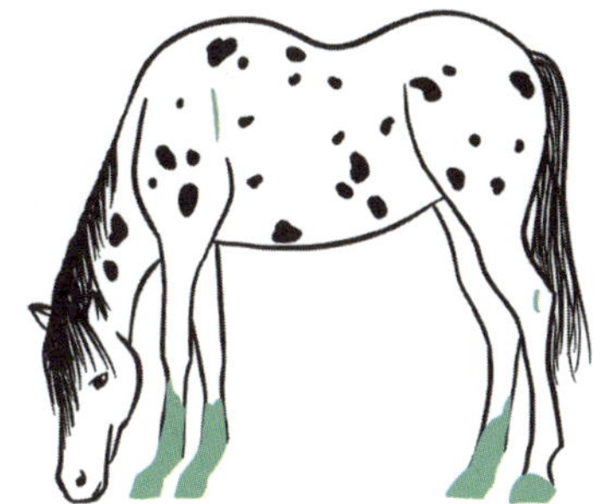

STEP 7

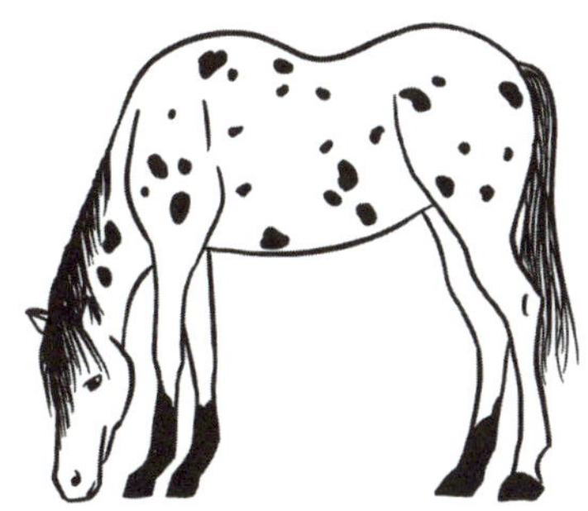

FUN FACT!

No two Appaloosas have exactly the same color pattern.

Spirit Bear / Kermode Bear

Ursus americanus kermodei

STEP 1

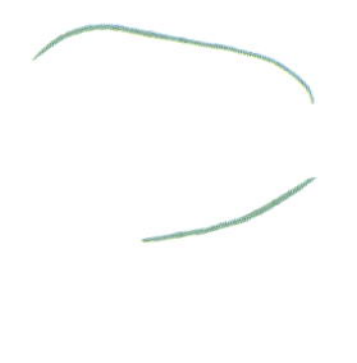

STEP 2

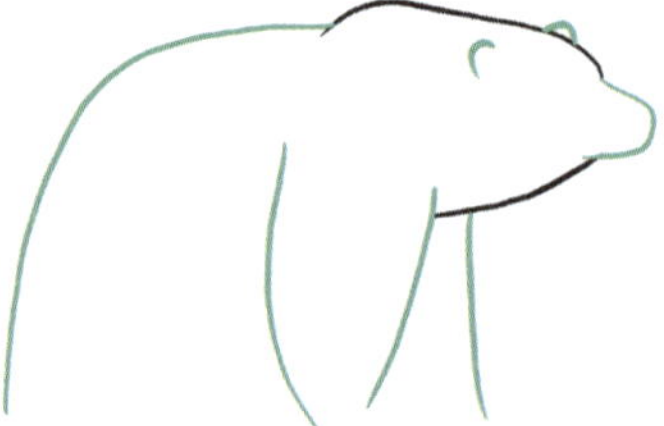

STEP 3

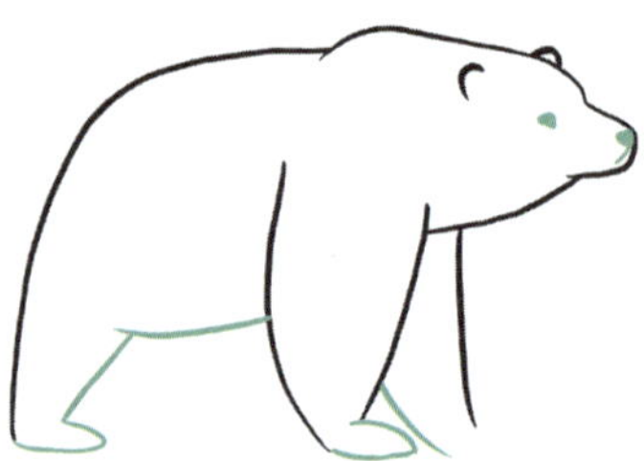

STEP 4

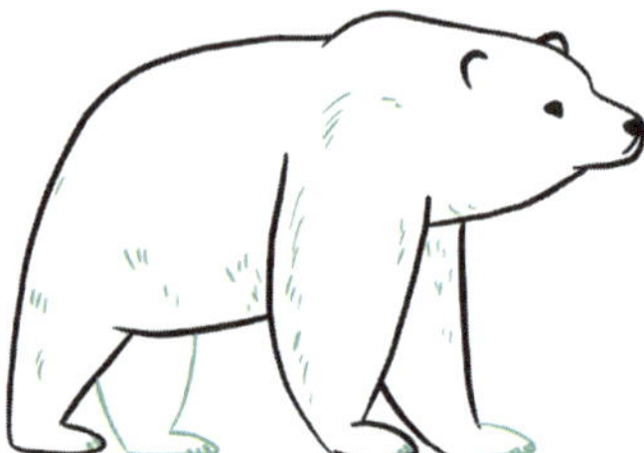

STEP 5

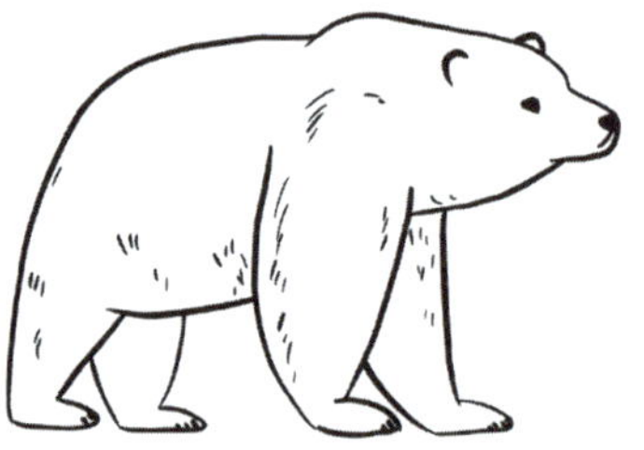

FUN FACT!

These rare white-coated bears are culturally significant to some Native people.

Columbian White-Tailed Deer (Fawn)

Odocoileus virginianus leucurus

STEP 1

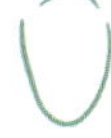

STEP 2

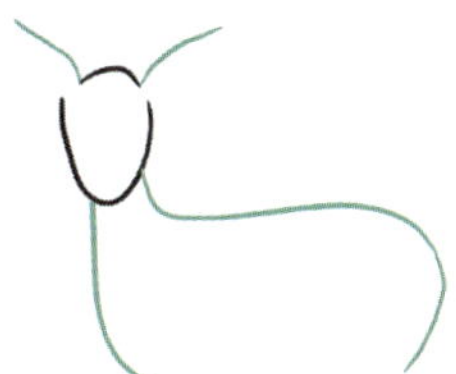

STEP 3

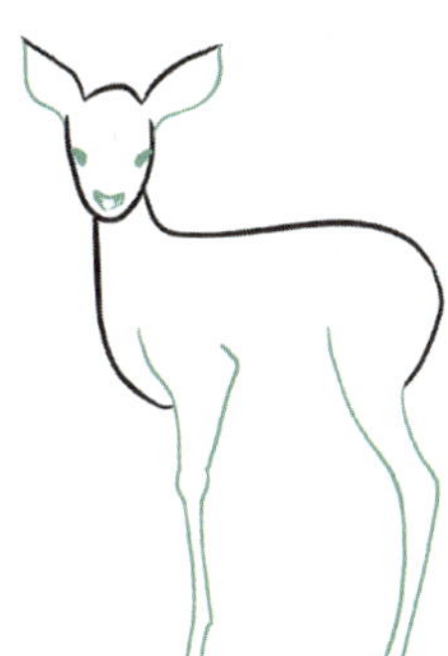

STEP 4

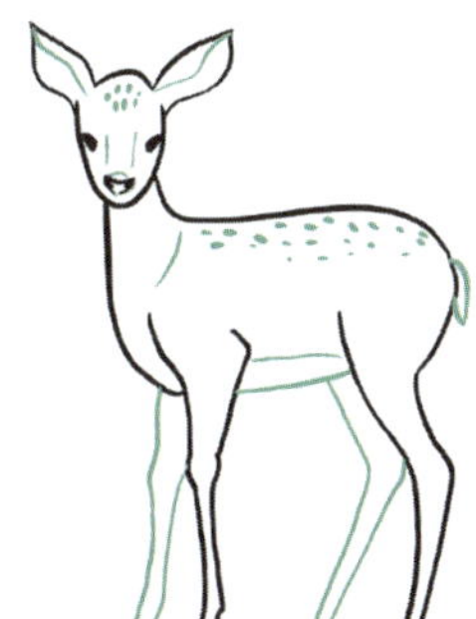

STEP 5

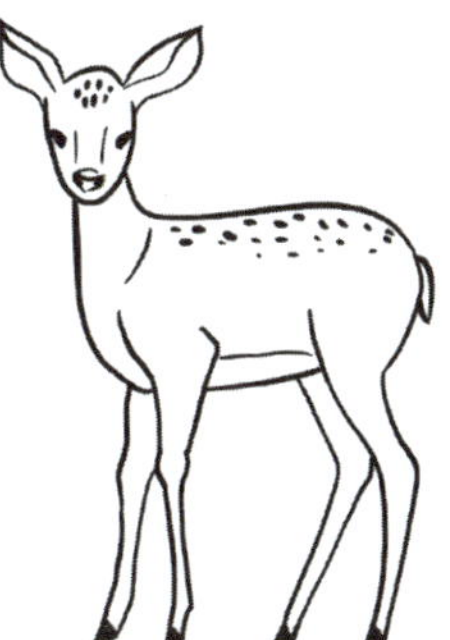

FUN FACT!

White-tailed deer aid in seed dispersal and affect plant community compositions through their grazing habits.

Gray Wolf

Canis lupus

STEP 1

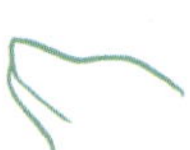

STEP 2

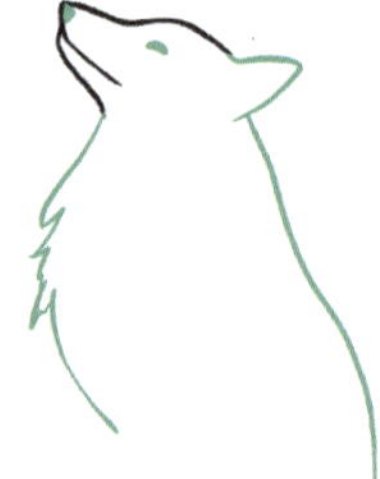

STEP 3

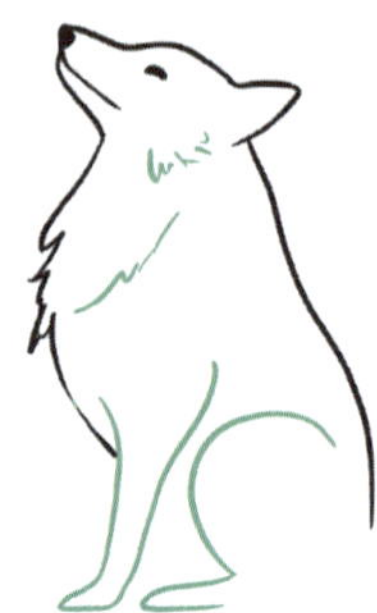

STEP 4

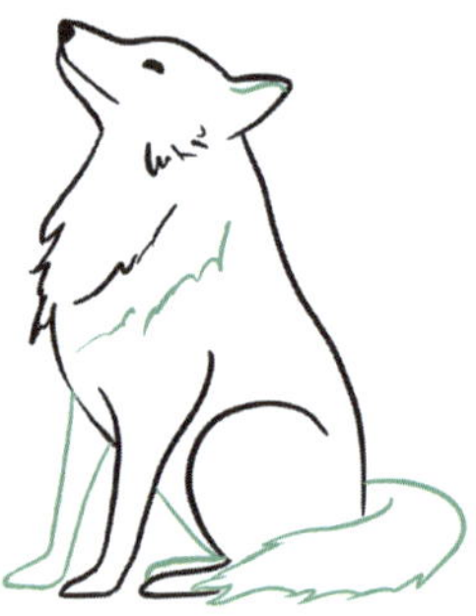

STEP 5

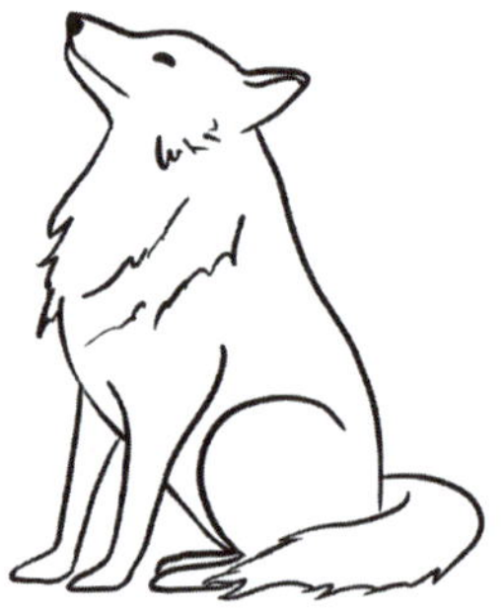

FUN FACT!

As the largest living wild canine species, this wolf is the ancestor of all domesticated dogs.

Mountain Goat

Oreamnos americanus

STEP 1

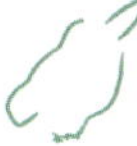

STEP 2

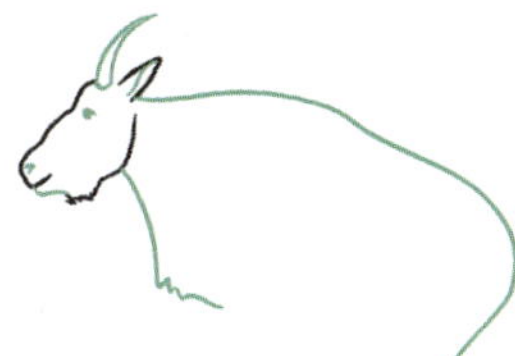

STEP 3

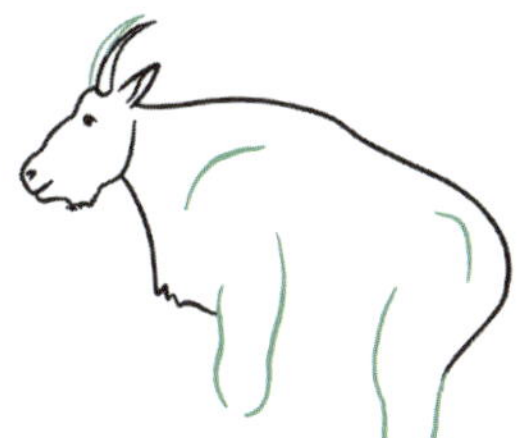

STEP 4

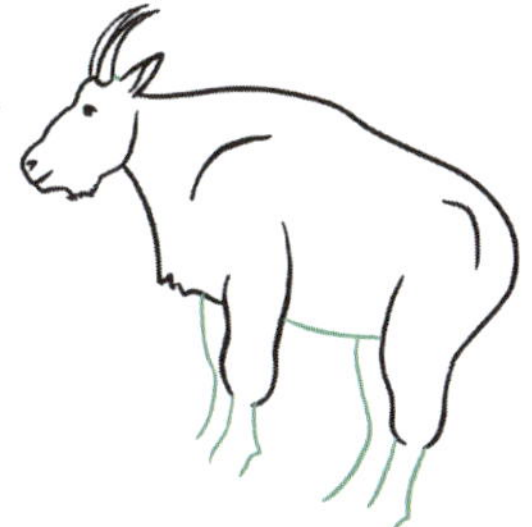

STEP 5

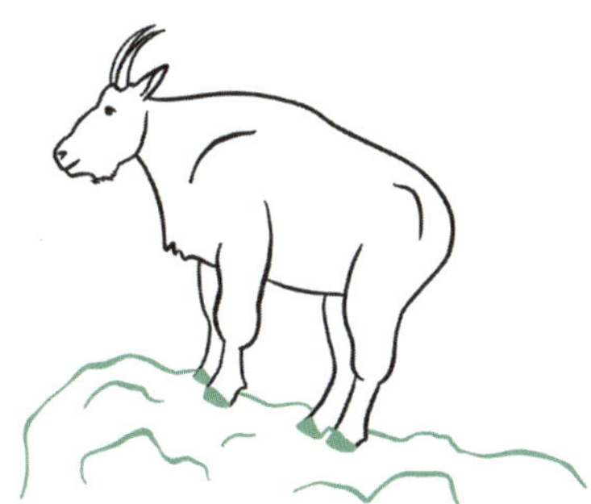

STEP 6

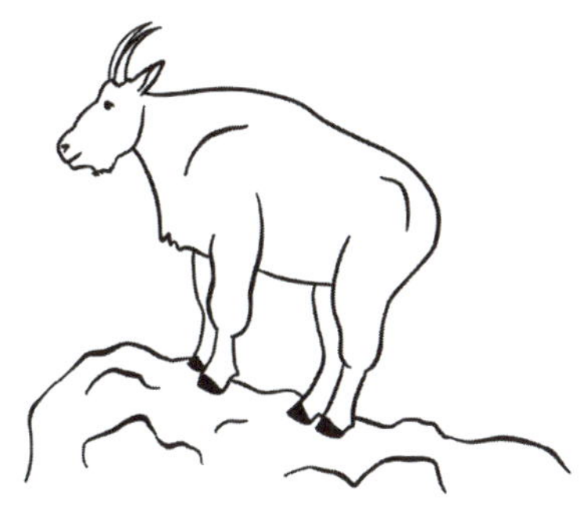

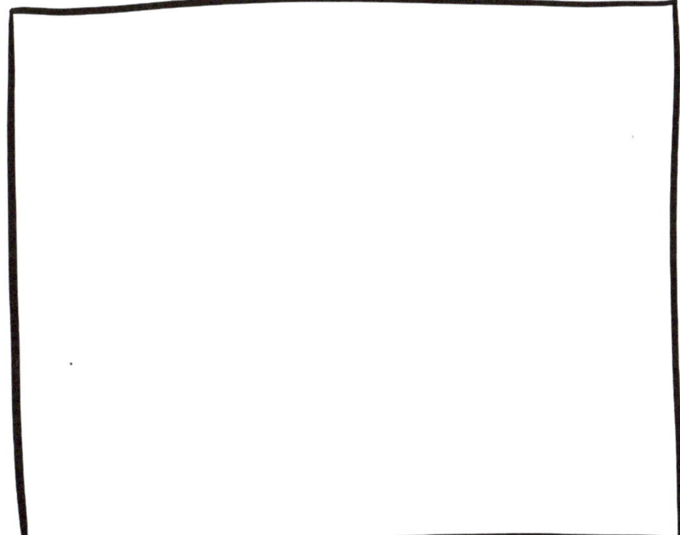

FUN FACT!

When mountain goats get together, they are called a band.

Elk

Cervus canadensis

STEP 1

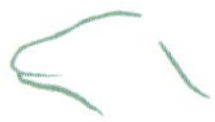

STEP 2

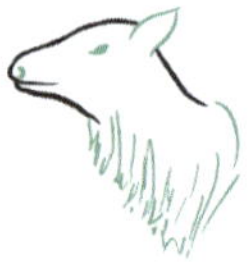

STEP 3

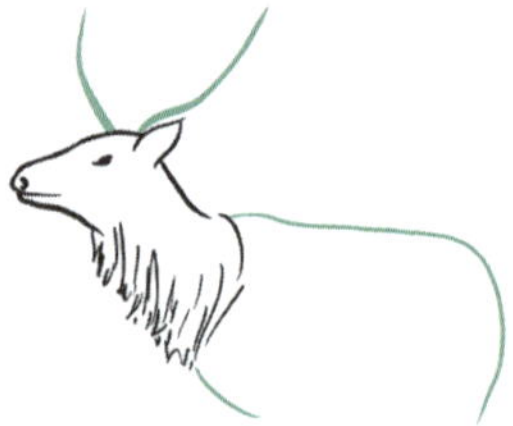

STEP 4

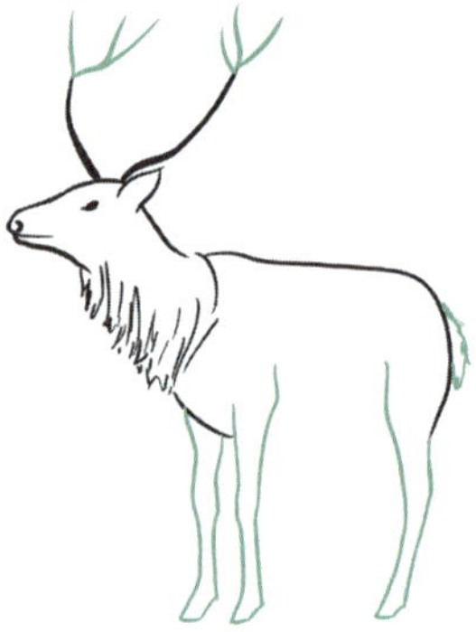

STEP 5

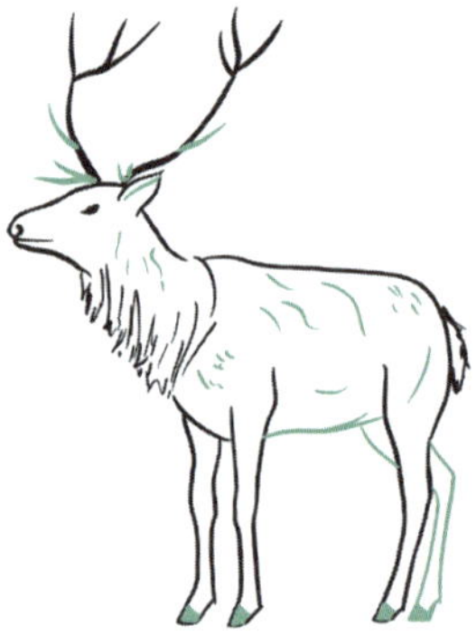

STEP 6

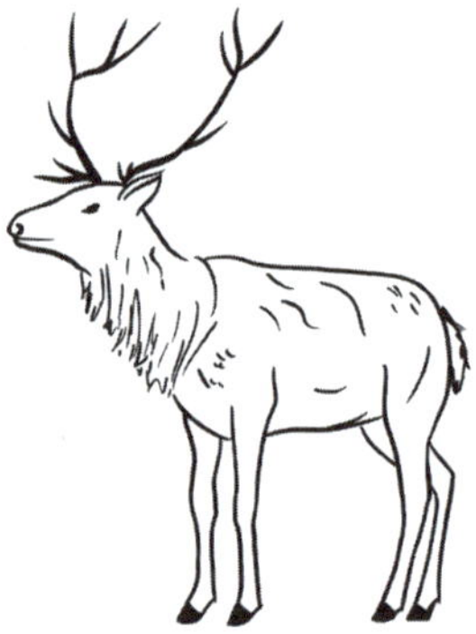

FUN FACT!

Weighing up to seven hundred pounds, the North American elk is one of the biggest deer species in the world.

Cascade Red Fox

Vulpes vulpes cascadensis

STEP 1

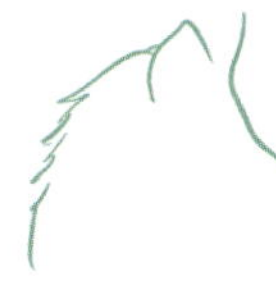

STEP 2

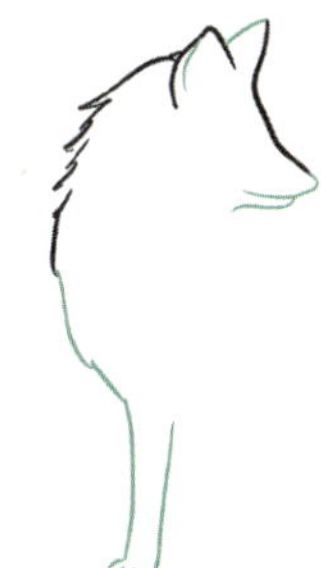

STEP 3

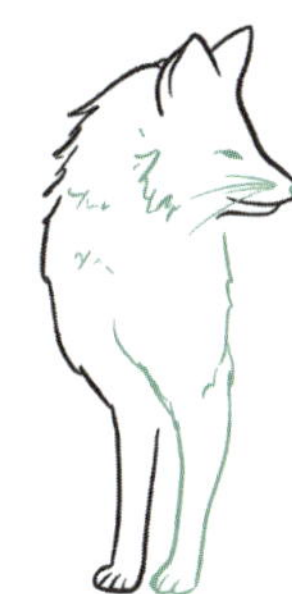

STEP 4

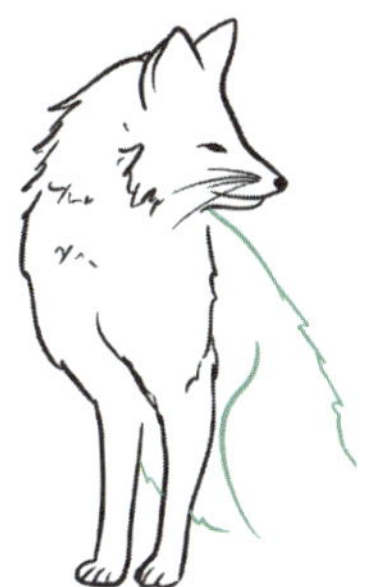

STEP 5

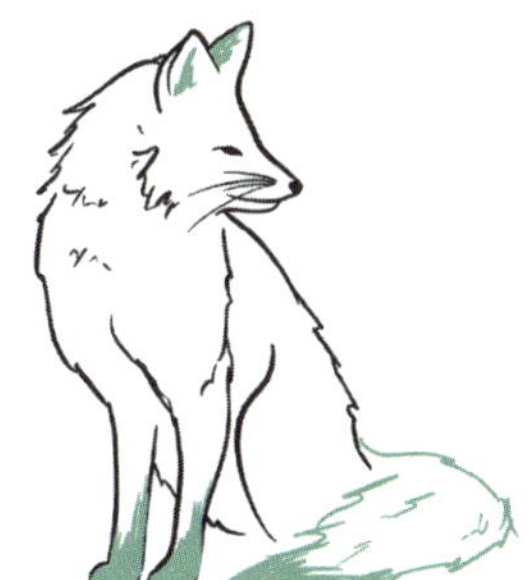

STEP 6

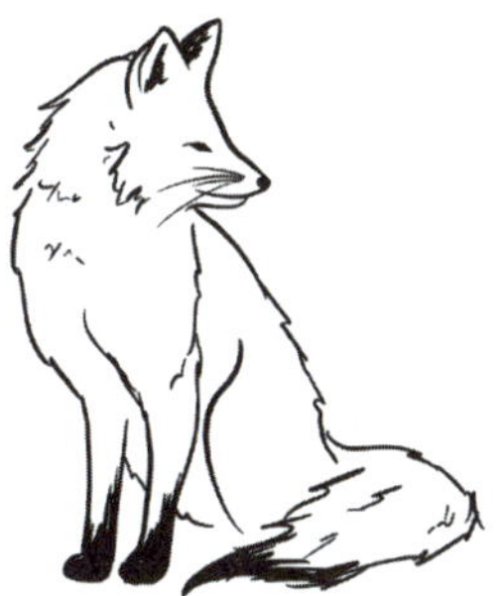

FUN FACT!

This subspecies of fox has extraordinary hearing and is considered endangered.

Bald Eagle

Haliaeetus leucocephalus

STEP 1

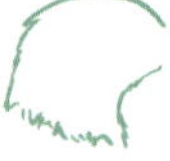

STEP 2

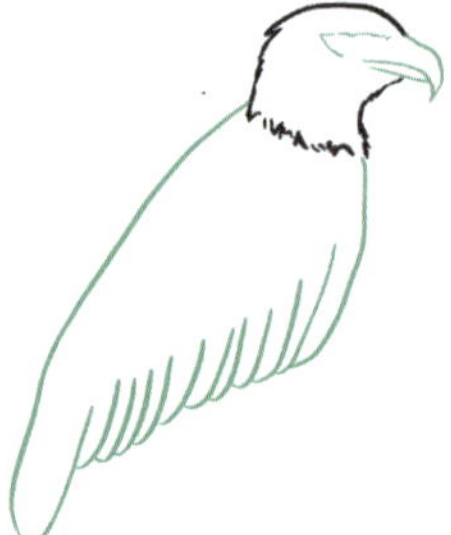

STEP 3

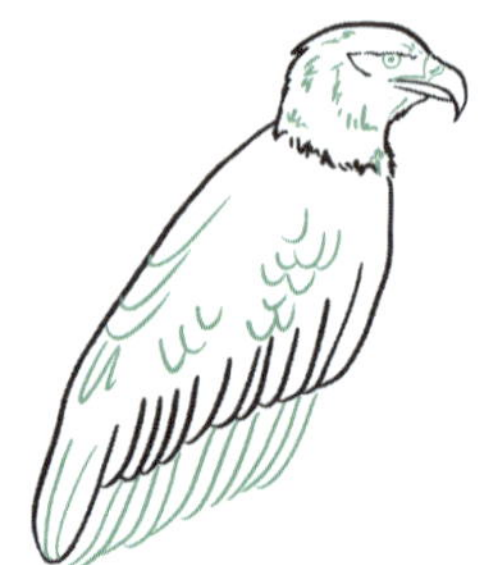

STEP 4

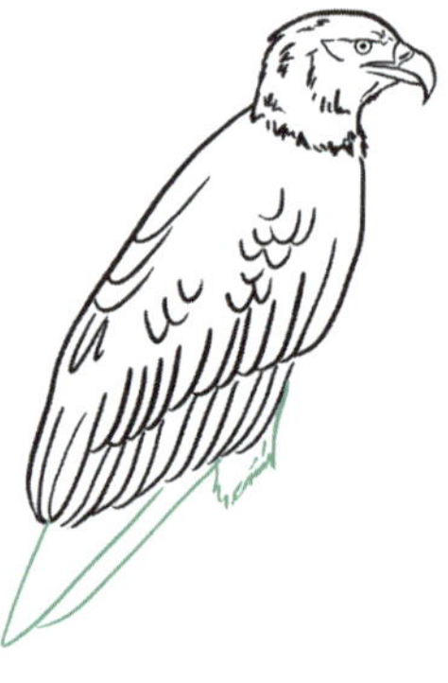

STEP 5

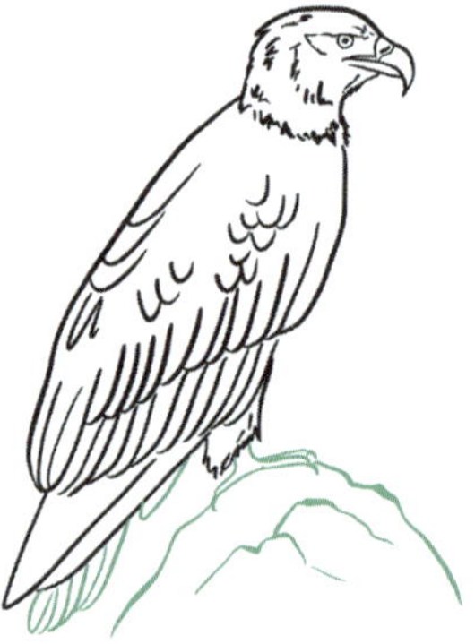

STEP 6

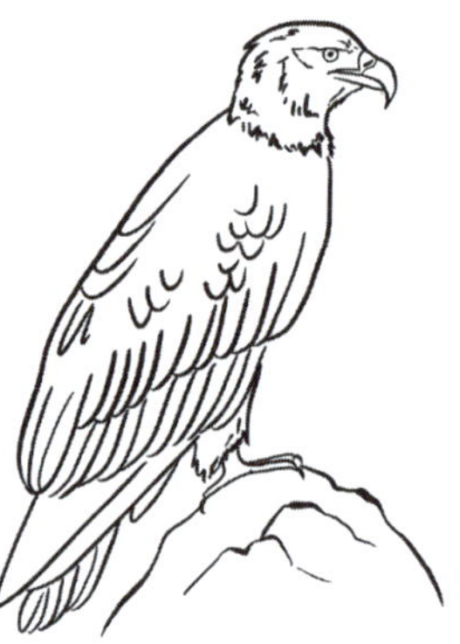

FUN FACT!

This eagle got its name from the Middle English word *balde*, which means "white."

Western Meadowlark

Sturnella neglecta

STEP 1

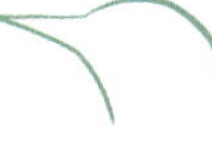

STEP 2

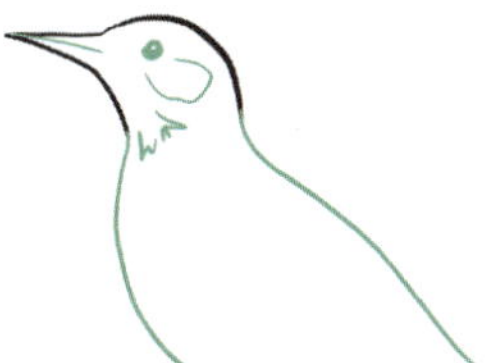

STEP 3

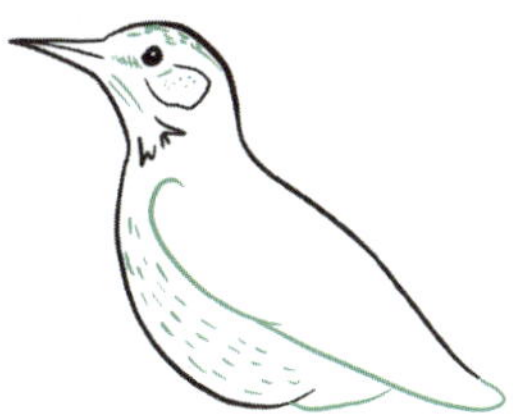

STEP 4

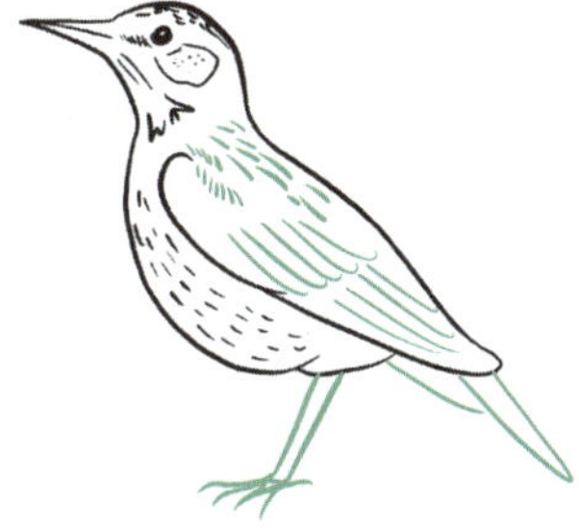

STEP 5

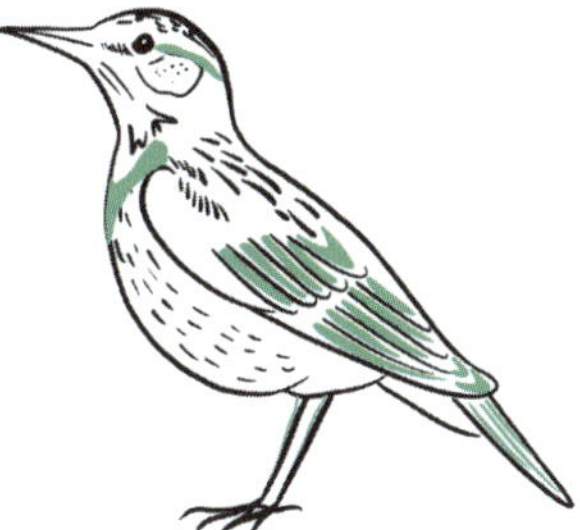

STEP 6

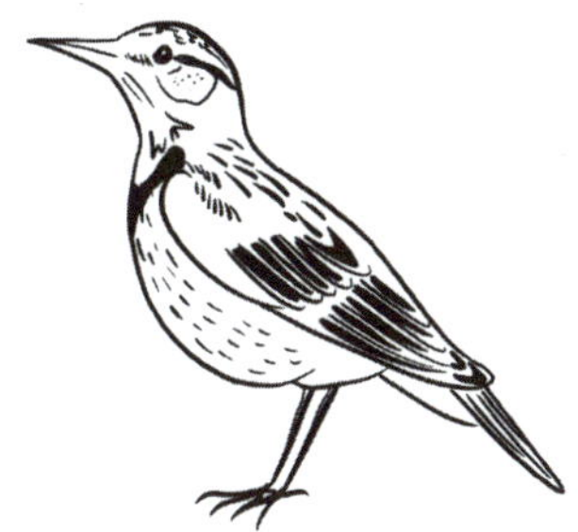

FUN FACT!

Though the males and females look alike to us, the feathers of the female reflect ultraviolet light in a different way than males, helping them differentiate each other.

Mountain Bluebird

Sialia currucoides

STEP 1

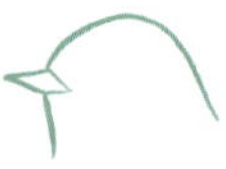

STEP 2

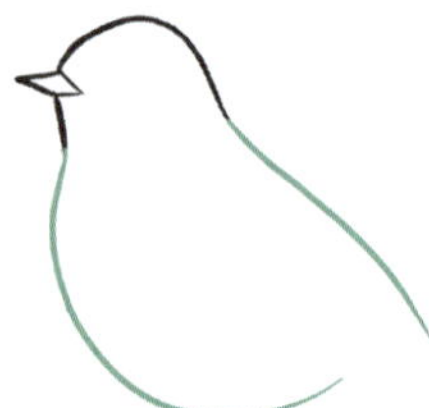

STEP 3

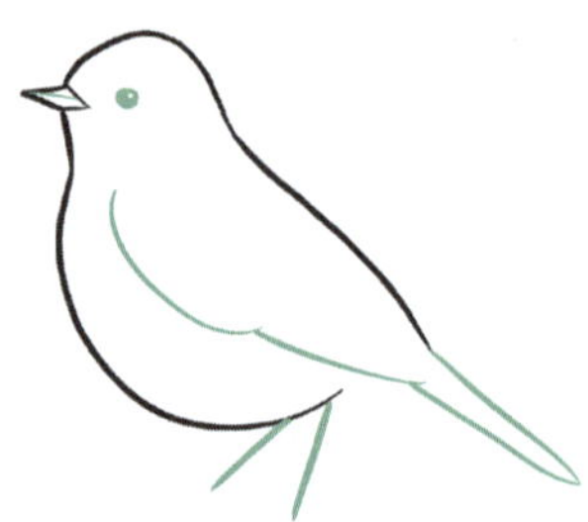

STEP 4

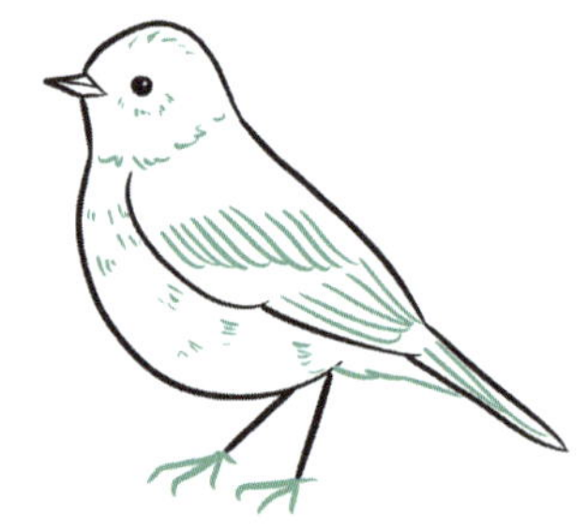

STEP 5

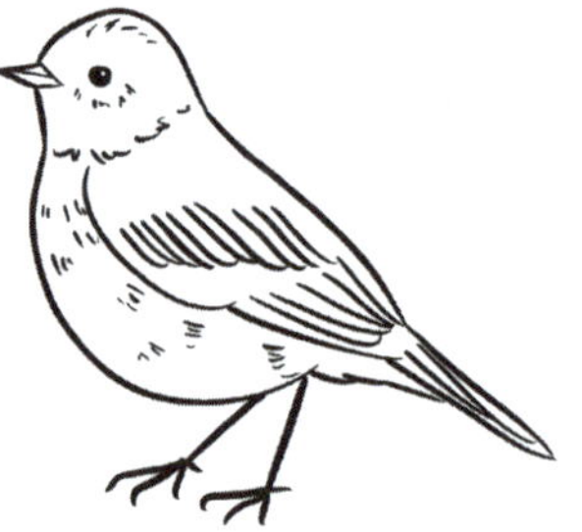

FUN FACT!

This little bird can fly at speeds of up to forty-five miles per hour!

Steller's Jay

Cyanocitta stelleri

STEP 1

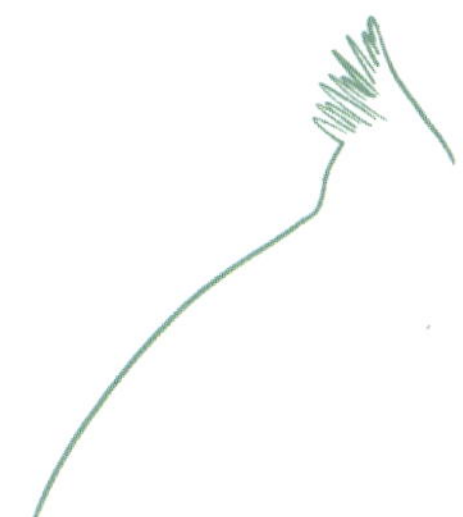

STEP 2

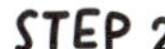

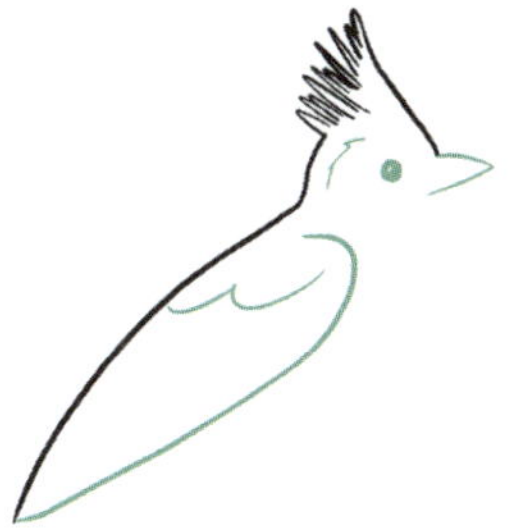

STEP 3

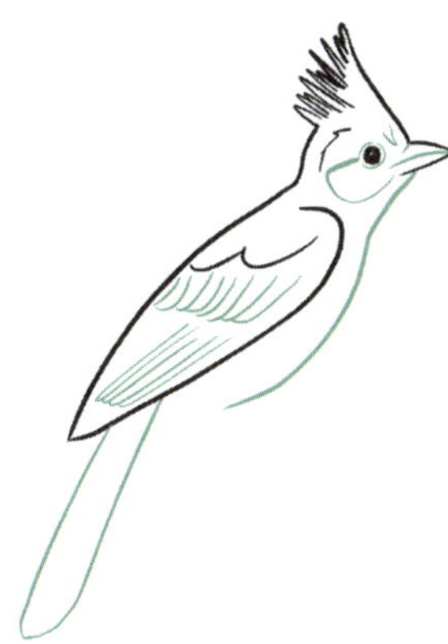

STEP 4

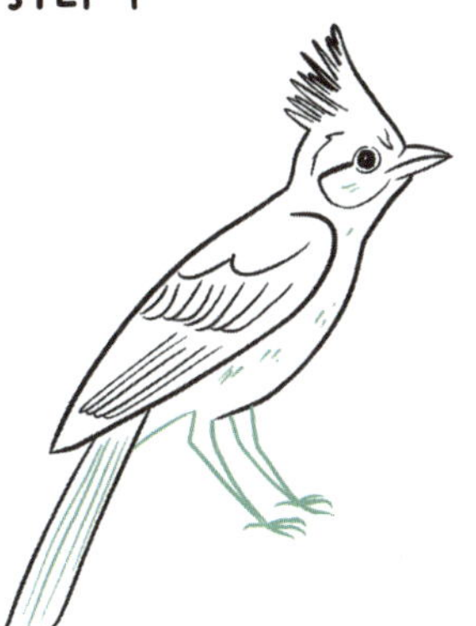

STEP 5

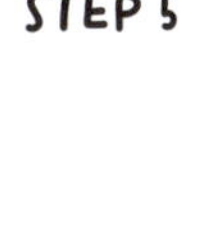

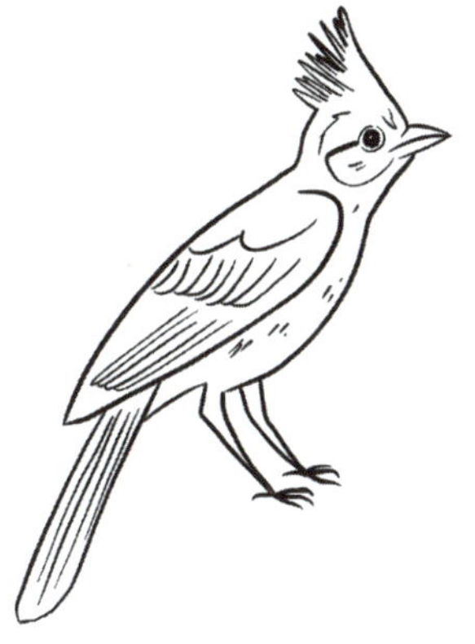

FUN FACT!

A Steller's jay can imitate other birds, cats, dogs, squirrels, chickens, and even some mechanical sounds.

American Goldfinch

Spinus tristis

STEP 1

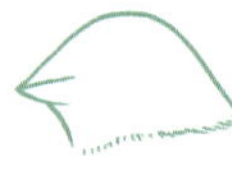

STEP 2

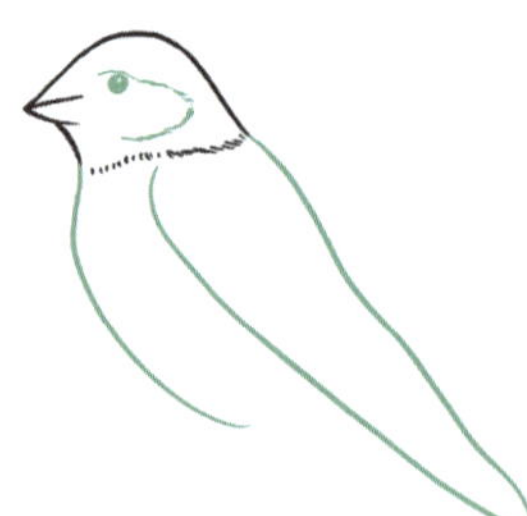

STEP 3

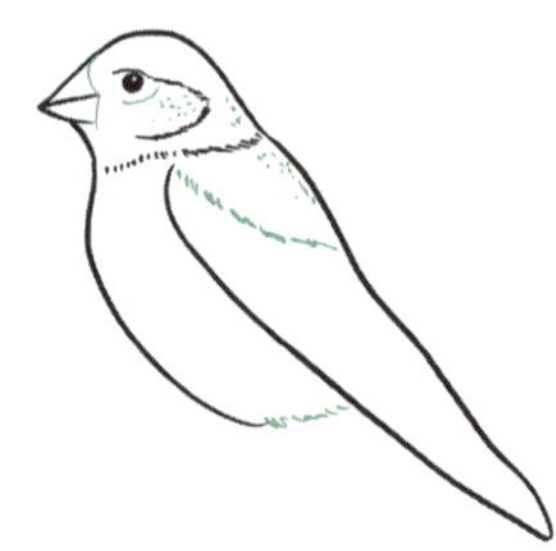

STEP 4

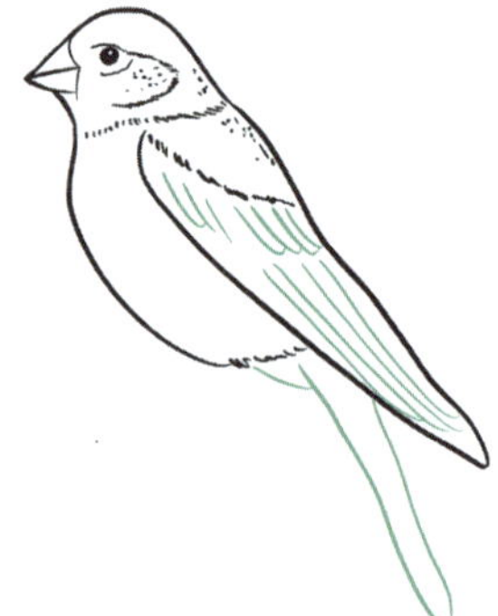

STEP 5

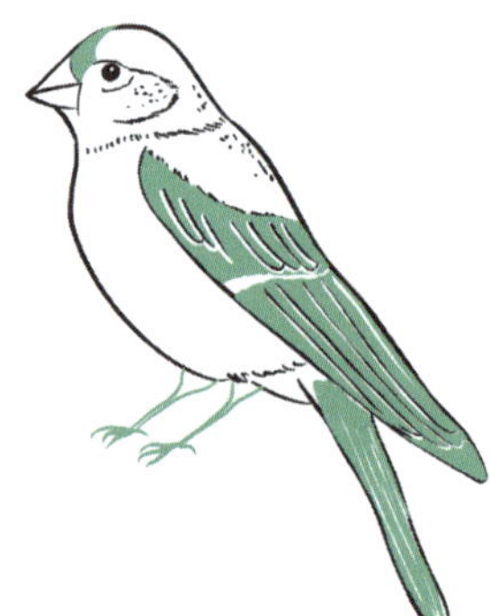

STEP 6

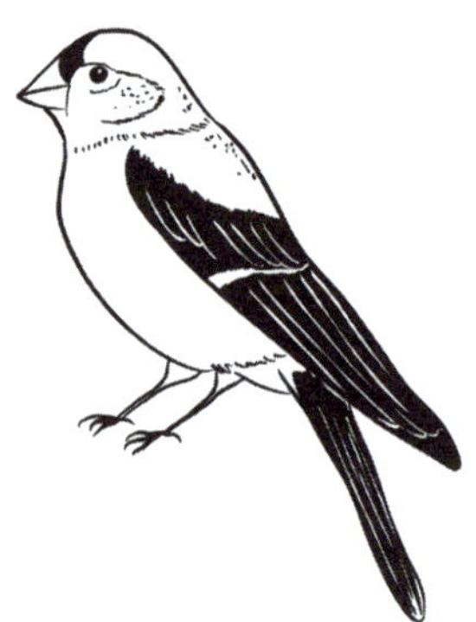

FUN FACT!

This little yellow bird is the official state bird of Washington.

Pileated Woodpecker

Dryocopus pileatus

STEP 1

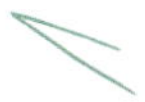

STEP 2

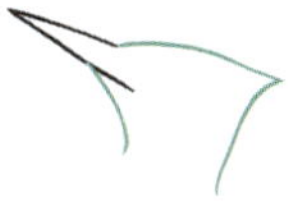

STEP 3

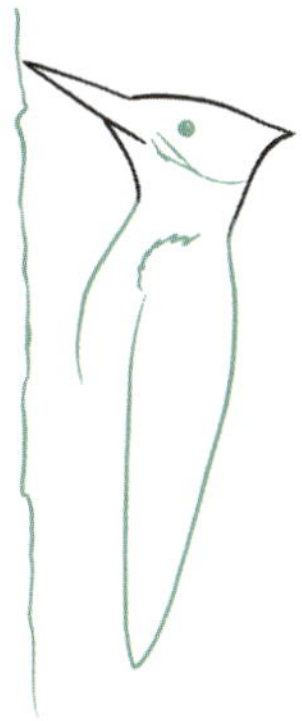

STEP 4

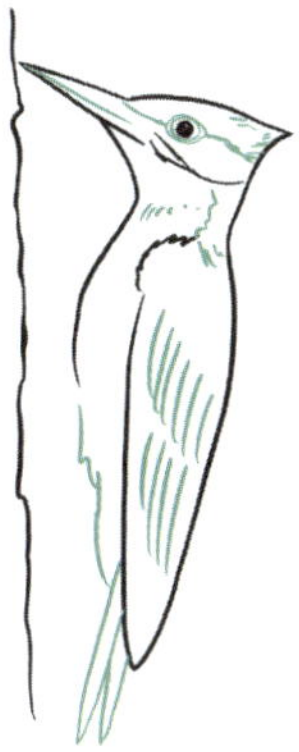

STEP 5

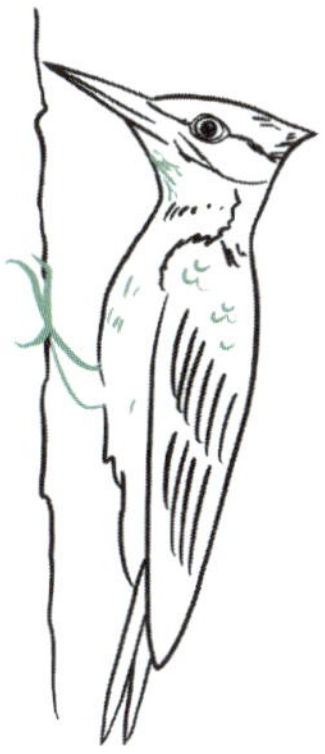

STEP 6

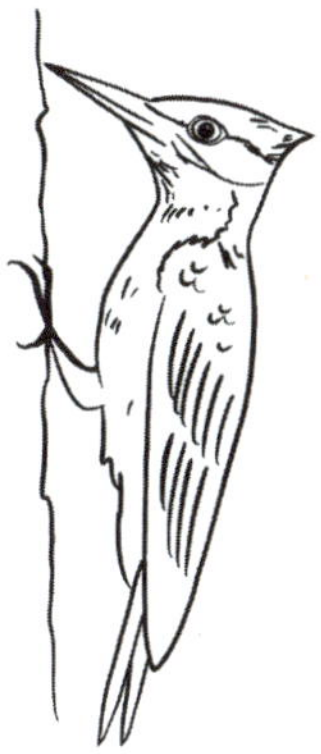

FUN FACT!

At sixteen to nineteen inches long, it's the largest woodpecker species in North America.

Northern Spotted Owl

Strix occidentalis caurina

STEP 1

STEP 2

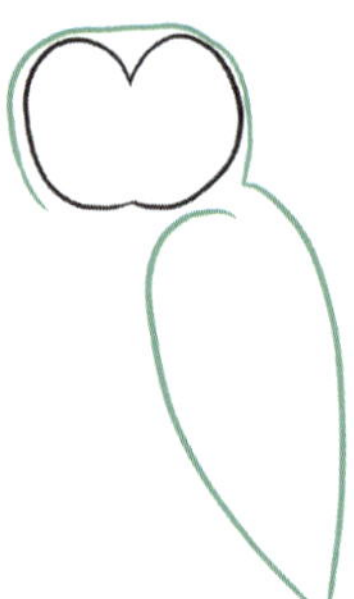

STEP 3

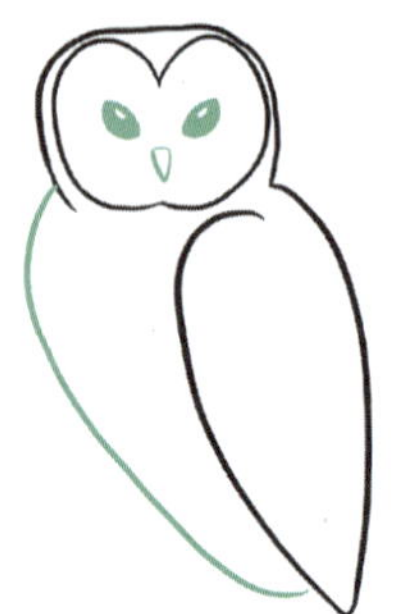

STEP 4

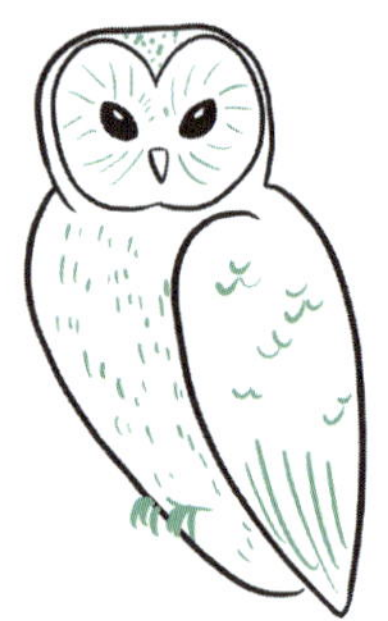

STEP 5

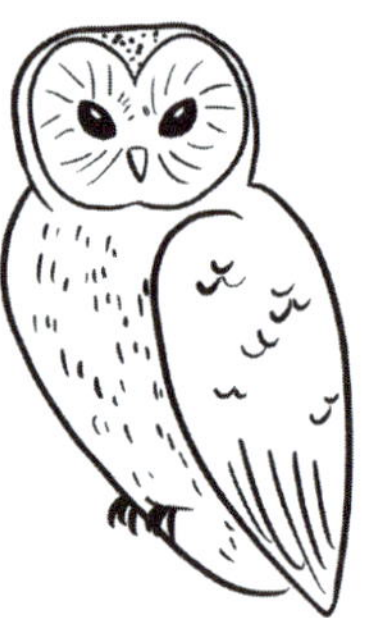

FUN FACT!

A vital indicator of the health of a forest, this species of owl can live to be up to seventeen years old.

Tufted Puffin

Fratercula cirrhata

STEP 1

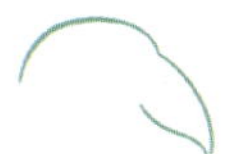

STEP 2

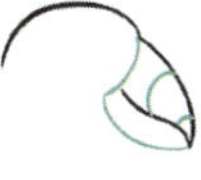

STEP 3

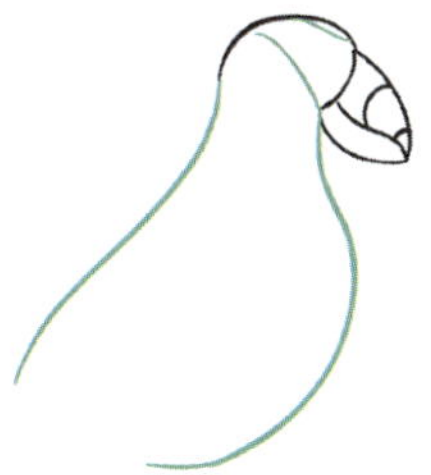

STEP 4

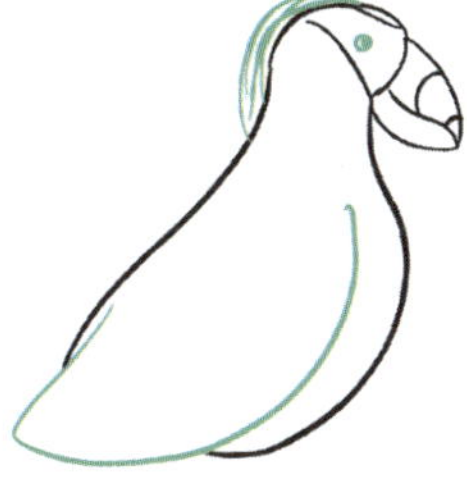

STEP 5

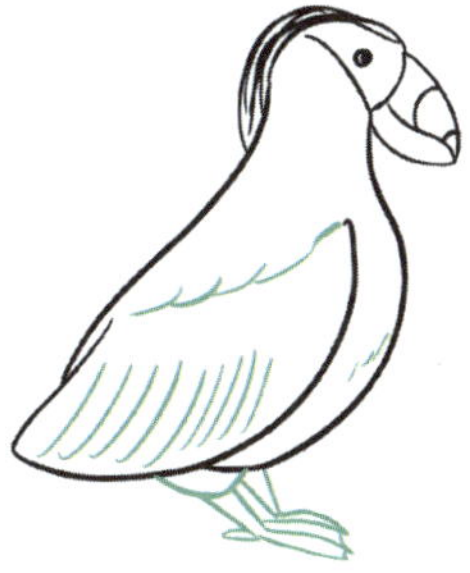

STEP 6

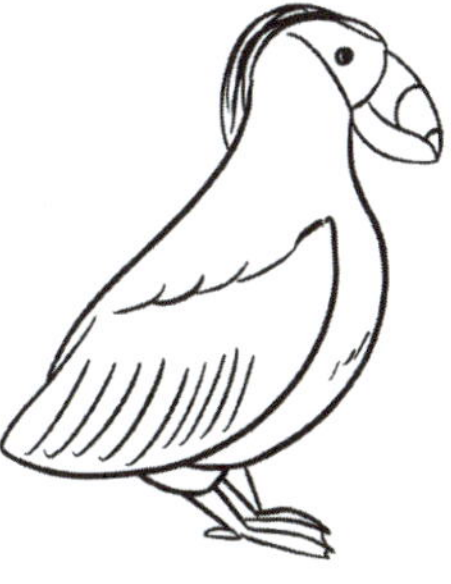

FUN FACT!

Nicknamed "parrot of the sea," the puffin can hold many fish in its beak at once.

Orca

Orcinus orca

STEP 1

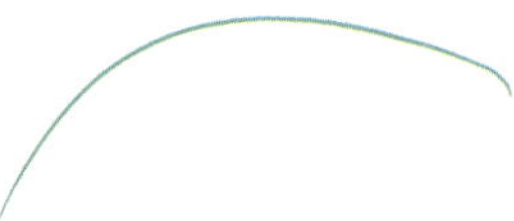

STEP 2

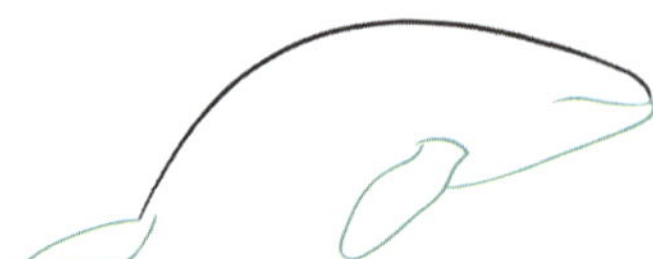

STEP 3

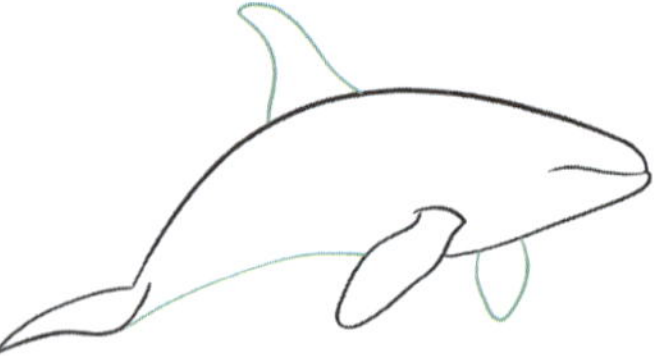

STEP 4

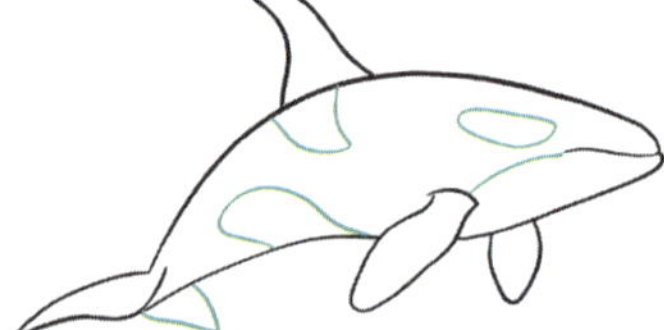

STEP 5

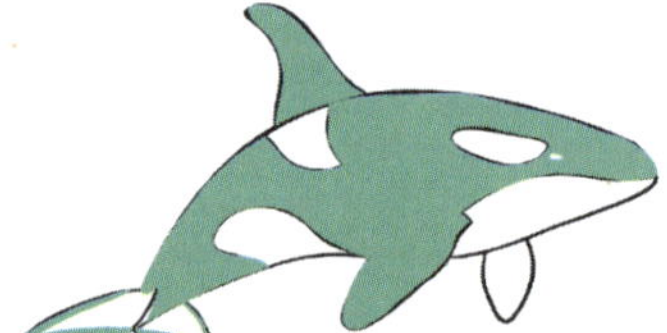

STEP 6

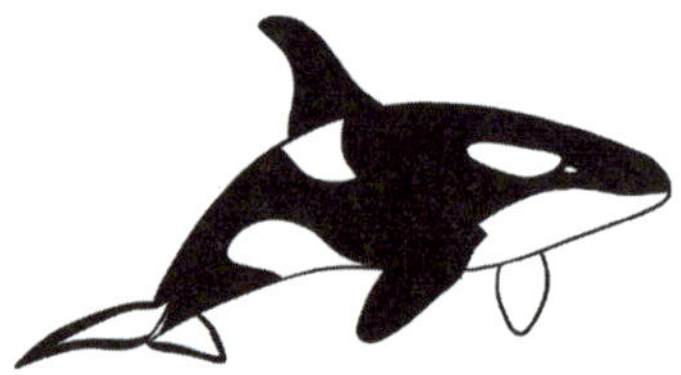

FUN FACT!

The largest member of the dolphin family, orcas live in every ocean of the world.

Raccoon

Procyon lotor

STEP 1

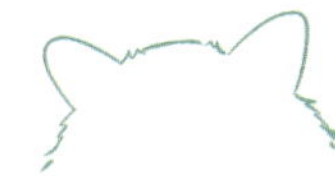

STEP 2

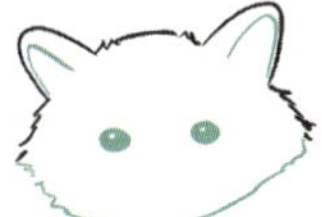

STEP 3

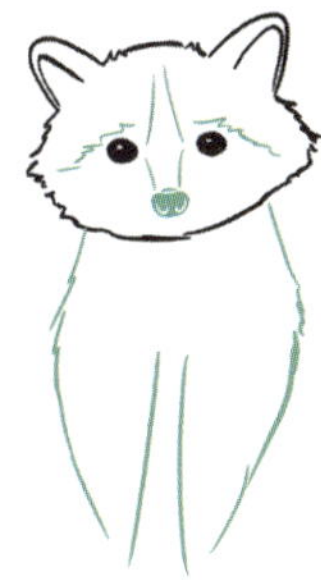

STEP 4

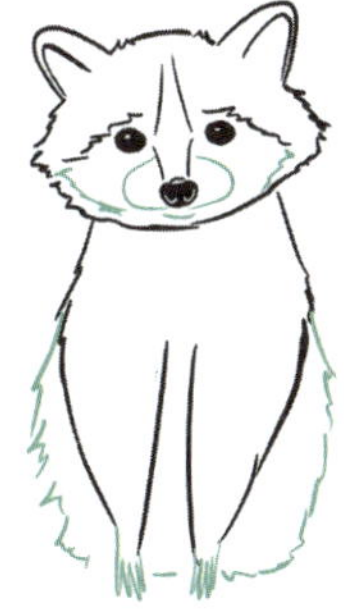

STEP 5

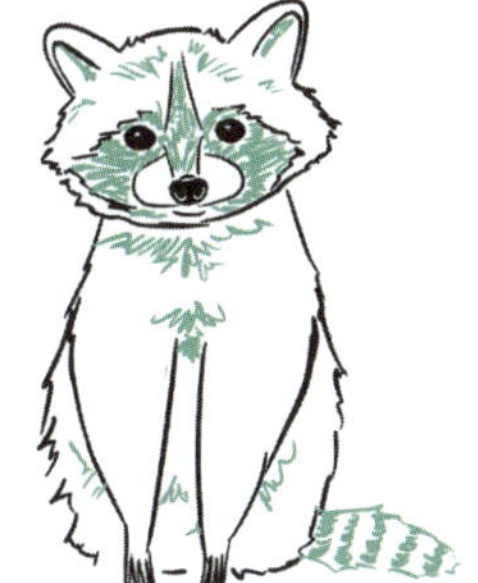

STEP 6

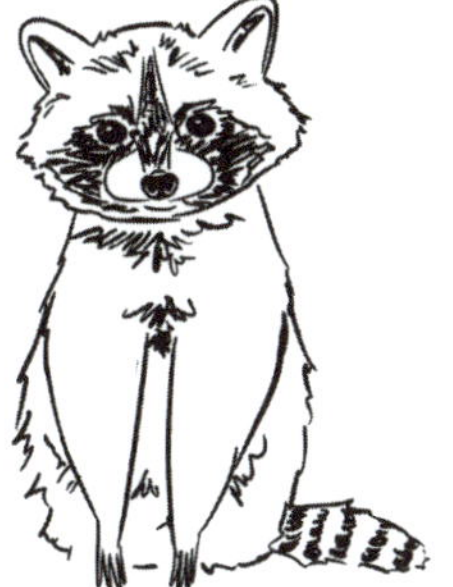

FUN FACT!

These opportunistic eaters are present in almost every environment, and multiple studies have documented their intelligence.

Pygmy Rabbit

Brachylagus idahoensis

STEP 1

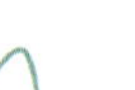

STEP 2

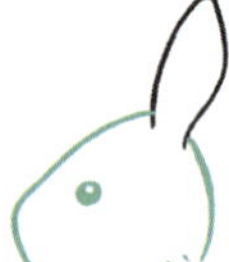

STEP 3

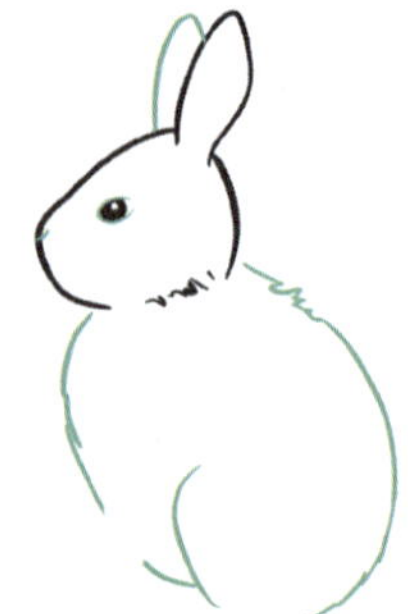

STEP 4

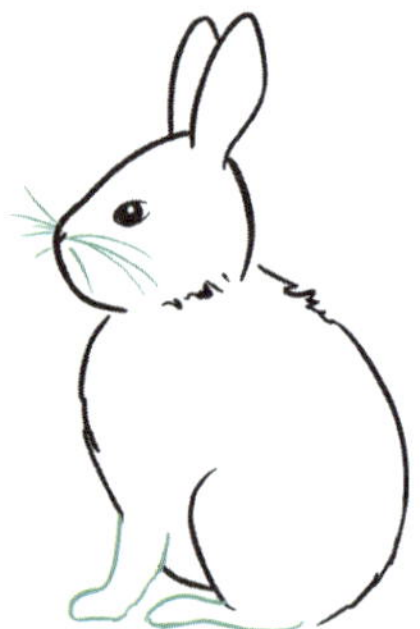

STEP 5

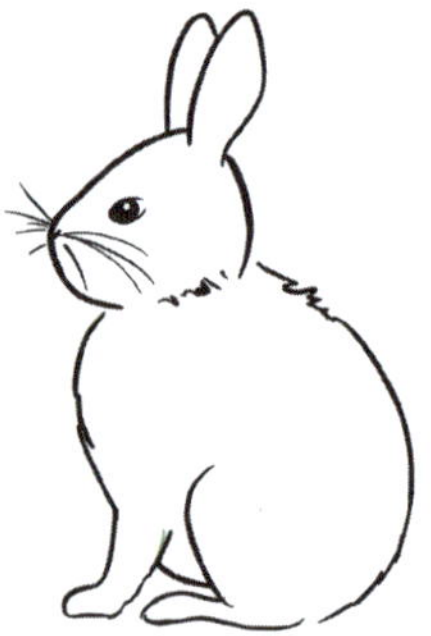

FUN FACT!

This rabbit species is the smallest in North America, with adults weighing under one pound.

Douglas Squirrel

Sciurus niger

STEP 1

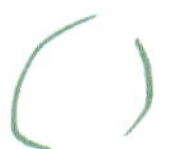

STEP 2

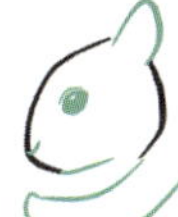

STEP 3

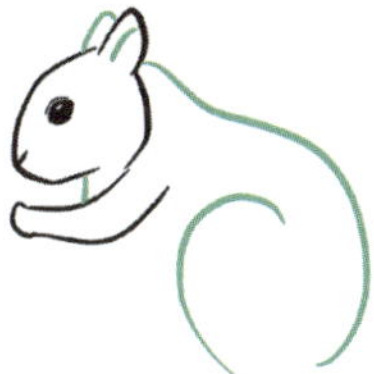

STEP 4

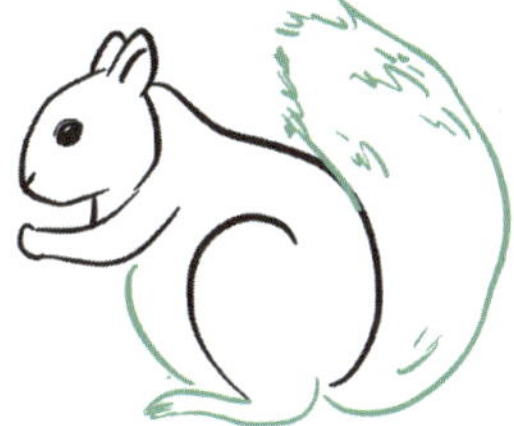

STEP 5

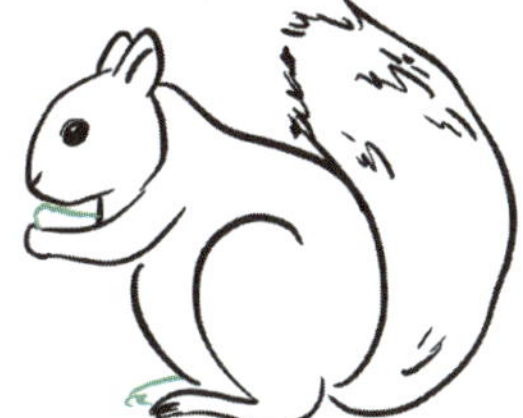

STEP 6

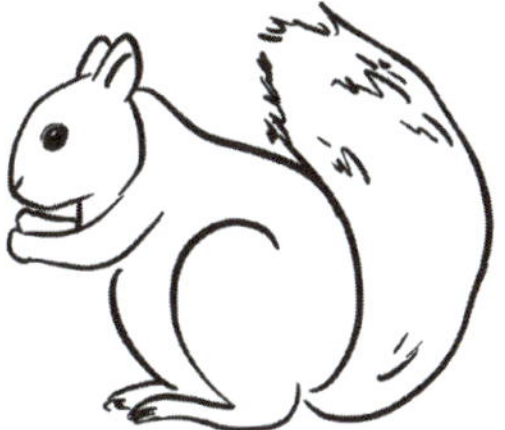

FUN FACT!

Douglas squirrels are "larder hoarders," storing large caches of seeds and cones in moist, underground areas or tree cavities for later use.

American Shrew Mole

Neurotrichus gibbsii

STEP 1

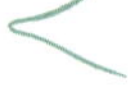

STEP 2

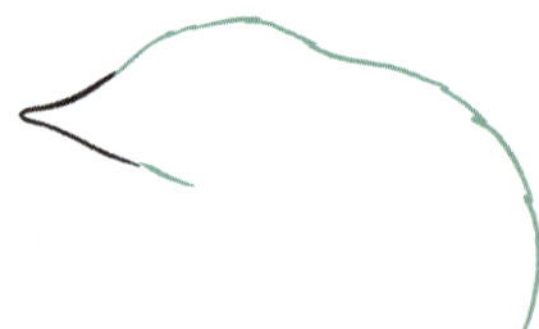

STEP 3

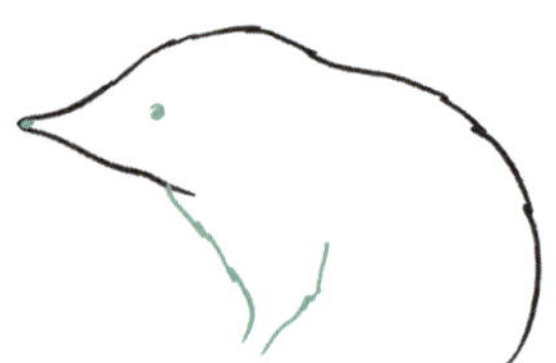

STEP 4

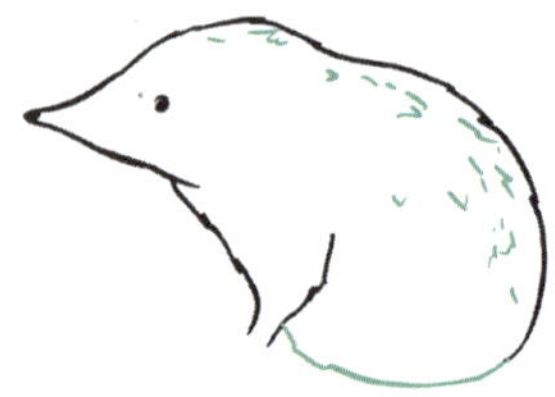

STEP 5

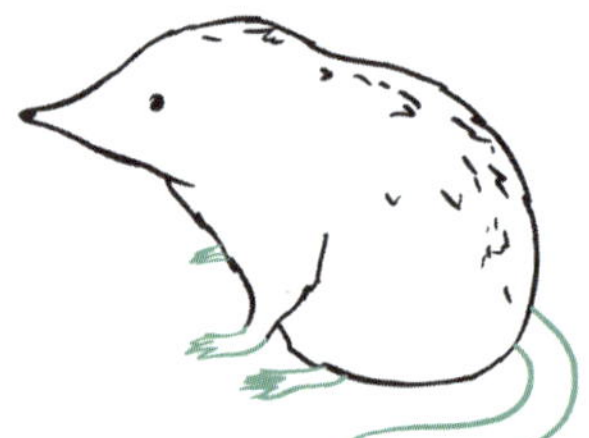

STEP 6

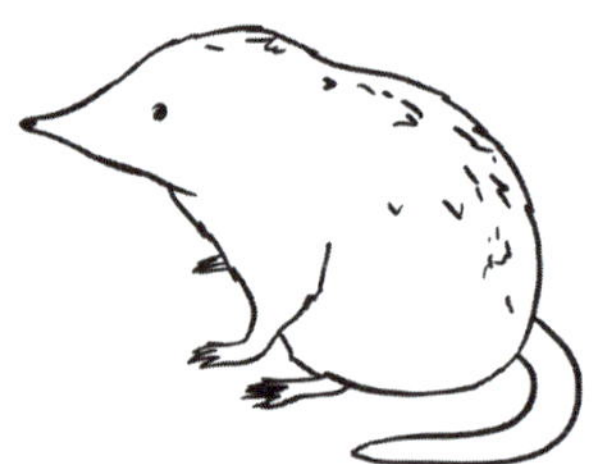

FUN FACT!

The smallest species of mole does not have great eyesight, so it relies on its exceptional hearing and sense of touch.

Cougar

Puma concolor

STEP 1

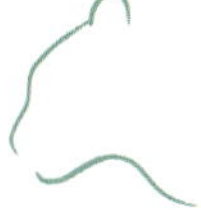

STEP 2

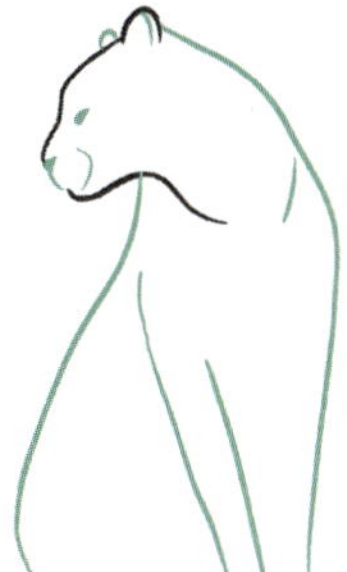

STEP 3

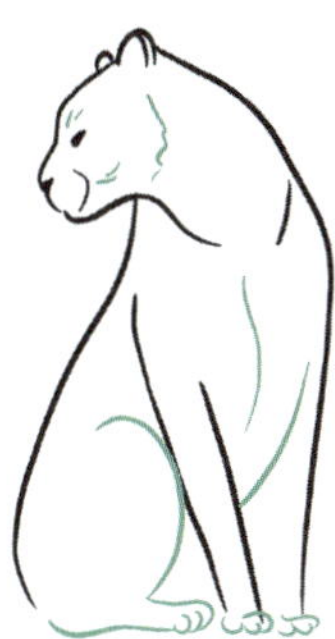

STEP 4

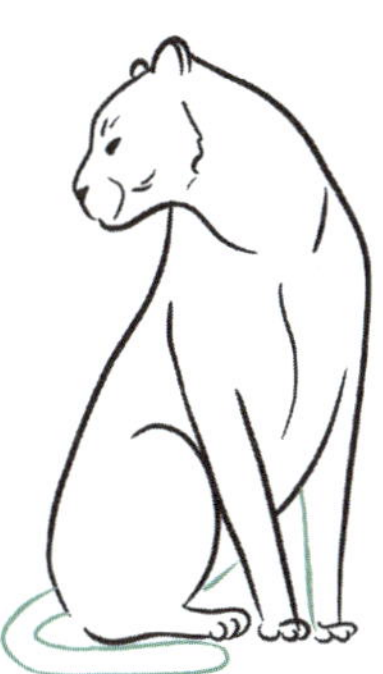

STEP 5

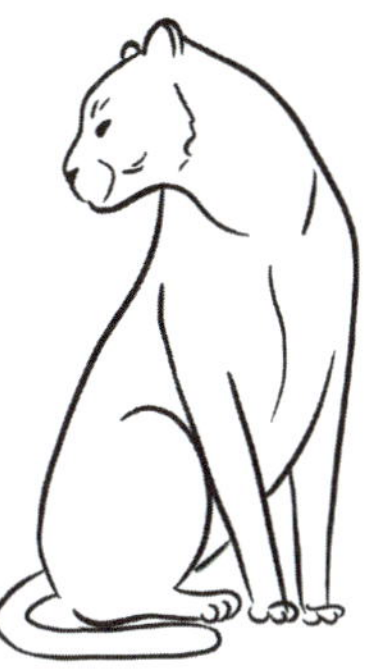

FUN FACT!

The cougar is the fourth largest cat in the world. Kittens are born with spots to help them hide, but those spots disappear after a year.

Western Tiger Swallowtail

Papilio rutulus

STEP 1

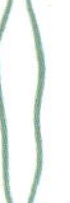

STEP 2

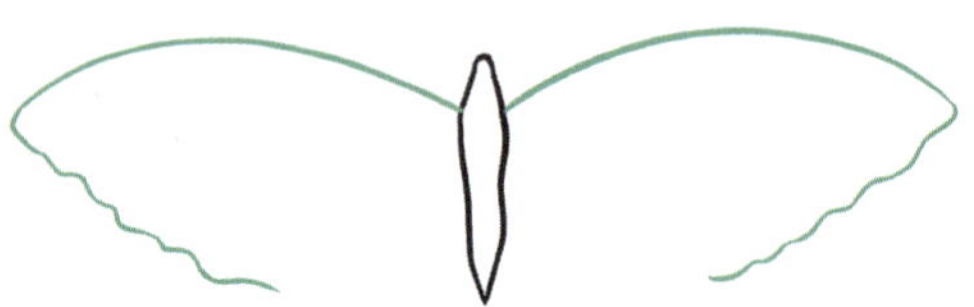

STEP 3

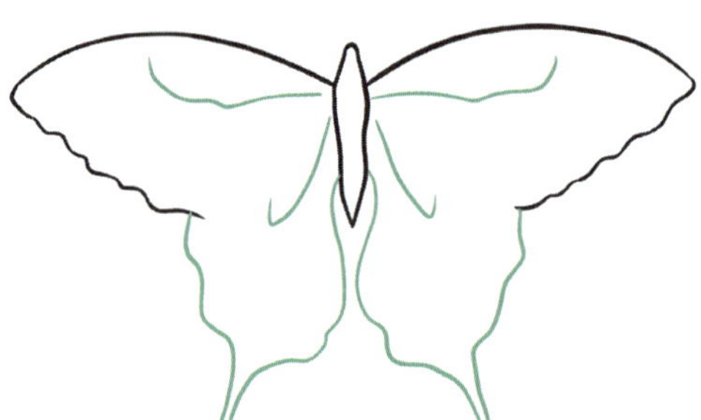

STEP 4

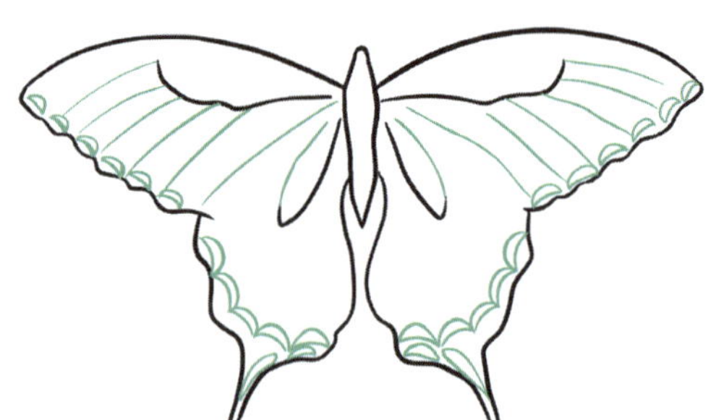

STEP 5

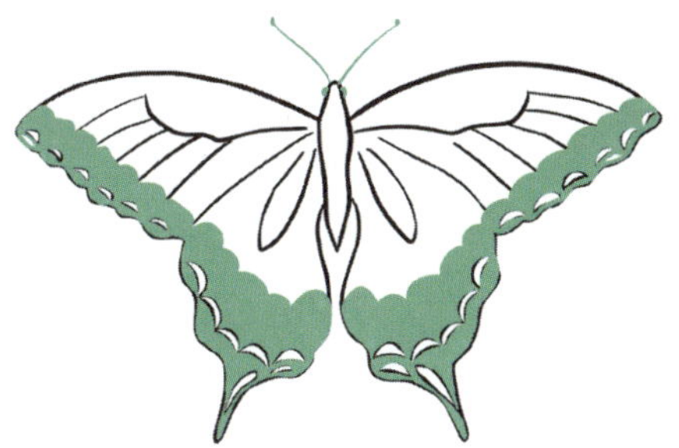

STEP 6

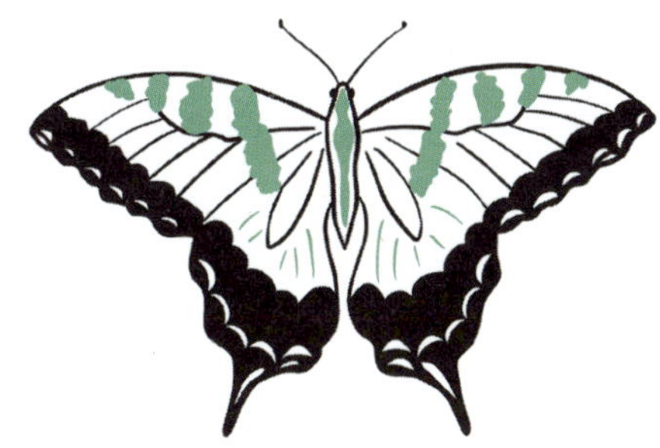

STEP 7

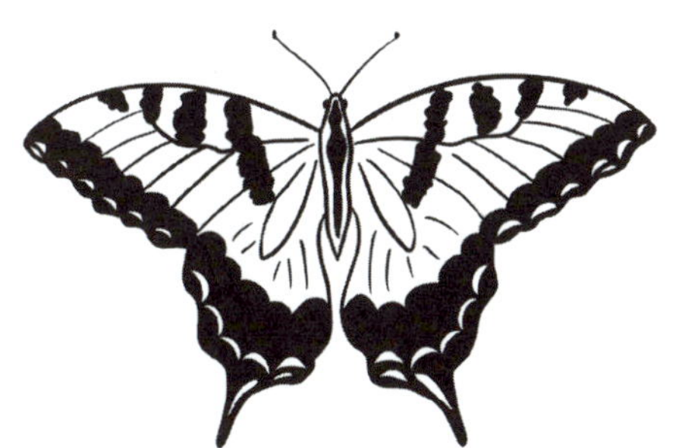

FUN FACT!

These yellow-winged insects are the most common butterfly in the Pacific Northwest.

Cabbage White

Pieris rapae

STEP 1

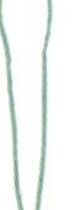

STEP 2

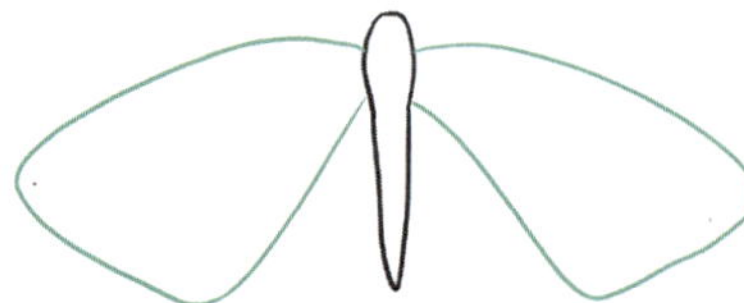

STEP 3

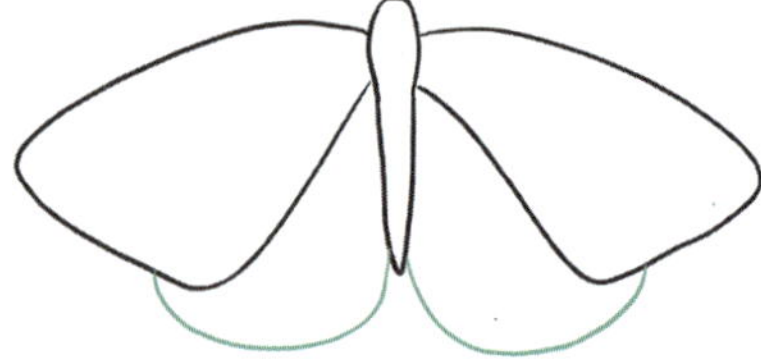

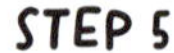

STEP 4

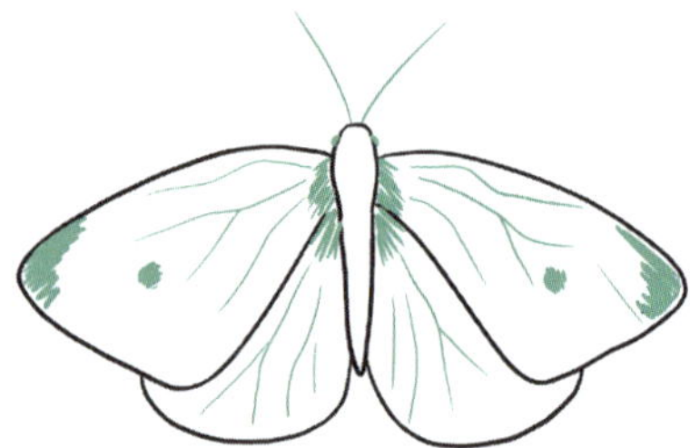

STEP 5

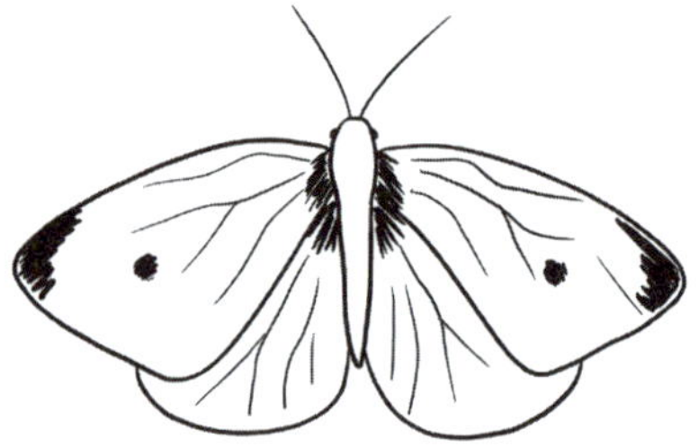

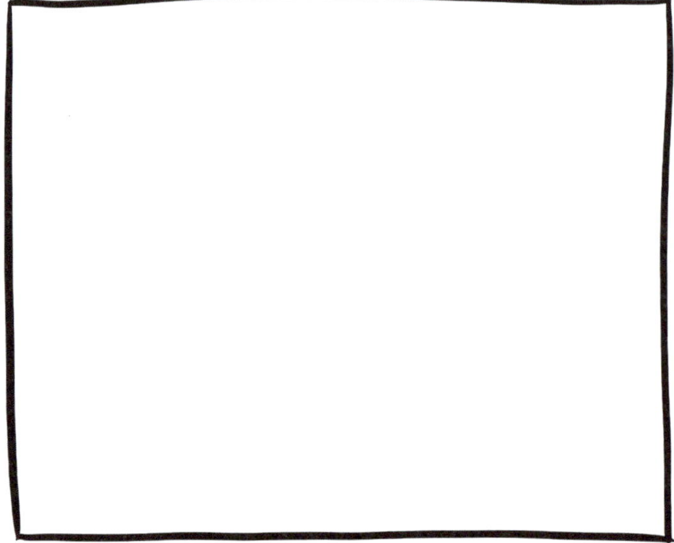

FUN FACT!

This butterfly was accidentally introduced to North America from Europe and is now common across the continent.

Island Marble Butterfly

Euchloe ausonides insulanus

STEP 1

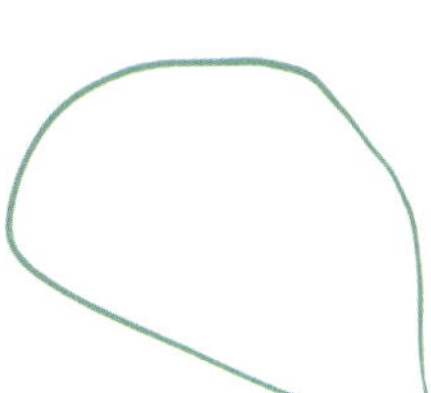

STEP 2

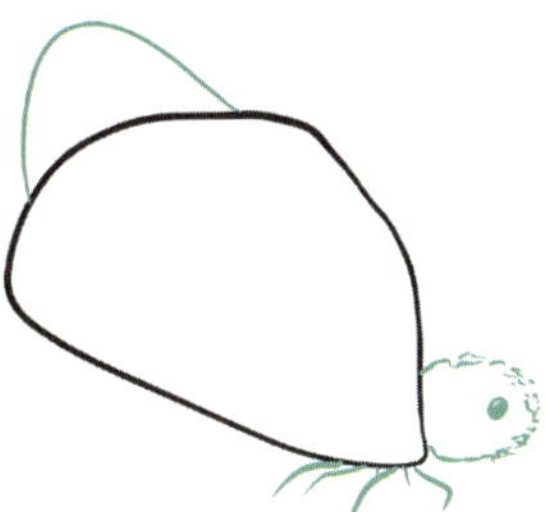

STEP 3

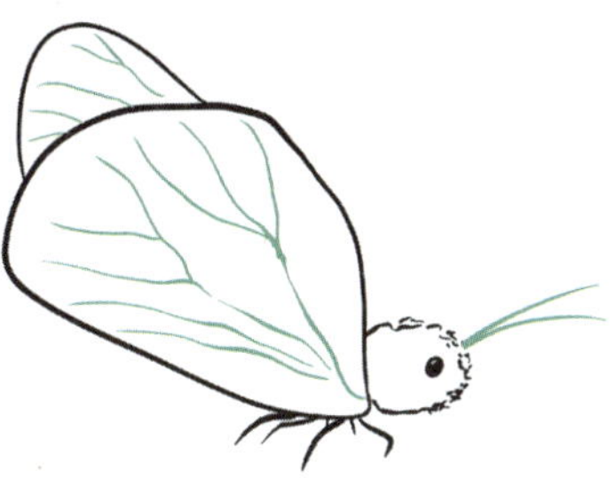

STEP 4

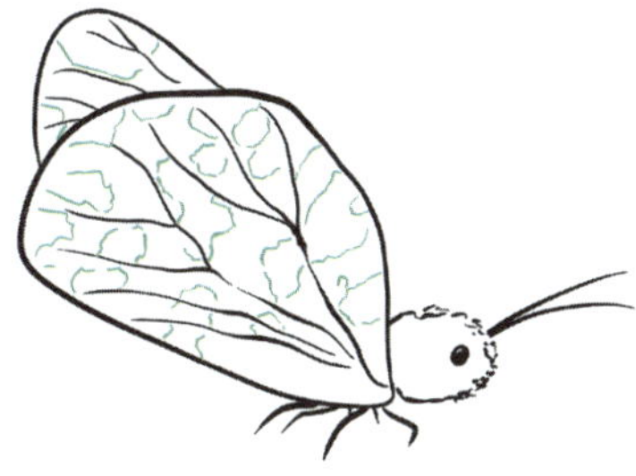

STEP 5

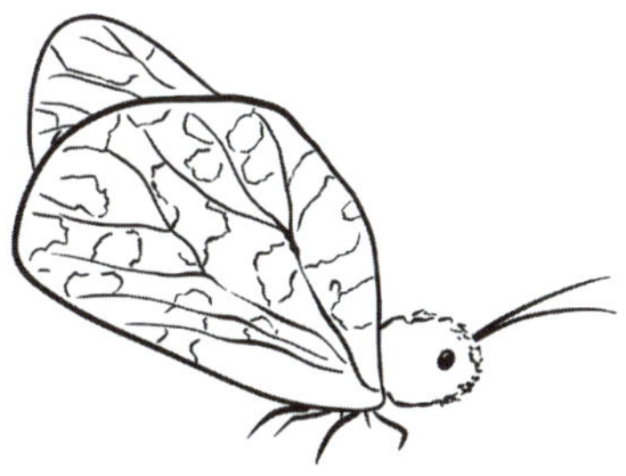

FUN FACT!

This unique white and green butterfly, once thought to be extinct, is currently endangered and lives only on San Juan and Lopez Islands in Puget Sound.

Puget Blue

Icaricia icarioides blackmorei

STEP 1

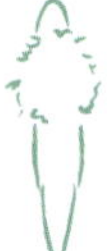

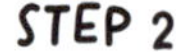

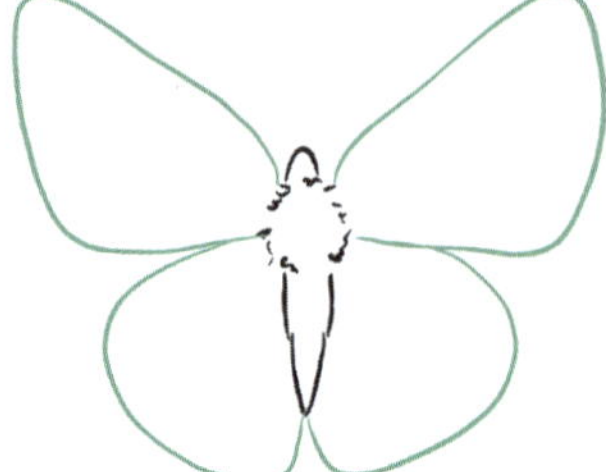

STEP 3

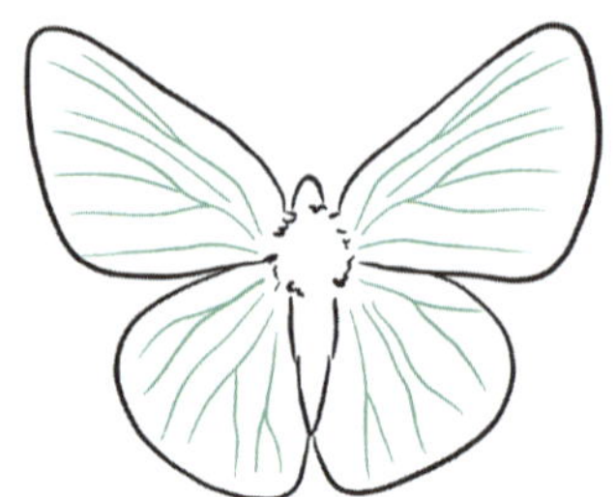

STEP 4

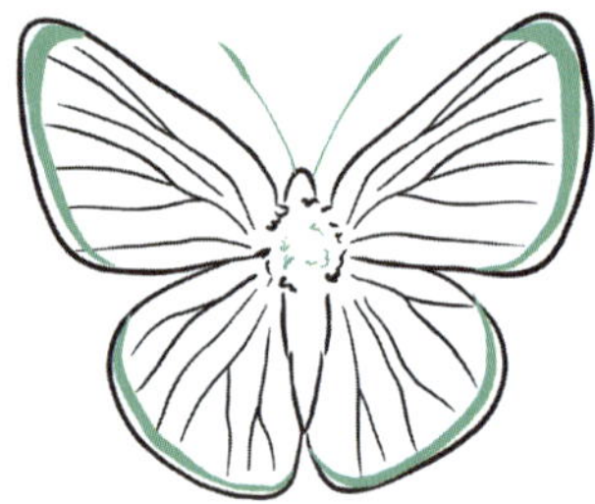

STEP 5

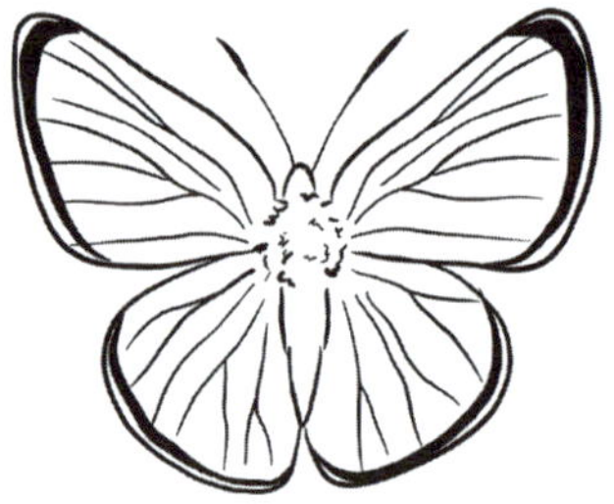

FUN FACT!

These butterflies, while not yet declared endangered, are a subspecies specific to the Puget Sound region.

Harlequin Duck

Histrionicus histrionicus

STEP 1

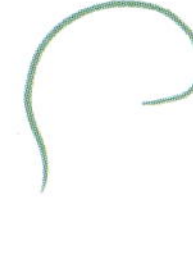

STEP 2

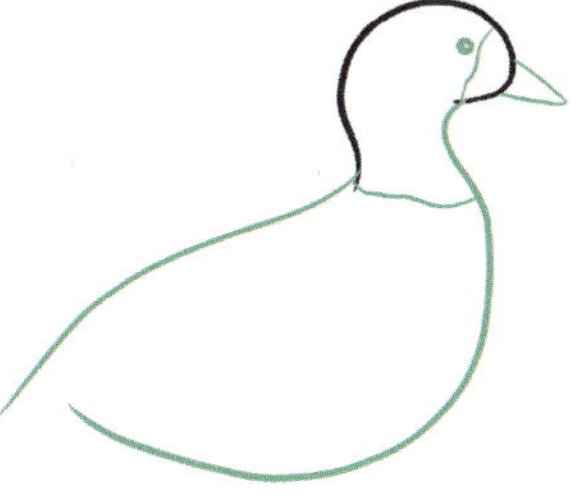

STEP 3

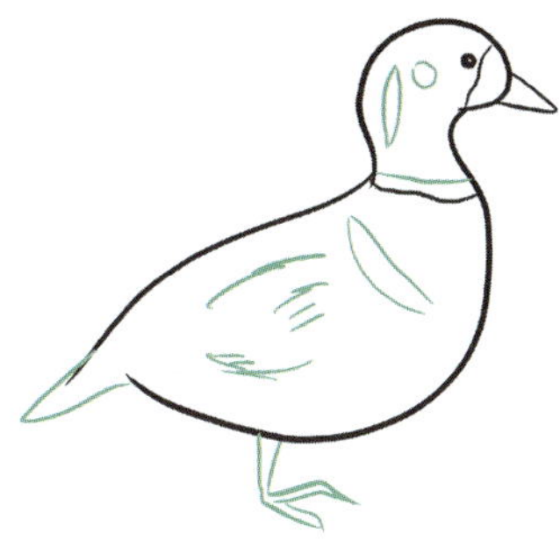

STEP 4

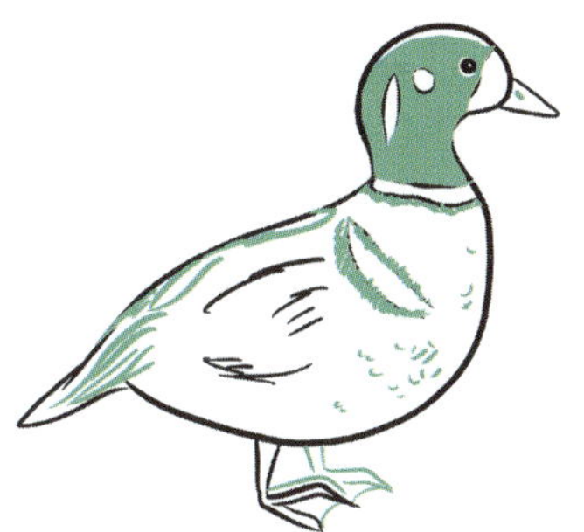

STEP 5

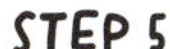

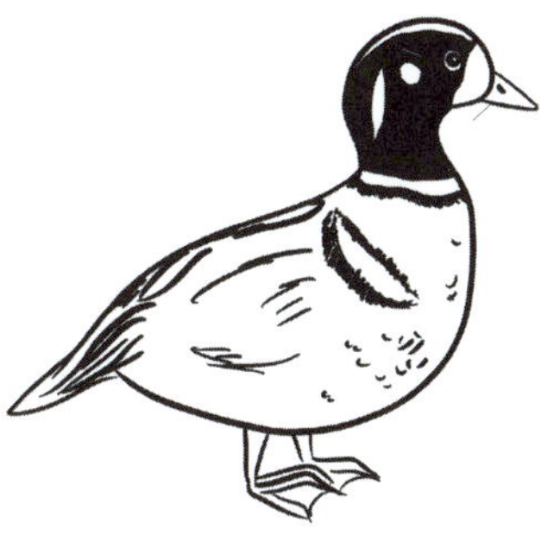

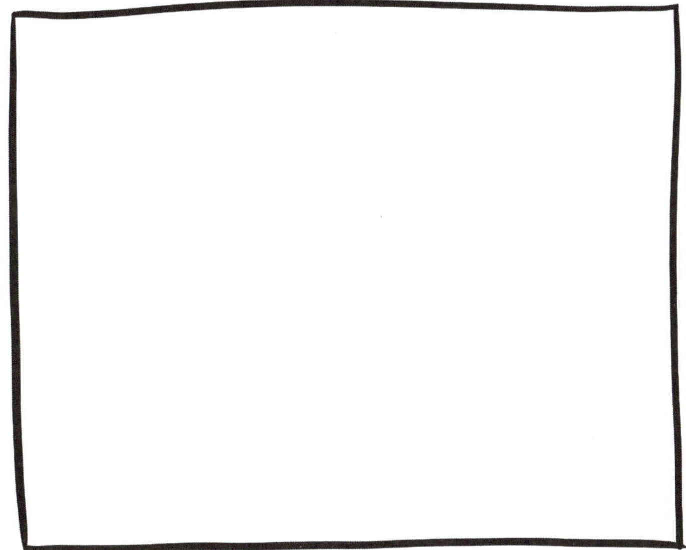

FUN FACT!

Nicknamed "sea mouse," this duck produces unduck-like squeaks when communicating.

Rufous Hummingbird

Selasphorus rufus

STEP 1

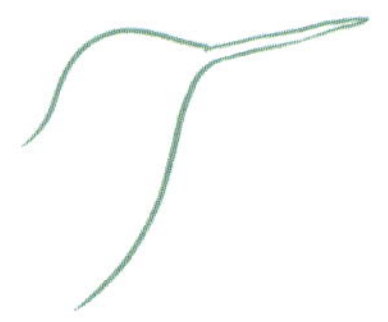

STEP 2

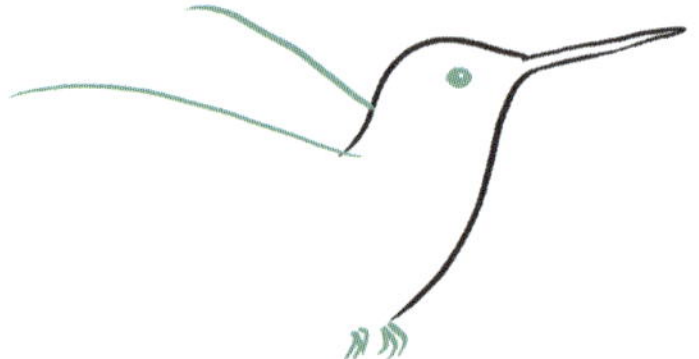

STEP 3

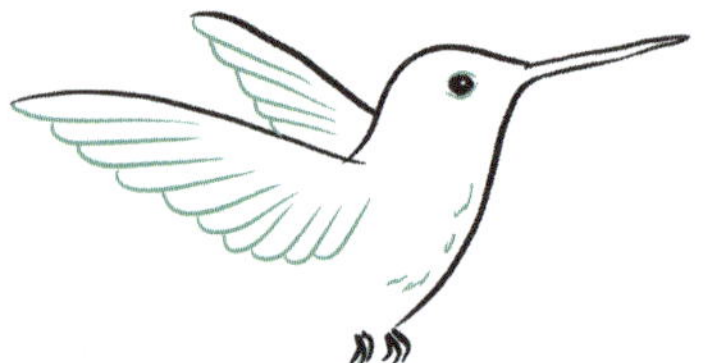

STEP 4

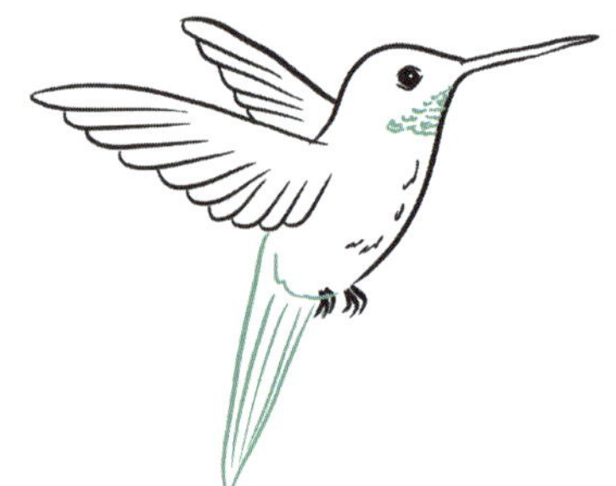

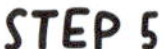

STEP 5

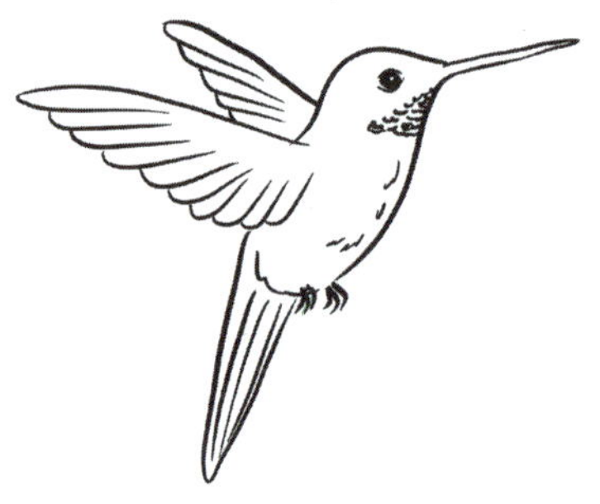

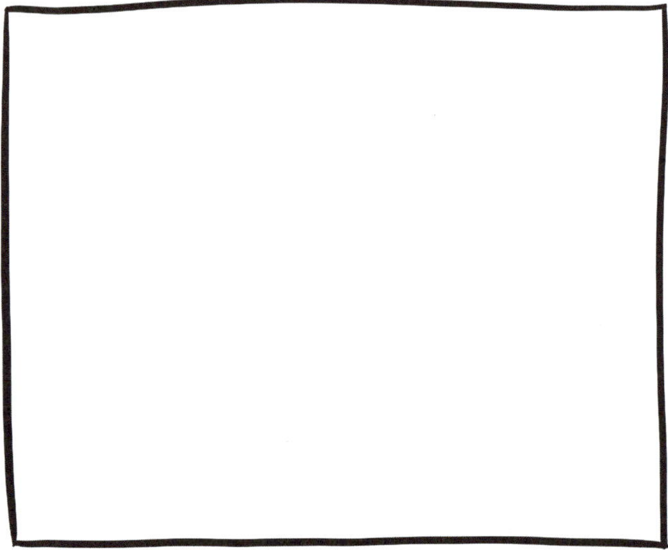

FUN FACT!

This hummingbird flies annually from Mexico to Alaska and back, which is the longest bird migration relative to body size.

Salmon

Oncorhynchus spp.

STEP 1

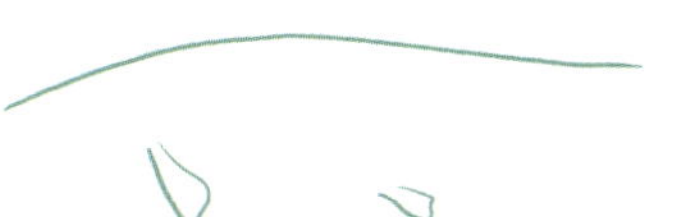

STEP 2

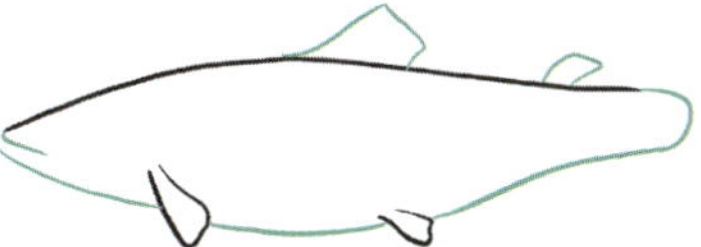

STEP 3

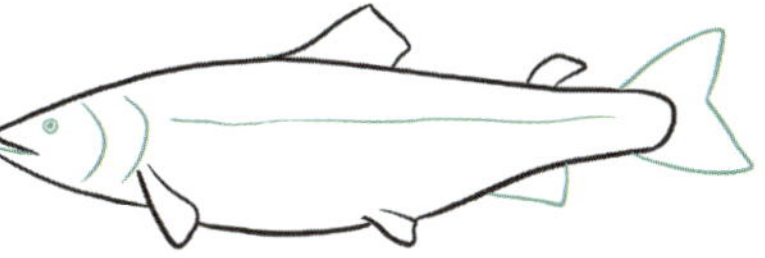

STEP 4

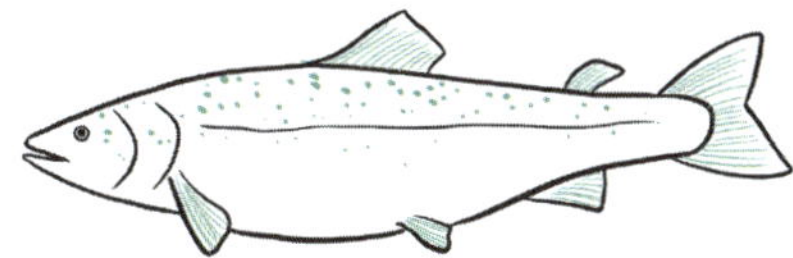

STEP 5

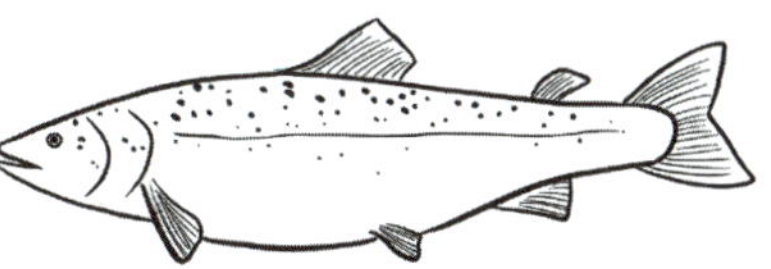

FUN FACT!

Its life cycle takes it from freshwater rivers to the ocean and then back to its natal rivers.

Steelhead Trout

Oncorhynchus mykiss

STEP 1

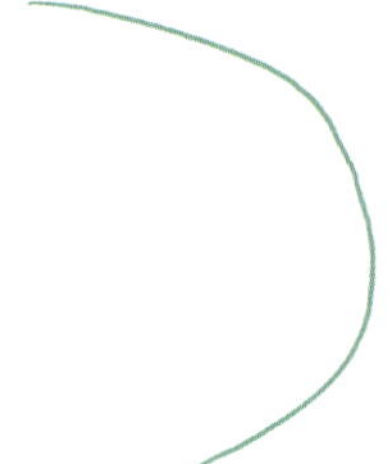

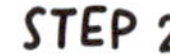

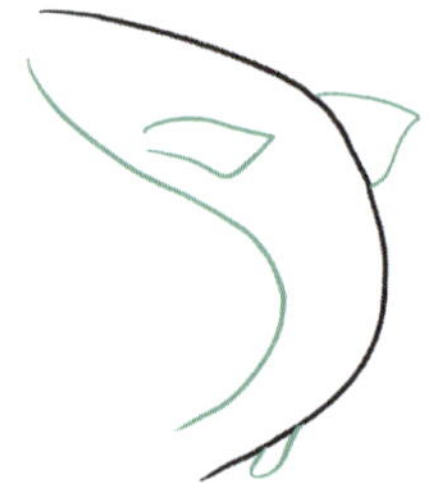

STEP 3

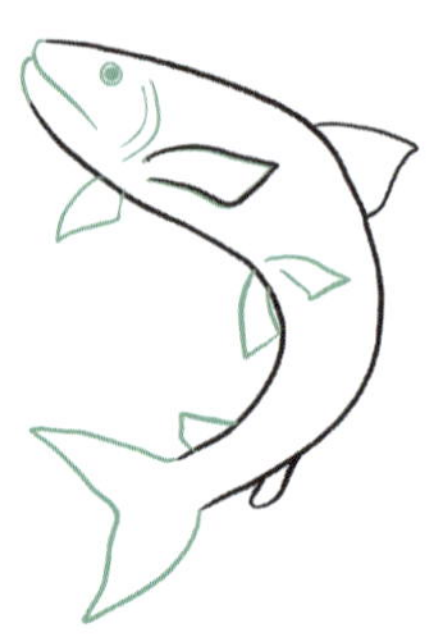

STEP 4

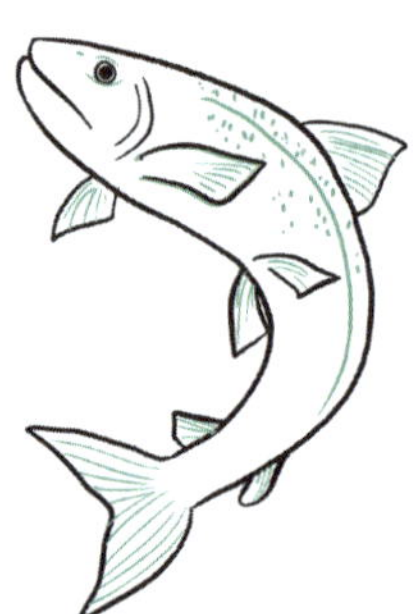

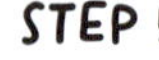

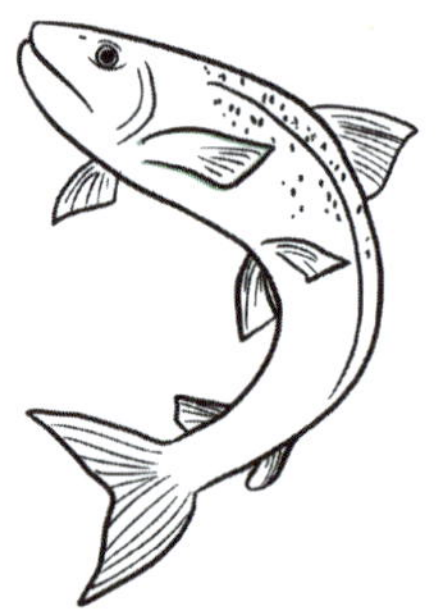

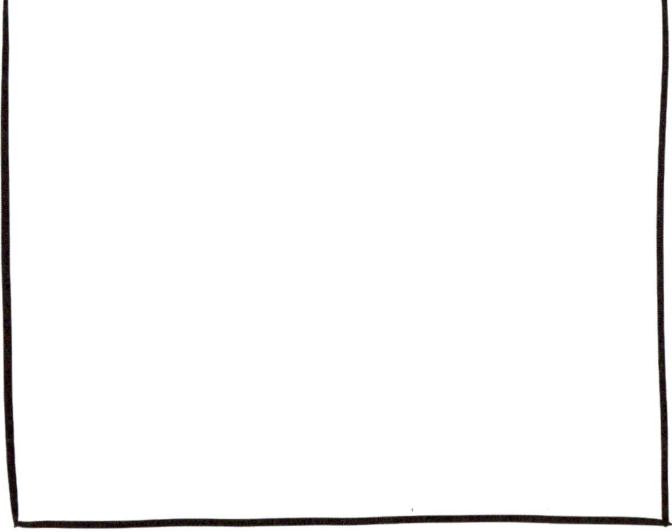

FUN FACT!

Trout and other fish have *otoliths* or "ear stones" in their head, which help them with balance and hearing.

River Otter

Lontra canadensis

STEP 1

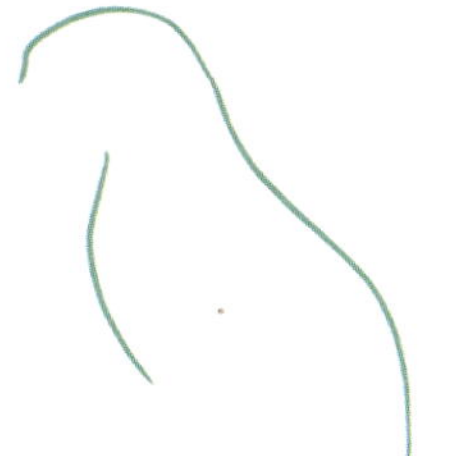

STEP 2

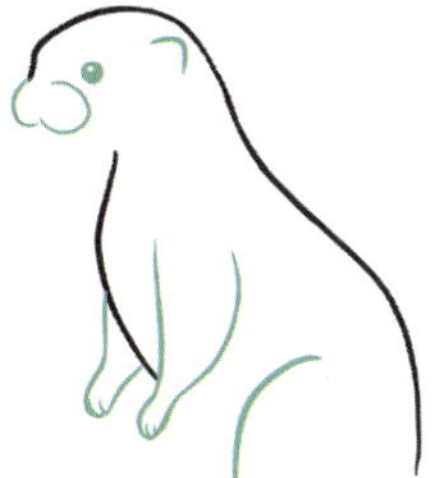

STEP 3

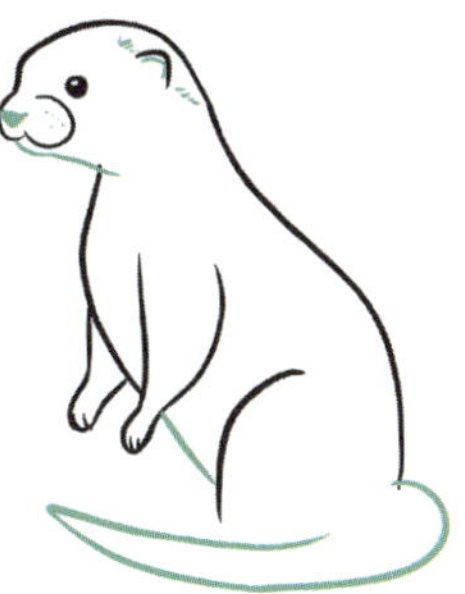

STEP 4

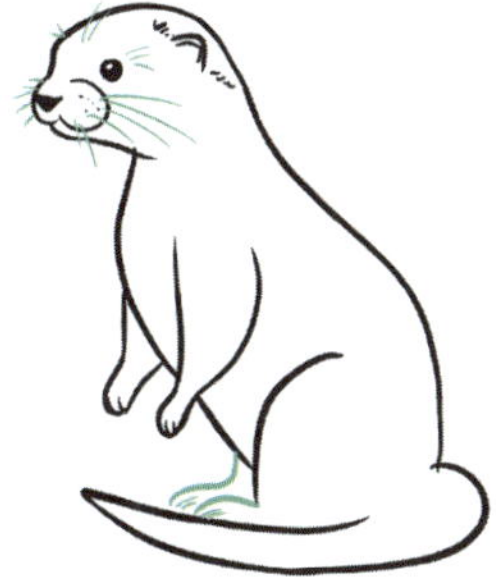

STEP 5

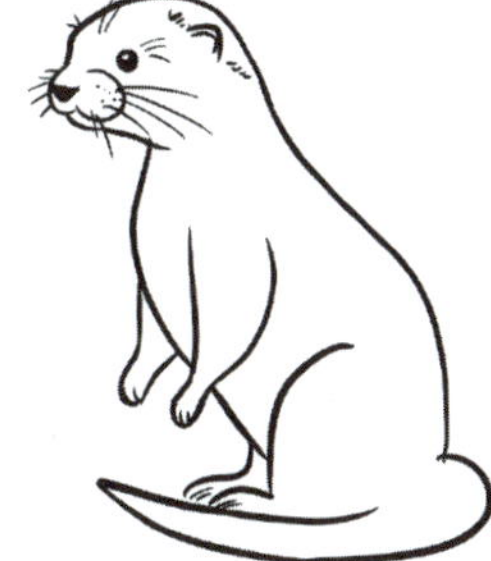

FUN FACT!

River otters can hold their breath underwater for up to eight minutes and dive to sixty feet deep.

Pacific Lamprey

Entosphenus tridentatus

STEP 1

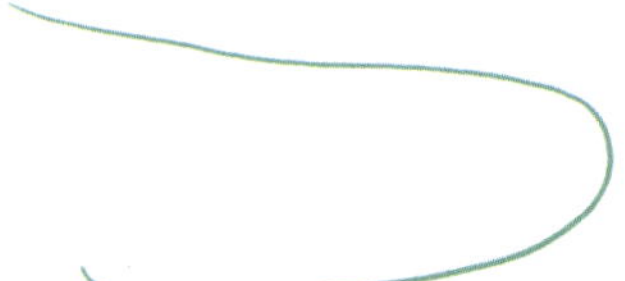

STEP 2

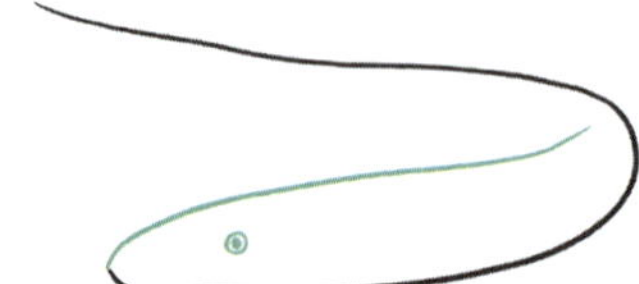

STEP 3

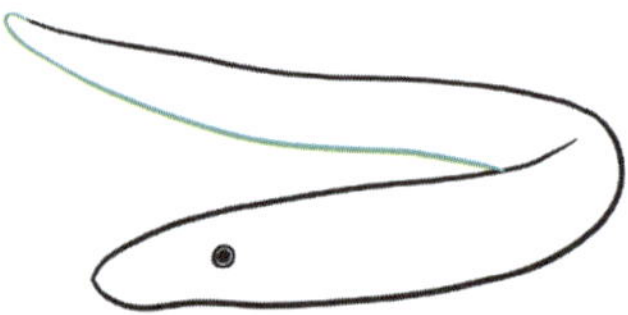

STEP 4

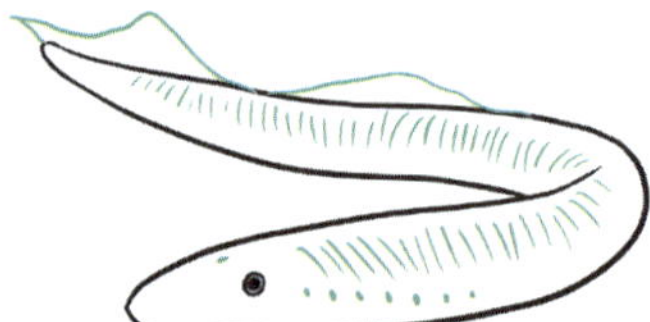

STEP 5

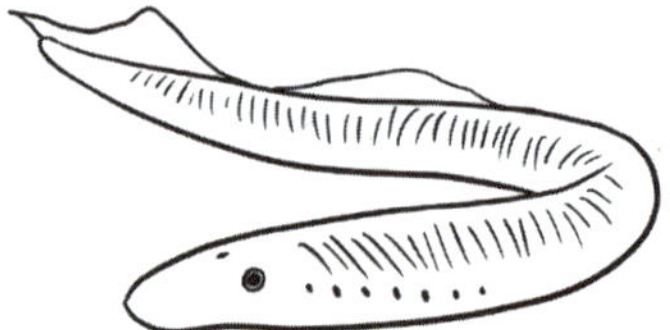

FUN FACT!
Because adult lampreys die within four days of spawning, the females lay up to one hundred thousand eggs that can be fertilized externally.

Pacific Sideband Snail

Monadenia fidelis

STEP 1

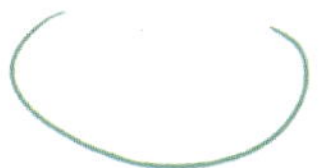

STEP 2

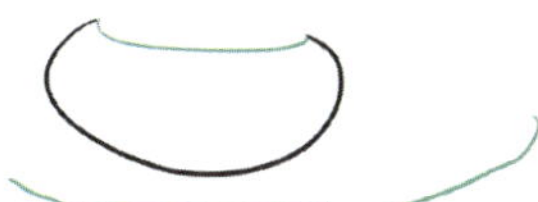

STEP 3

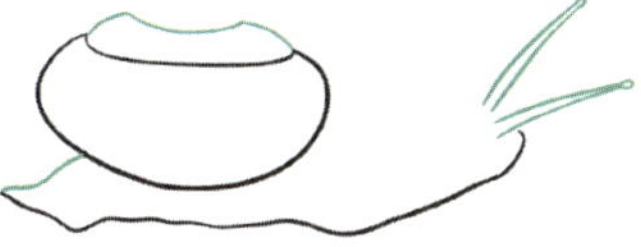

STEP 4

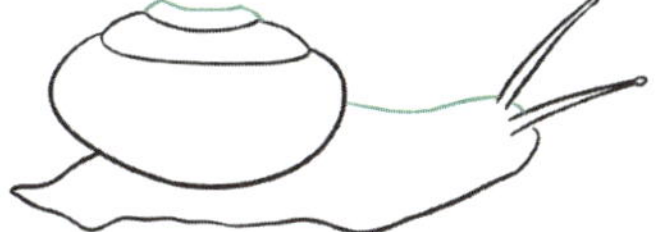

STEP 5

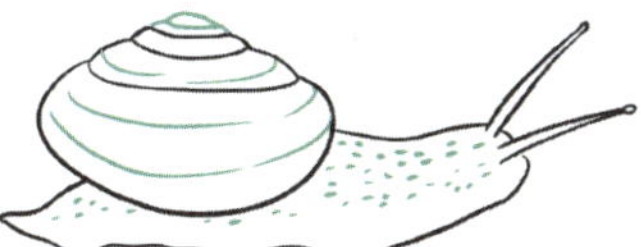

STEP 6

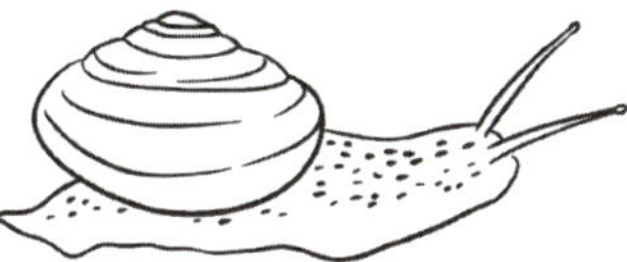

FUN FACT!

This snail breathes through a single hole on the right side of its body.

Giant Pacific Octopus

Enteroctopus dofleini

STEP 1

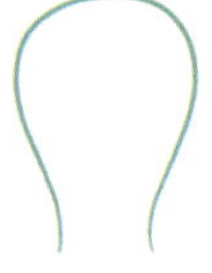

STEP 2

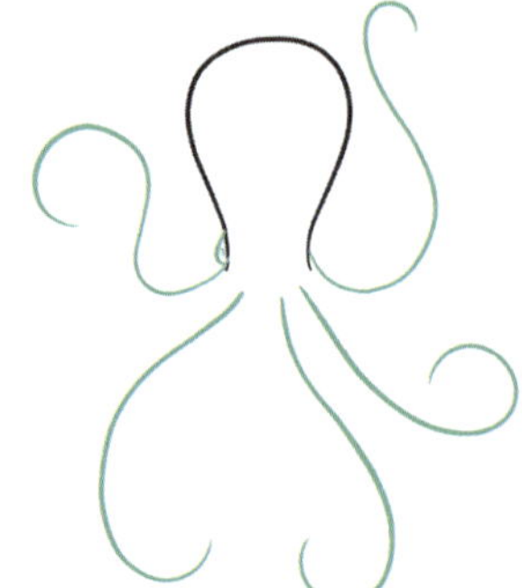

STEP 3

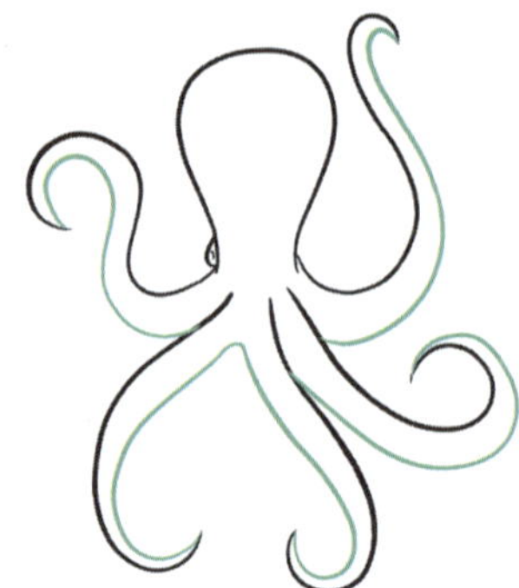

STEP 4

STEP 5

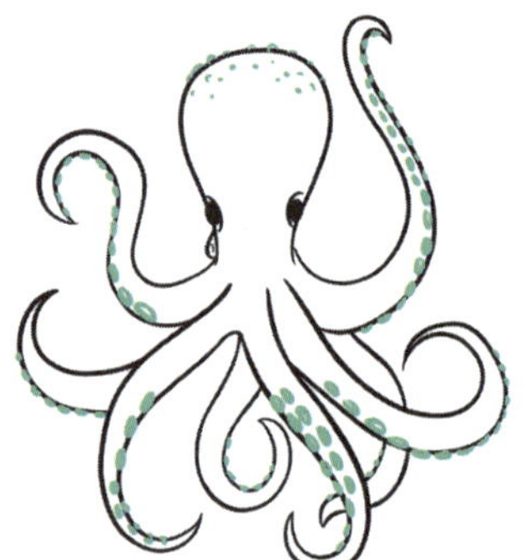

STEP 6

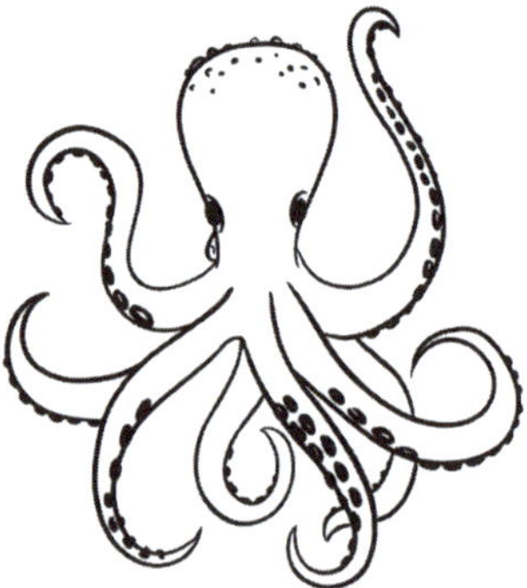

FUN FACT!

The largest species of octopus in the world, it spends most of its life alone. With three hearts and nine brains, the octopus is one of the most unusual creatures on Earth.

Pacific Banana Slug

Ariolimax columbianus

STEP 1

STEP 2

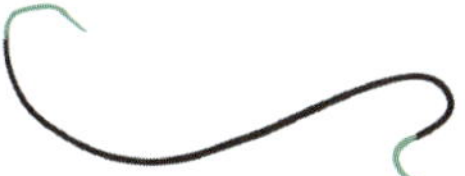

STEP 3

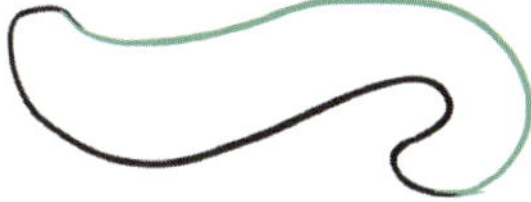

STEP 4

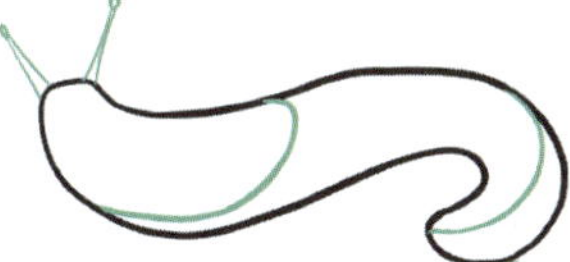

STEP 5

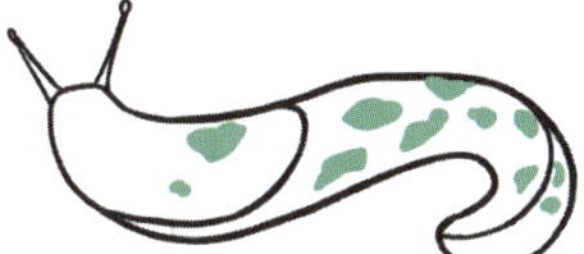

STEP 6

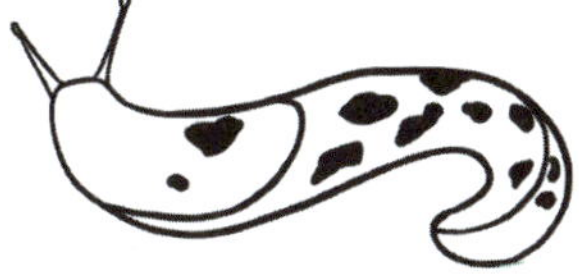

FUN FACT!

One of the largest slug species, it's named for its yellow color, which resembles a ripe banana.

Cascades Frog

Rana cascadae

STEP 1

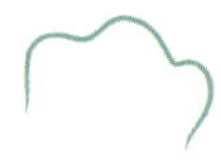

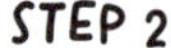

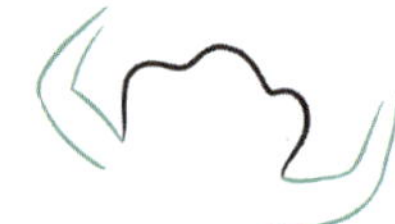

STEP 3

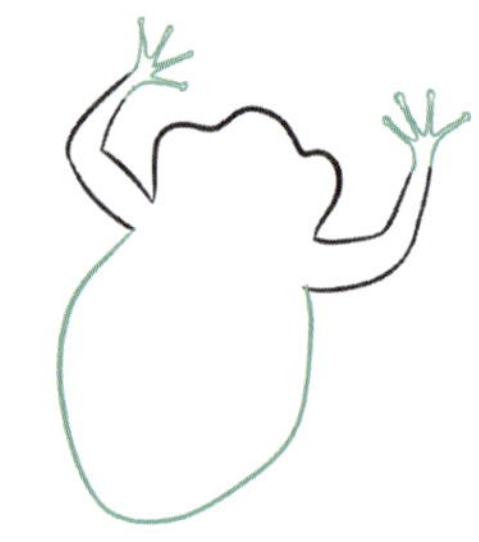

STEP 4

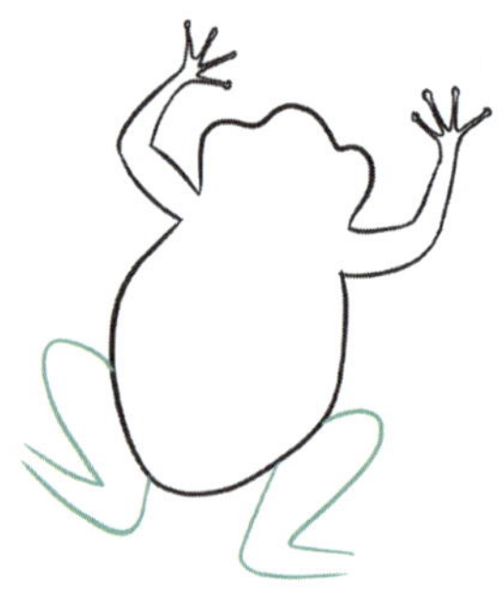

STEP 5

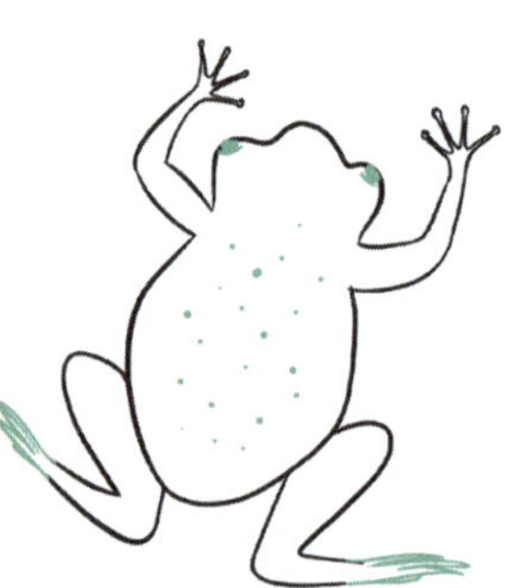

STEP 6

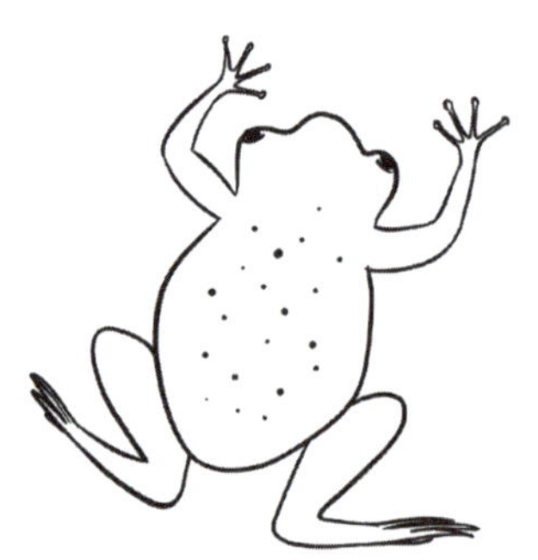

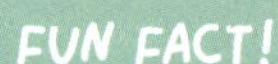

Found primarily at high elevations, this frog is named for its home region, the Cascade Mountains.

Common Nighthawk

Chordeiles minor

STEP 1

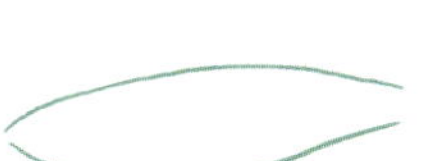

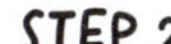

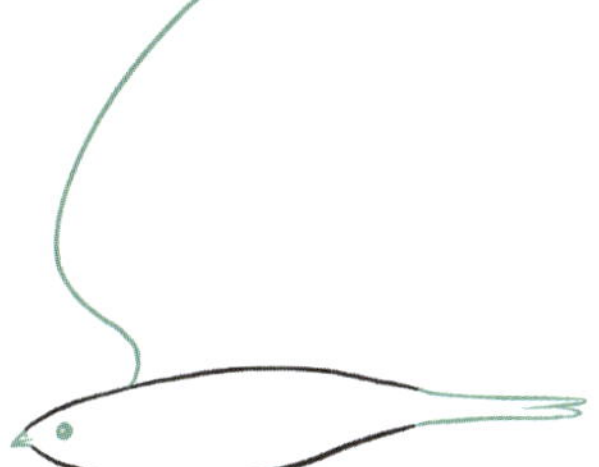

STEP 3

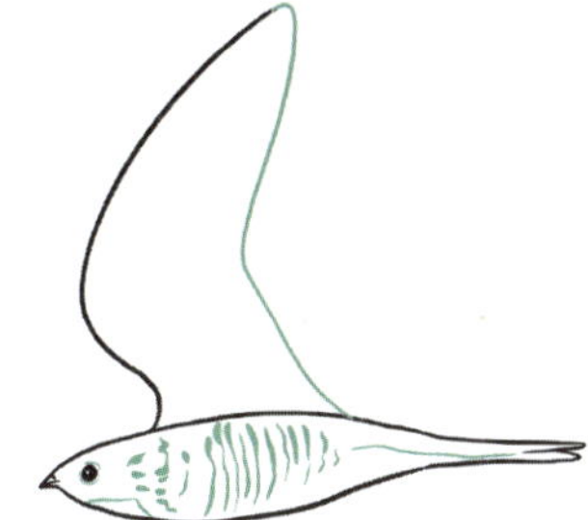

STEP 4

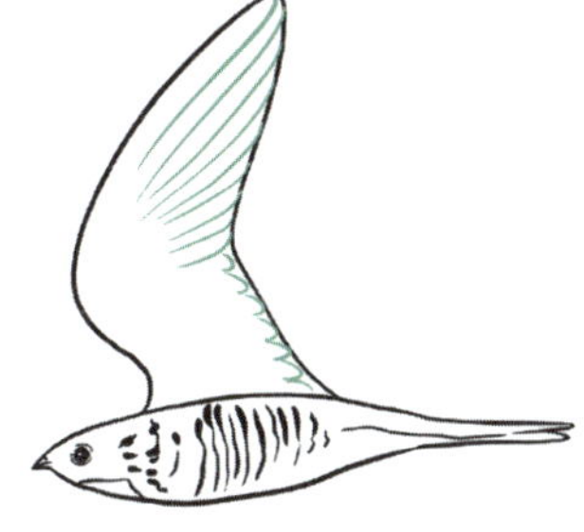

STEP 5

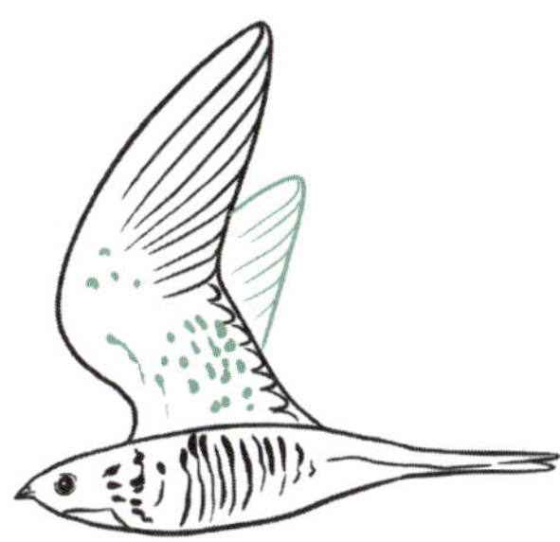

STEP 6

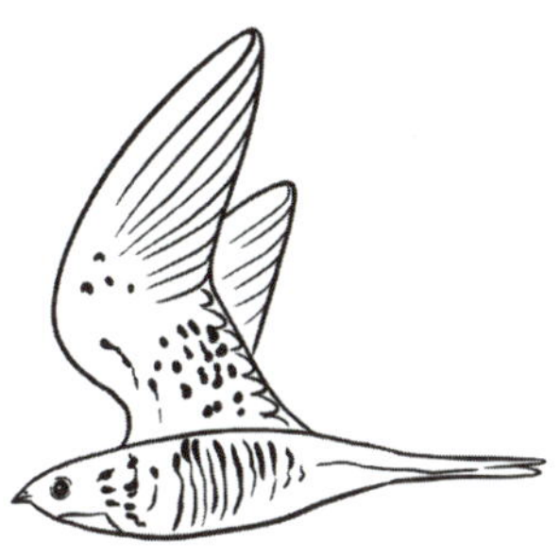

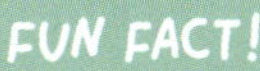

Despite its name, the nighthawk is not a hawk but a dusk-flying insect-eating bird.

Rough-Skinned Newt

Taricha granulosa

STEP 1

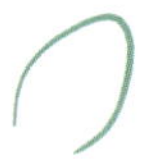

STEP 2

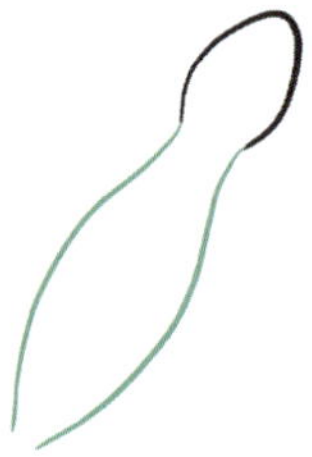

STEP 3

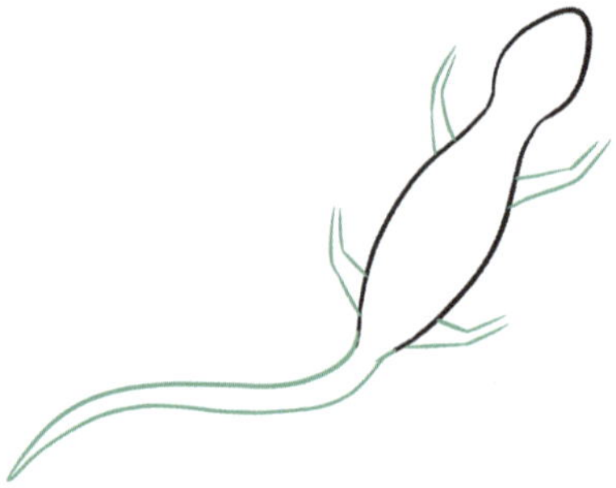

STEP 4

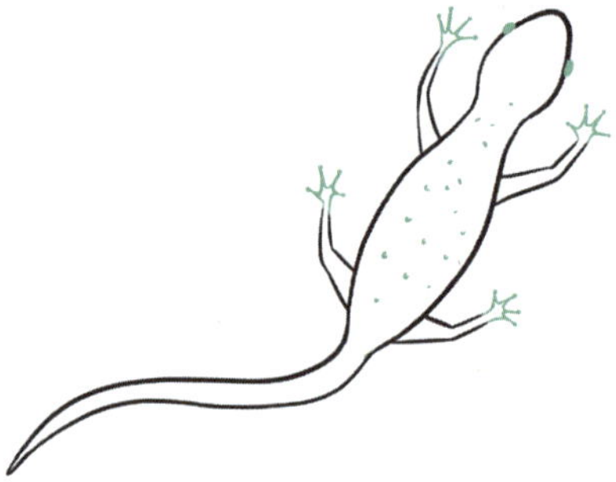

STEP 5

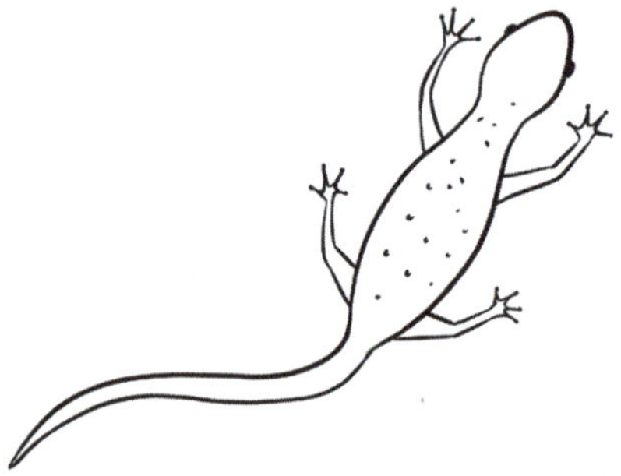

FUN FACT!

Be careful if you encounter this amphibian—its skin is covered in a substance that is toxic to animals and humans.

Townsend's Big-Eared Bat

Corynorhinus townsendii

STEP 1

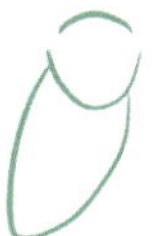

STEP 2

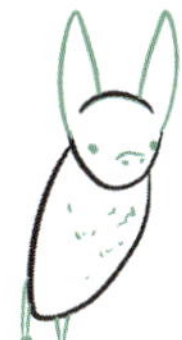

STEP 3

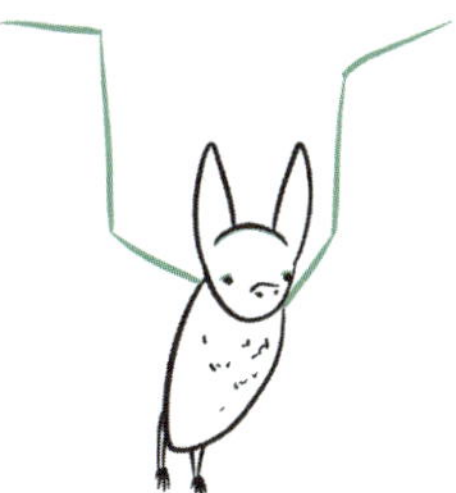

STEP 4

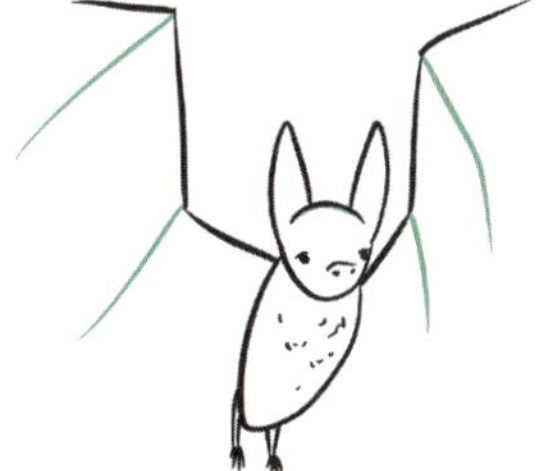

STEP 5

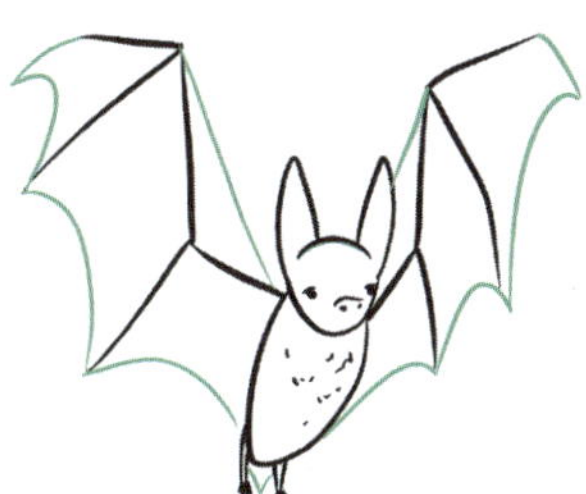

STEP 6

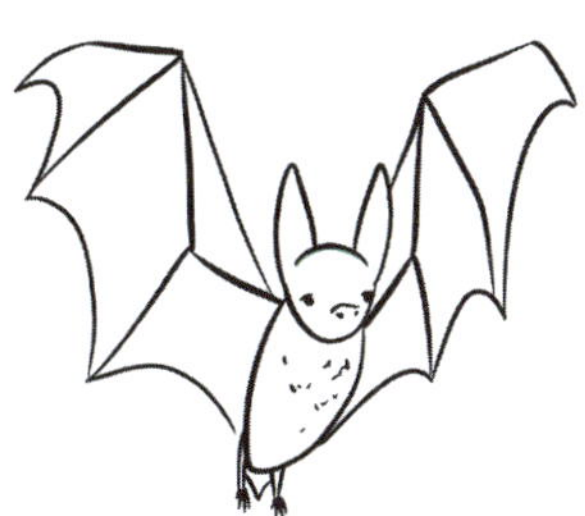

FUN FACT!

This charismatic species with characteristically large ears primarily feeds on moths.

Spotted Sandpiper

Actitis macularius

STEP 1

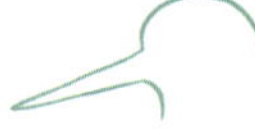

STEP 2

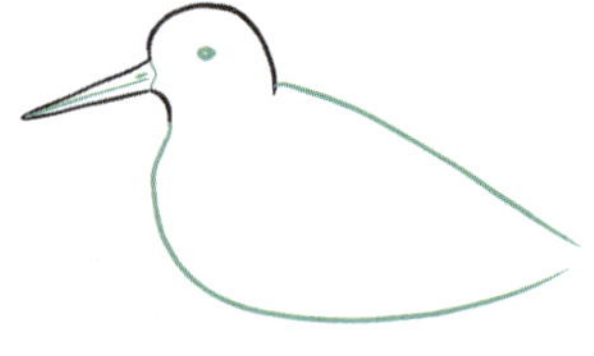

STEP 3

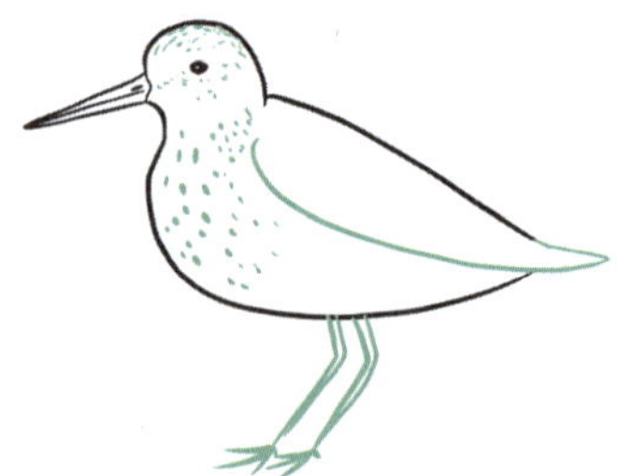

STEP 4

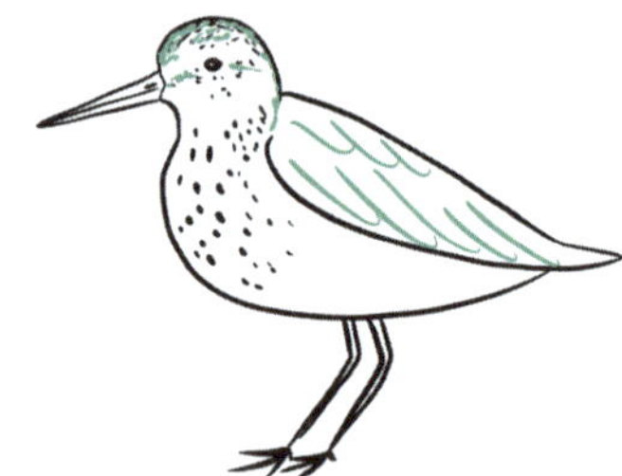

STEP 5

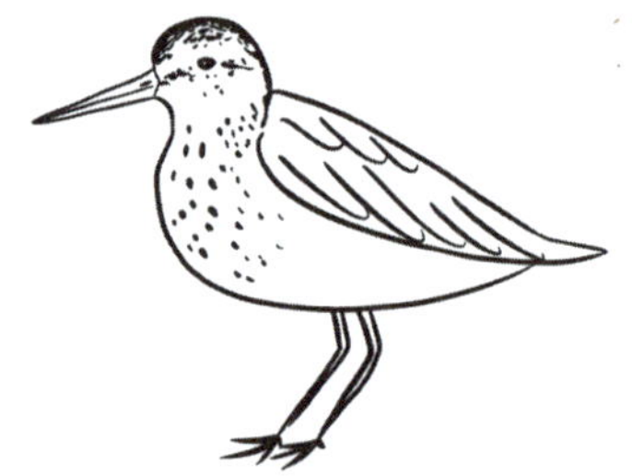

FUN FACT!

Known for their long-distance migrations, these birds fly all the way from the Arctic to South America every year!

Harbor Seal

Phoca vitulina

STEP 1

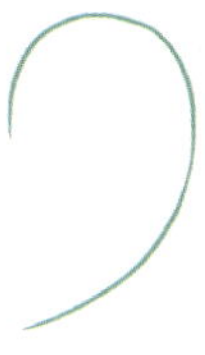

STEP 2

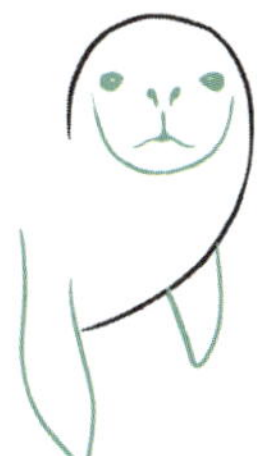

STEP 3

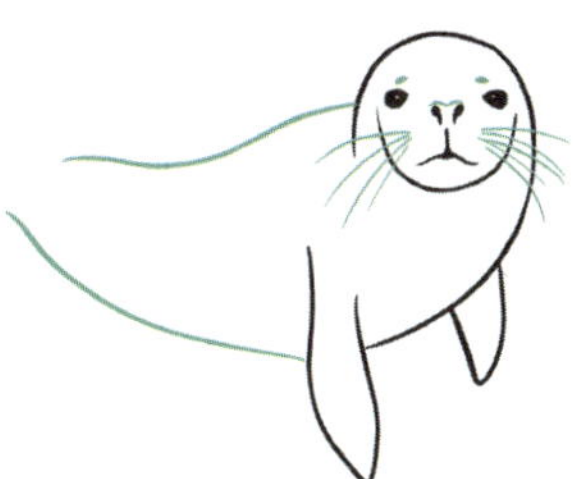

STEP 4

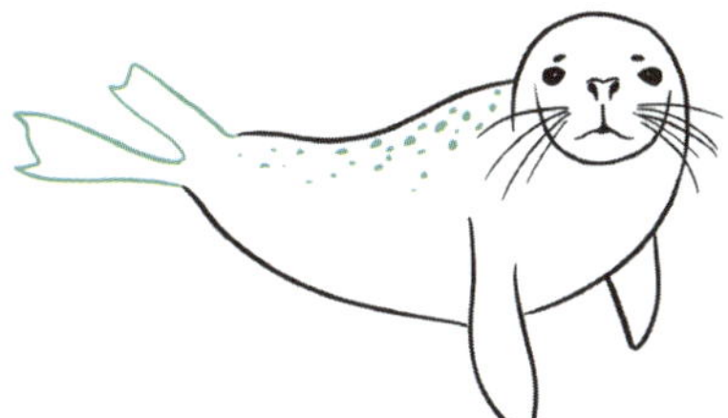

STEP 5

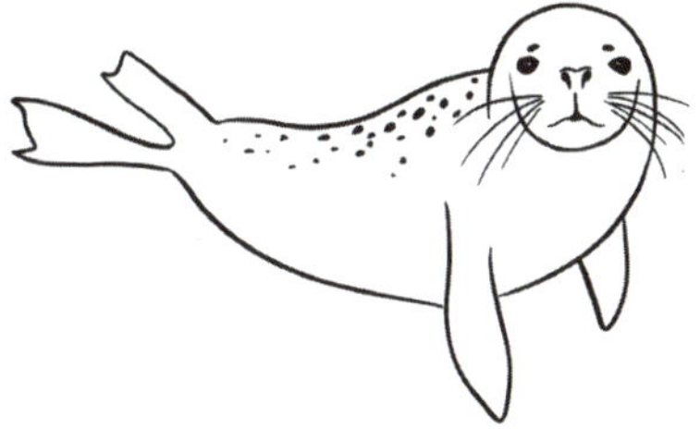

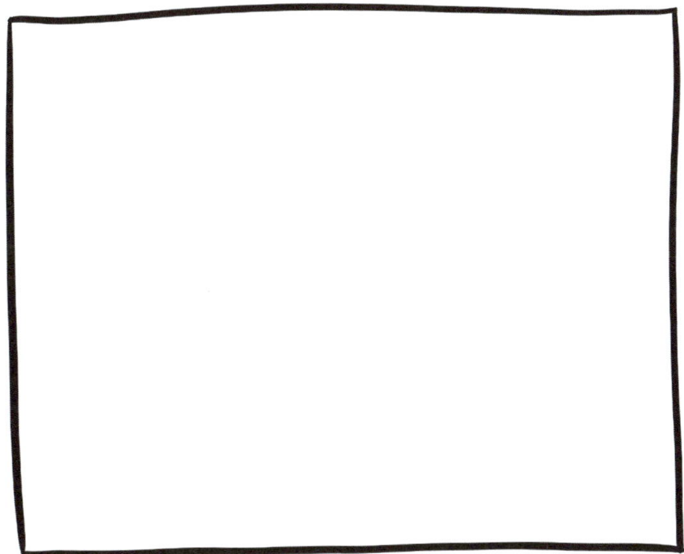

FUN FACT!

The seal's hearing is fourteen times more powerful underwater than a human's.

Harbor Porpoise

Phocoena phocoena

STEP 1

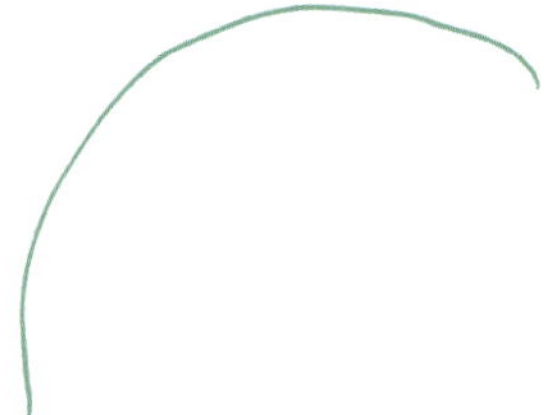

STEP 2

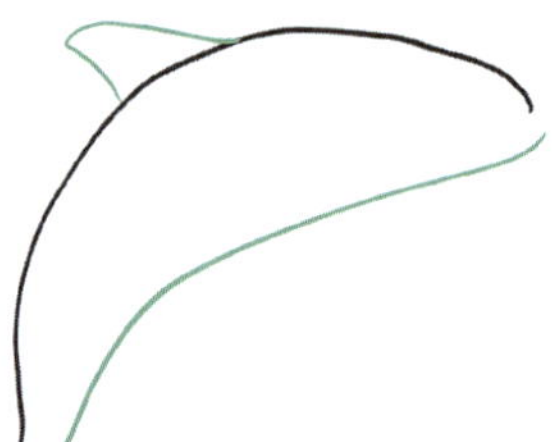

STEP 3

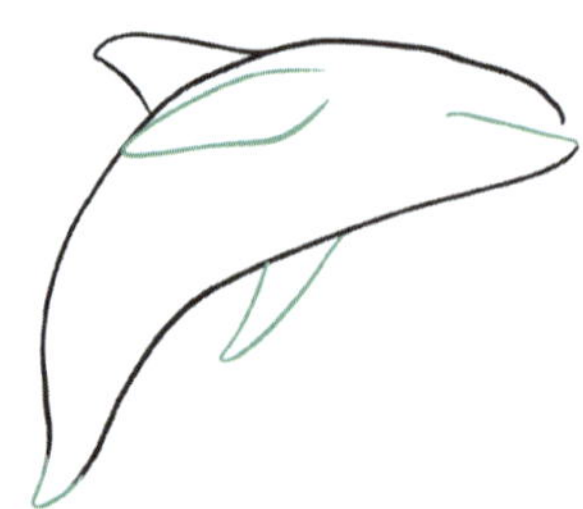

STEP 4

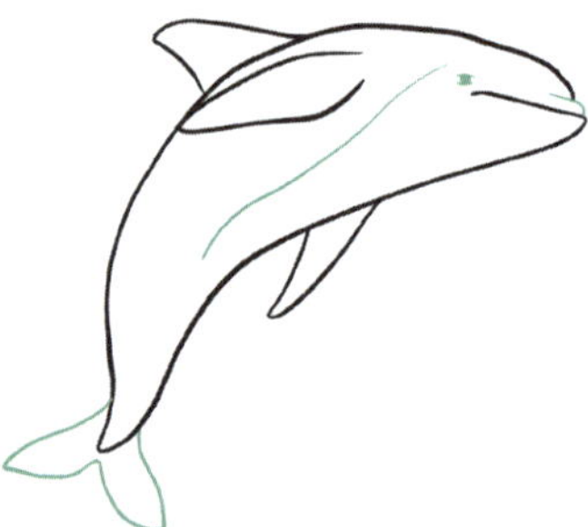

STEP 5

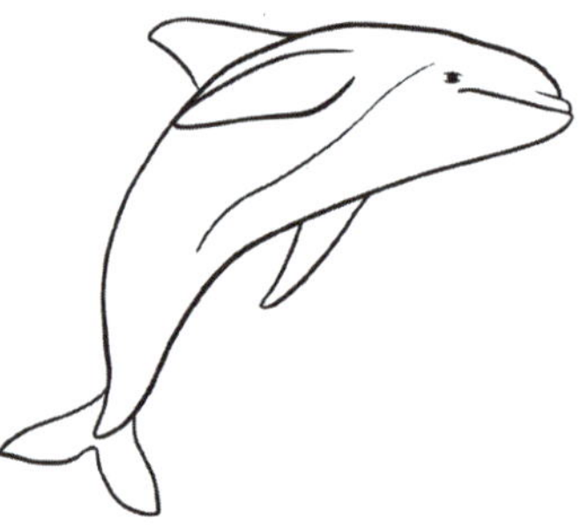

FUN FACT!

These shy animals use echolocating clicks to help them navigate and find prey.

Salmon Shark

Lamna ditropis

STEP 1

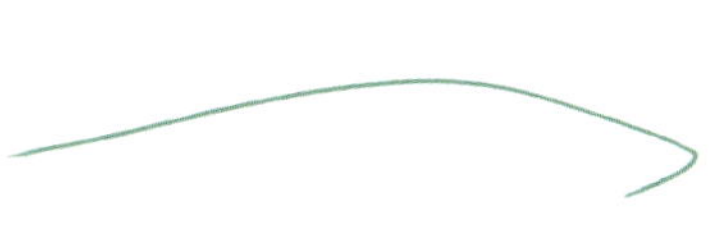

STEP 2

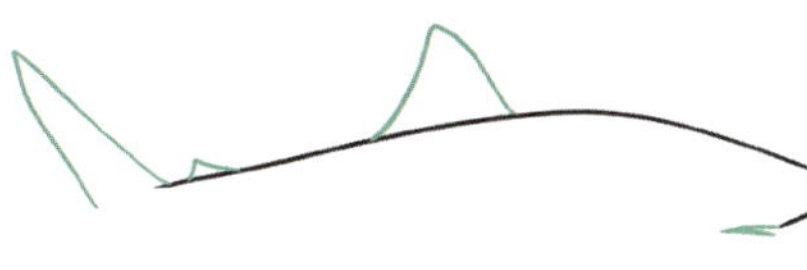

STEP 3

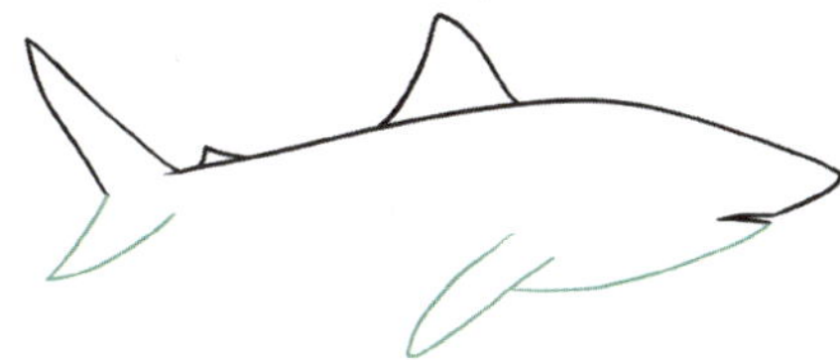

STEP 4

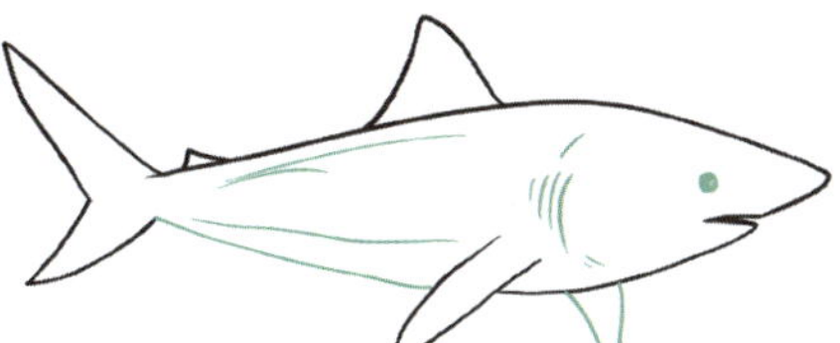

STEP 5

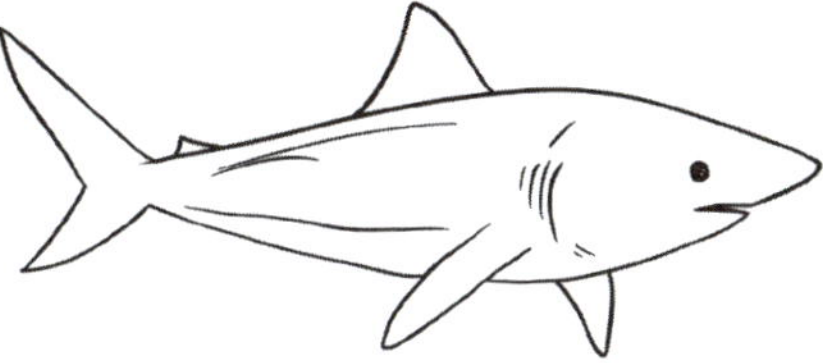

FUN FACT!

Unlike other sharks, salmon sharks are very social creatures, and they prefer to stay in groups.

Steller Sea Lion

Eumetopias jubatus

STEP 1

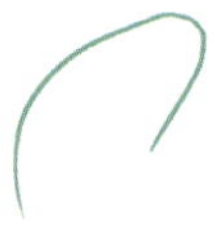

STEP 2

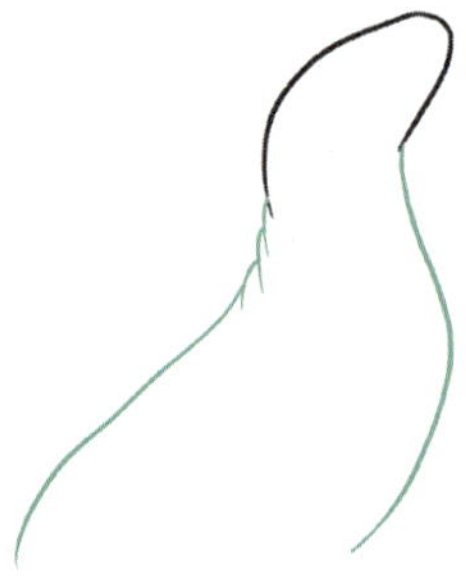

STEP 3

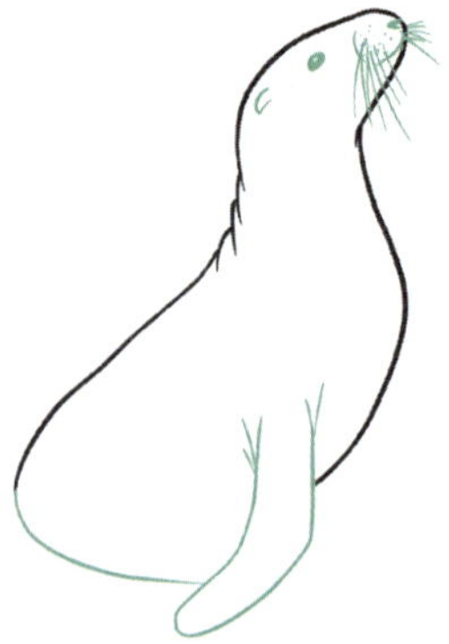

STEP 4

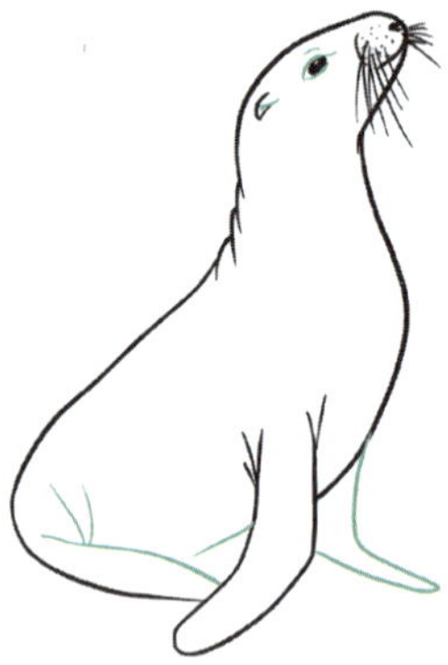

STEP 5

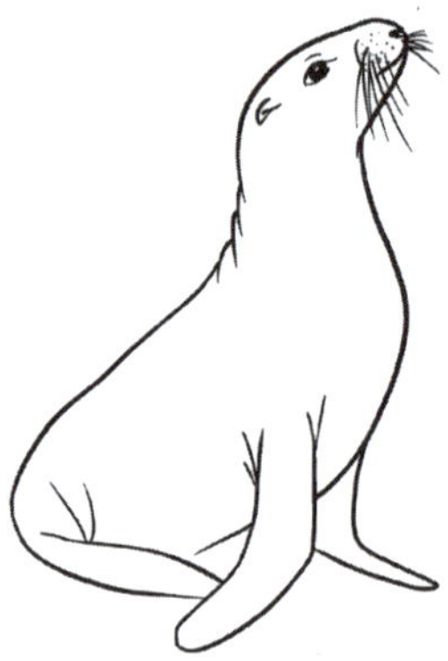

FUN FACT!

These mammals are amazing divers and can hold their breath underwater for sixteen minutes!

Marbled Murrelet

Brachyramphus marmoratus

STEP 1

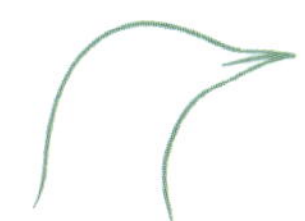

STEP 2

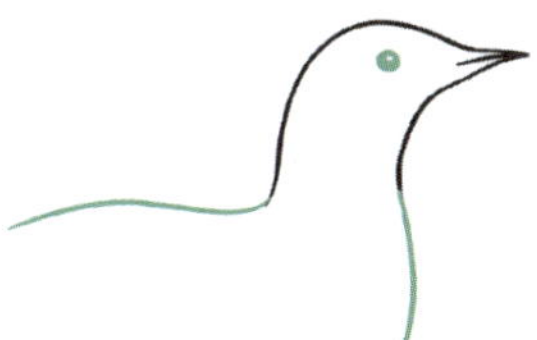

STEP 3

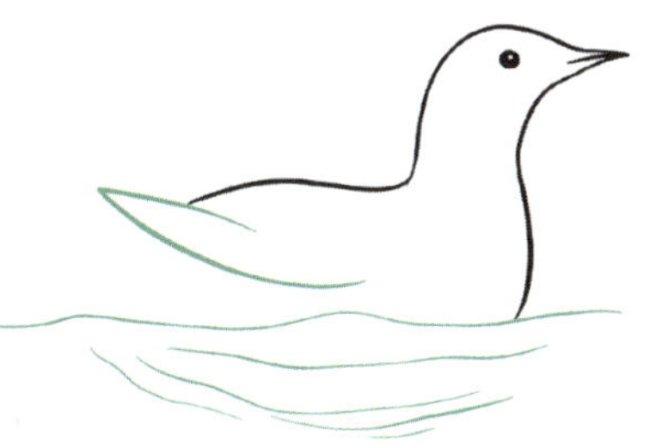

STEP 4

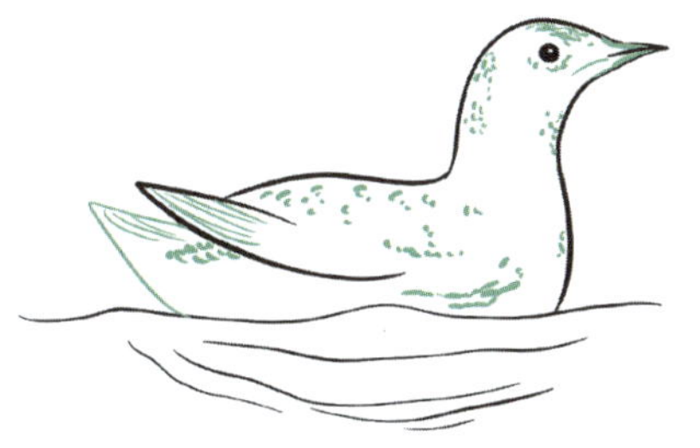

STEP 5

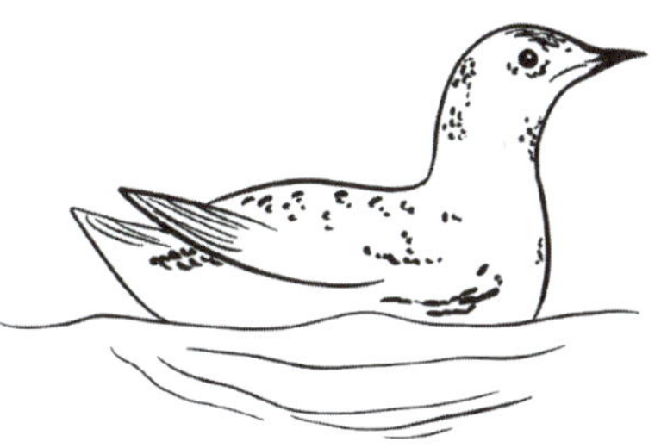

FUN FACT!

These robin-sized birds nest alone high in old-growth conifers, unlike most seabirds, which nest colonially on coastal rocks and cliffs.

Gull

Larus spp.

STEP 1

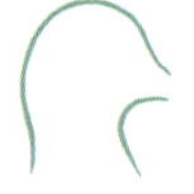

STEP 2

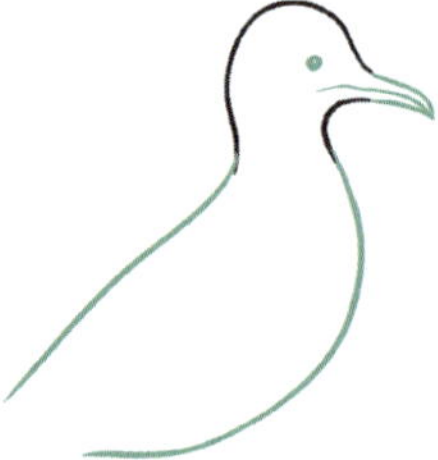

STEP 3

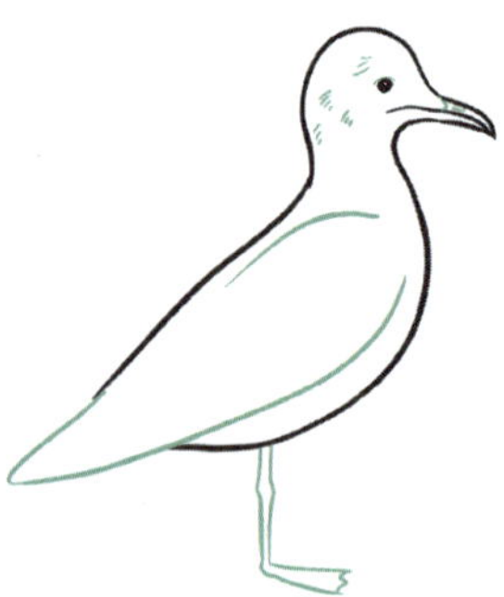

STEP 4

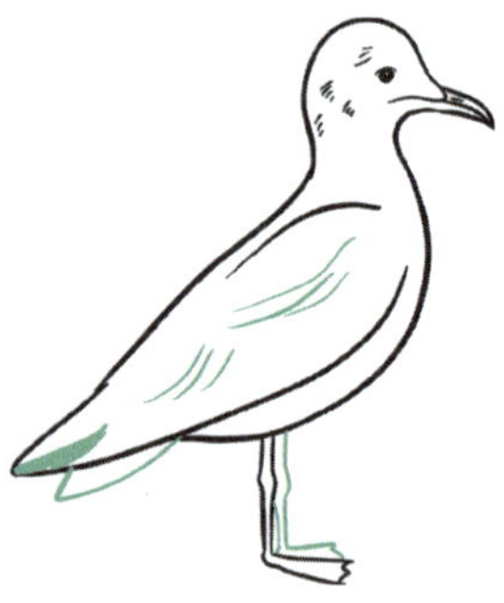

STEP 5

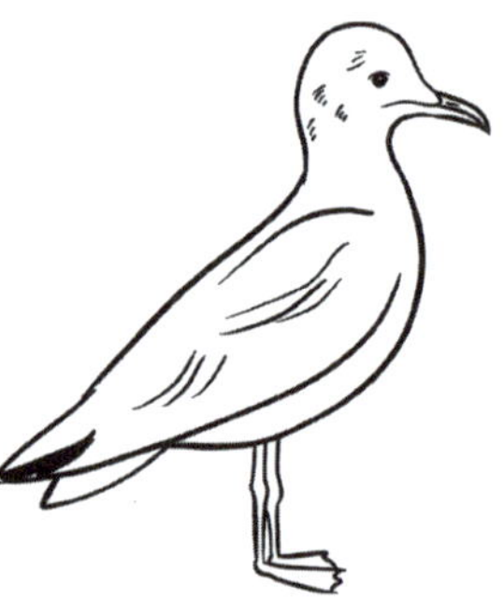

FUN FACT!

Thriving in the cities, gulls are expert food thieves and will eat nearly anything they encounter.

Sand Dollar

Echinarachnius parma

STEP 1

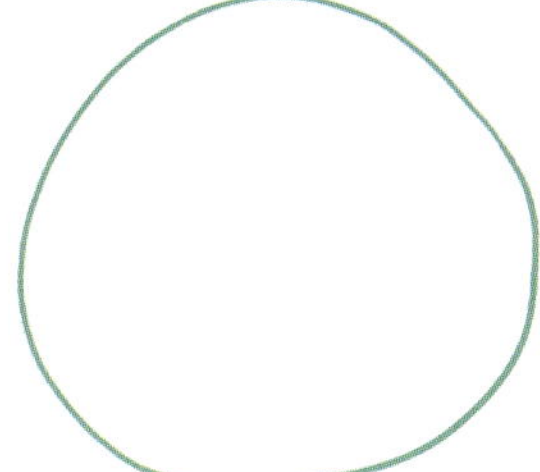

STEP 2

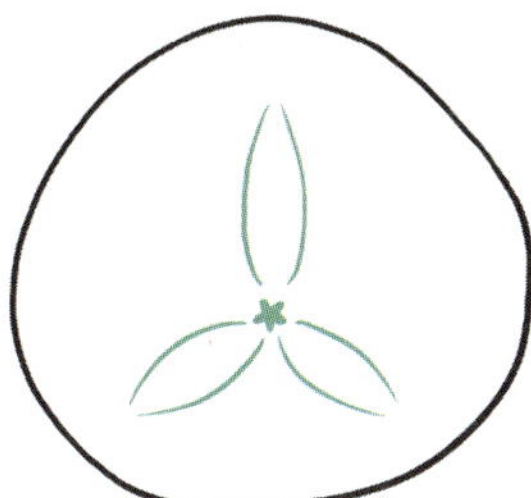

STEP 3

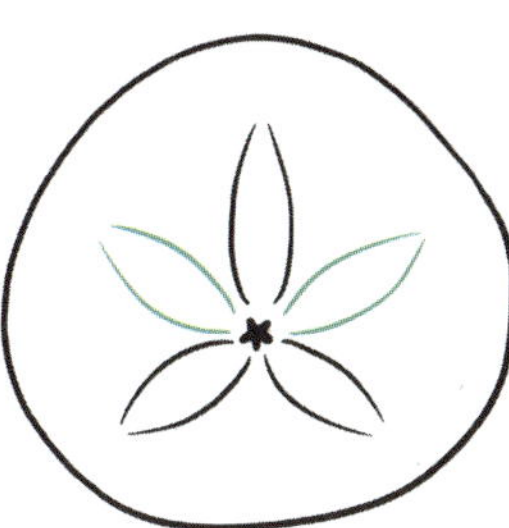

STEP 4

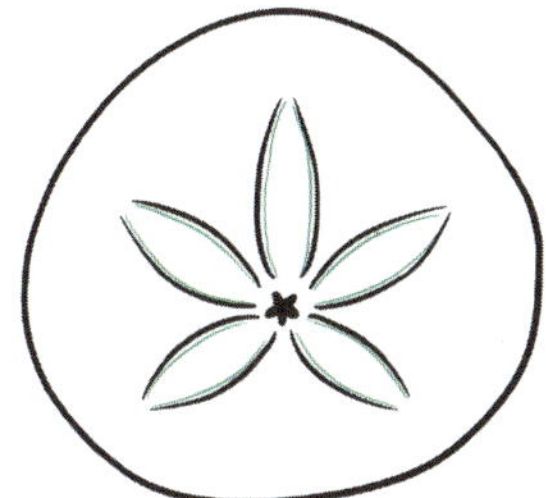

STEP 5

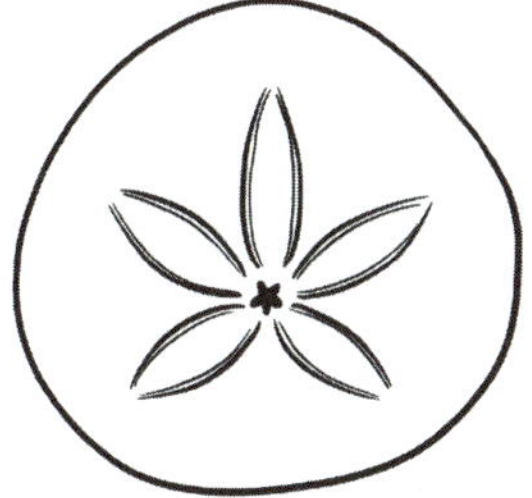

FUN FACT!

Similar to a tree, you can tell the age of a sand dollar by the rings on its exoskeleton. They typically live between six and ten years.

Dungeness Crab

Metacarcinus magister

STEP 1

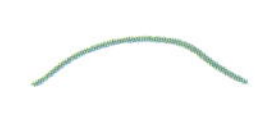

STEP 2

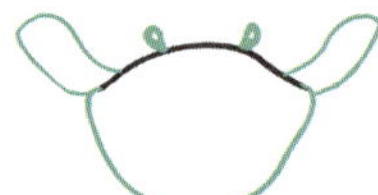

STEP 3

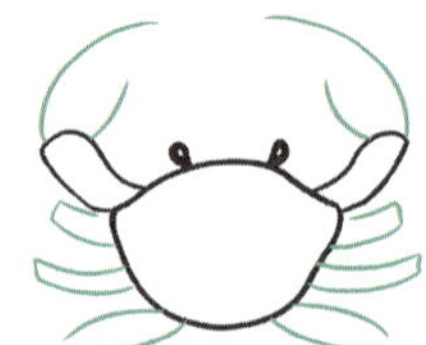

STEP 4

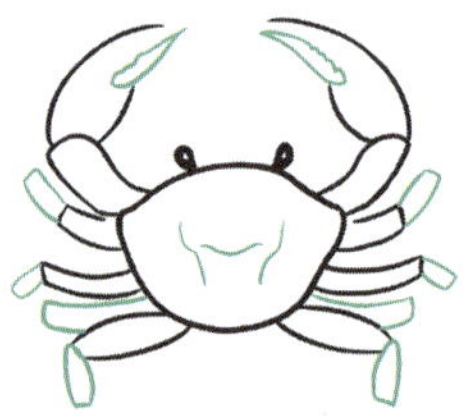

STEP 5

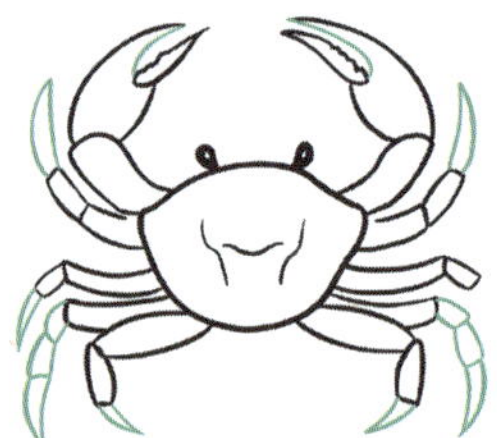

STEP 6

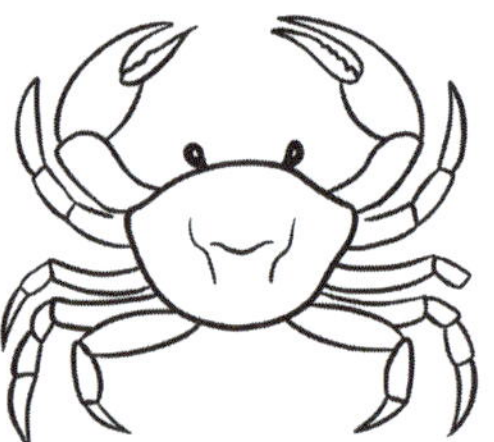

FUN FACT!

This crab species got its name from the Dungeness Spit, a sand spit in the Strait of Juan de Fuca in Washington.

Ochre Sea Star

Pisaster ochraceus

STEP 1

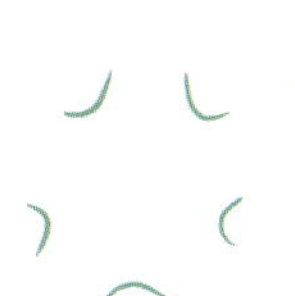

STEP 2

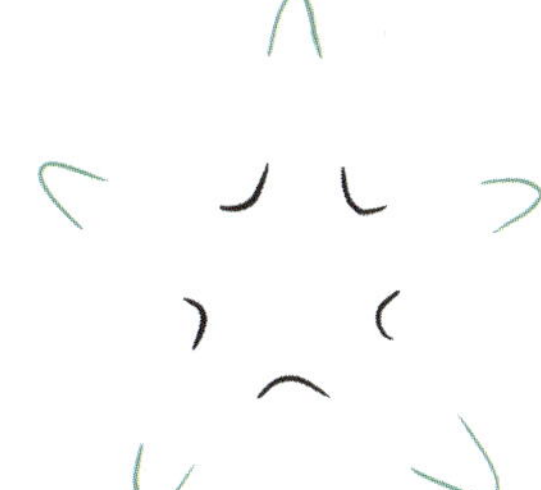

STEP 3

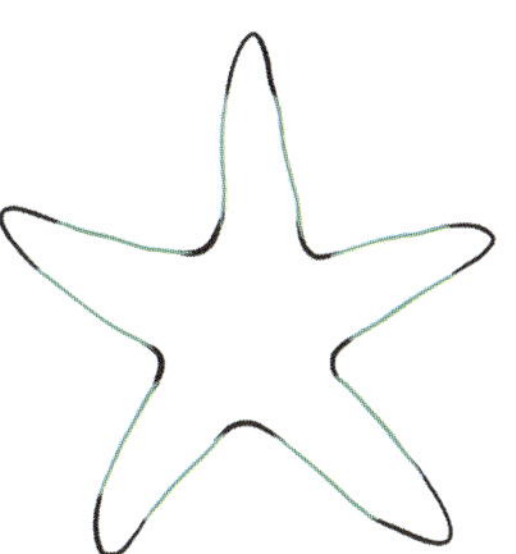

STEP 4

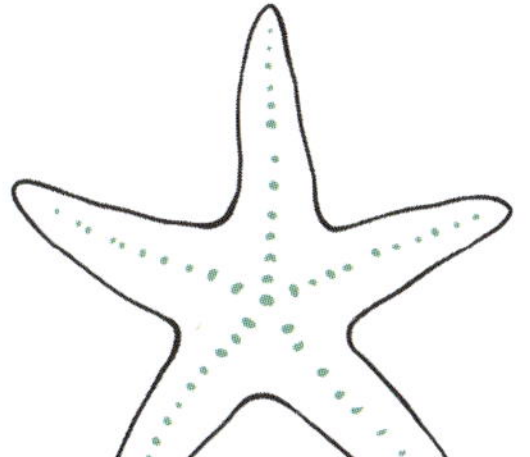

STEP 5

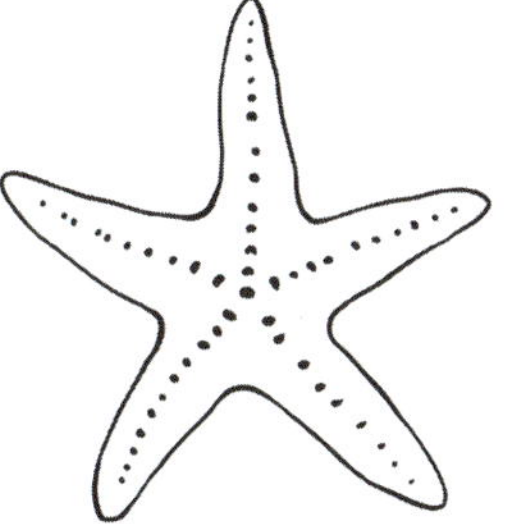

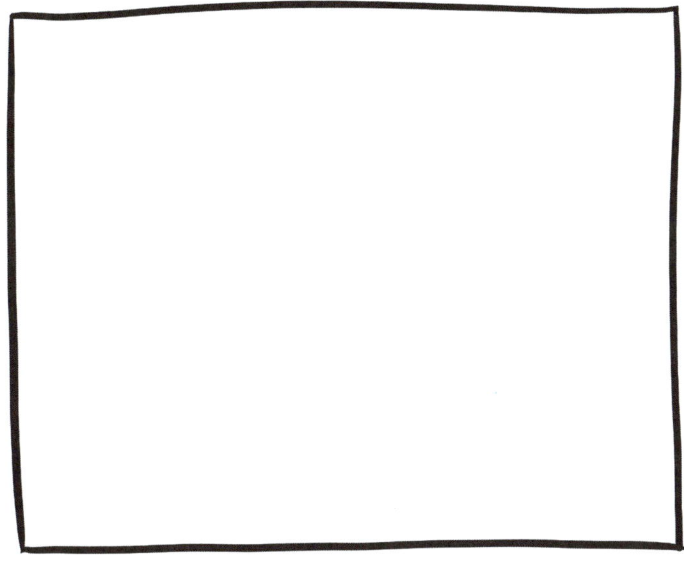

FUN FACT!

Lost limbs are not a problem for this sea star, as it can easily regrow them.

Pacific Purple Sea Urchin

Strongylocentrotus purpuratus

STEP 1

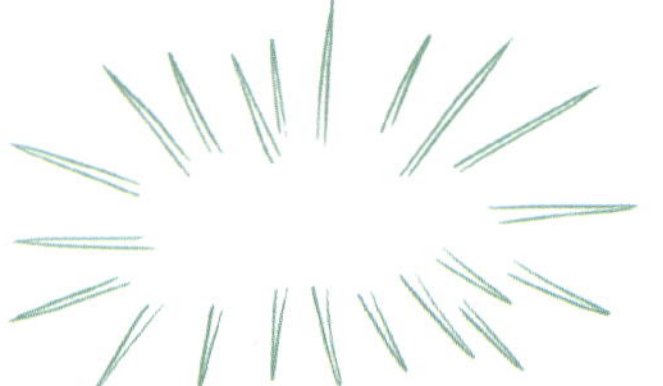

STEP 2

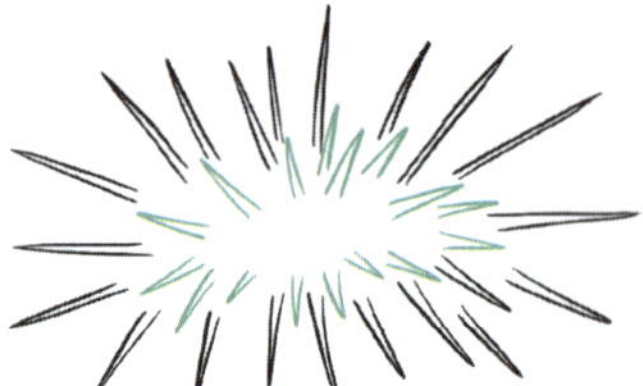

STEP 3

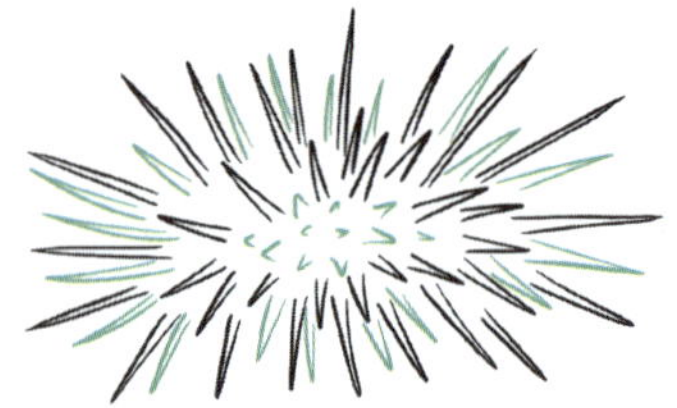

STEP 4

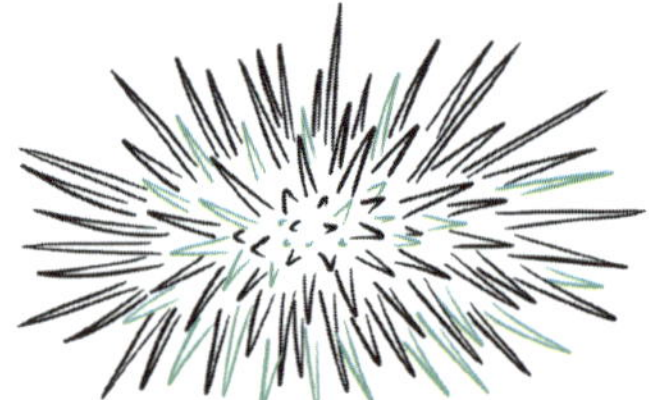

STEP 5

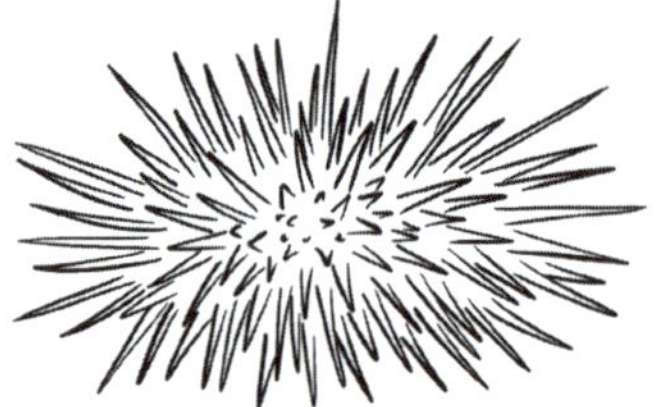

FUN FACT!

This spiny creature uses internal hydraulic pressure to move its tube feet and "walk" around its rocky habitat.

Landmarks

The Pacific Northwest is rich in both cultural and natural landmarks, each telling a part of its diverse and dynamic story. From historic bridges connecting communities across rugged terrain to awe-inspiring vistas carved by volcanic activity and glacial movements, the Northwest offers an abundance of iconic sites—and they're easier to draw than you might think!

As you re-create these iconic scenes, consider how the interplay of natural and human-made elements shapes the visual landscape. Your line drawings will capture not just the physical features, but also the spirit and history embedded in each landmark.

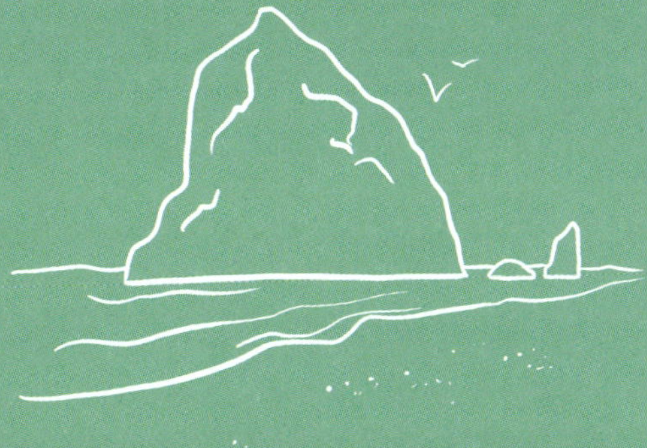

Multnomah Falls

Columbia River Gorge, Oregon

STEP 1

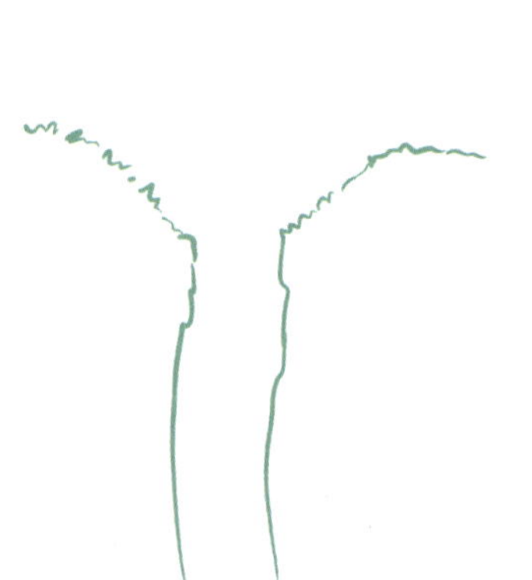

STEP 2

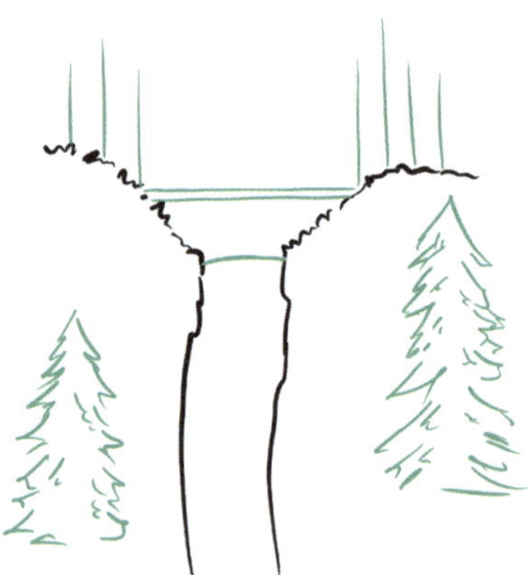

STEP 3

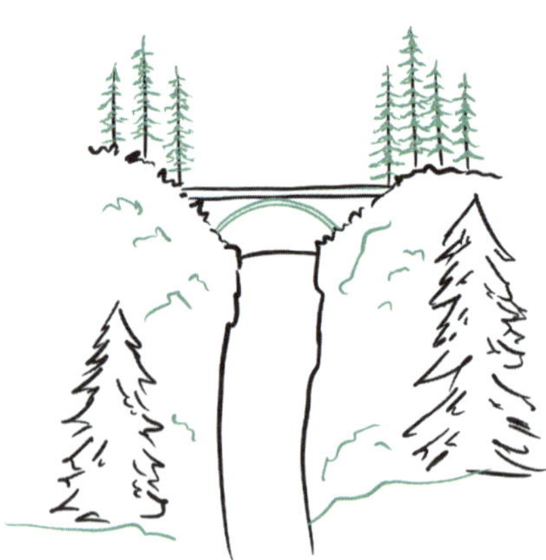

STEP 4

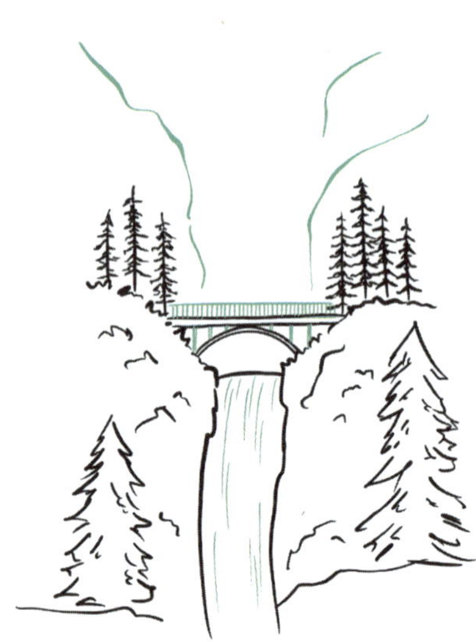

STEP 5

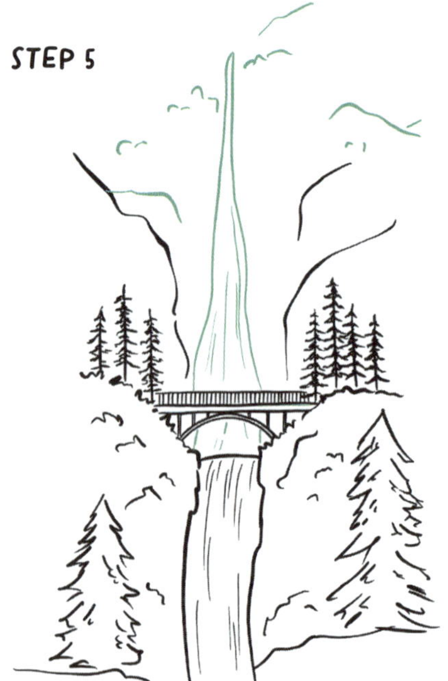

STEP 6

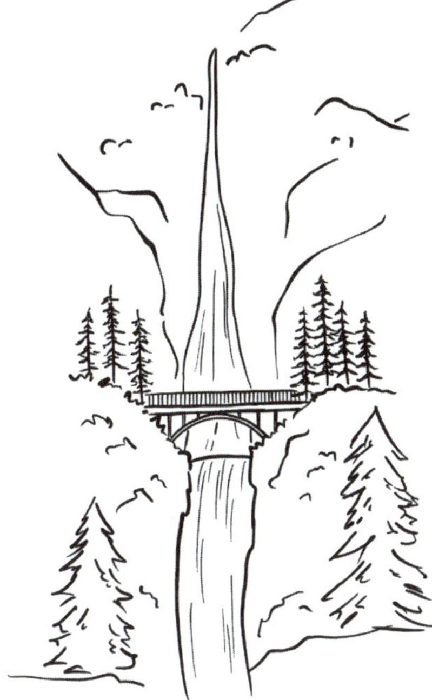

FUN FACT!

Formed by cataclysmic floods beginning fifteen thousand years ago and standing at 620 feet, it's the tallest waterfall in Oregon and one of the most visited tourist sites in the area.

Crater Lake

Southern Oregon

STEP 1

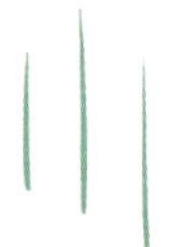

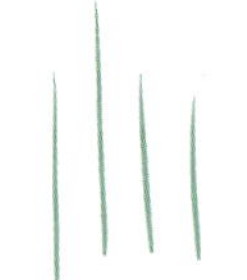

STEP 2

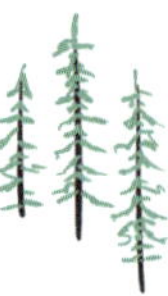

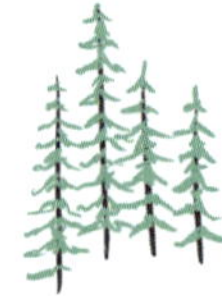

STEP 3

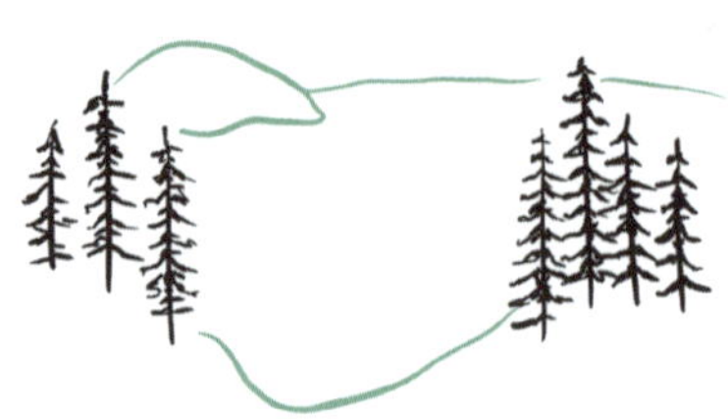

STEP 4

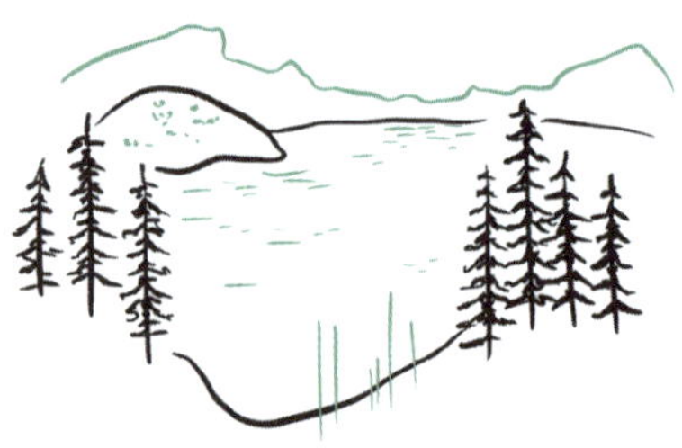

STEP 5

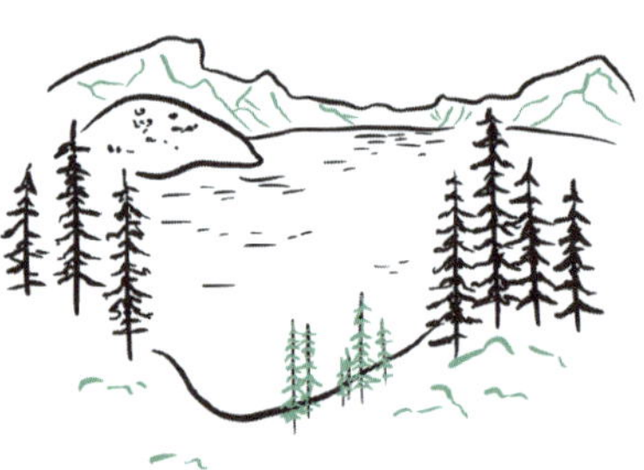

STEP 6

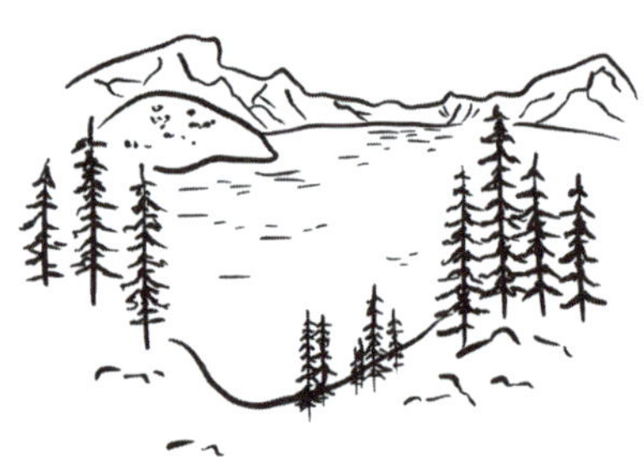

FUN FACT!

Crater Lake is the deepest lake in the United States and is Oregon's only national park.

Haystack Rock

Cannon Beach, Oregon

STEP 1

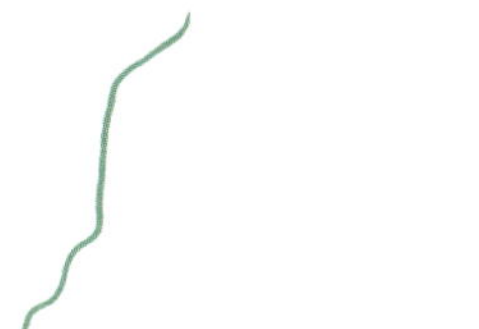

STEP 2

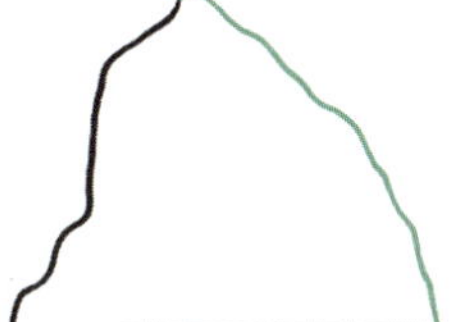

STEP 3

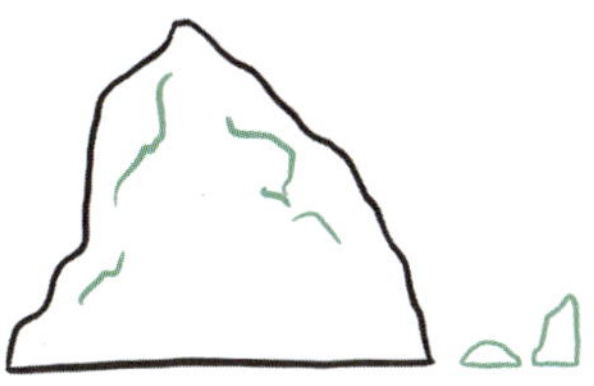

STEP 4

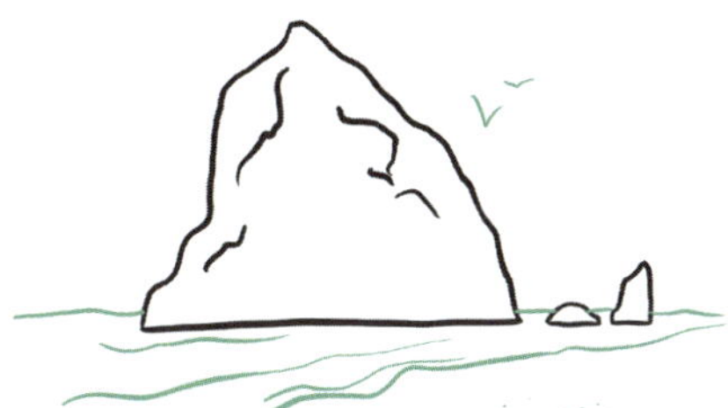

STEP 5

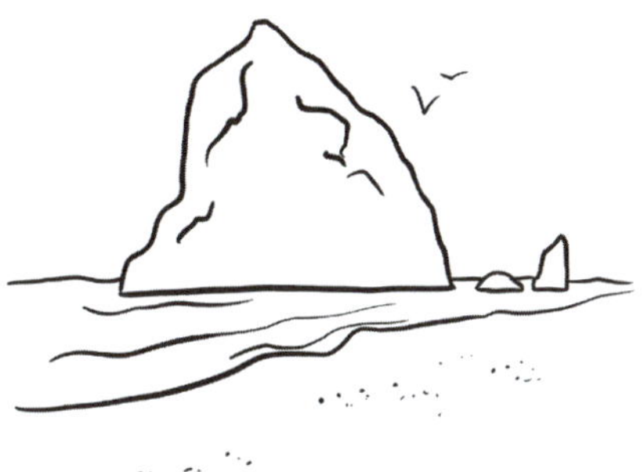

FUN FACT!

This irregular rock formation was created by lava flowing through the old Columbia River drainage system.

Hells Canyon

Borders Oregon, Washington, and Idaho

STEP 1

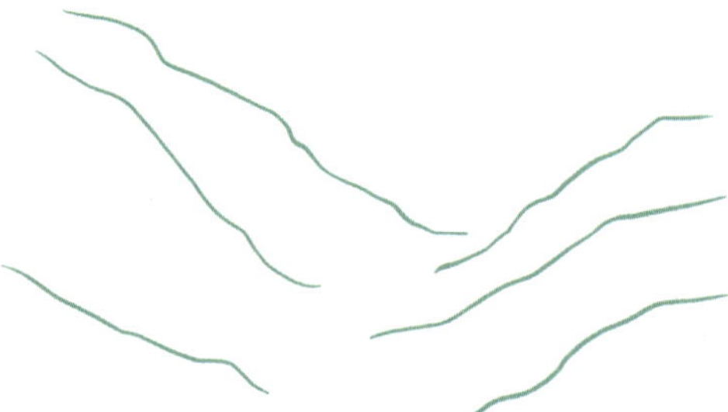

STEP 2

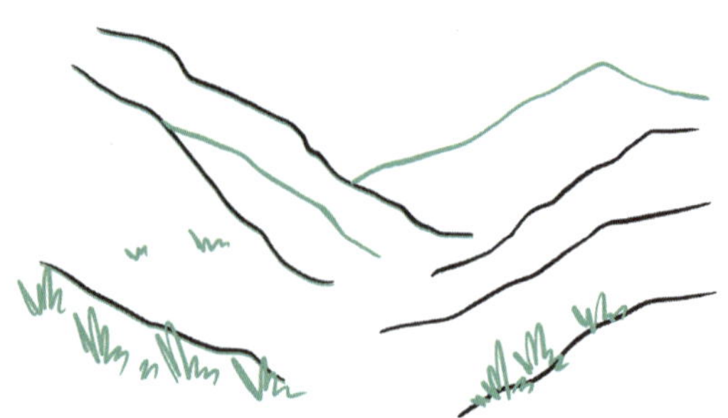

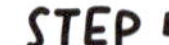

STEP 3

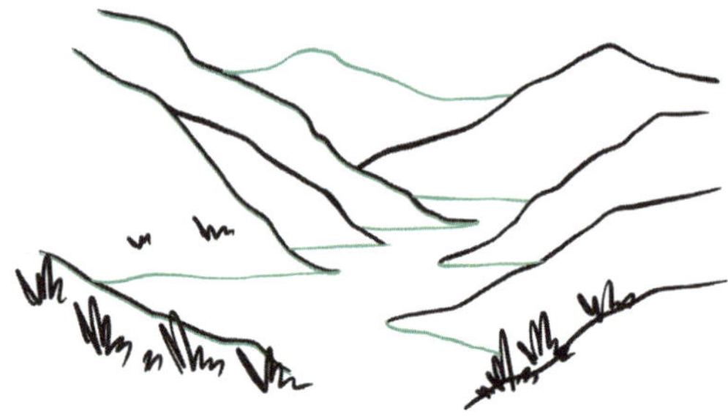

STEP 4

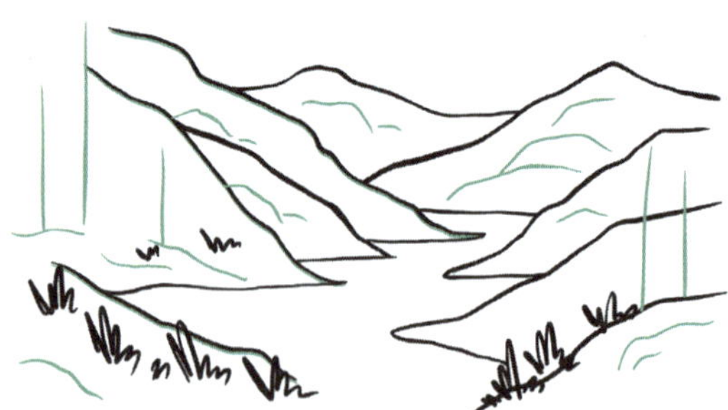

STEP 5

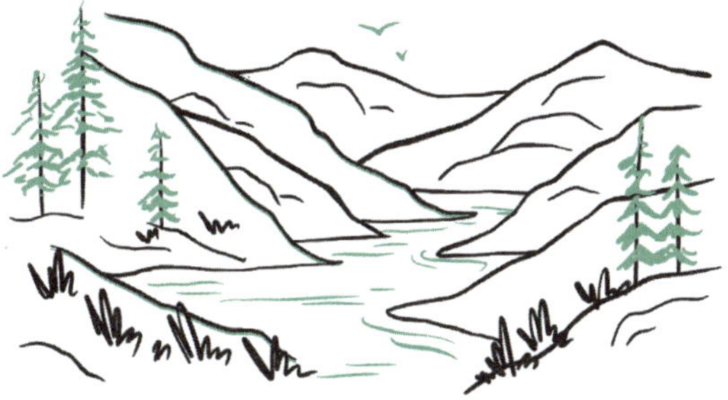

STEP 6

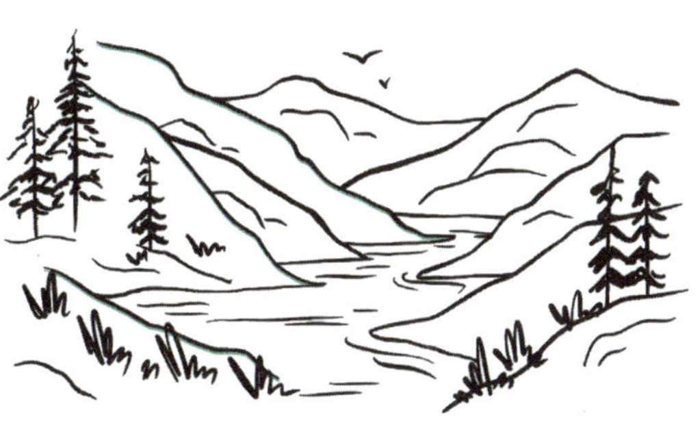

FUN FACT!

Carved by the Snake River, this canyon is the deepest in North America (yes, it's deeper than the Grand Canyon by almost two thousand feet!).

Snake River Canyon

Magic Valley, Idaho

STEP 1

STEP 2

STEP 3

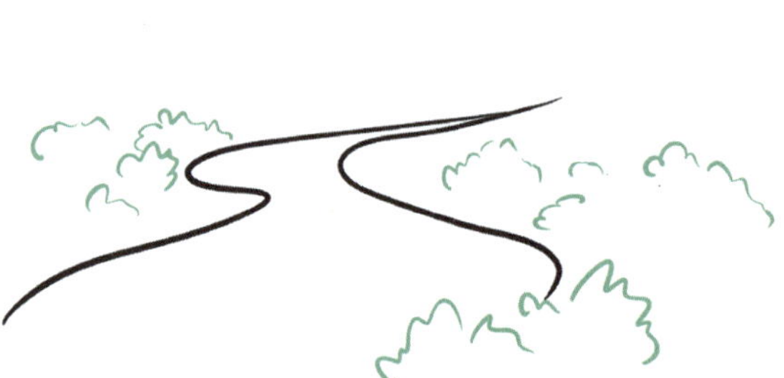

STEP 4

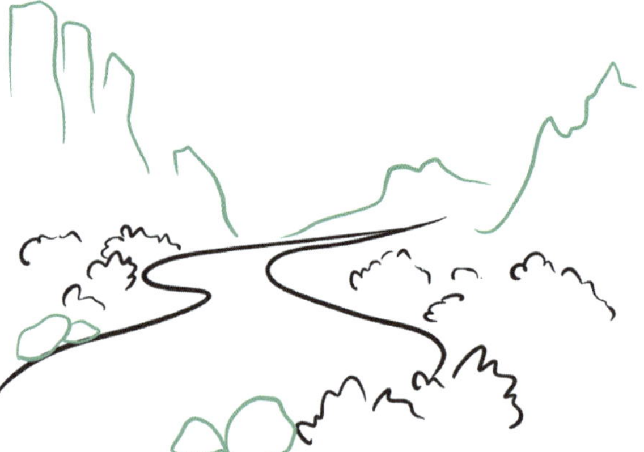

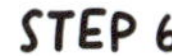

STEP 5

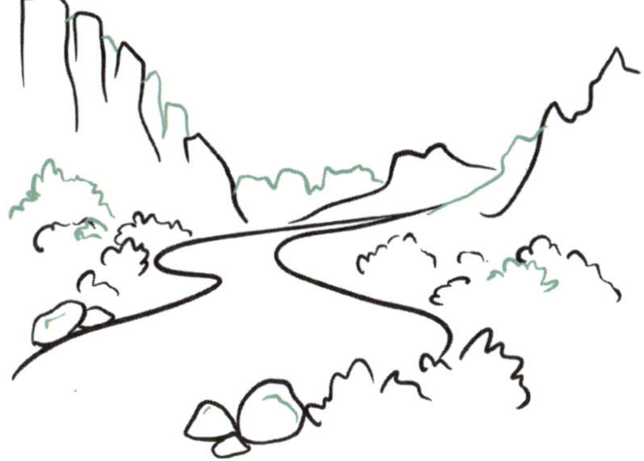

STEP 6

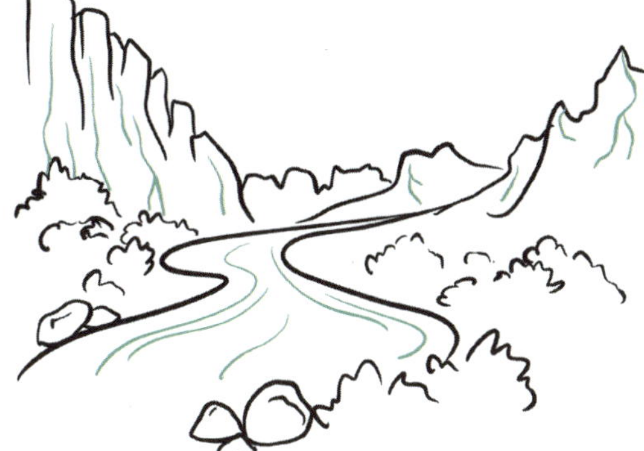

STEP 7

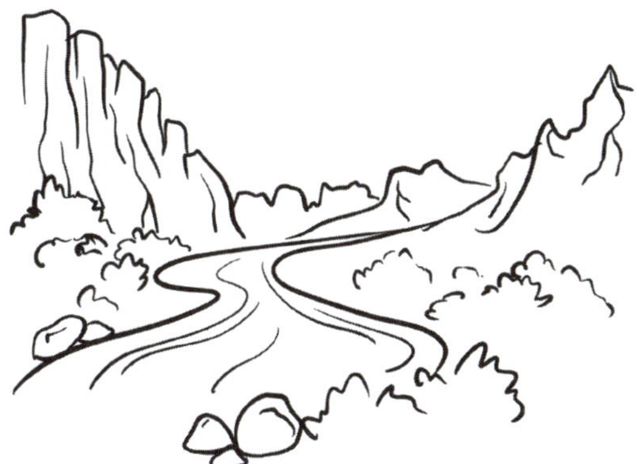

FUN FACT!

This river's claim to fame is Evel Knievel's attempt to cross it on a steam-powered rocket.

Lassen Peak
Northern California

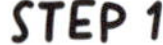

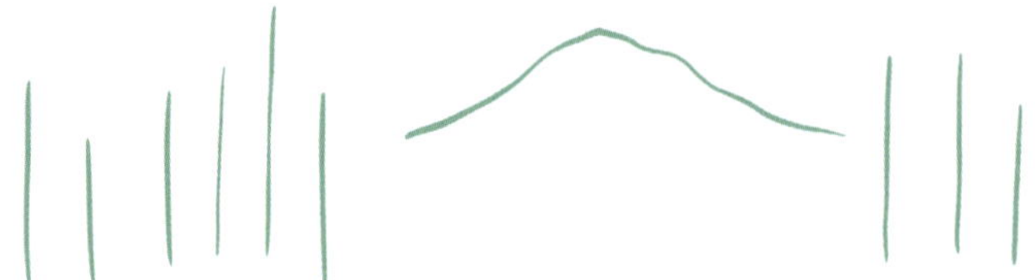

STEP 2

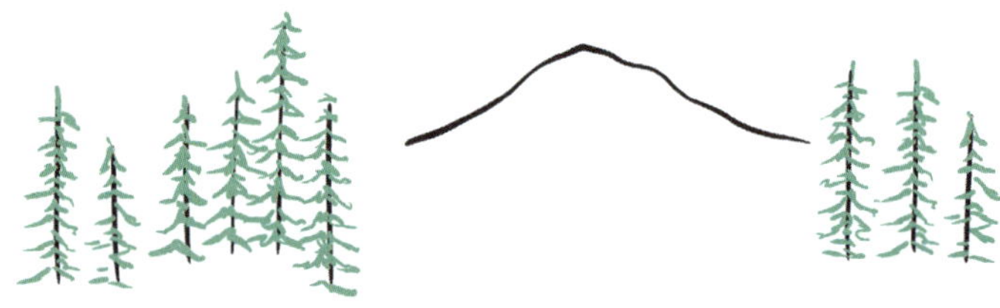

STEP 3

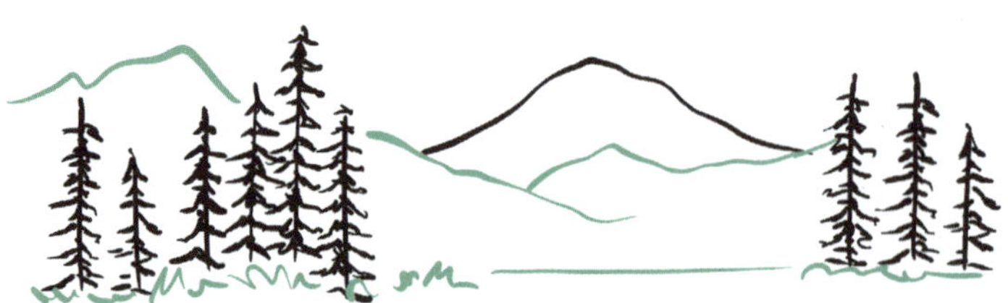

STEP 4

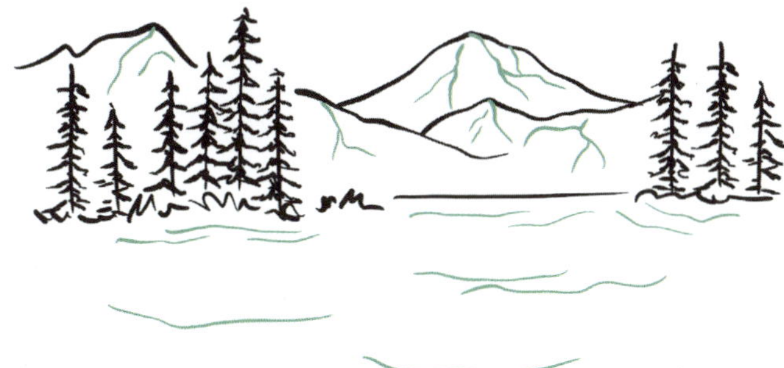

FUN FACT!

The main attraction of Lassen Volcanic National Park is Lassen Peak, the largest plug dome volcano in the world.

STEP 5

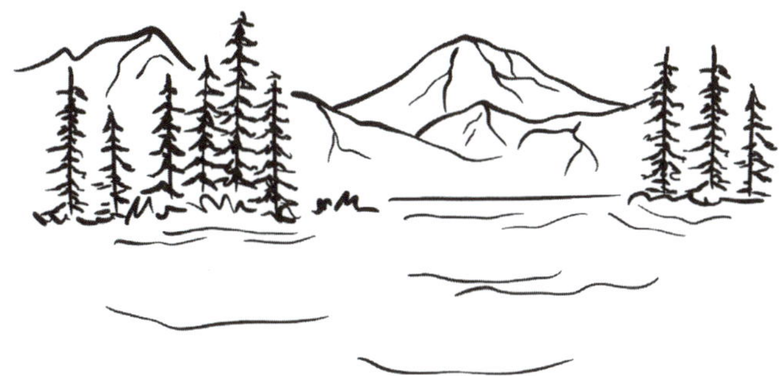

Mount St. Helens

Cascade Mountains, Washington

STEP 1

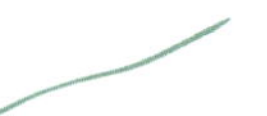

STEP 2

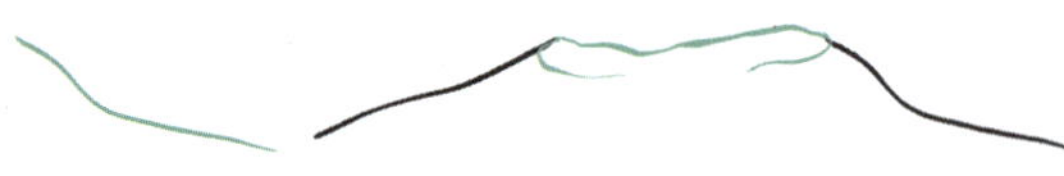

STEP 3

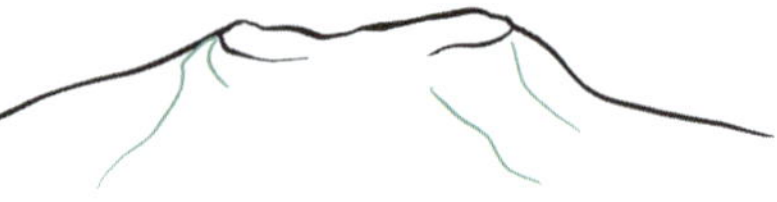

STEP 4

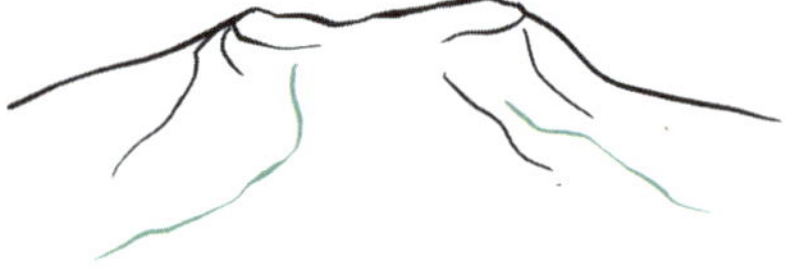

STEP 5

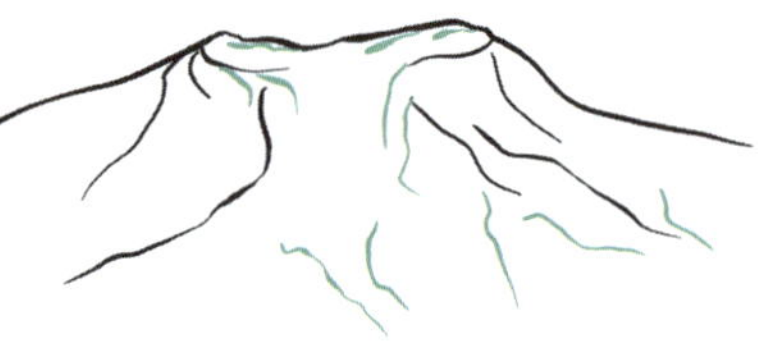

STEP 6

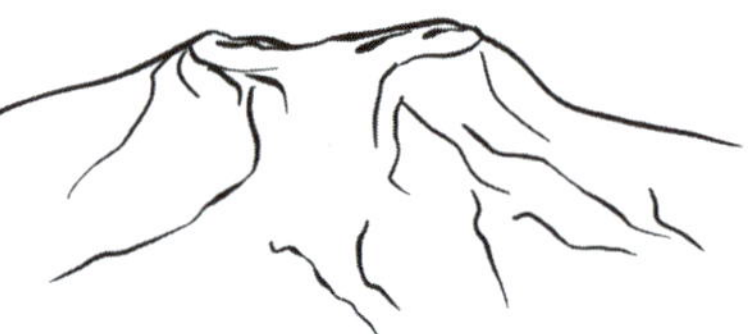

FUN FACT!

This forty-thousand-year-old stratovolcano is most recognized for its eruption on May 18, 1980, which remains the deadliest and most economically destructive eruption in US history.

Mount Rainier

Cascade Mountains, Washington

STEP 1

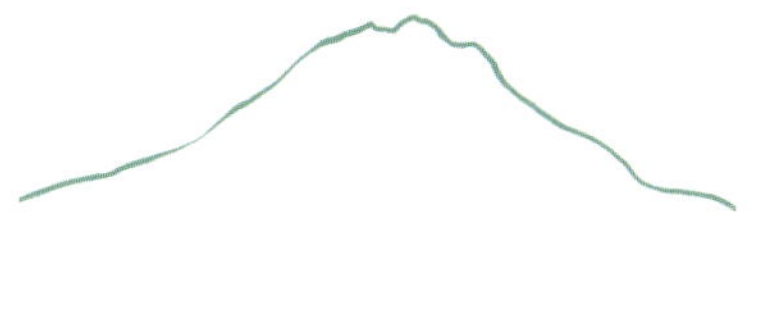

STEP 2

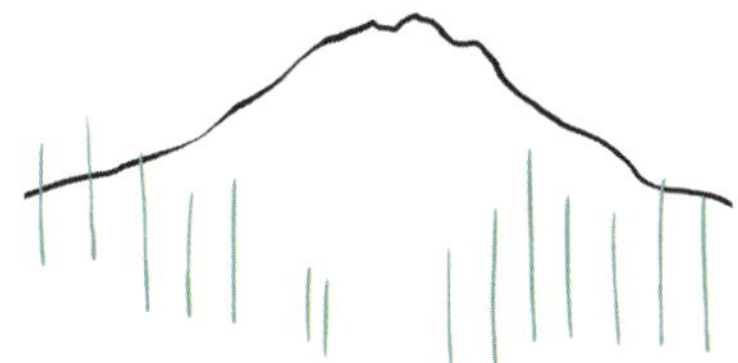

STEP 3

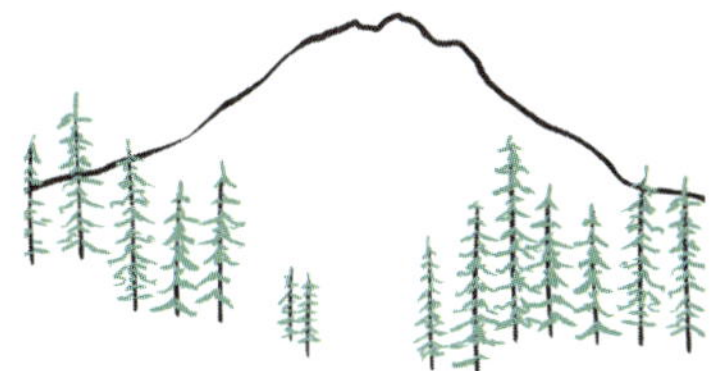

STEP 4

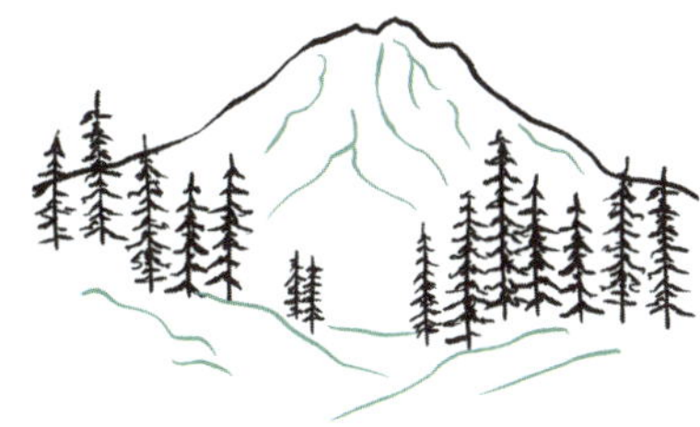

STEP 5

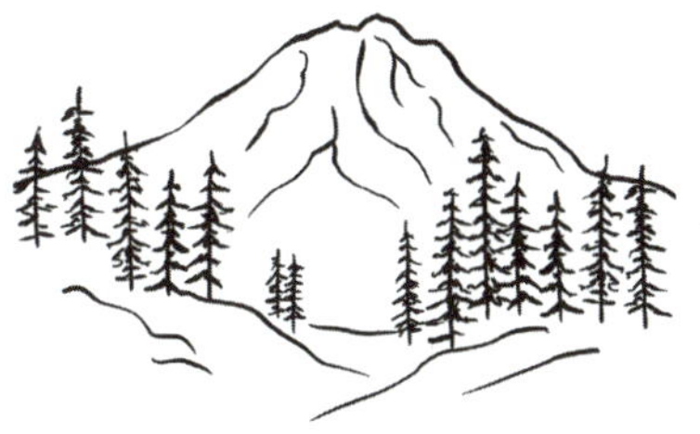

FUN FACT!

The highest mountain in Washington, it is considered to be one of the most dangerous volcanoes in the world due to its large amount of glacial ice, which could produce massive lahars (volcanic mudflows) in the event of an eruption.

Mount Hood

Cascade Mountains, Oregon

STEP 1

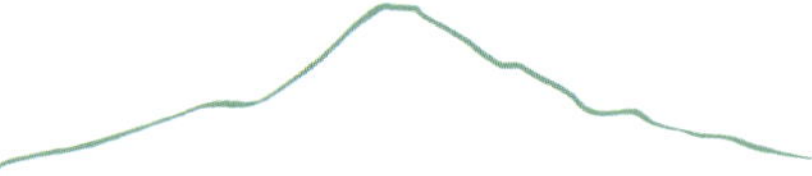

STEP 2

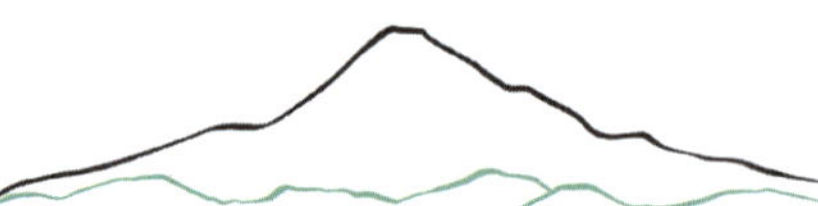

STEP 3

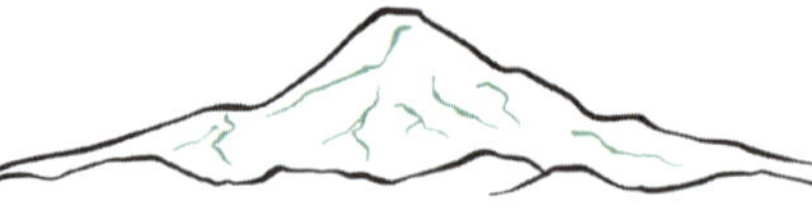

STEP 4

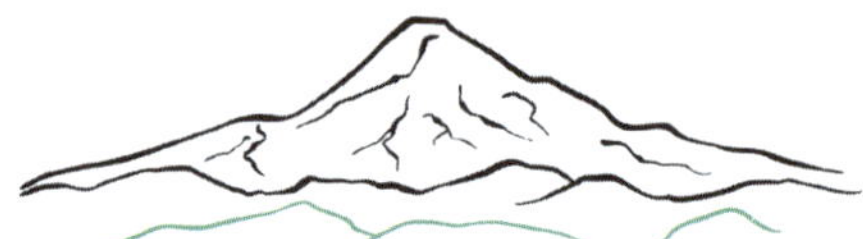

STEP 5

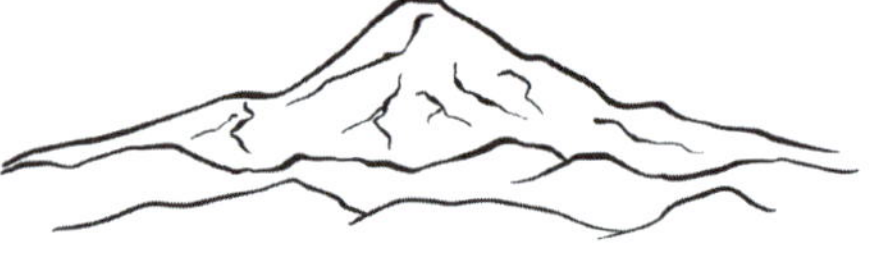

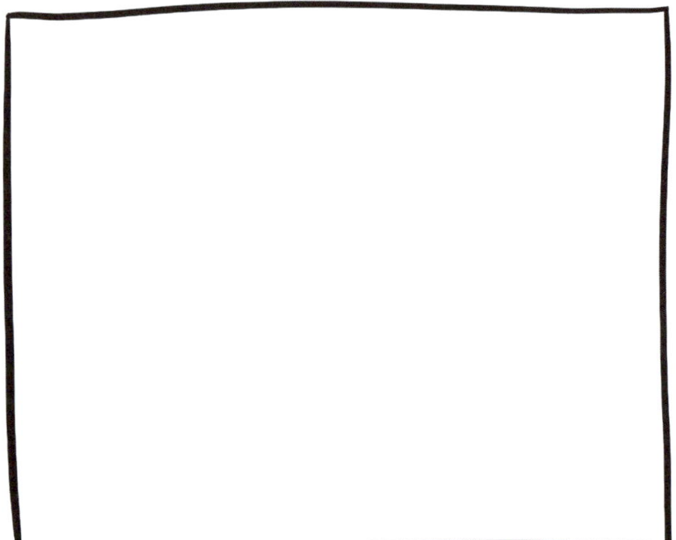

FUN FACT!

This mountain is the only one in Oregon that offers year-round skiing!

Mount Shasta

Northern California

STEP 1

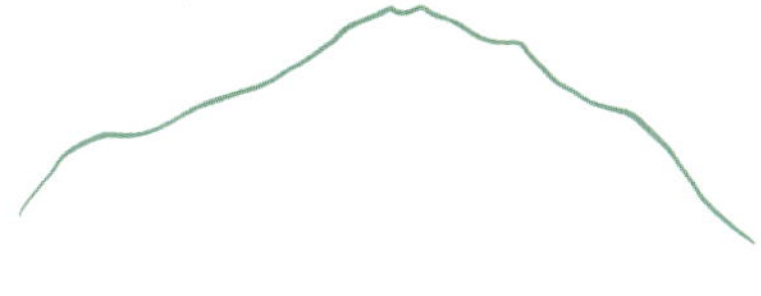

STEP 2

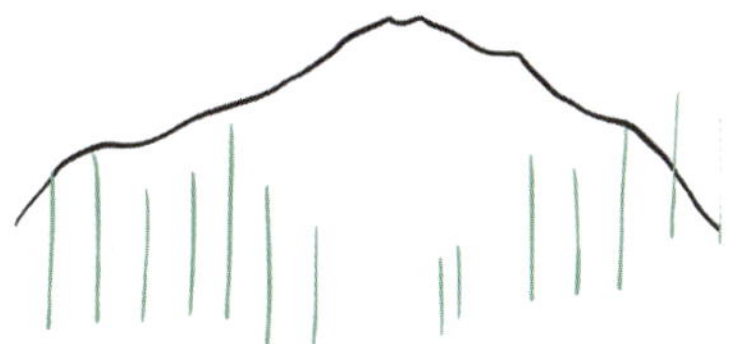

STEP 3

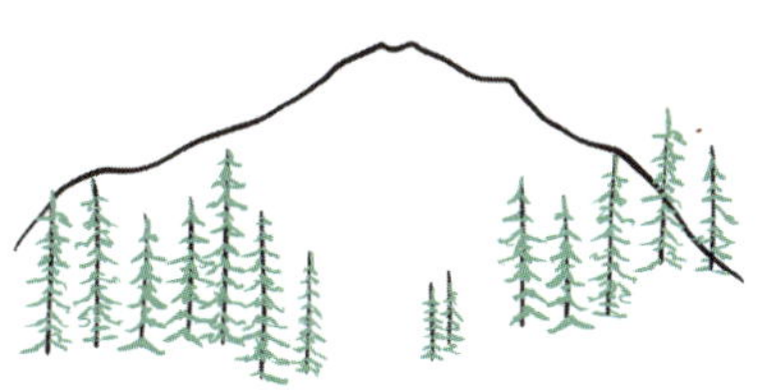

STEP 4

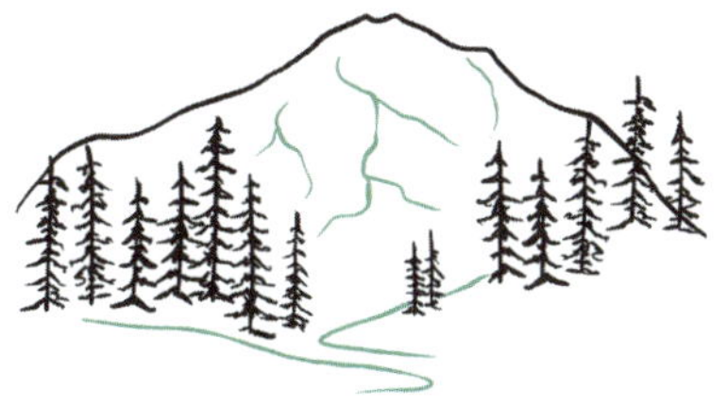

STEP 5

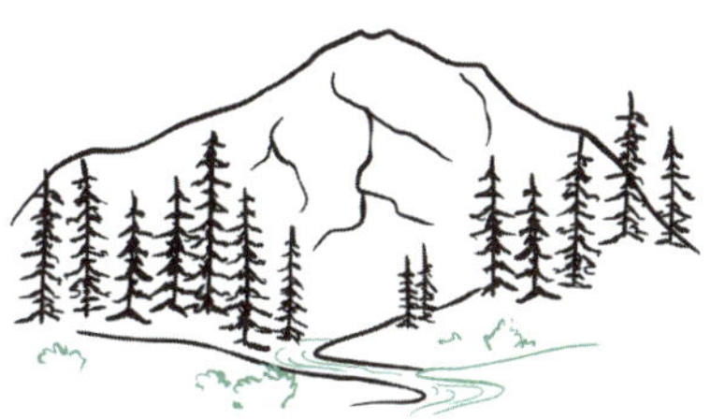

STEP 6

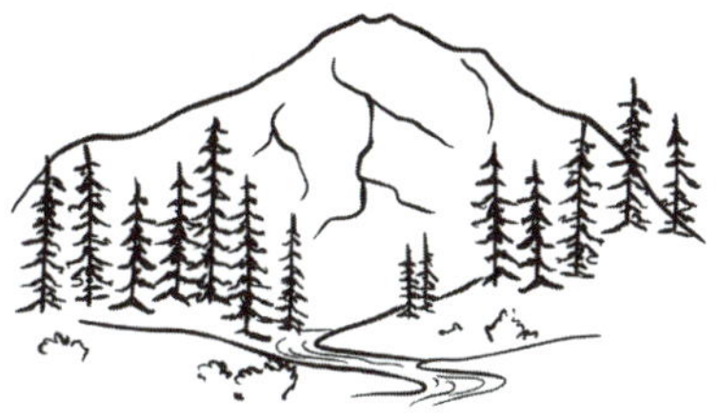

FUN FACT!

This mountain is the subject of many tales, from Native American creation stories to metaphysical accounts of hidden cities and spiritual beings said to reside on the mountain.

Snoqualmie Falls

Snoqualmie, Washington

STEP 1

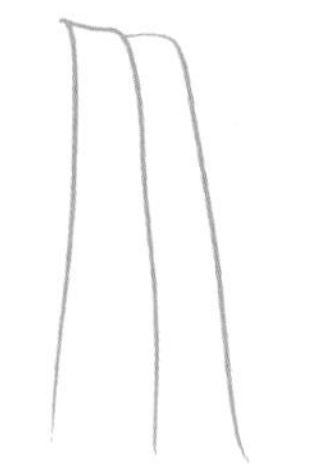

STEP 2

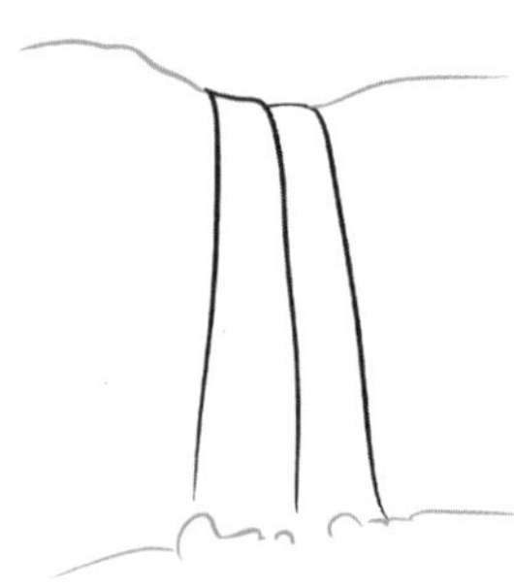

STEP 3

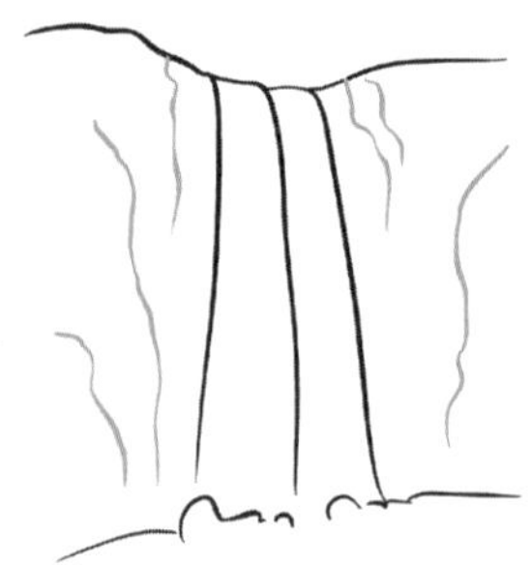

STEP 4

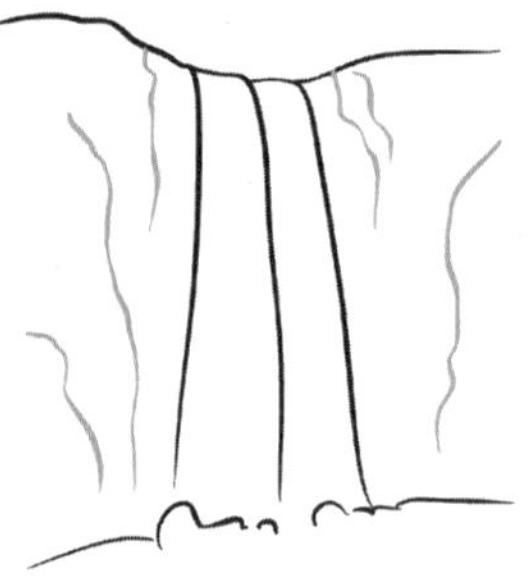

STEP 5

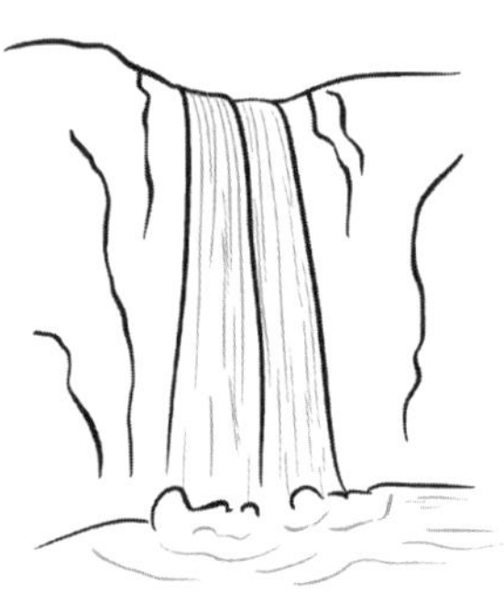

STEP 6

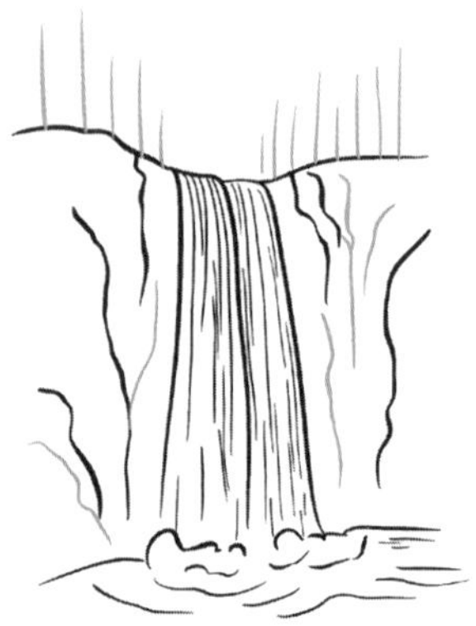

STEP 7

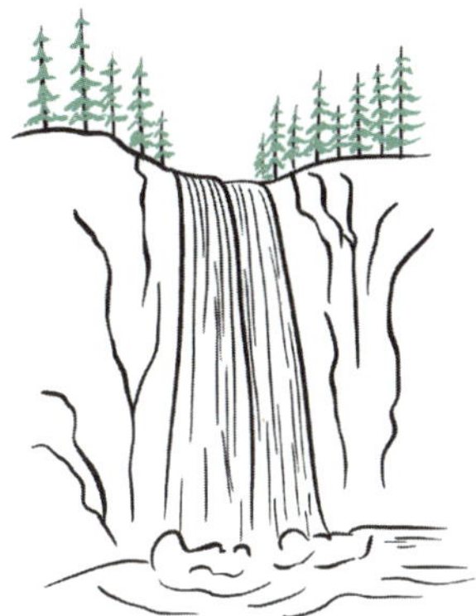

STEP 8

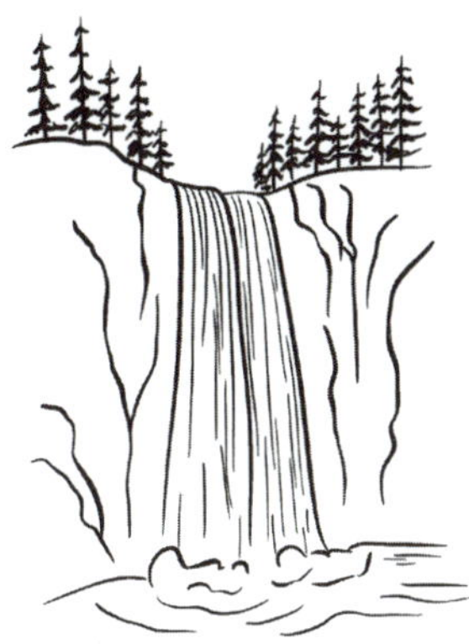

FUN FACT!

Standing more than one hundred feet higher than Niagara Falls, this place is considered sacred to the Snoqualmie Tribe as the site of creation.

Painted Hills

John Day Fossil Beds National Monument, Oregon

STEP 1

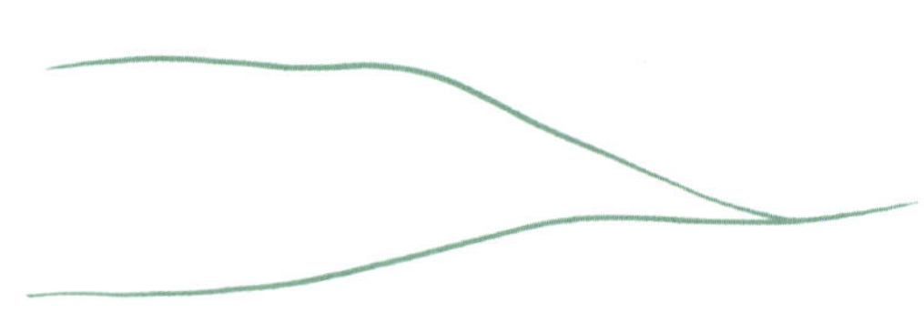

STEP 2

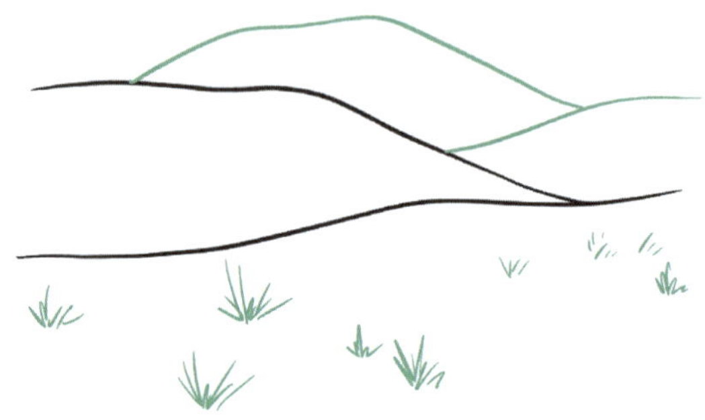

STEP 3

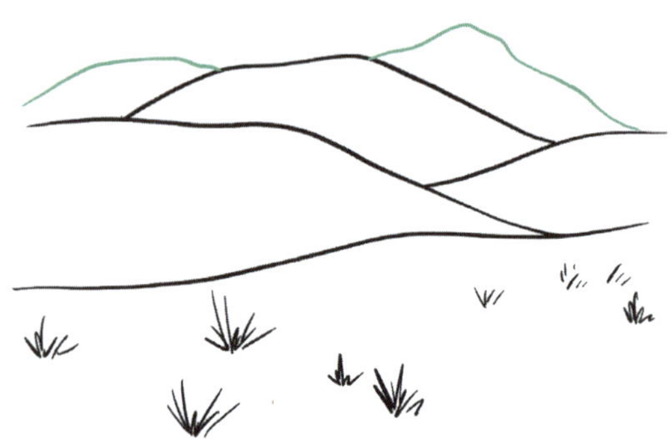

STEP 4

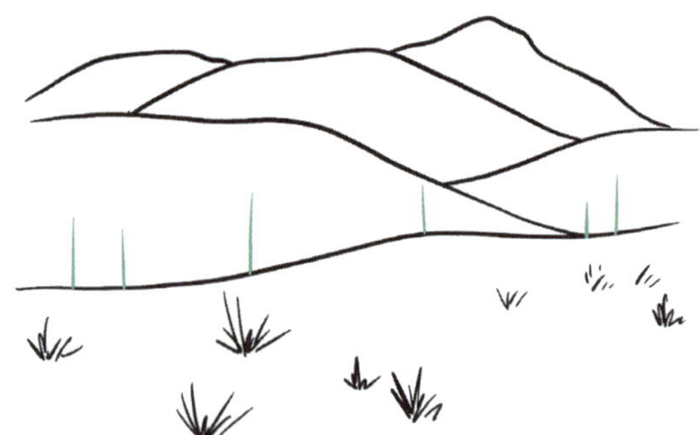

STEP 5

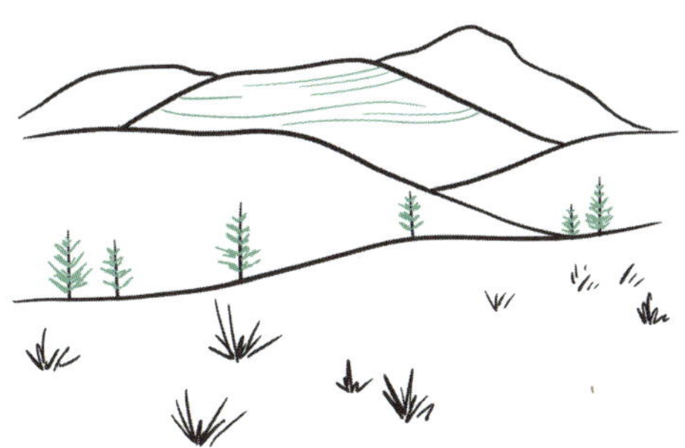

STEP 6

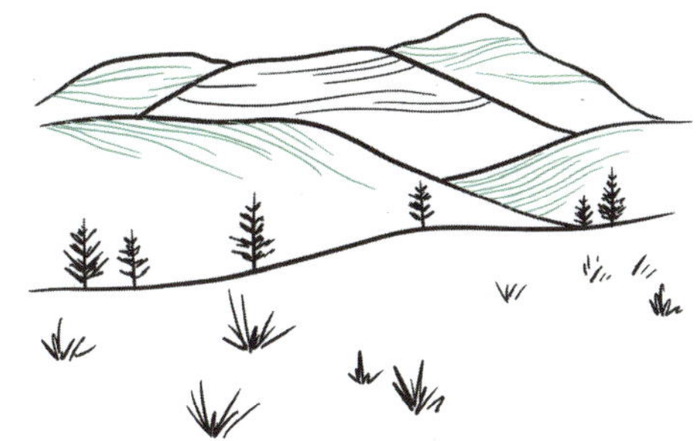

STEP 7

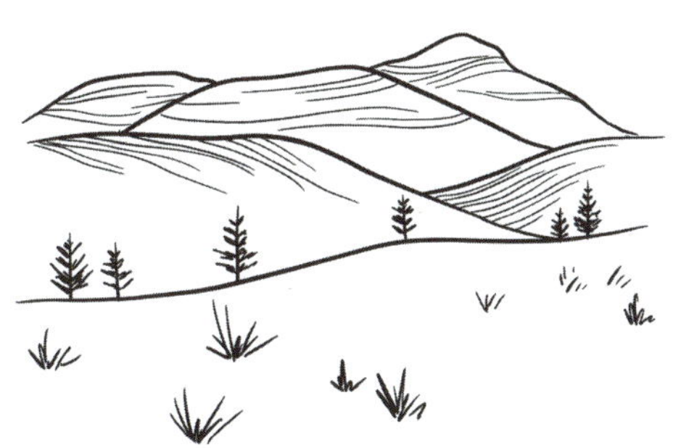

FUN FACT!

This stunning site started forming thirty-five million years ago following a volcanic eruption. Depending on the amount of moisture, the light reflections create striking color variations.

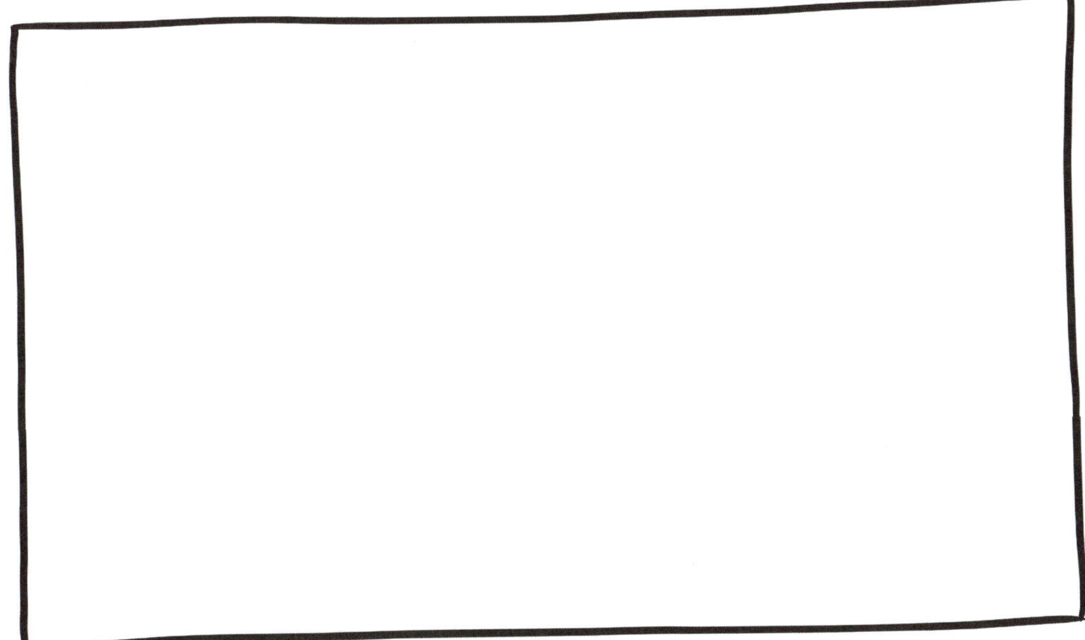

Butchart Gardens

Victoria, British Columbia

STEP 1

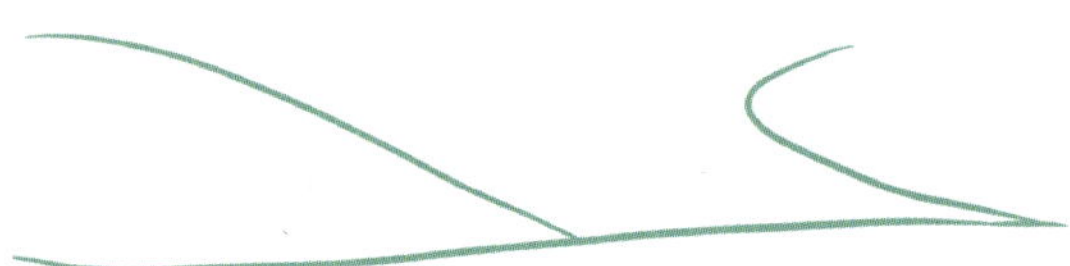

STEP 2

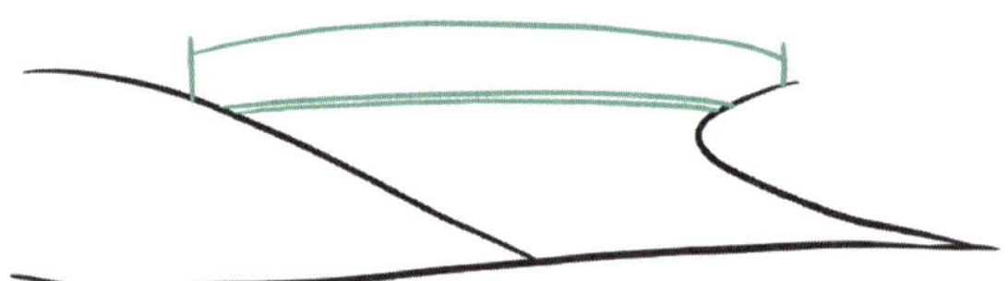

STEP 3

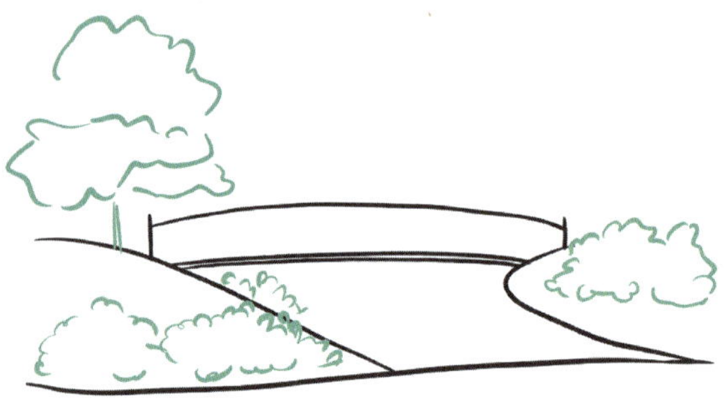

STEP 4

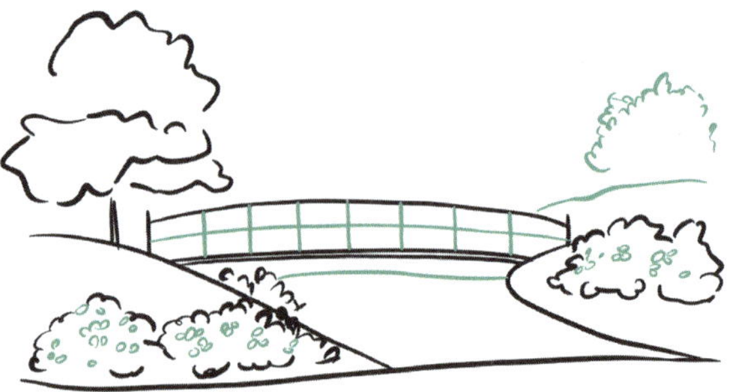

STEP 5

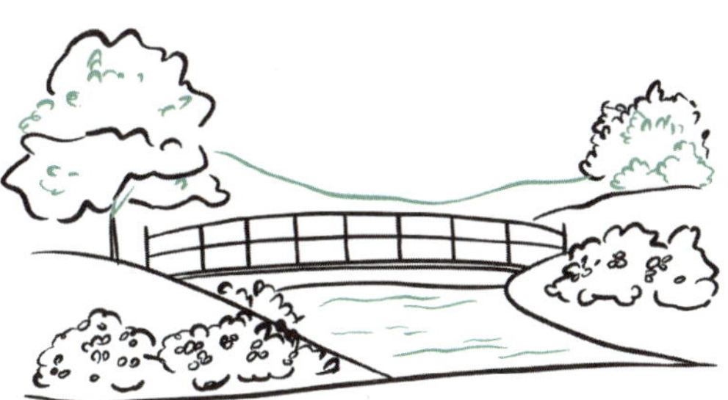

STEP 6

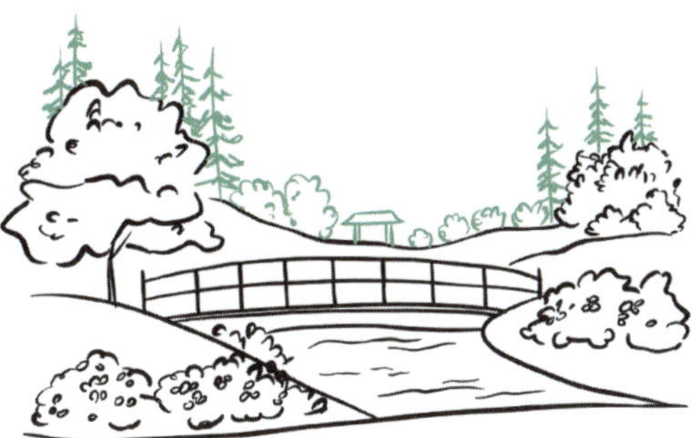

STEP 7

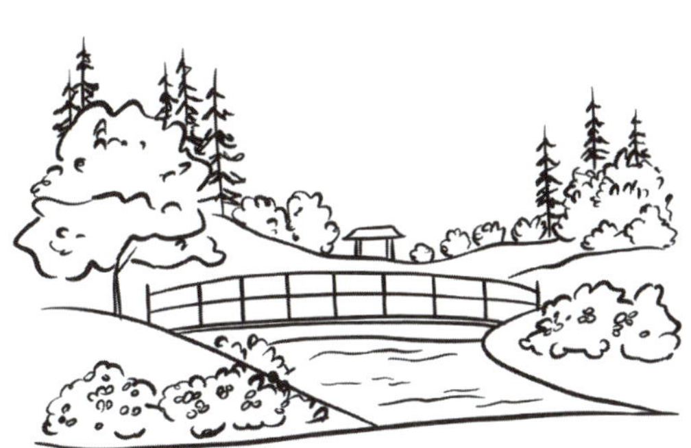

FUN FACT!

Receiving almost one million visitors a year, the gardens are still owned by the founding family. They also served as inspiration for Epcot at the Walt Disney World Resort in Florida.

St. Johns Bridge

Portland, Oregon

STEP 1

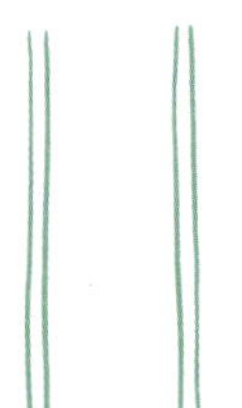

STEP 2

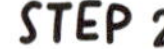

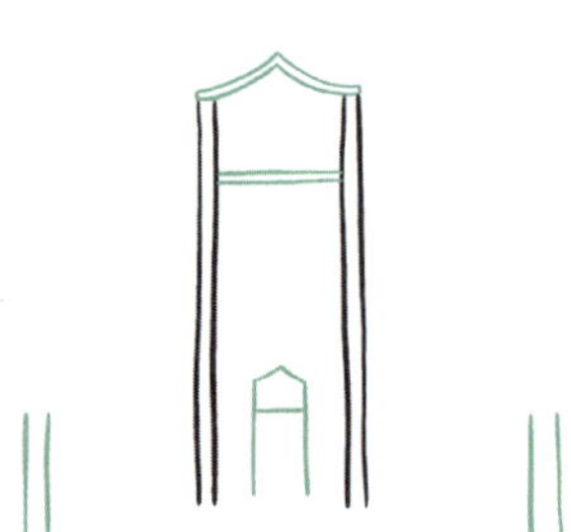

STEP 3

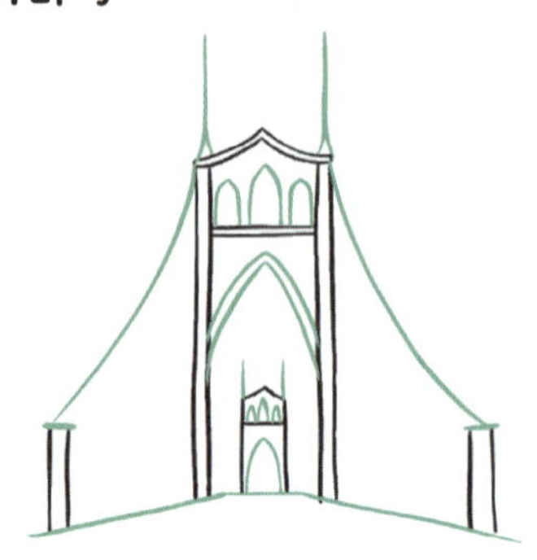

STEP 4

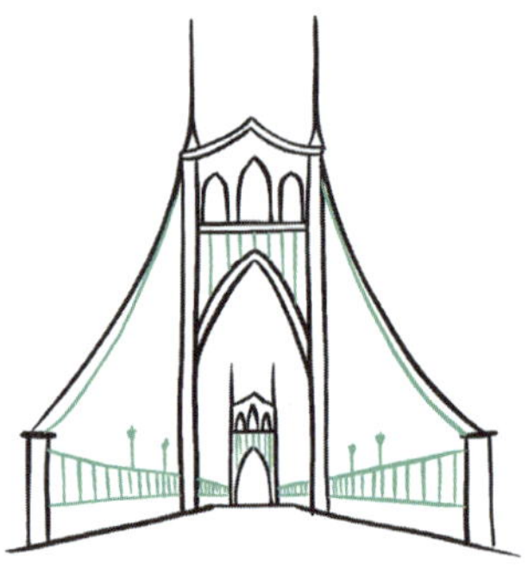

STEP 5

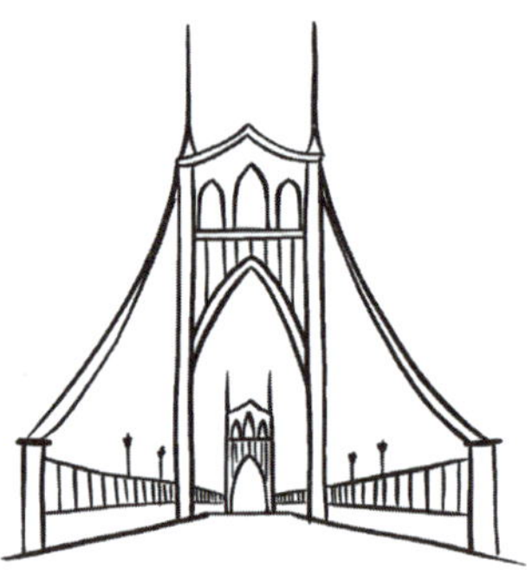

FUN FACT!

When it was constructed in 1931, the St. Johns Bridge was the longest suspension bridge west of the Mississippi River.

Space Needle

Seattle, Washington

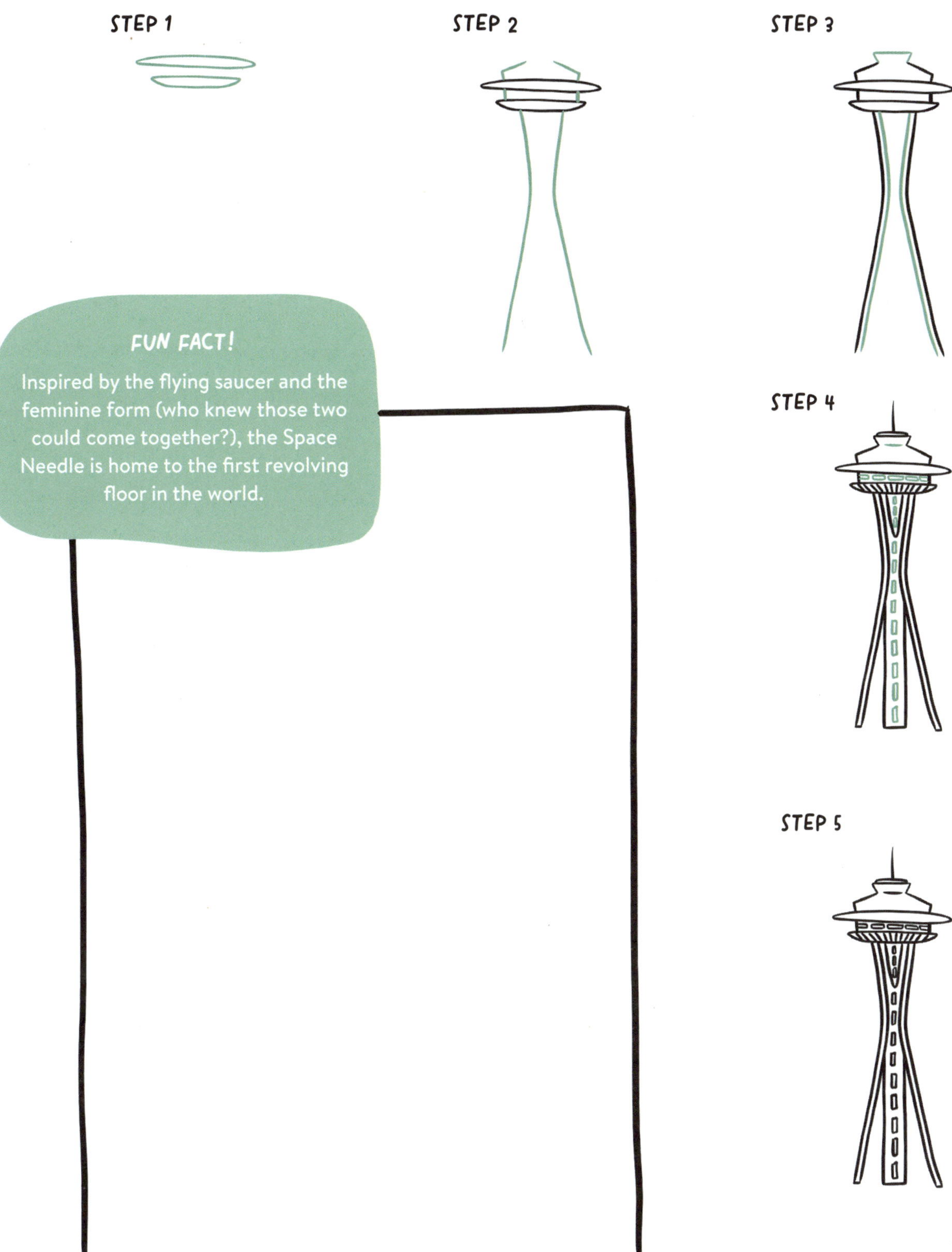

Portland Skyline

STEP 1

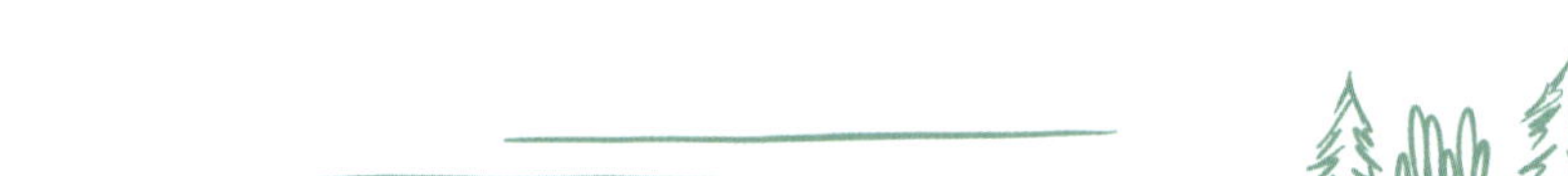

STEP 2

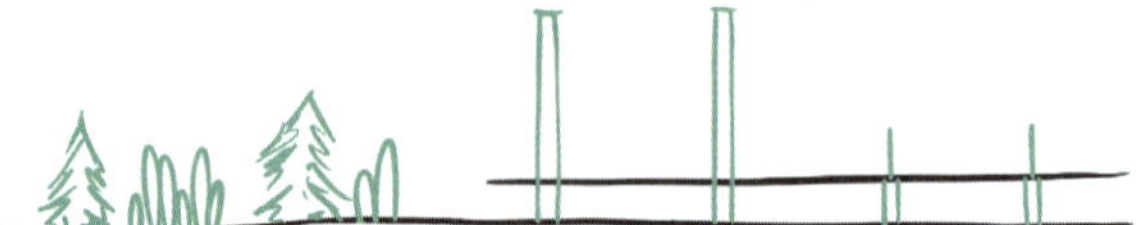

STEP 3

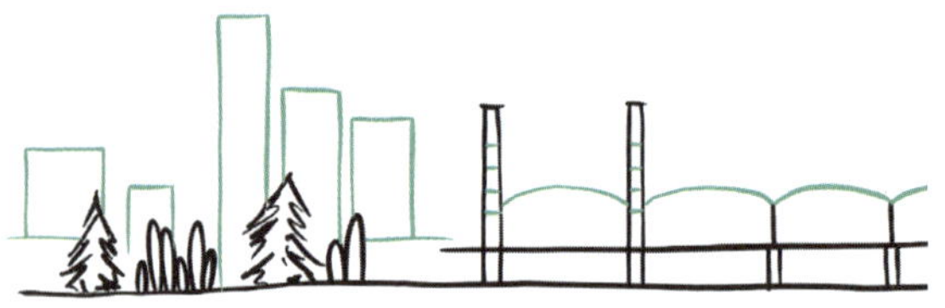

STEP 4

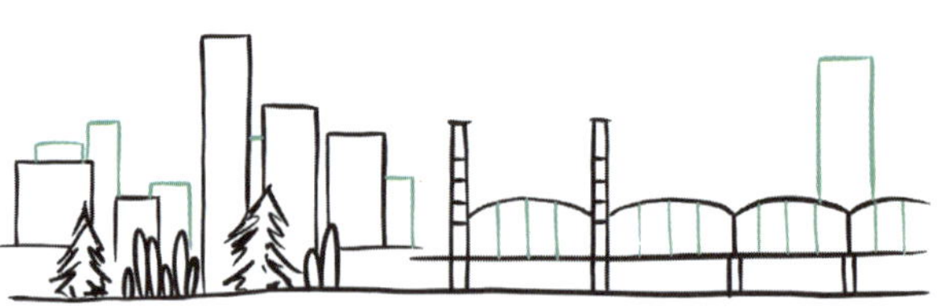

STEP 5

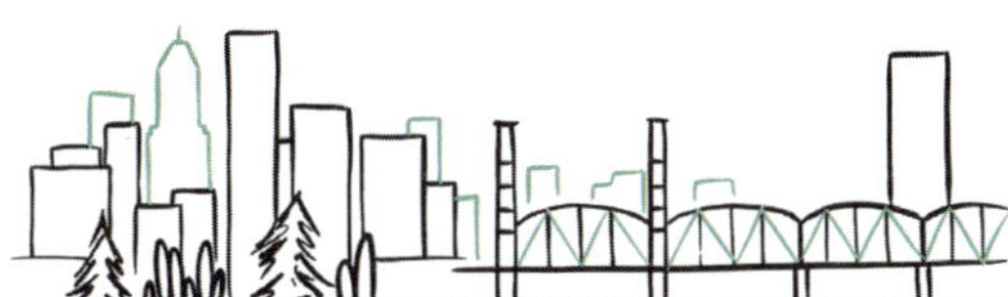

STEP 6

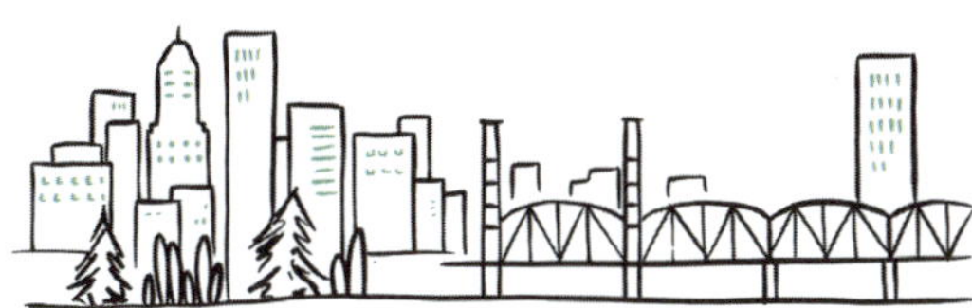

STEP 7

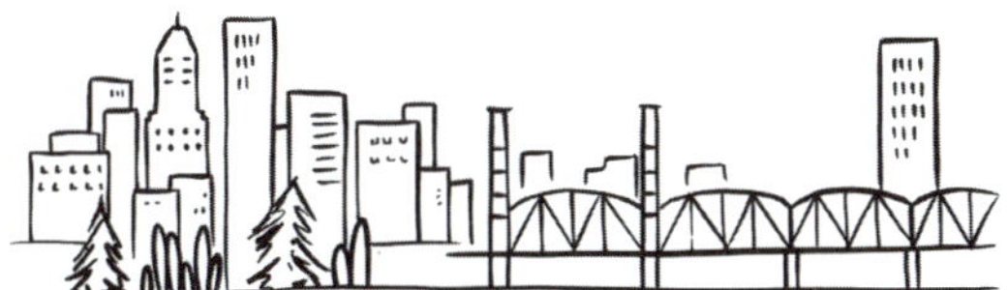

FUN FACT!

The famous "Portland Oregon Old Town" sign greets travelers on the Burnside Bridge with a prancing deer whose nose glows red from Thanksgiving through the holidays.

Seattle Skyline

STEP 1

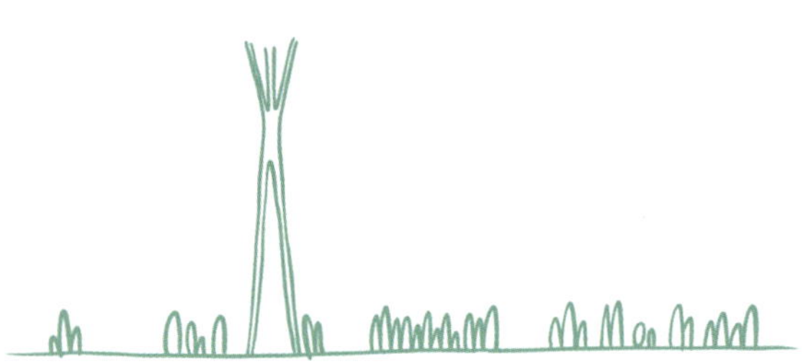

STEP 2

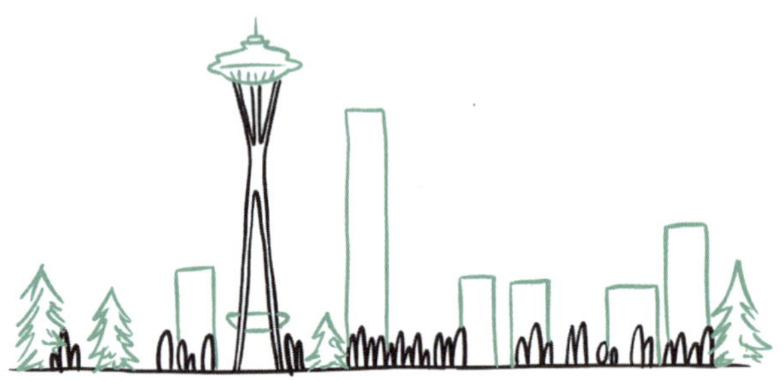

STEP 3

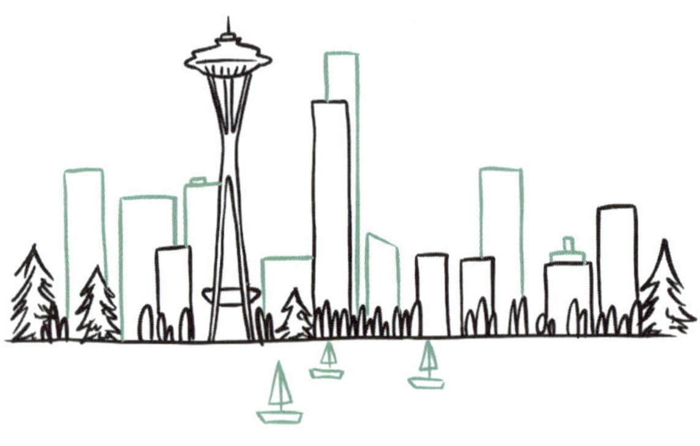

STEP 4

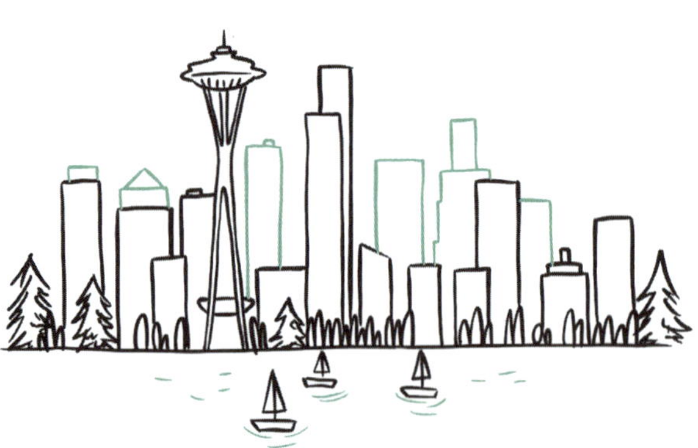

STEP 5

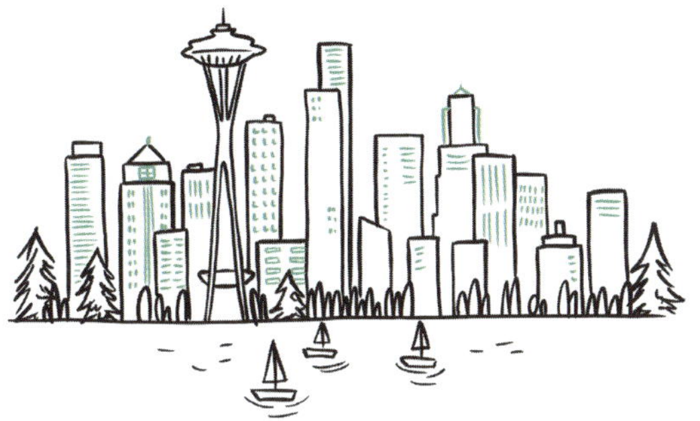

STEP 6

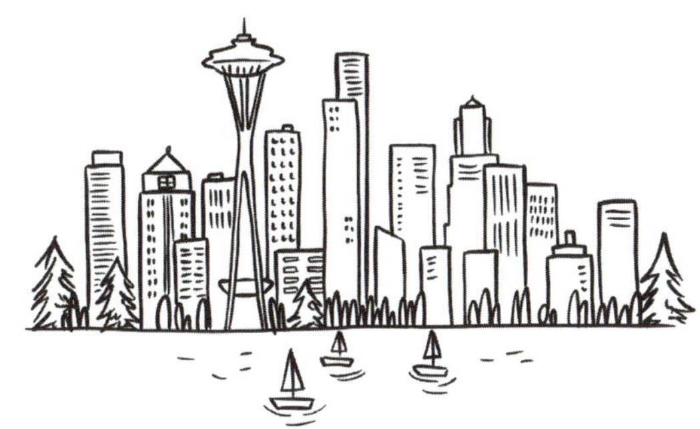

FUN FACT!

From the 73rd floor of the Sky View Observatory, you can take in a 360-degree panoramic view of all that Seattle, Puget Sound, and Lake Washington have to offer.

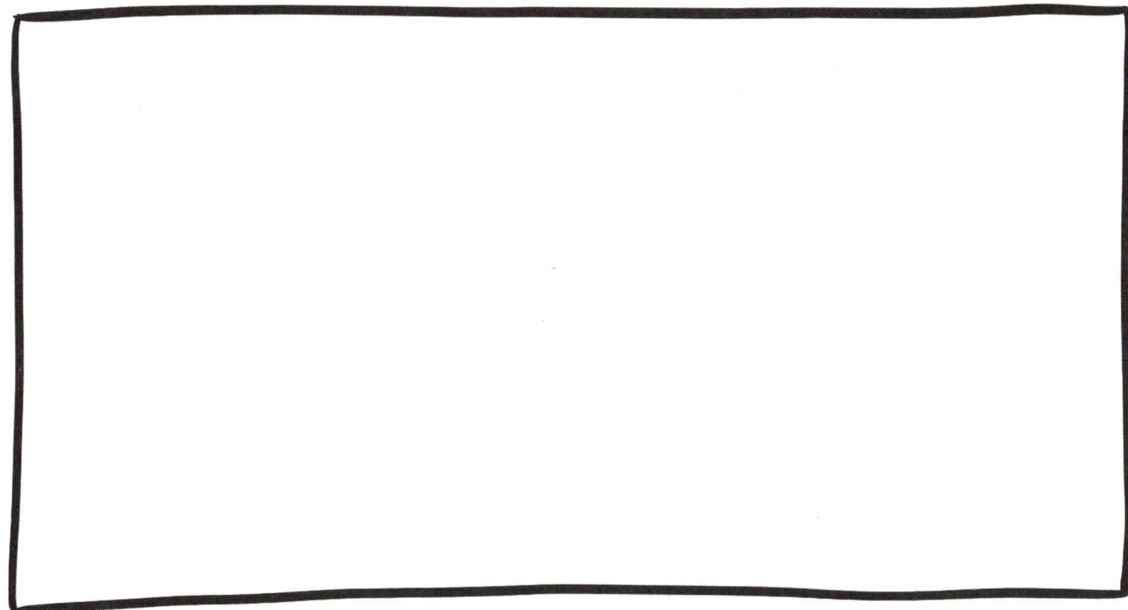

Farmers Market

STEP 1

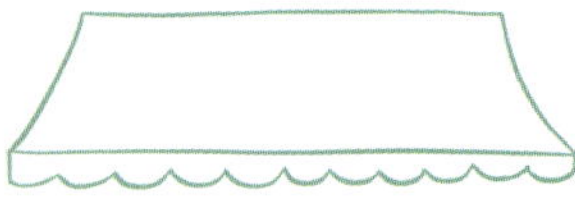

STEP 2

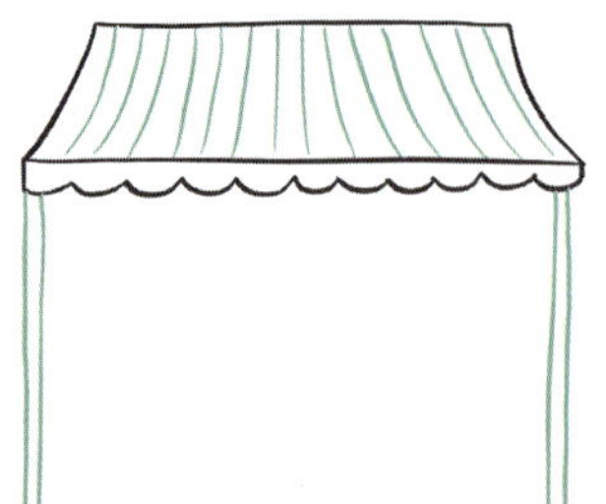

STEP 3

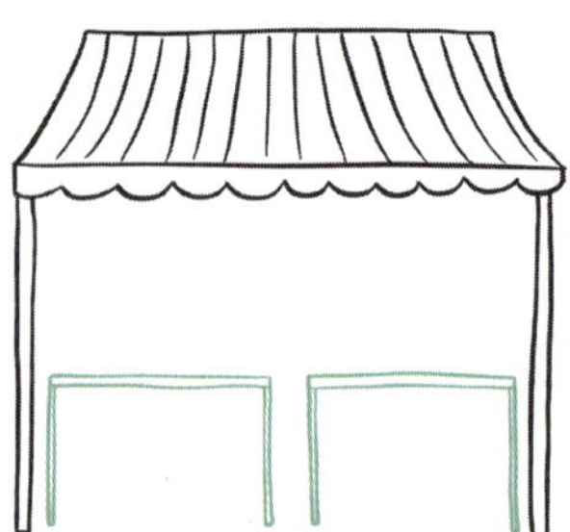

STEP 4

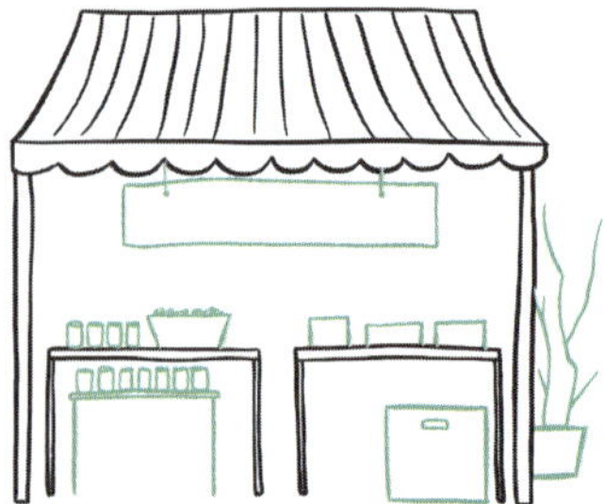

STEP 5

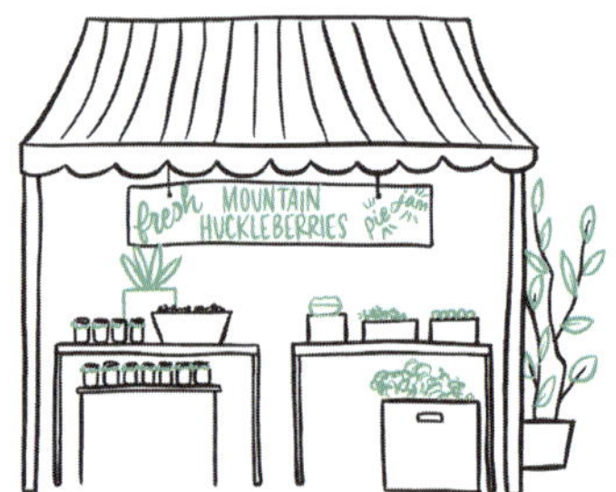

STEP 6

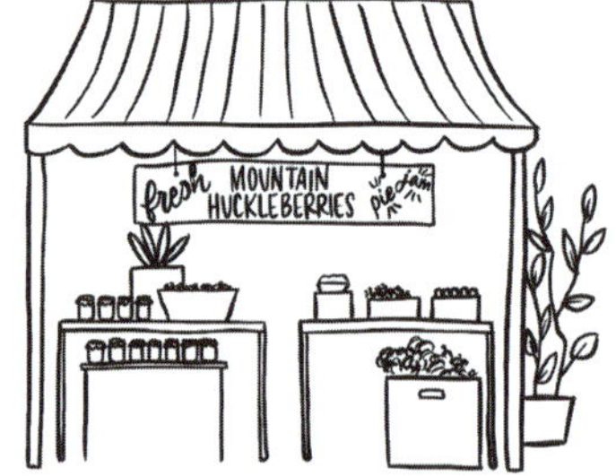

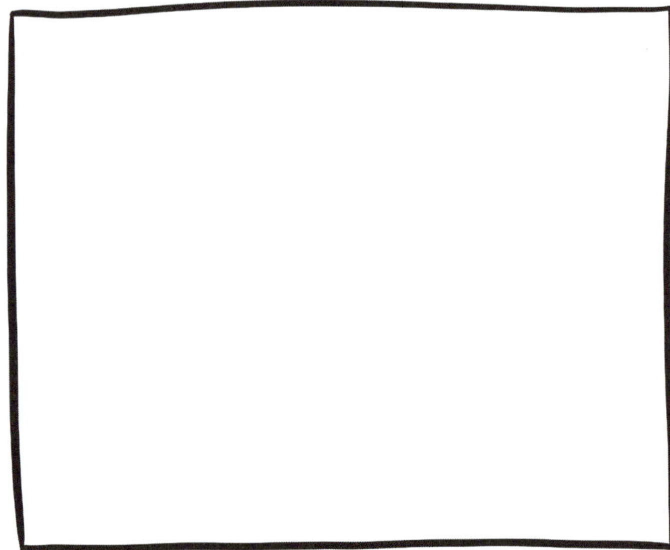

FUN FACT!

Farmers markets in the Pacific Northwest go beyond selling fresh produce. Some feature cooking demonstrations, live music, and even workshops on gardening and sustainability.

A Parting Note

With its majestic mountains, verdant forests, and vibrant cities, the Pacific Northwest provides inspiration and a challenge to our perception and creativity. Hopefully, you've found that in capturing its beauty, you've also discovered new layers of your ability and broadened your horizon of expression.

As you hone your skills, consider the journey ahead as an ongoing process of learning and discovery. Here are some ideas to further develop your artistic capabilities.

Drawing Techniques, Resources & Tips

- Practice observational drawing: Spend time in nature or urban settings, sketching directly from life. Observing real-life scenes enhances your ability to capture details and understand perspectives. Check out my book *Mindful Sketching* for more on this.
- Explore different mediums: Experiment with pencils, ink, charcoal, and watercolors to discover how each can best express what you see around you, from the subtle shades of a foggy morning to the vibrant hues of a sunset.
- Utilize online classes: Come visit me at ThePigeonLetters.com—I'd love to see you in class!
- Participate in art communities: Art communities, whether online or in-person, can provide support, inspiration, and opportunities to share your work with others who are passionate about creativity.

Now that you've completed this journey through the Pacific Northwest, I encourage you to keep your artistic momentum going. Set a goal to draw something new each day, even if it's just for a few minutes. Share your creations on social media using #PNWLineDrawing, and join our community of artists celebrating the beauty of this region. Remember, every line you draw is a step forward in your artistic journey. Keep exploring, keep creating, and most importantly, keep enjoying the process!

Practice your skills here

Practice your skills here

Practice your skills here

Practice your skills here

Practice your skills here

Practice your skills here

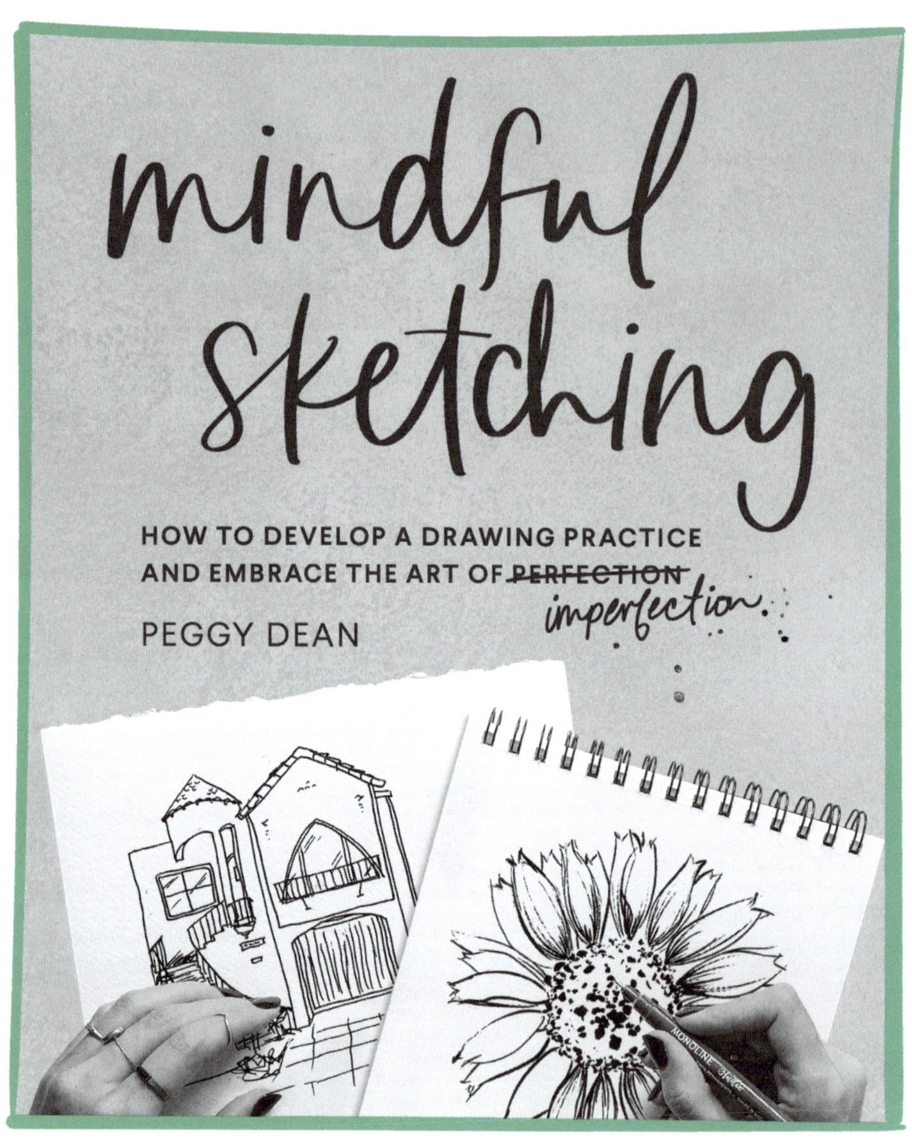

Embrace imperfection with *Mindful Sketching*, also by Peggy Dean!

Combine the mental-health benefits of mindfulness with the joy of sketching. This life-changing drawing practice helps you to stay in the moment while expressing your own creativity. Learn the basic skills of sketching as you practice the art of being present while you draw—and enjoy your work without self-criticism.